The Complete Book of Drafting
for Handweavers

by
Madelyn van der Hoogt

ShuttleCraftBookS

UNICORN
BOOKS AND CRAFTS, INC.

1338 Ross Street ♦ Petaluma, CA 94954 USA
Phone: 707-762-3362 ♦ Fax: 707-762-0335
E-Mail: unicorn@unicornbooks.com

Copyright © 1993 Madelyn van der Hoogt
First printing 1993
Second printing 1994
Third printing 2000

All rights reserved. Permission is granted to photocopy practice exercises for personal use.

Printed in the United States of America.

Library of Congress Catalog Number 92-060840
ISBN: 0-916658-51-1

Table of Contents

♦ Acknowledgements ♦

♦ Introduction ♦

Part I: The Basic Weaves 1

♦ The Family Tree of Weaves ♦ 2

Chapter 1 ♦ Reading Drafts ♦ 4

Lesson ♦ Writing Drafts ♦ 12

Chapter 2 ♦ Understanding the Basic Weaves ♦ 15

Lesson ♦ Drafting Twills and Color-and-Weave ♦ 24

Part II: Blocks 25

♦ Keys to Block Weaves ♦ 26

Chapter 3 ♦ Reading Profile Drafts ♦ 28

Lesson ♦ Writing Profile Drafts ♦ 36

Chapter 4 ♦ Understanding Overshot ♦ 39

Lesson ♦ Drafting Overshot ♦ 50

Chapter 5 ♦ From Blocks to Units ♦ 53

Part III: Unit Weaves 58

Chapter 6 ♦ Understanding Lace Weaves ♦ 59

Lesson ♦ Drafting Lace ♦ 67

Chapter 7 ♦ Understanding Damask ♦ 69

Lesson ♦ Drafting Damask ♦ 74

Chapter 8 ♦ Understanding Tied Unit Weaves ♦ 77

Lesson ♦ Drafting Tied Unit Weaves ♦ 93

Chapter 9 ♦ Understanding Patterned Double Weave ♦ 95

Chapter 10 ♦ Understanding Stitched Double Cloth ♦ 100

Chapter 11 ♦ Understanding Lampas ♦ 104

Lesson ♦ Drafting Double Weave ♦ 108

Part IV: Extras 111

Chapter 12 ♦ Understanding Turned Drafts ♦ 111

Chapter 13 ♦ Understanding Blended Drafts ♦ 114

Chapter 14 ♦ Understanding Network Drafting ♦ 116

Chapter 15 ♦ Understanding Fabric Analysis ♦ 119

♦ Answers ♦ 120

♦ For Further Study ♦ 126

♦ Graph Paper and Design Sheets ♦ 128

♦ Index ♦ 134

Acknowledgements

As a weaver, I have often felt like a small child, seeing the world by standing on her father's shoulders. The shoulders of centuries of weavers before me provide the knowledge and perspective in this small book. I'd like to think that its existence might help some future weaver climb a little higher.

The Complete Book of Drafting brings together most of what I've learned about weaving in more than ten years of passionate study. In every sentence in this book I recognize the words of my teachers, my students, and my weaving friends. I thank them all.

I would especially like to thank David Xenakis for so patiently and joyfully sharing his knowledge and discoveries with me, not only about weaving, but also about every aspect of working with words and graphics on a computer. If it weren't for David, I'd never have survived 'Copy a:*.* c:\WP50,' let alone tied up my countermarch loom.

I'd also like to acknowledge with gratitude the many weavers whose theories influence the presentation of the weave structures in this book: David Xenakis for damask tie-up design, development of piqué design techniques and graph paper, and original extensions and applications of many weave structures; Clotilde Barrett for groundbreaking monographs on double two-tie unit weave and shadow weave; Doramay Keasbey for explanations of half-units in damask and turned twill and steps for designing stitched double cloths and for blending drafts; Ruth Morrison for huck lace design techniques and graph paper; and Alice Schlein for clear translations and original applications of network drafting. I am indebted to Ruth Holroyd for publication of the work of Jacob Angstadt, whose 4-block profile draft is interpreted in this book in over a dozen different weaves. I'm grateful to Jane Evans for sharing with me the Latvian terms 'paired-tie' and 'tied-float' weaves and to Traudi Bestler for suggesting 'template' as a term for tie-up modules.

Thanks also go to the patient readers who proofed the final copy of this book and caught (we hope!) the errors that persistently creep into weaving drafts and language: Mildred McCloskey, Margaret Windeknecht, Suzanne Ramsey, Virginia I. Harvey, Susan Huffman, Lynda Lee, and William Dyer.

The drafts and other graphics in this book are prepared on a Macintosh IIci in Adobe Illustrator by the author, but owe their clarity to lessons and templates provided by David Xenakis and Carol Skallerud of Golden Fleece Publications (since this author can't manage to read a computer manual in the way that she intends for you to read this book).

These pages are produced with desktop publishing program Quark Xpress, and I thank Alexis Xenakis, Elaine Rowley, and **Weaver's** Magazine for teaching me Quark's quirks. The back cover photo is by Alexis Xenakis.

All of the impeccably woven samples interpreting the 4-block Angstadt profile draft are woven by Ruth Morrison over a period of four months. This task required re-threading the loom more than a dozen times in addition to weaving and finishing the samples. The 8-shaft overshot samples are woven by Margaret Heller, who is also responsible for developing some of the treadling variations they illustrate. Two of the piqué samples are woven by Sue Beevers.

The most difficult challenge in writing a book on drafting is to express so clearly the complex and abstract principles of weaving that they can be understood by even a beginning weaver. I know I could do a better job next year and an even better one in ten years — after I've practiced explaining them to greater numbers of students. To every student who has been brave enough to say, "I don't understand what you are talking about," I give my heartfelt appreciation. I hope you understand most of the sentences in this book.

Last and most, I'd like to thank Lee Anderst. She was the one who said, "How'd you like to write a little monograph on drafting for Shuttle-Craft Books?" "Sure," I said. "I think I could do that in about two months." Two years later she became temporary secretary, cook, go-fer, proofer, and mom to see that *The Complete Book of Drafting* finally reaches your hands.

Madelyn

Introduction

It took only a second to make me a weaver. I *was* an English teacher. Teachers were assigned 'extra-curricular activities' where I taught, and one of the extra duties in my last year of teaching was to supervise a craft show. Local craftspeople were invited to exhibit their work in order to expose the students to the arts and crafts. They exposed *me* and lost a teacher.

What caught my eye and changed my life that day was a page in Mary Atwater's *Shuttle-Craft Book of American Hand-Weaving*. It lay open beside a Dorothy table loom whose owner was weaving overshot pot holders. The page showed black-and-white drawings of snowball and pine tree coverlets, and the idea that held me transfixed was: *I* could weave them. My reasoning went like this: she is weaving pot holders based on information from this book. She is a normal person in the 20th century. This book tells how to weave snowball and pine tree coverlets. I am a normal person in the 20th century. Therefore: I can weave snowball and pine tree coverlets if I have this book and a loom.

I signed up for classes. Since I was interested only in snowball and pine tree coverlets, I neglected to concentrate on some of the apparently irrelevant course work. I learned the basics, like the bottom row is '1.' I astutely grasped the fact that I needed a wider loom than the Dorothy for my coverlets. A few months went by (I learned that time has a different meaning in a weaver's life). I read all the loom ads about friction brakes and easy tie-up systems, and not knowing very much about any of these features, I ordered my loom because it was made of cherry.

Finally, I had both the loom and the book. On somebody's recommendation ('you can weave anything you'd ever want on a 4-shaft loom') my loom had four shafts. This was OK with me because one of the coverlet patterns I liked showed four rows in what I thought was the threading draft. Ready to begin, I puzzled over the draft. It called for ten warp threads in a row to be threaded on shaft 1. *My* question: where do I put the blue warp threads and where do I put the white warp threads? Weaving was so much magic and mystery to me that I wasn't worried at all about those ten consecutive threads on shaft 1.

As a last resort I decided to *read* Mary Atwater's book. I am by long habit not much of a reader of introductions, nor do I usually read a book by starting at the beginning. I like to go straight to the good parts. It took many sittings of struggling through chapter after chapter to learn that my chosen draft was a profile draft, not a threading draft, and that I would need 16 shafts for my coverlet.

It took four years to assemble the necessary knowledge and equipment to weave it. Many times since, I have felt the same joy in dreaming of something I wanted to make and the same frustration from lacking the necessary knowledge or tools. Weaving is such an astoundingly complex field; a lifetime is not enough to learn all one needs to know, let alone enough to weave all one wants to weave. It is to save you a little bit of time that I write this book. In it are all the things I needed to know in that second I decided I wanted to weave snowballs and pine trees.

If you are reading this introduction *after* you have already read the chapter on profile drafts or overshot or network drafting, you might be someone like me. Try to alter your habit for this book, and start with Chapter 1. Your understanding of the vocabulary and concepts in later chapters depends on the information that comes before them.

A weaving teacher once told me, 'Everything in weaving is so simple after you understand it, but before you do, it seems so hard.' Remind yourself as you struggle with concepts that feel complicated, they are simpler than they seem. If you persevere, you'll learn the special joy of sudden understanding — which will bring a special joy to me.

Part I
The Basic Weaves

How to use this book

The Complete Book of Drafting includes all of the ways in which weave structures can be illustrated on paper. If you've just bought a computer weaving program, you might wonder why you need to know how to graph a weave. Isn't that what a computer program is supposed to do? The answer is that although you can generate a drawdown with a computer weaving program, you won't be able to use the drawdown unless you understand how the weave structure works. The process of preparing a draft for weaving is the most important step towards that understanding. A computer program will save you lots of hours of work *after* you know how to write a draft.

The Complete Book of Drafting is divided into four parts. You shouldn't expect to read it in a weekend. If you are a beginning weaver, plan to spend a lot of time on Part I: The Basic Weaves. Even if you think you already understand the material in Part I, you should read it carefully. Parts II, III, and IV presume that you have learned the specific weaving vocabulary and techniques presented in Part I. Part II explains block theory and profile drafting. A thorough understanding of the material in Part II is a prerequisite for Part III.

Part III shows how to translate a profile draft into a real draft for almost every unit weave. Learn how to use threading, tie-up, and treadling keys to open the door to new designing freedom. Once you understand the process, you can choose to study each unit weave in sequence or in any order. Also use Part III as a handy reference book of pattern weaves.

Part IV presents some special drafting techniques that can increase your weaving repertoire.

Most of the chapters are followed by lessons with exercises. The exercises are an important learning tool. Use them to evaluate your understanding. Check your work in the answer section, pages 120-125.

Pages 128-133 give examples of special design and graph papers. Instead of using these sheets for practice work, photocopy them to use as needed.

The language of weaving is not easy to understand nor easy to write. Most of the weaving words we use are a part of our non-weaving vocabulary: pattern, unit, block, simple, shadow, fancy, satin, plain, tie, profile, halftone, turned. You may not recognize the very specific ways these ordinary words are used in a sentence about weaving. To help you understand the text, each chapter is preceded by 'Words to Know,' giving definitions of the important weaving vocabulary used in the chapter. Study the definitions before reading the chapter even though you may not completely understand them. As you read the chapter, refer back to the definitions. A complete list of 'Words to Know' and the pages on which to find their definitions is included in the index on page 136.

How to use Part I

Part I covers the basic weave structures and principles of drafting. You'll learn how to prepare a drawdown and a drawup, how to tell the difference between a warp and weft drawdown, and how to recognize the connection between a draft and the corresponding setup on the loom. You'll also learn to read and write a cross section. Drawdowns and cross sections represent what the threads do in a weave structure.

Refer often to the definitions in 'Words to Know.'

The 'Family Tree of Weaves,' p. 2, groups all weave structures into three categories. Refer to this chart as you read Parts I-IV. Keep the three categories in mind as you examine fabrics. With practice, you'll learn to identify their construction. Understanding weave structures gives you the power to choose how you want your own fabrics to be.

The Family Tree of Weaves

Simple weaves

One warp and one weft

plain weave
    warp-faced and weft-faced
        ('rep') weaves
    basket weave

twill
    straight, point, broken,
        and fancy twills
    warp-faced and weft-faced
        twills

satin

Weaves that produce blocks of pattern
    warp-faced and weft-faced
        ('rep') weaves
    M's and O's
    spot weaves
        spot Bronson
        Swedish lace

Weaves that produce blocks of pattern with units
    multishaft M's and O's
    Bronson lace
    huck lace
    turned twill
    turned satin (damask)

Weaves with compound sets of elements

More than one warp
More than one weft

Supplementary weft or warp

Weaves that produce blocks of pattern
    overshot
    crackle

Weaves that produce blocks of pattern with units
    two-tie weaves
        summer and winter and others:
            (ratios of tie-down ends to
            pattern ends 1:1, 1:2, 1:3,
            1:4, 2:4, etc.)
    three-tie weaves
        'Bergman,' 'half satin'
    four-tie weaves
        'Quigley'
    warp and weft pile weaves
        velvet
        terry

Complementary weft or warp
    Bedford cord
    swivel

Weaves that produce blocks of pattern with units
    warp-faced compound tabby
        and twill
    weft-faced compound tabby
        and twill (taqueté, samitum)

Compound weaves

More than one weave

Double weave

Layer-exchange double weave
    two independent and equal
    structures are connected by
    exchanging faces

        also called patterned, figured,
        or block double weave

Stitched double cloths
    two independent structures
    (face and back) do not change
    faces but are connected
    by stitching with:

        warp from bottom layer over
            weft from top layer
        warp from top layer under weft
            from bottom layer
        extra warp
        extra weft

Lampas
    two independent but unequal
    structures (main and secondary)
    are connected where the weft of
    the secondary weave passes
    over the main weave

    The two structures can either:
        form free double cloth where
        main structure is on the top
        or
        interweave throughout (main
        structure is stitched to
        secondary wherever main
        structure is on top)

Basic Drafting: Words to Know

draft: usually refers to the complete draft for weaving and includes the threading draft, tie-up, treadling order, and drawdown (or drawup).

drawdown: prepared on graph paper, the drawdown is a graphic representation of the cloth, showing either warp threads passing over weft threads (warp drawdown) or weft threads passing over warp threads (weft drawdown).

fabric analysis: deriving the threading, tie-up, and treadling order of a piece of woven cloth. First the warp threads and weft threads of a complete repeat are picked apart in order to diagram the interlacement in drawdown form. The other components of the draft can then be determined.

harness: in North America 'harness' has often been used as the name of the frame that carries the heddles. In Europe, however, 'harness' is used to identify a *set* of frames (also called shafts, heddle frames, or leaves). According to this definition, a two-harness loom is a loom with two sets of shafts, or two 'mountings,' such as the pattern harness and ground harness on a drawloom. To avoid ambiguity, shaft is used in this book to refer to an individual frame; a harness is a set of shafts.

interlacement: the crossing of warp threads (or 'ends') with weft threads (or 'picks') to produce a fabric. For each weave structure there is a specific order of interlacement.

plain weave: the simplest of all interlacements. In plain weave each weft pick passes over one warp end and under one end. The next weft pick reverses the actions of the first. Two warp ends and two weft picks complete the interlacement.

rising shed: refers to looms that raise shafts in order to form a shed. Jack looms are rising-shed looms.

satin: a weave with warp floats on one surface of the cloth and weft floats on the other. In twill, a diagonal line is produced when each successive weft pick interlaces with a warp end directly adjacent to the warp end that interlaced in the preceding pick. To eliminate the diagonal line and produce a smooth, uniform cloth surface, in satin each succeeding weft thread interlaces with a *non-adjacent* warp thread. In each pick, the interlacing warp end is the *same number* of ends away from the end that interlaced in the preceding pick.

shaft: one of at least two frames equipped with heddles. Selected warp ends are threaded through the heddles so that they can be lifted or lowered together to form the sheds for weaving.

shed: the opening created by raised and lowered warp threads through which a weft pick passes.

sinking shed: refers to looms that lower shafts to form the shed. Counterbalance looms are often called 'sinking-shed' looms, although shafts also rise as a result of their connection to lowered shafts over pulleys.

tabby: a synonym for plain weave, used especially to distinguish a plain weave weft from a pattern weft.

threading draft: shows the order in which the warp ends are threaded through the heddles on the shafts.

tie-up: indicates the shafts that are lifted and lowered to form each shed.

treadling sequence (or order): the order in which the sheds are formed.

twill: a weave in which each weft pick passes over or under more than one warp end in the interlacement sequence (and each warp end over or under more than one weft pick). In each successive pick, the same interlacement begins on an adjacent warp end, either to the left or to the right, creating a diagonal line.

warp: a set of threads or 'ends' all of which interlace in the same way with a set of weft threads. A fabric has 'two warps' when one set of warp ends interlaces in one way, in plain weave order, for example, and another set interlaces in a different way, such as floating to form pattern.

warp drawdown: a drawdown in which black squares represent warp ends passing over weft picks.

warp end: an individual working thread in a warp (more than one strand can be threaded through a heddle to be used as a single working warp end).

weft: a set of threads which interlace in the same way with a set (or sets) of warp threads. A fabric has 'two wefts' when one set of weft threads interlaces in one way in plain weave order, for example, and another set interlaces in a different way, such as floating to form pattern as in overshot.

weft drawdown: a drawdown in which black squares represent weft picks passing over warp ends.

weft pick: the thread or group of threads passing through a single shed.

Chapter 1
Reading Drafts

THE BASIC DRAFT

The draft is the handweaver's blueprint. It tells how to thread the warp, how to tie up the treadles, and in what order to use the treadles for a particular weave structure. *Figure 1* shows the four parts of a basic draft: the threading, the tie-up, the treadling order, and the drawdown. Note the black square where the four parts meet. Think of it as the 'you are here' of the draft. Begin reading each of the four parts from this point.

The threading

The threading draft gives the order in which the warp ends are threaded through heddles on specific shafts. It is always written horizontally to reflect the position of the heddles on the shafts. The bottom row represents shaft 1, the second row shaft 2, etc. From the 'you are here' square, read the threading in *Figure 1*: 1-2-3-4-1-2-3-4, etc.

The tie-up

The tie-up shows which shafts must be raised and which lowered to produce each of the sheds required by the weave structure. On a floor loom, treadles are connected to lamms that move the shafts. On some looms the lamms *raise* shafts (most jack looms), on some they *lower* shafts (counterbalance looms), and on still others they both *raise and lower* shafts (countermarch looms). Any tie-up can be used for any type of loom. Discover from the tie-up which shafts must be up and which down for each shed, and do to the loom whatever is required to get them there.

When the tie-up is written with numerals, the numerals represent raised shafts; the blank spaces represent shafts that are down. In *Figure 1* treadle 1 raises shafts 1 and 2, treadle 2 raises shafts 2 and 3, treadle 3 raises shafts 3 and 4, and treadle 4 raises shafts 1 and 4.

The treadling order

The treadling diagram shows the order in which the treadles are depressed. Each symbol in the treadling diagram represents a weft pick. The first pick in *Figure 1,* for example, is made by depressing treadle 1; shafts 1 and 2 are raised. In the second pick, shafts 2 and 3 are raised, etc. The treadling diagram is always vertical to correspond to the successive rows of picks.

1. The four parts of a draft

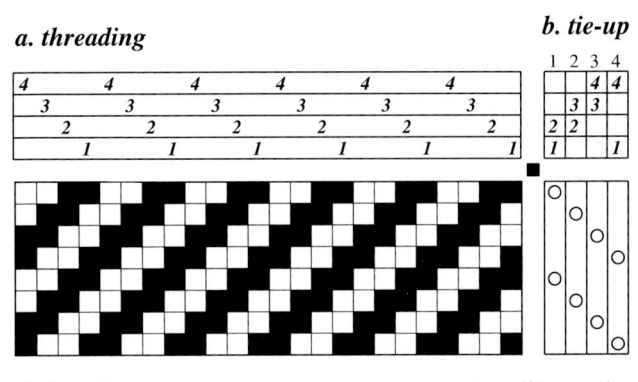

a. threading   *b. tie-up*

d. drawdown   *c. treadling order*

The drawdown

The drawdown is a graphic representation of the cloth. It shows how the warp threads and the weft threads interlace with each other. In the drawdown in *Figure 1*, black squares represent raised warp threads and white squares represent weft threads. Read this drawdown starting at the 'you are here' square, from top to bottom. In the first pick, shafts 1 and 2 are raised. Since warp threads on shafts 3 and 4 are down, the weft covers them but passes under the raised threads on shafts 1 and 2. In the next row, shafts 2 and 3 are raised. Notice that each thread on shaft 2 is up for the first two rows; the two corresponding (vertical) black squares represent a warp thread that floats for two picks. Remember that although they look like empty squares, two adjacent (horizontal) white squares represent a weft thread that passes over two warp ends.

THE DRAFT AND THE LOOM

Figure 2 shows the way in which the draft in *Figure 1* is used to set up the loom and weave the cloth. Imagine that you are standing in front of the loom, where you sit as you weave. The first warp end on the right is threaded through a heddle on shaft 1, as indicated by the threading draft (see arrow); the second through a heddle on shaft 2, etc. The loom can be threaded from either direction. If you start at the left, thread the first end through a heddle on shaft 4, the second through a heddle on shaft 3, etc.

2. From the draft to the loom

 a. *threading*
 b. *tie-up*
 c. *treadling order*
 d. *cloth*

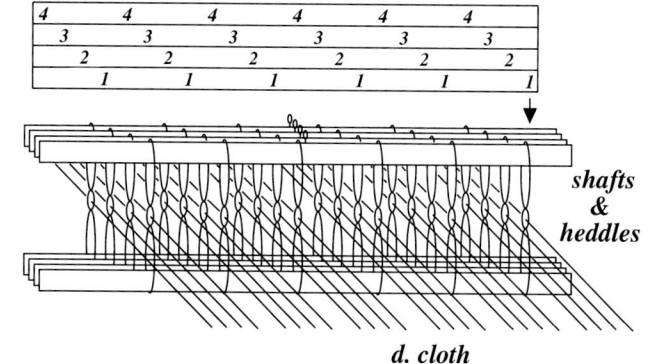

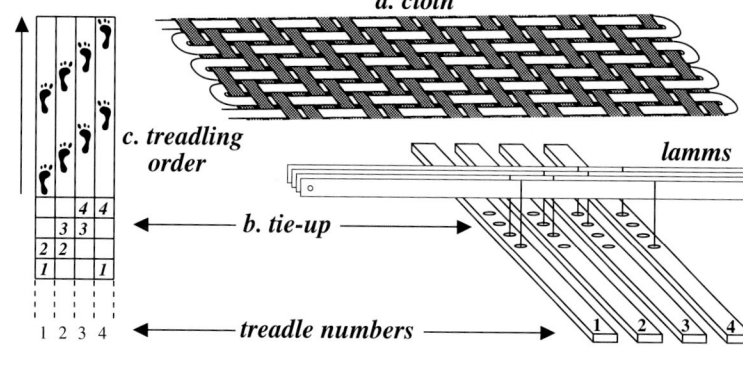

a. threading

d. cloth

c. treadling order

b. tie-up

treadle numbers

shafts & heddles

lamms

Use the tie-up diagram to tie the treadles to the lamms. *Figure 2* shows the treadles of a jack loom tied to lift 1-2, 2-3, 3-4, 1-4.

While the threading and tie-up diagrams tell how to set up the loom, the treadling order tells how to weave the cloth. The weft symbols in the treadling diagram in *Figure 1* show which treadles to depress. Locate again the first pick in *Figure 1*. Now imagine that you are suspended in air, looking down at the loom in *Figure 2*. The shafts and threaded heddles are at the top of this picture and the treadles and tie-up at the bottom. The first pick in the cloth is the bottom one, the one closest to the weaver. The cloth is woven from 'bottom to top.' Follow the footprints and compare the eight picks in *Figures 1* and *2*. Notice that in the cloth, the twill moves in one direction, from bottom right to top left, but in the top-to-bottom drawdown in *Figure 1*, the twill moves in the opposite direction. Since it is easiest to make a drawdown by starting with the pick nearest to the threading, most drafts are written with a top-to-bottom drawdown as in *Figure 1*, even though the twill diagonal moves in the opposite direction from the actual direction in the cloth.

VARIATIONS IN DRAFT FORMATS

Just about the time you think you understand how to read a draft in one format, you'll find a draft that looks completely different. Don't be discouraged! Take a deep breath and say to yourself 'I *can* figure this out.' Remember that whatever the format, every draft reveals the same information: the threading order, the combinations of raised and lowered shafts that form the sheds, and the order in which the sheds are made.

The direction of the draft

Most of the confusion comes from drafts presented in an unaccustomed direction. In Scandinavian drafts, the threading appears at the bottom. In some sources the tie-up appears in the upper left corner instead of the right so that the threading can be read from left to right the way we read a book. Whatever the direction, position an imaginary 'you are here' square at the point where threading, tie-up, and treadling meet, and read each of the components moving away from it.

Study the four drafts in *Figure 3*. Notice that the direction of the twill changes whenever *one* component of the draft is reversed. Compare *3a* and *3b*: reversing the threading reverses the twill direction. Writing the treadling order from bottom to top instead of top to bottom also reverses the direction of the twill (compare *3a* and *3c*; *3b* and *3d*). If the loom is threaded, tied up, and treadled exactly as *3c* or *3d* is written, the direction of the twill in the

3. *Draft formats: four directions*

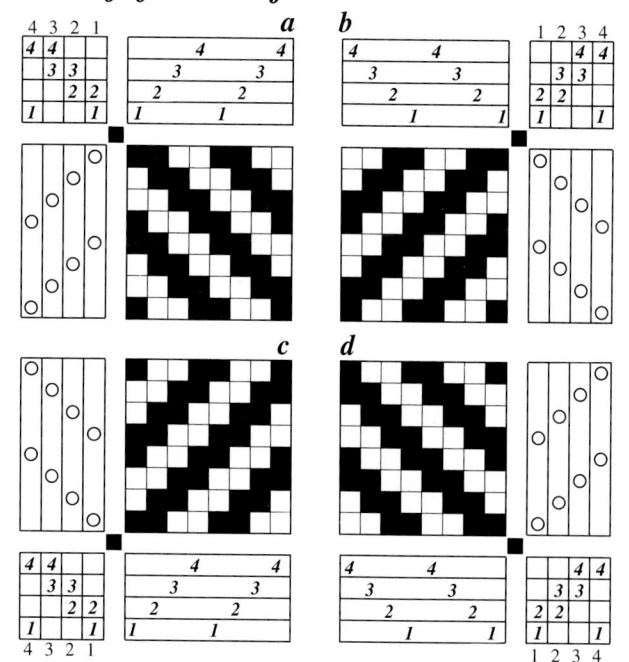

 a   *b*

 c   *d*

5

cloth and in the drawdown — or draw*up* in this case — exactly match.

Most of the time the direction of the twill doesn't matter. You are not likely to begin weaving and throw down your shuttle in despair, exclaiming: 'But I expected a *right*-hand twill, not a *left*-hand twill!' Simply reverse the treadling order if you need a different twill direction.

WARP OR WEFT DRAWDOWN?

The drawdowns in the drafts we have examined so far are 'warp' drawdowns: black squares indicate raised warp ends passing over weft picks. White squares represent weft picks passing over warp ends that are down. When used with a jack — or 'rising shed' — loom, a warp drawdown directly portrays the action of the shafts: warp ends on the shafts that are raised are black in the drawdown. Warp drawdowns are commonly used for plain weave, twills, satins, and laces, where the number of picks per inch is equal to the number of ends per inch.

A warp drawdown can easily be identified by examining the first pick. If a black square appears directly under a warp end threaded on a shaft that is raised, the drawdown is a *warp* drawdown. In **Figure 4a**, the weft symbol in the treadling order indicates that shaft 1 is raised for the first pick. Black squares appear under ends threaded on shaft 1; therefore **Figure 4a** shows a warp drawdown. If a square for an end on the raised shaft is white, as in **Figure 4b**, the drawdown is a *weft* drawdown. In weft drawdowns, black squares appear under every warp end that is *not* raised to indicate that a weft passes over that warp end. It is more difficult to do a weft drawdown than a warp drawdown since all the squares in a weft drawdown are marked *but* those indicated in the tie-up.

Confusion about warp vs. weft drawdowns occurs for several reasons. We associate the squares in the drawdown with the colors of the warp and weft threads, dark vs. light. The drawdown indicates warp and weft *function*, not color, however. Any similarity between the actual colors of warp and weft threads and the black or white in the drawdown is coincidental. Notice that the weft threads in **4b** are white, but the weft drawdown shows them as black to indicate that they pass over the warp threads.

We tend to read all drawdowns as weft drawdowns (even though most are not) because blank white squares do not resemble the horizontal slash of a weft thread; they seem instead like empty squares. We see (and draw) the black rows as horizontal rows rather

4a. Warp drawdown

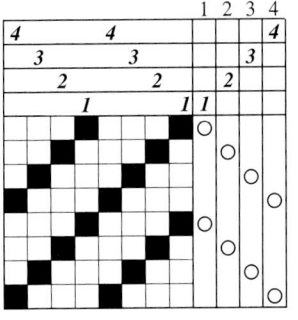

Black squares indicate the warp threads that are raised in each pick.

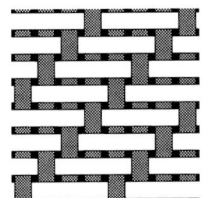

4b. Weft drawdown

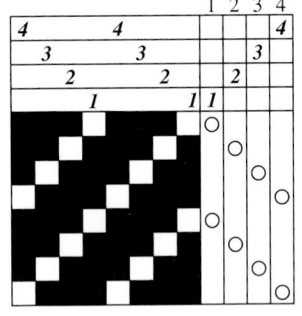

Black squares indicate weft threads passing over warp threads.

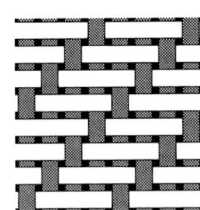

4c. Vertical or horizontal marks represent warp threads or weft threads

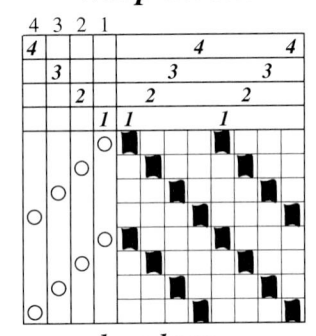

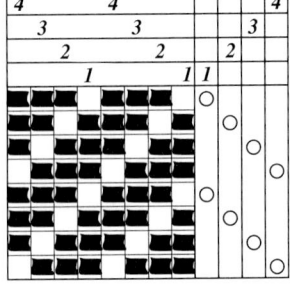

warp drawdown   weft drawdown

than vertical rows. We also have a habit of picturing warp threads as more often white than black, which encourages us to think of black squares as weft threads forming pattern against a white background. When preparing drawdowns, mark squares with a flat-tipped marking pen so that a vertical mark indicates a warp thread and a horizontal mark indicates a weft thread as in **Figure 4c**. The marks can then be connected to depict accurately a warp or weft float.

It is not really very important that you are able to recognize whether a drawdown is a warp or weft drawdown. It *is* important, however, that you understand what the threads are supposed to do and that you are able to operate your loom so that they do it.

WARP AND WEFT CROSS SECTIONS

For some weave structures, a drawdown does not give a true picture of the cloth. A drawdown cannot show two layers effectively. It does not distinguish between thick threads and thin threads, nor between close and loose setts. When it is necessary to understand an interlacement and accurately portray the size and behavior of the threads, a cross section is the ideal graphic form. Cross sections look technical, but they are nothing more than a simple picture of what one thread — warp or weft — does in a structure. Believe it or not, one day you'll find yourself intently drawing squiggly lines to puzzle out an exciting idea.

Examine the draft for plain weave in *Figure 5a*. At the side and at the bottom of the drawdown there is a cross section. The cross section at the side (*a*) is a *weft* cross section: the weft threads are 'sliced' in order to show the behavior of the warp thread. (It is an annoying source of confusion that the *warp* is studied in a *weft* cross section and vice versa.) The cross section at *a* shows the path of the last warp end, threaded on shaft 2. Consider that the face or top of the cloth is on its left. In other words, the warp thread passes over a weft when it is on the left of it and under a weft when it is on the right of it. Follow its path under the first weft, over the second, under the third, etc. Compare the warp thread in the cross section with the warp thread in the drawdown and cloth diagram. The warp cross section (warp ends are sliced) at *b* shows the path taken by the last weft pick. It passes over the first warp end threaded on shaft 1, under the second, over the third, etc.

Familiarize yourself with all of the parts of the draft. Compare the two cross sections with their counterparts in the drawdown and in the cloth diagram. Take the time to identify warp threads and weft threads by their respective symbols: black and white squares in the drawdowns, black and white circles for the sliced threads, and black and white lines for the threads represented in the cross sections. Knowing how to identify and interpret the symbols used in this draft and its corresponding cross sections is a very important step toward understanding more complicated drafts.

Study the draft for twill in *Figure 5b* and the draft for weft-predominant satin in *Figure 5c*. Match each of the cross sections with its counterpart in the drawdown and cloth diagram. Observe, for example, that the warp thread in the weft cross section in *5c* passes under the first three weft threads, over one, under four, over one, and under one.

5a. Warp drawdown with cross sections: plain weave

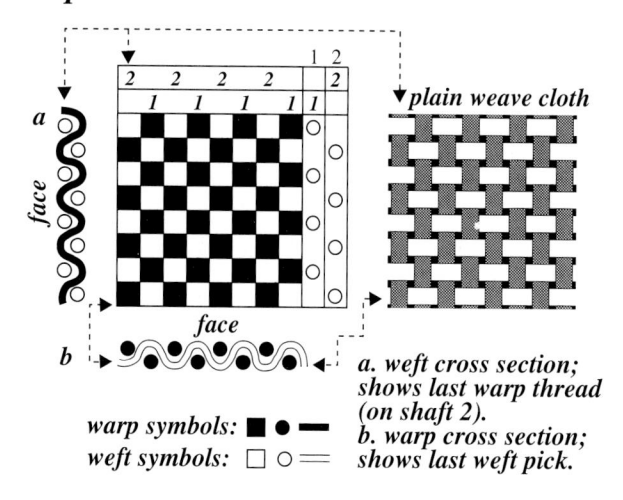

warp symbols: ■ ● ▬
weft symbols: □ ○ ═

a. weft cross section; shows last warp thread (on shaft 2).
b. warp cross section; shows last weft pick.

5b. Warp drawdown with cross sections: twill

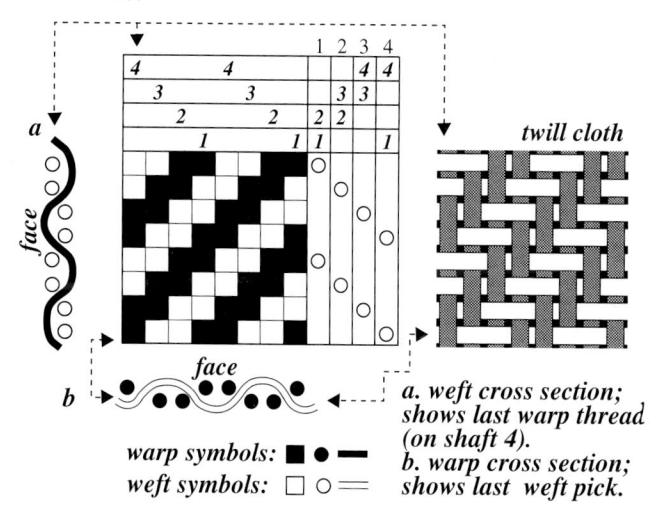

warp symbols: ■ ● ▬
weft symbols: □ ○ ═

a. weft cross section; shows last warp thread (on shaft 4).
b. warp cross section; shows last weft pick.

5c. Warp drawdown with cross sections: satin

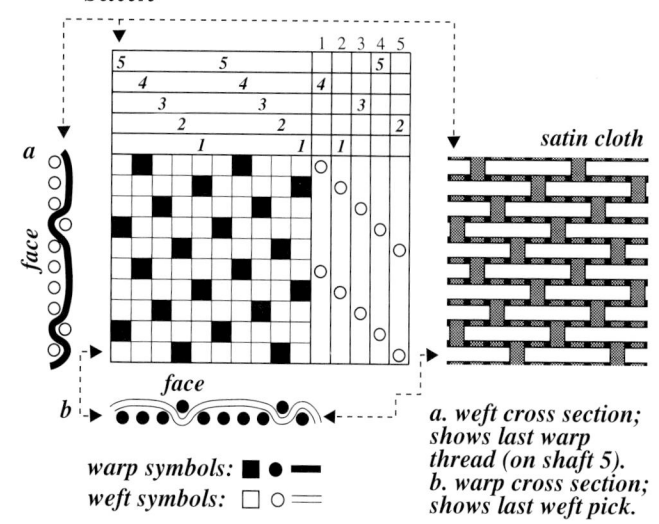

warp symbols: ■ ● ▬
weft symbols: □ ○ ═

a. weft cross section; shows last warp thread (on shaft 5).
b. warp cross section; shows last weft pick.

VARIATIONS IN DRAFT SYMBOLS

Draft formats employ a variety of symbols to indicate threading and treadling instructions. Most 4-shaft drafts in older weaving texts use vertical marks for the threading (as in the Marguerite Davison draft in *Figure 6a*) or filled-in black squares. In current texts, the threading is usually given in numbers. Drafts with numbers are much easier to use when threading the loom, particularly if the draft is for eight or more shafts. Note in *6a* that when a threading draft is long and must be continued on a second line, the second line is read in the same direction as the first, in this case, from right to left. (Remember to start reading the threading from an imaginary 'you are here' square, away from the tie-up.)

Sometimes the choice of threading or treadling symbols acts to abbreviate the draft. In the overshot draft in *Figure 6a*, a number in the treadling diagram indicates the number of supplementary-weft pattern picks for each block. The tabby picks that weave the plain weave ground cloth are not shown in the treadling diagram. 'Use tabby' instructs the weaver to alternate the tabby weft with the pattern weft

Symbols can effectively indicate color, fiber, and/or relative size of warp and weft threads, as in *Figures 6b* and *7*. A key is usually included with the draft that explains what the symbols mean.

To save space, brackets often enclose sections of a draft that are to be repeated. To thread the *Figure 7* draft from right to left: begin with two floating selvedge threads. [Thread blue on shafts 1-4 five times (20 ends) and green on shafts 1-3-2-4 five times (20 ends).] Repeat between brackets two times (80 ends). Thread red on shafts 1-4 five times (20 ends). End with two floating selvedge threads (144 total ends). Weave 4 violet picks using treadles 1-4 five times (20 picks); then weave three violet picks (treadles 1-2-3). Weave 4 yellow picks (treadles 1-5-3-6) four times (16 picks; 39 total picks).

7. Brackets enclose repeated sections.

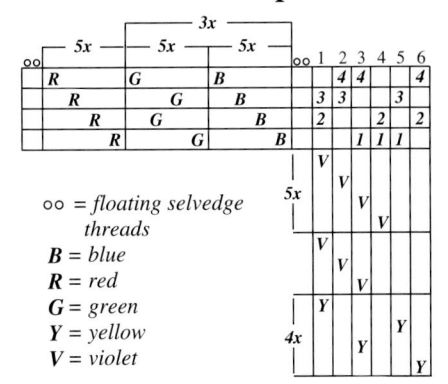

∞∞ = *floating selvedge threads*
B = *blue*
R = *red*
G = *green*
Y = *yellow*
V = *violet*

6a. Treadling shows pattern picks only.

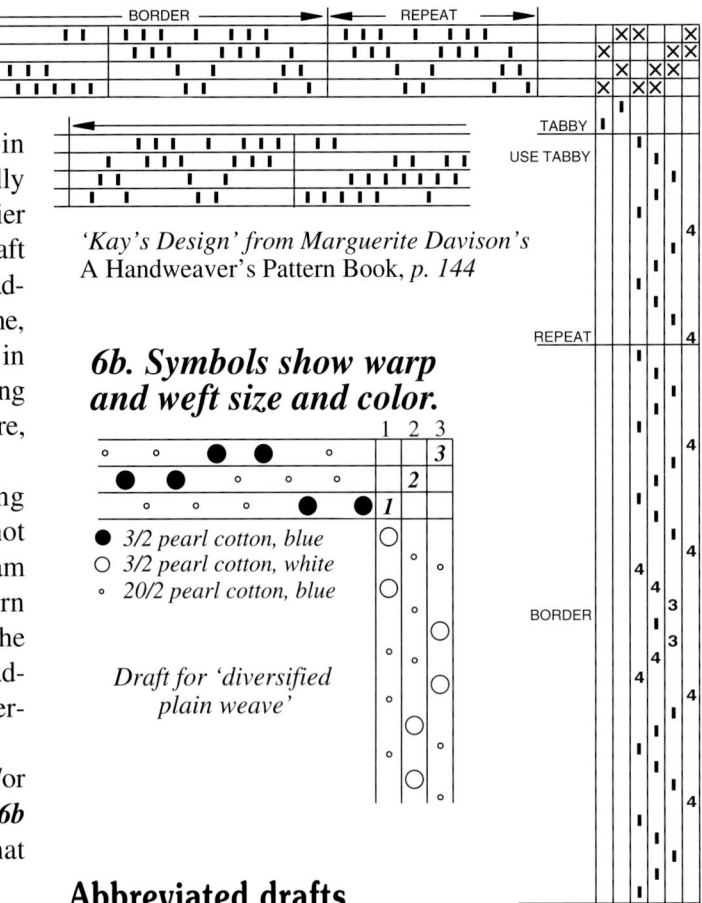

'Kay's Design' from Marguerite Davison's
A Handweaver's Pattern Book, p. 144

6b. Symbols show warp and weft size and color.

● *3/2 pearl cotton, blue*
○ *3/2 pearl cotton, white*
∘ *20/2 pearl cotton, blue*

Draft for 'diversified plain weave'

Abbreviated drafts

Weavers have devised many ways to abbreviate threading and treadling orders. Some of the most unusual abbreviations were developed long ago to save precious paper and time. *Figure 8a* shows a threading draft from the world's second published weaving text (Nathaniel Lumscher, *Neu eingerichtetes Weber Kunst und Bild Buch*, 1708, republished in *Ars Textrina*, vol. XIV, ed. by Pat Hilts). A 20-shaft threading is divided into two sections. Lines indicate straight- or point-twill threadings; a circle marks the starting shaft for each line. Begin reading at the left: 20-19-18-17, etc., to shaft 5, then back to shaft 20; then 4-3-2-1 three times, etc. Four-shaft twill threading and treadling drafts can be abbreviated in the same way, see *8b*.

8. Lines indicate twill threading and treadling orders.

8

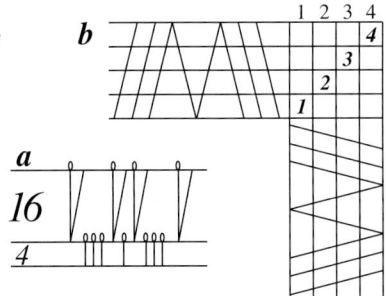

9a. Summer and winter: weft drawdown includes tabby picks

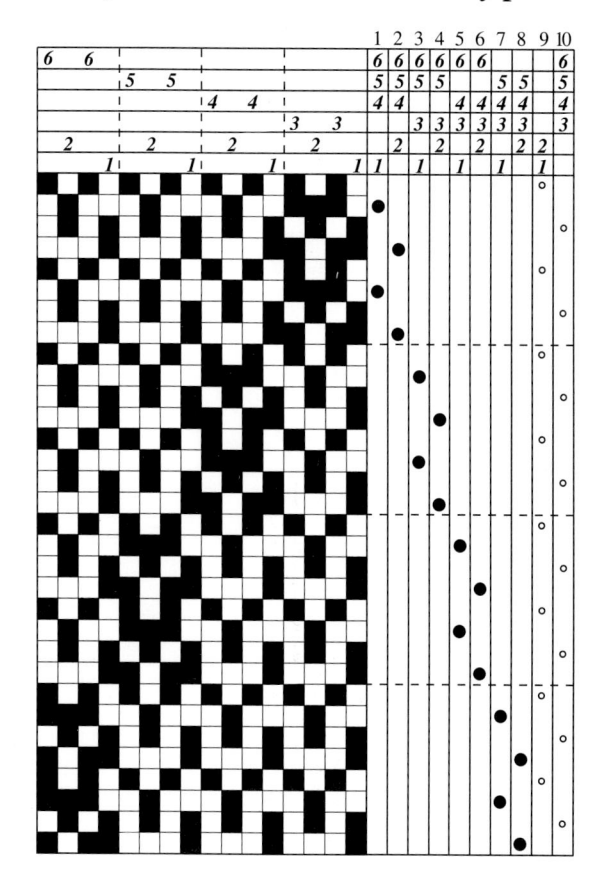

9b. Cloth diagram

In summer and winter, a heavy pattern weft floats on a plain weave cloth. Twice as many weft picks as warp ends form each 'square' of the design.

9c. Weft drawdown: tabby omitted

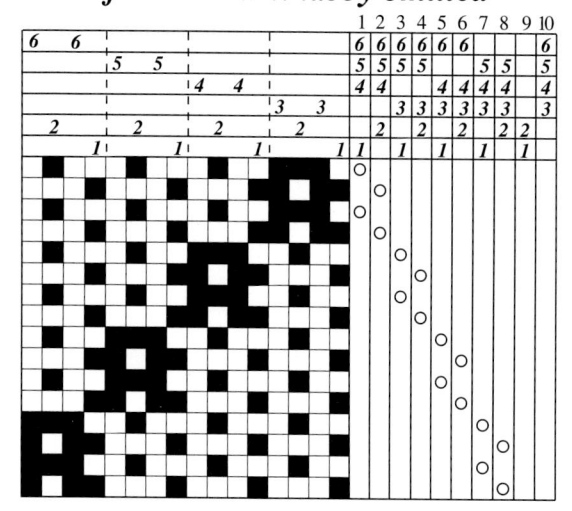

DRAWDOWN VARIATIONS

In graphed drawdowns, squares of the same size indicate thin threads and thick threads, which misrepresents the appearance of the cloth even while accurately showing the behavior of the threads. Compare the summer and winter *weft* drawdown in **Figure 9a** with the drawing of the cloth in **Figure 9b**. A heavy pattern weft alternates with a fine tabby weft. The black squares for the tabby picks in the drawdown (every other pick beginning with the first pick) are as prominent as the squares for the pattern weft.

A weft drawdown that includes only the pattern picks (see **Figure 9c**) resembles the patterned cloth more closely. Note that a warp drawdown, since it does not show the pattern weft, would not be effective. Drafts for summer and winter, overshot, and structures with supplementary pattern wefts often omit the tabby picks from the treadling instructions. The draft instead includes the words: 'Use tabby' as in 'Kay's Design,' **Figure 6a**. You might have noticed these words and misunderstood their significance. You learn their significance the hard way if you omit tabby rather than 'use' it!

ALL ABOUT TIE-UPS

Of all of the parts of a draft, the tie-up can seem the most mysterious. The connection between the threading, the tie-up, and the interlacement is not always clear. Remember: a tie-up tells nothing more complicated than which shafts must be up and which down for each shed.

Direct tie-up

Sometimes there are not enough treadles on the loom to tie up all of the required combinations of shaft lifts for a particular weave. Treadling diagrams in which two weft symbols appear in the same horizontal row indicate that two treadles are depressed together. The 4-shaft tie-up in **Figure 10** is a 'direct' tie-up: each treadle raises one shaft. All of the sheds on a 4-shaft loom can be formed with a direct tie-up using two feet. For some of the sheds, two feet depress three treadles: 123, 124, 134, 234.) A *full* tie-up for all of the possible sheds requires 14 treadles.

10. Direct tie-up

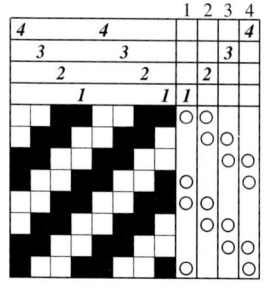

Skeleton tie-up

A direct tie-up is only practical on a 4-shaft loom — more shafts would require more feet! A 'skeleton' tie-up can often be devised so that using two or more treadles together provides the necessary sheds.

11. Summer and winter: a. full tie-up, b. skeleton tie-up

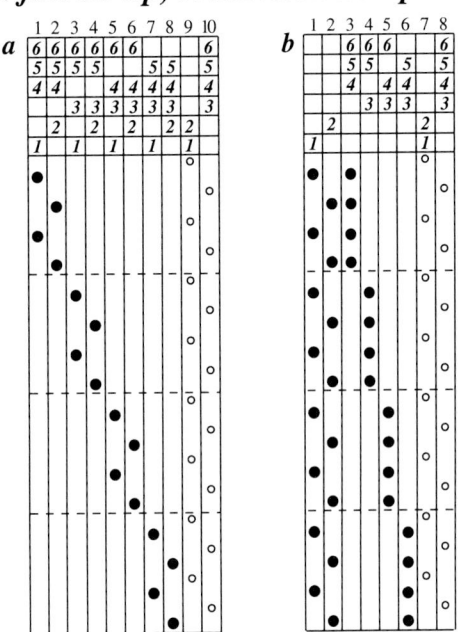

Variations in tie-up format

Tie-up symbols reflect the shedding action of the loom: rising, sinking, or rising-*and*-sinking. Because of the current predominance of jack looms, most tie-ups show the shafts that are raised for each shed.

If you learned to weave in the early years of the 'Age of the Jack Loom,' you used texts written for looms with sinking action. Not knowing the significance of an 'x' in the tie-up, you may have raised the shafts that are supposed to sink. Perplexed by the failure of the cloth to look as it should, one day you dropped a shuttle, and bending to retrieve it, discovered the correct interlacement on the underside!

Tie-ups are usually written in one of four ways:

12. Standard tie-up formats

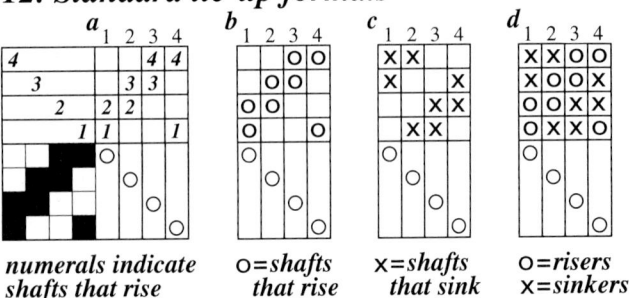

a. numerals indicate shafts that rise
b. o = shafts that rise
c. x = shafts that sink
d. o = risers x = sinkers

13a. Jack loom

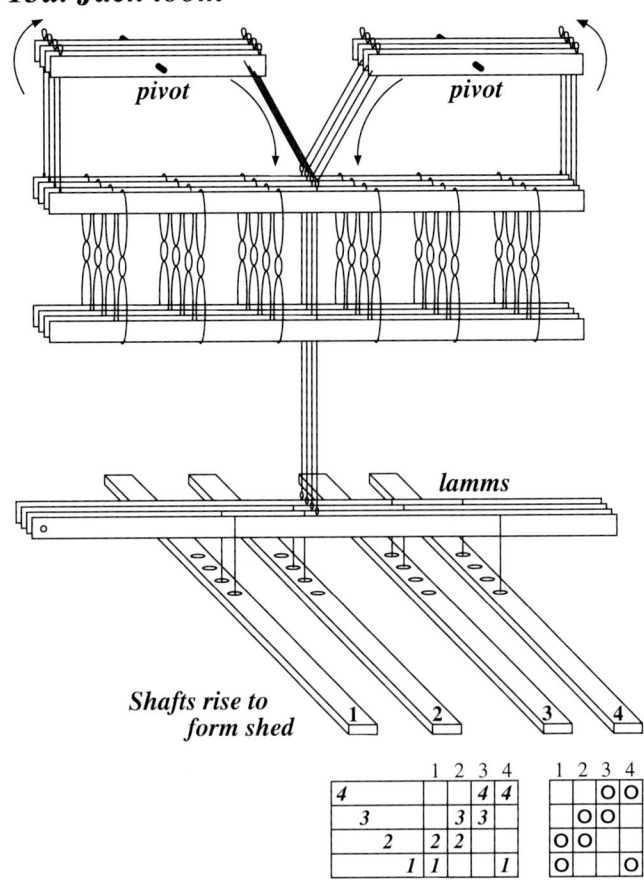

pivot   *pivot*

lamms

Shafts rise to form shed

Jack looms

An 'o' in the tie-up always indicates a shaft that rises (just as a number does). With tie-ups such as **12a** and **12b**, tie the treadles to the lamms for the marked shafts. Convert a tie-up with x's by tying the unmarked shafts (blank squares) to rise. (A handy hint: if you have trouble remembering which symbols mean what, think of the o's as balloons and the x's as anchors.)

The position of the treadles in the tie-up is usually determined by the structure: tabby treadles are on one side; treadles for twill are arranged in twill sequence; the treadles for each block are grouped together, etc. This is not always the most convenient order in which to operate the treadles. Treadle 1 in the tie-up need not be treadle 1 on the loom. Many weavers place tabby treadles on opposite sides; tie the heaviest lifts in the center; align skeleton treadles so that one foot can operate two treadles, freeing the other foot for a third; or arrange the treadles in 'walking' order: left foot, right foot, left foot, right foot, etc. Choose a convenient arrangement, but follow the correct shedding order indicated in the treadling sequence.

Table looms are 'rising-shed' looms. For each shed, move the levers that raise the shafts listed in the tie-up above the weft symbol in the treadling diagram.

13b. Counterbalance loom

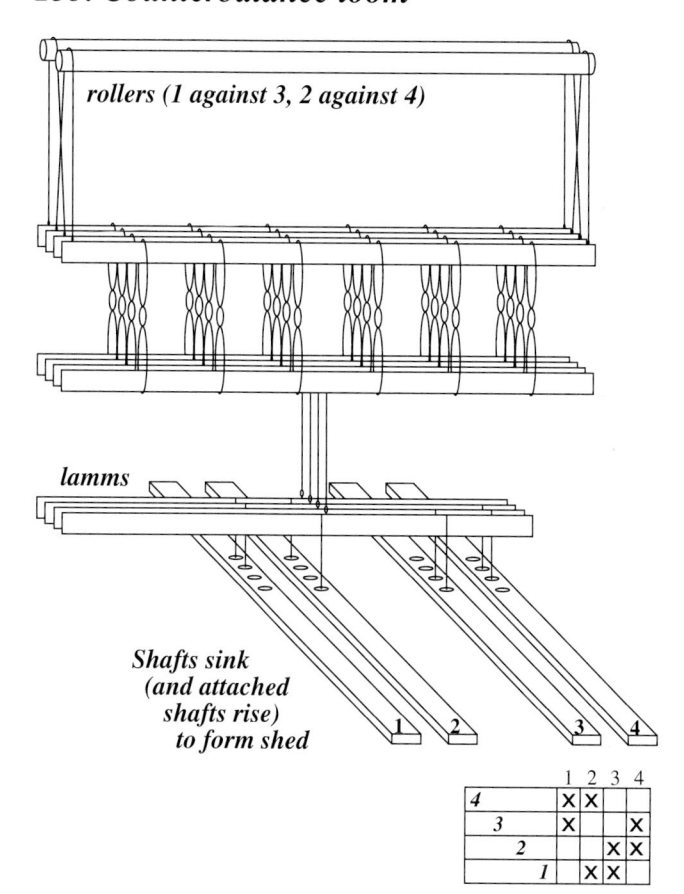

	1	2	3	4
4	x	x		
3	x			x
2			x	x
1		x	x	

13c. Countermarch loom

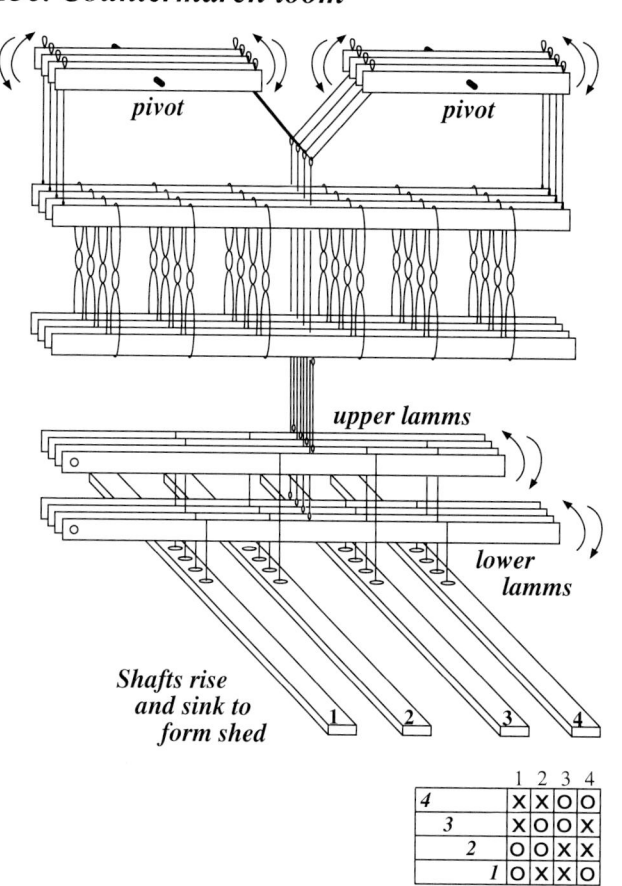

	1	2	3	4
4	x	x	o	o
3	x	o	o	x
2	o	o	x	x
1	o	x	x	o

Counterbalance looms

Counterbalance looms, misleadingly called 'sinking shed' looms, influenced North American tie-up format for the first half of the 20th century. In these tie-ups, an 'x' designates a shaft that sinks as in *12c*. (Tie-ups are sometimes written with filled-in black squares. In Scandinavian texts, black squares usually indicate shafts that sink. In other sources, such as computer-generated drawdowns, black squares signal shafts that rise.)

On a counterbalance loom each shaft is connected to another shaft by a cord passing over rollers or pulleys at the top of the loom. Pulling down a lamm causes one shaft to sink and its connected shaft to rise. (The *shed* does not sink.) Blank, or white, squares in the tie-up represent shafts that rise. In *Figure 13b*, shaft 1 is connected to shaft 3 and shaft 2 is connected to shaft 4. Treadle 1 lowers shafts 3 and 4 but at the same time *raises* shafts 1 and 2. Notice that the tie-up in *12c* gives the same information as *12a*. The same shafts must be up and the same shafts down for each shed in both.

So you need not ponder whether you have a 'sinking-shed' loom or a 'rising-shed' loom or a 'sinking-shed' tie-up or a 'rising-shed' tie-up. Determine which shafts are up and which down for each of the required sheds and tie your treadles to move them there.

Countermarch looms

Countermarch looms are equipped with two sets of lamms. The lower lamm causes shafts to rise and the upper lamm causes shafts to sink. Observe the ties to lamms in *Figure 13c* and compare them with the marks in the tie-up: treadle 1 is tied to the lower lamms for shafts 1 and 2 and to the upper lamms for shafts 3 and 4. When the treadles are at rest, the warp is positioned in the middle of the shed. When a treadle is depressed, all the shafts are moved, either up or down. If a shaft is not tied to go up or down, the warp ends threaded on it remain in the middle of the shed.

Use any tie-up format with a countermarch loom. For tie-ups *12a* and *12b*, tie the marked squares to rise and the blank squares to sink. For *12c*, tie the x's to sink and the blank squares to rise.

You can use skeleton tie-ups on a countermarch loom with one limitation: no single shaft can be asked both to rise *and* to sink. (Use the skeleton tie-up in *14* with the treadling sequence in *11*.) Treadles 7 and 8 weave tabby. Use treadles 1 and 2 with the pattern treadles; all shafts are raised or lowered; none are in conflict.

14. Countermarch skeleton tie-up

	1	2	3	4	5	6	7	8
			o	o	x	o		
			o	x	o	x		
		o	x	o	x	o		
	x	o	o	o	x	o		
	x	o					o	x
	o	x					o	x

Lesson: Writing Drafts

If you can read a weaving draft, you can use a multitude of sources for interesting projects. If you can write a weaving draft you can design unique pieces. Drafts are usually written from two different starting points. In the first, the threading, tie-up, and treadling order are given, and the drawdown is generated to check effectiveness. In the second, the drawdown or interlacement is known, and the threading, tie-up, and treadling order are derived. This second process, known as 'fabric analysis,' is explored in Chapter 15.

Make a warp drawdown.

Step 1. Select a draft such as the twill draft in *Exercise 1*. When you have completed this exercise, practice with a variety of twill or lace drafts from weaving magazines or books. Use 8 sq/in graph paper (see p. 128).

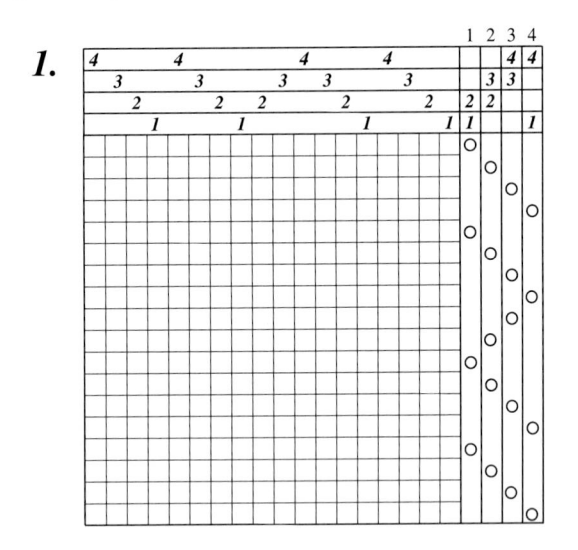

Step 2. Look at the first row in the drawdown (remember the 'you are here' square?). Then note the first mark in the treadling sequence under the tie-up. It appears in the treadle 1 column: shafts 1 and 2 are raised. Move across the weft row, shading in all the squares under threads on shafts 1 and 2. Remember that in a *warp* drawdown the warp threads that are raised for each pick are black in the drawdown. For the next row, shade squares under 2 and 3, for the next row 3 and 4, etc. (When doing a warp drawdown, avoid filling in squares with horizontal strokes; the filled-in squares then look like weft threads. Use a calligraphic pen or marker with a wide, flat point and mark each square with a vertical stroke.) When you have completed the drawdown, take time to study the connection between threading order, treadling order, and drawdown. Compare your drawdown with the drawdown in the answer section (p. 120).

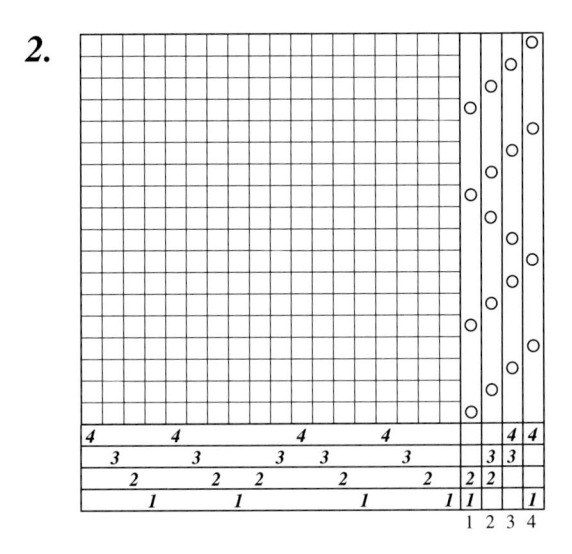

Make a draw*up* by following the directions in Step 2. You will move up from the imaginary 'you are here' square instead of down to fill in squares above the threads that are raised for each succeeding row.

Make a weft drawdown.

Using the same grid as in the first exercise, do a *weft* drawdown. Instead of shading warp threads that are raised, shade squares for threads that are *not* raised to represent weft threads passing *over* warp threads. Make *horizontal* strokes when filling a square.

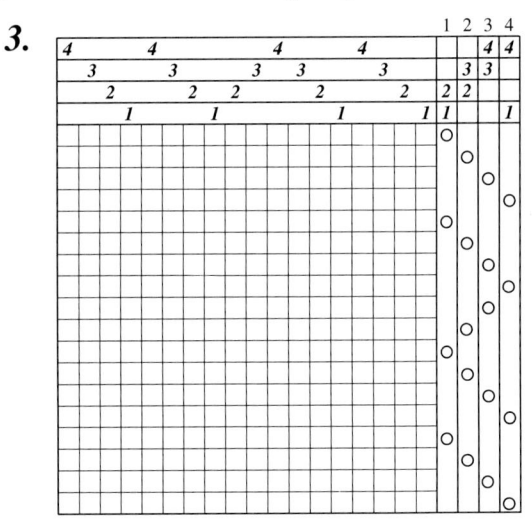

Draw a weft cross section.

If you're like me, you have wished you'd never have to do a cross section. If you persevere, however, you'll be amazed by how simple they really are. Cross sections are an important tool for understanding interlacements that can't be diagrammed accurately any other way. Let's start with an easy one. Study the twill draft in **4**.

Bisected weft threads are shown to the left of the draft in **4**, at *a*. Draw the path of the last warp end, on shaft 4. Consider that the face, or top of the cloth, is to the left: if the warp thread is up for a pick, it passes to the left of the weft; if it is down, it passes to the right.

✎ **Step 1.** Determine whether the warp thread is up or down for the first pick.

✎ **Step 2.** If it is up, begin drawing its path to the left of the top weft. If it is down, begin drawing its path to the right of the top weft. Continue, crossing from left to right of the weft threads as the warp thread is raised or lowered respectively.

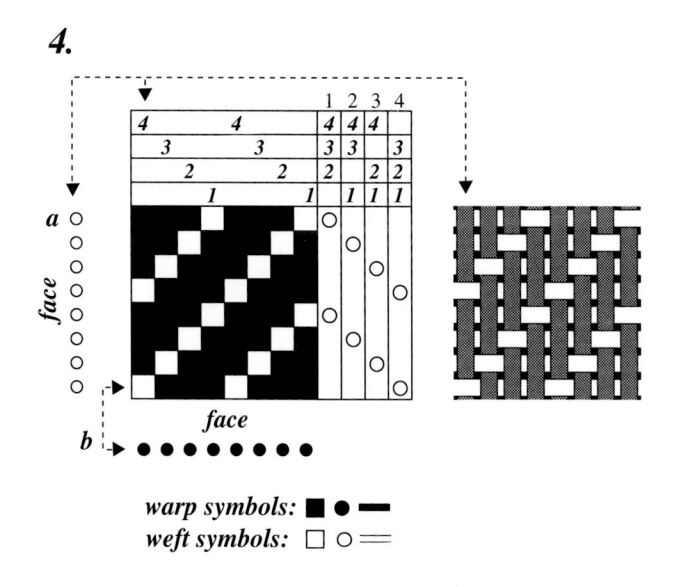

4.

warp symbols: ■ ● ▬
weft symbols: □ ○ ═

Draw a warp cross section.

Bisected warp threads are shown below the draft in **Figure 4** at *b*. Complete the warp cross section by drawing the path of the last (eighth) weft pick. The face of the cloth is on the top.

✎ **Step 1.** Determine whether each warp thread is up or down.

✎ **Step 2.** Draw the weft's path under all raised warp ends and over all warp ends that are not raised. Compare your warp and weft cross sections with the cross sections in the answer section (p. 120).

More cross sections

Now let's try a harder one. Study the draft in **5a**. To give you a little help, a cloth diagram is included that shows the thick and thin warp and weft threads.

5a.

warp symbols: ■ ● ▬
weft symbols: □ ○ ═

weft cross section; shows first warp thread (on shaft 1).

face   back

warp cross section; shows first weft pick.

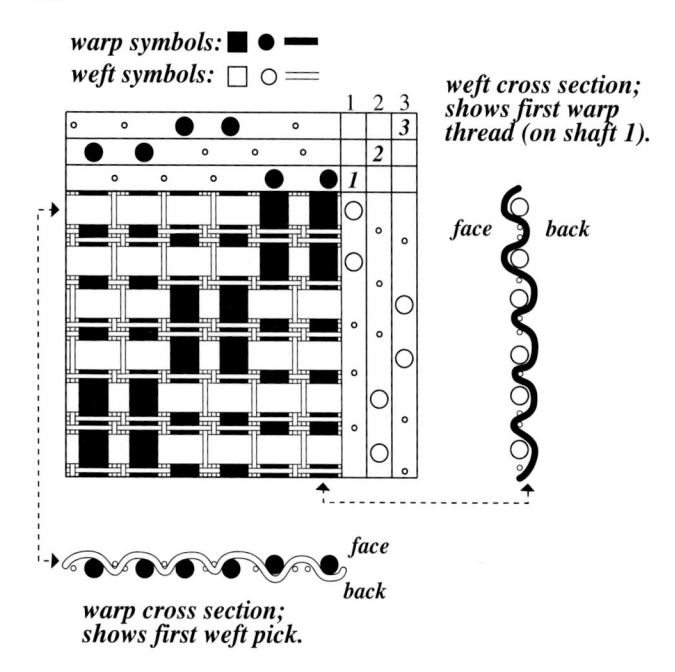

This time the first warp thread on shaft 1 is shown in a sample weft cross section to the right of the draft. The first weft pick is shown in the warp cross section at the bottom of the draft.

5b.

face   back

Complete the weft cross section in **5b** for the sixth warp end in the draft, a heavy black thread on shaft 3. If the warp thread is up for the pick, it passes to the left of the weft; if it is down, it passes to the right. Next, complete the warp cross section in **5c** for the sixth pick in the draft, a heavy white thread inserted with treadle 3. If a warp thread is down the weft passes over it; if it is up, the weft passes under it.

5c.

face

back

13

Basic Weaves: Words to Know

basket weave: a derivation of plain weave in which two, three, or four adjacent warp threads and two, three, or four adjacent weft threads form the alternate plain weave sheds instead of single warp threads and weft threads.

broken twill: describes twill threading or treadling orders that reverse (as point twills do) but skip one or more shafts in the threading and/or one or more treadles in the treadling, causing a visible break in the diagonal twill lines.

color-and-weave: refers to the alternation of dark and light warp ends and weft picks that produces a visual effect different from the structural interlacement. The alternation can be one-and-one, two-and-one, two-and-two-and-one-and-one, or many other combinations. Color-and-weave effects are usually produced with plain weave or twill threadings, but can be produced by a variety of other weave structures.

extended point twill: describes twills in which the point is extended when the threading progresses in one direction more than one time through the shafts available before reversing, i.e., 1-2-3-4-1-2-3-4-3-2-1-4-3-2-1; or 1-2-3-4-5-6-7-8-1-2-3-4-3-2-1-8-7-6-5-4-3-2-1.

fancy twill: describes 50/50 weave structures produced with twill threading and treadling orders but with tie-ups that cannot be expressed as a twill ratio.

hopsack: see basket weave.

log cabin: a color-and-weave effect in which vertical and horizontal pin stripes are produced with a plain weave draft. Dark warp ends and light warp ends alternate in the threading, and dark weft picks and light weft picks alternate in the treadling. Placing two adjacent dark (or light) warp ends in the threading and two adjacent dark (or light) weft picks in the treadling causes the pin stripes to change vertical or horizontal direction.

point twill: describes twill threading and treadling orders that begin on the first shaft (or treadle) in use and move through the shafts (or treadles) to the last and then reverse and return to the first. If a twill is threaded and treadled in a point, cross ('x') or diamond motifs are formed. If a twill is threaded in a point but treadled in straight order, a horizontal zigzag is formed; if threaded in straight order but treadled in point order, a vertical zigzag design is formed.

repeat twill: a term used in older weaving texts to describe twill-based threadings in which pairs of shafts are repeated, such as in overshot 1-2-1-2-1-2-3-2-3-2-3. It is inaccurate, since almost all structures that use 'repeat' threadings are not twills.

satin counter: indicates the number of warp ends the weft skips in each succeeding interlacement in a satin unit so that the interlacements are distributed in a regular way over all of the warp ends and do not form the diagonal line characteristic of twill; also called the distribution factor. (The actual number used for the counter is the number of ends *away* the interlacing end is from the previous interlacing end rather than the number *skipped*.)

shadow weave: refers to the color-and-weave effect produced with a twill threading when dark warp ends forming one twill alternate with light warp ends forming the same twill but beginning on a different shaft. The structure is mostly plain weave. Vertical and horizontal pin stripes progress in diagonal directions, producing twill designs.

simple weave: a weave with one warp and one weft, i.e., one set of warp ends that perform the same function and one set of weft picks that perform the same function. Plain weave, twills (including turned twills), satins (including damask), lace weaves, and spot weaves are simple weaves. Overshot, which has two wefts (a tabby weft and a pattern weft) is not a simple weave.

straight draw: the shafts in use are threaded in succession, from the first to the last or from the last to the first (1-2-3-4-5-6-7-8-1-2-3-4-5-6-7-8 or 8-7-6-5-4-3-2-1-8-7-6-5-4-3-2-1, etc.).

warp-faced vs. warp-predominant: when warp threads are so closely set as to completely hide the weft threads, the fabric is warp-faced. When weft threads completely hide warp threads, the fabric is weft-faced. 'Warp-predominant' and 'weft-predominant' describe interlacements that show more warp than weft as in 3/1 twill or more weft than warp as in 1/3 twill. Warp-predominant and weft-predominant twills are sometimes called warp twills and weft twills; warp-predominant and weft-predominant satins are sometimes called warp satins and weft satins.

50/50 weave: weave structures in which the number of picks per inch equals the number of ends per inch, such as plain weave, twill, satin, and lace weaves.

Chapter 2
Understanding the Basic Weaves

Weave structures can be grouped into three main categories, those with: a) one warp and one weft; b) more than one warp, more than one weft, or more than one of both; and c) more than one weave. These groups have been labeled by Irene Emery in *Primary Structures of Fabrics* as a) simple weaves, b) weaves with compound sets of elements, and c) compound weaves. The words 'warp' and 'weft' in these categories do not identify individual threads, but instead refer to a set of threads. A single thread is a 'warp end' or a 'weft pick.'

Refer to the 'Family Tree of Weaves,' p. 2, for a chart that places most of the weave structures used by handweavers into the three categories.

SIMPLE WEAVES: THE ROYAL FAMILY

Although 'simple' does not mean 'easy' when used to describe weave structures, working with simple weaves *is* easier than working with structures in the other categories. Simple weaves have one set of warp threads and one set of weft threads. A 'set' consists of threads that have the same function. Consider plain weave, for example. Each weft pick weaves alternately over and under all of the warp ends. The adjacent weft pick does the same job but in the opposite order: under and over. All of the warp ends have the same function — over-and-under alternating with under-and-over — and all of the weft picks have the same function. To understand the difference between a simple weave and one with more than one warp or weft, compare plain weave and overshot. Overshot has one warp and *two* wefts: one weft function is to weave plain weave with the warp, and the other weft function is to float over or under groups of warp ends to form pattern or background. The fact that two shuttles are required is frequently a clue to the presence of two wefts.

Most simple weaves belong to what I like to call the Royal Family: plain weave, twill, and satin. Examine again the drafts for these three structures in ***Figure 1***. Think of their respective interlacements as *order*s. Plain weave is alternate order (every other one), twill is sequential order (one, then the next, then the next, etc.), and satin is a regularly interrupted sequential order (such as: take one, skip two, take one, skip two, etc.). For example, in the twill draft in *1b*, in the first pick the weft travels under two over two. That

1. Plain weave, twill, and satin

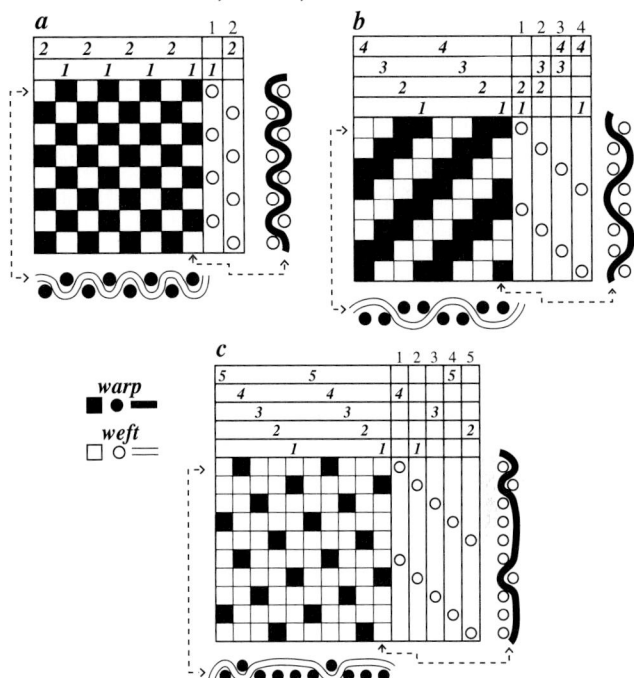

same under-two-over-two happens in the second pick, but it begins on warp 2 instead of 1. The interlacement moves over one end in each pick. Now examine the satin draft in *1c*. Warp end 4 is raised in the first pick. In the next pick warp end 5 is skipped and warp end 1 is raised. In the third pick warp end 2 is skipped and warp end 3 is raised. One end is skipped in each pick.

Keep these orders in mind as we investigate other structures, and you will see that most of the principles of interlacement can be related to them: alternation, sequence, and regular interruption of the sequence.

The King: plain weave

The unlimited variations of true plain weave are achieved not through changes in structure, but through the use of color, warp and weft size, sett, or a combination of these. Heavier warp threads and closer setts create horizontal ribs — warp color predominates. Heavier weft threads and looser setts create vertical ribs — weft color predominates. Drafting techniques that show structure are not useful for designing these variations. Instead, use colored pencils to diagram stripes or plaids and to develop pleasing proportions. Drafting techniques *are* useful for planning special kinds of color effects such as occur in log cabin.

2a. Color-and-weave drawdown: log cabin

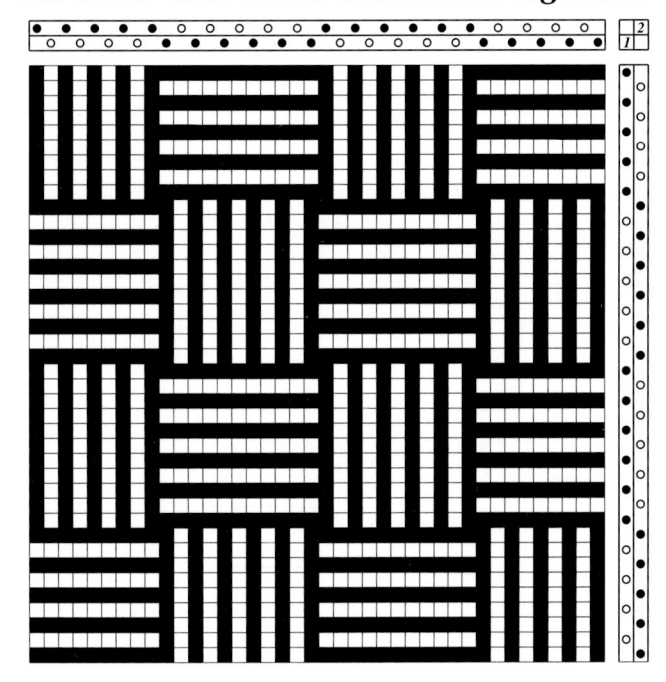

2b. Drawdown grid for color-and-weave

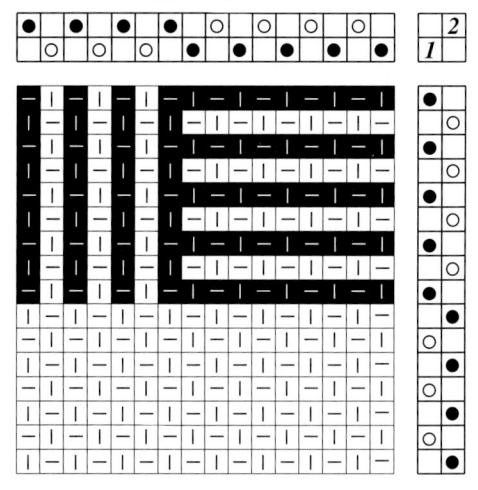

Finish filling in the squares to show the color-and-weave effects (see p. 120). On graph paper, discover new patterns by varying the arrangement of dark and light threads. Better yet, use a computer and make color-and-weave drawdowns with a keystroke.

Log cabin: color-and-weave effects with plain weave

Alternating dark and light threads in both warp and weft can create a visual image that is very different from the structural interlacement. The color alternations can be one-and-one, two-and-two, or innumerable others. To form horizontal pin stripes with the 'log cabin' draft in *Figure 2a*: raise dark warp ends and weave with a dark weft; on alternate picks raise light warp ends and weave with a light weft. To form vertical pin stripes raise dark warp ends and weave with a light weft; on alternate picks raise light warp ends and weave with a dark weft. To produce areas of vertical pin stripes adjacent to horizontal pin stripes, thread two adjacent dark ends or two adjacent light ends at intervals across the warp. To change the direction of the pin stripes in the treadling, weave with two consecutive dark or light weft picks as in *Figure 2a*.

A drawdown of the structure of plain weave shows only a checkerboard. To diagram a color-and-weave effect, mark a drawdown grid lightly with vertical and horizontal marks to show the warp ends *and* weft picks that appear on the face of the cloth, see *Figure 2b*. Look at the weft symbols in the treadling diagram to identify the dark weft picks. For every dark weft, darken each square in its horizontal row that shows a horizontal mark. Next look at the threading diagram to identify the dark warp ends. Darken every square in the vertical column that shows a vertical mark. No marks need be made for light ends and picks.

Other plain weave variations

Basket weave, or hopsack, is produced when *two* weft picks pass over *two* warp ends and under *two*, and the next *two* picks reverse the actions of the first two. Basket weave variations include alternating three ends and three picks, or four and four, or mixing the numbers of grouped ends and picks so that two threads alternate with one, or three with one, etc. In all variations, plain weave order is maintained in threading and treadling.

When the warp is so closely sett that the weft is not visible, one half of the warp (every other thread) is seen when one of the plain weave sheds is formed and the other half of the warp is seen when the other plain weave shed is formed. When two colors alternate in the warp (dark, light, dark, light), narrow *horizontal stripes* occur as the two warp colors surface on alternate picks. The thicker the invisible weft, the wider the horizontal stripe. Color arrangements can be planned that include *vertical stripes* when all warp ends in one area of the warp are one color and in another area a different color. All of these variations are planned in the color order of the warp. A drawdown of the structure shows only the checkerboard of plain weave interlacement. Plan warp-faced plain weave by using colored marking pens to design stripes.

Weft-faced plain weave produces solid *horizontal stripes* when one weft color is used for one section of weaving and in other sections other colors are used. Narrow *vertical stripes* are produced when one weft color alternates with a second weft color.

16

3. Twill ratios

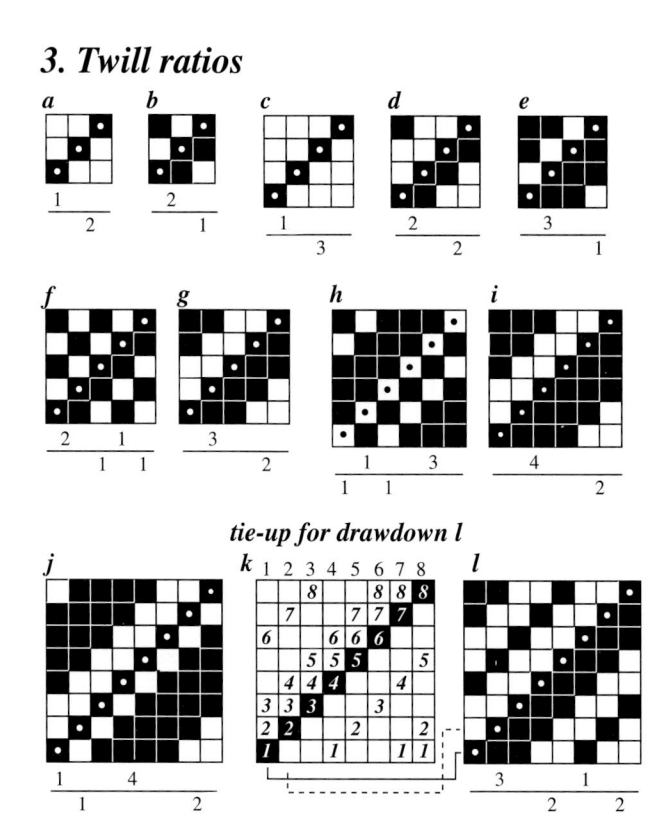

a 1/2 *b* 2/1 *c* 1/3 *d* 2/2 *e* 3/1

f 2/1/1/1 *g* 3/1/1 *h* 1/2/1/2 *i* 1/3/1/2 (4/2)

j 1/4/1/2 *k* tie-up for drawdown l (3/1/2/2) *l* 3/1/2/2

Read twill ratios horizontally in drawdowns (number of ends above and below each weft pick) but vertically in tie-ups (number of shafts raised and lowered for each pick). The ratio moves 'over-and-up' in each succeeding pick. A white dot marks the start of the ratio in the drawdowns, black squares mark the start of the ratio in the tie-up in 3k. Compare 3k and 3l.

The Queen: twill

Twill, the most illustrious member of the Royal Family, provides a stable structure and an astonishing range of patterning. Each warp thread passes over or under *more* than one weft thread, and each weft thread over or under *more* than one warp thread in the interlacement sequence. A minimum of three warp ends and three weft picks is therefore required: the weft passes under one end and over two, or under two ends and over one (**3a-b**). Each successive pick begins *the same interlacement* on an adjacent warp end, either to the left or to the right, creating a diagonal line. The twill warp drawdowns in *Figure 3* show 'right' twills: each succeeding pick moves the interlacement one warp to the right. (When drawdowns are isolated in text from threading and treadling orders, they are usually treated as draw*ups* and are read from bottom to top, though we still refer to them as drawdowns. Isolated threadings in text are usually read from left to right.)

Twill directions: don't get lost!

Included with each twill drawdown (draw*up*) in *Figure 3* is a key showing the ratio of warp ends *up* to ends *down* for each pick in the sequence. Read the key *horizontally*, from left to right, as though the line represents the weft at the bottom of the drawdown. In **3j**, for example, 1 end is up, 1 down, 4 up, 2 down for each of the eight picks. The warp end that begins the ratio in each pick is marked by a dot.

Read the twill ratio *vertically* in a tie-up. In **3k**, 3 shafts are up, 2 down, 1 up, 2 down. Each new treadle begins the ratio one shaft above the previous starting shaft; see black squares in **3k**. Compare the vertical treadles in the tie-up in **3k** with the horizontal picks in **3l**.

The twill circle: a symbol of repetition

Threadings, tie-ups, treadling orders, and drawdowns represent interlacements that are in continuous repetition across the width and length of a warp. The drawdown in *Figure 3l* represents eight warp ends, threaded continuously across a warp from left to right in straight order (1-2-3-4-5-6-7-8), one group of eight next to another, next to another, etc. When shafts 1, 2, and 3 are lifted, the first three warp ends of every group of eight are lifted. In the next pick, as the 3/2/1/2 twill progression moves to the right, the second, third, and fourth threads are lifted. The ratio now starts on the second warp end and stops on the first warp end in an adjacent group of eight. In marking the single group of eight in the drawdown, we return to the first thread in the same horizontal weft row to complete the ratio.

The same concept of repetition applies to the tie-up. Black squares mark where the ratio begins on each treadle in **3k**. As the ratio moves over one treadle and up one shaft for each pick, it is completed by returning to the first shaft. For example, the 3/2/1/2 ratio starts with the sixth shaft on treadle 6: shafts 6, 7, and 8 are lifted; shafts 1 and 2 are down; shaft 3 is lifted; and shafts 4 and 5 are down (3/2/1/2).

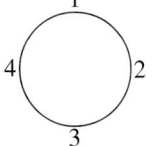

The concept of endless repetition is expressed in weaving texts by plotting shaft numbers on a circle. The circle makes it clear that a thread on shaft 1 is not *first*, and a thread on shaft 8 is not *last*. They are part of a continuously repeating sequence. The 8 is before the 1 in exactly the same way that the 1 is before the 2. Twill threading and treadling orders move around the circle in any direction and can reverse directions on any shaft.

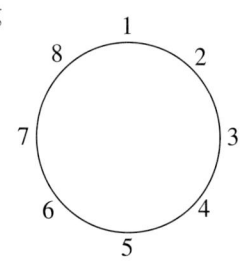

4a. 2/2 broken twill

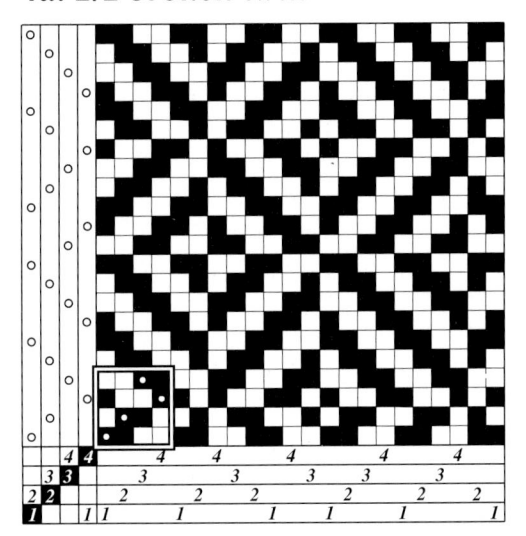

4b. 2/2 point twill

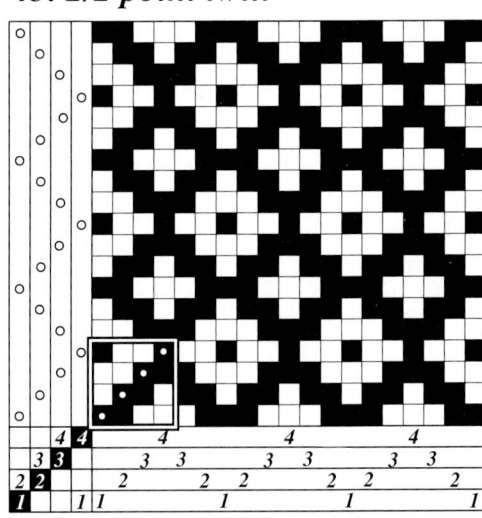

White dots mark the beginning of the twill ratio in the drawdown. Read the ratio horizontally in the highlighted square, from left to right. Black squares mark the beginning of the ratio in the tie-up. Read the ratio vertically in the tie-up, from bottom to top.

4c. 2/2 extended point twill

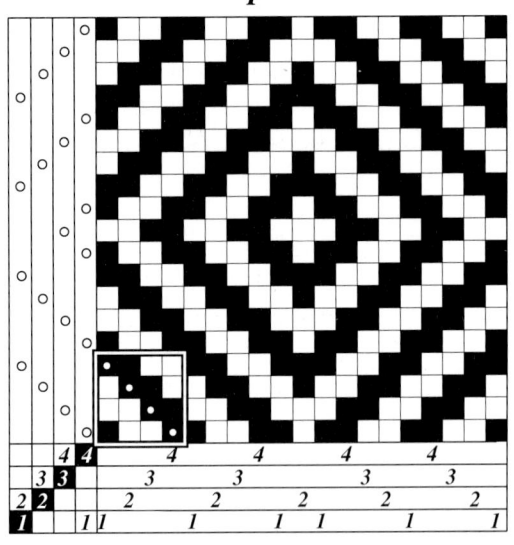

4d. 4-shaft fancy twill

The tie-ups in 4d and 4f do not show the regular progression of a twill ratio. The tie-up in 4d uses six sheds to form the fancy plaited-twill design.

4e. Extended point twill: 4/2/1/1

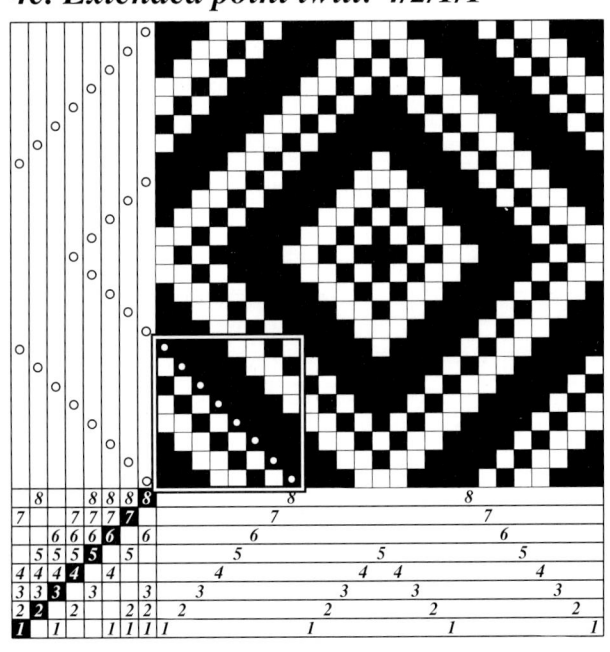

4f. Eight-shaft fancy twill

One more word about twill direction! Sometimes it *is* desirable to produce a twill fabric with a specific twill direction, right or left. 'Z' twist yarns, for example, show the twill lines more distinctly if woven in a left twill.

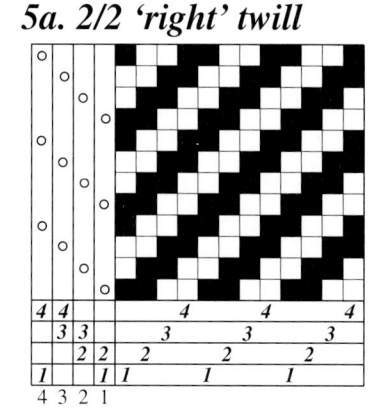

5a. 2/2 'right' twill

5b. 2/2 'left' twill

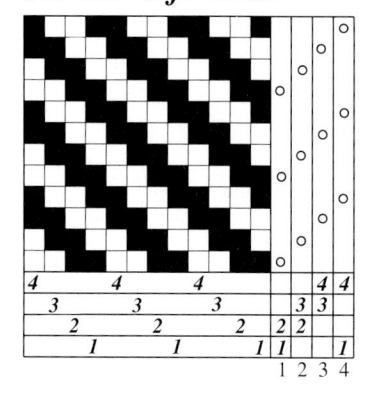

'S' twist yarns show the twill lines more distinctly in a right twill. 'Right' twill diagonals progress upward toward the right (from bottom to top); 'left' twill diagonals progress upward toward the left.

Twill variations

Twills provide endless design opportunities. Not only are there unlimited potential variations in threading, tie-up, and treadling orders, particularly when eight or more shafts are available, but variations in sett and fiber size, color, and texture add further dimension.

Drafting techniques are most useful for 'balanced' twills: twills with the same number of ends per inch as picks per inch. A drawdown then accurately shows the appearance of the cloth since there are the same number of squares per inch vertically and horizontally on the drawdown grid.

Threading and treadling orders

Most twills fall into one of four categories: straight, point, extended point, or broken. *Figures 5a* and *5b* show straight threading and treadling orders: the shafts are threaded in succession from first to last; the treadles are used in succession from first to last. *Figure 4b* shows point-twill threading and treadling orders: the shafts are threaded in succession, but the threading reverses on the last and first shafts. The same reversal appears in the treadling order. *Figures 4c* and *4e* show *extended* point threadings: the threading direction changes after all of the shafts have been threaded more than one time each. In *4c* ten warp ends are threaded in succession before the reversal on shaft 2. In *4e* 13 ends are threaded in succession before the twill direction reverses on shaft 5. Extended point-twill threading and treadling orders create a design of concentric diamonds. The more ends threaded before the twill reverses, the larger the diamond. In broken twills, a shaft or shafts are skipped at the reversal point. *Figure 4a* shows a 4-shaft broken twill: shaft 3 is skipped at one reversal; shaft 2 is skipped at another.

The labels 'straight,' 'point,' and 'broken' are applied to the threading and treadling orders, but not to the tie-up. The tie-up tells whether the twill is warp-dominant, weft-dominant, or 'even.' (In even twills total float length of warp and weft in a repeat is the same.) The twill in *Figure 4e*, for example, is warp-dominant. The twills in *Figures 4a-4c* are even: warp and weft floats pass over two, under two, throughout.

Regular and fancy twills

Twills are 'regular' when the tie-up can be expressed in a twill ratio. Examine the tie-ups in *4a, b, c,* and *e*. The black squares in the tie-up indicate the shaft on which the twill ratio begins for each treadle. Read the ratios vertically: 2/2 for *4a, b, c*; 4/2/1/1 for *4e*. The ratio can also begin on other treadles than those designated by black squares; on the third treadle from the left in *4e*, for example, the ratio is the same but begins with a different number: 1/1/4/2. Read all ratios in the drawdowns from left to right to correspond with the orientation of the threading in these particular drafts. Be sure to read the ratio within the highlighted square since the ratio is evident only in an area of the drawdown where the threading is in straight order.

Examine the drawdowns and tie-ups in *Figures 4d* and *4f*. Notice the absence of a diagonal line in *4f*. Neither of these tie-ups can be represented by a twill ratio; successive treadles lift *different* combinations of shafts. The unusual 4-shaft tie-up in *4d* uses six different sheds rather than the four usually required for a twill. These two irregular twills fall into a category that is sometimes called 'fancy' twills.

Designing 'fancy' twills on graph paper, particularly for eight or more shafts, can be very enjoyable. Look again at the threading in *4f*. Any design can be graphed in place of the star; the only limitation is its required symmetry around the center thread on shaft 8. Unfortunately, not every design that can be graphed can be woven. The longest float in the star design is the 4-thread weft float at the star's center (and a corresponding warp float on the back side.) Designs of this kind must be checked for overlong floats. Since the size of the design is limited to 15 warp ends per repeat, its scale in a fabric is likely to be very small.

6a. 3/2/1/2 twill: structure

6b. 3/2/1/2 twill: color drawdown

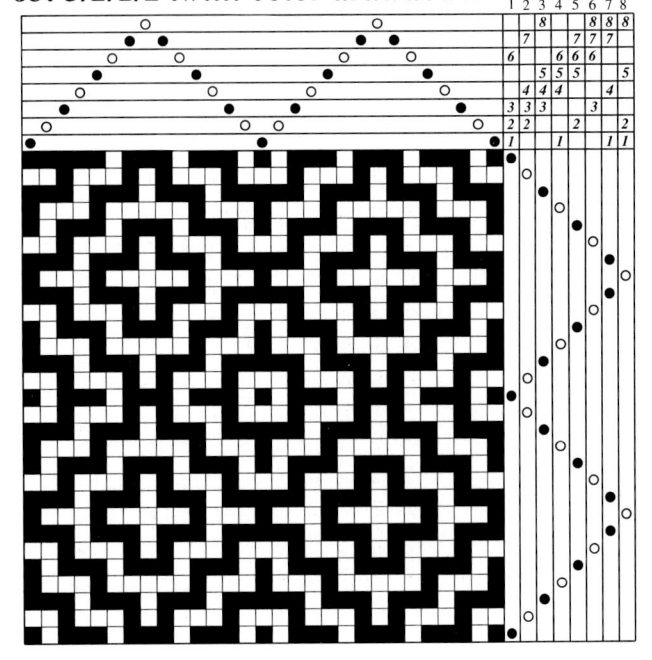

6c. 3/2/1/2 twill: color drawdown

6d. 3/2/1/2 twill: color drawdown

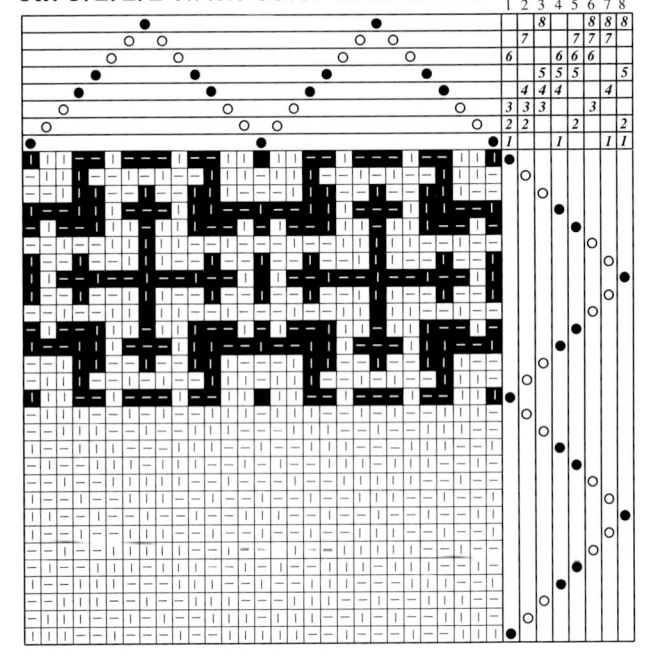

Twills: color-and-weave

Figures 6a-d all show the same 8-shaft point-twill threading, 3/2/1/2 twill tie-up, and point-twill treadling order. *Figure 6a* represents both the structure and the visual pattern if the warp is all dark and the weft all light. The drafts in *Figures 6b-6d* produce exactly the same structure, in which no float is longer than five threads. Alternation of light and dark threads, one-and-one, two-and-two, or any combination, in both warp and weft produce a pattern *different* from the interlacement. Examine the warp and weft color sequences in *6b-6d*. Color-and-weave drawdowns show the colors of both the light and dark warp *and* weft threads that appear on the face of the cloth instead of indicating warp and weft function.

Draft color-and-weave twills using the same process as for log cabin (p. 16). First place vertical marks for all raised warp ends in each weft row. Next pencil the unfilled squares with horizontal marks for the weft threads. For every *dark warp end* in the threading draft, darken the squares with vertical marks in the corresponding column (see *6d*). For every *dark weft symbol* in the treadling sequence, darken squares with horizontal marks in the corresponding weft row.

20

7a. Shadow weave color drawdown dark/light in warp and weft

7b. Shadow weave: color drawdown dark/light warp; light/dark weft

7c. Shadow weave structure: warp drawdown

Shadow weave

Shadow weave looks like twill, but the interlacement is really plain weave with scattered 2-thread floats. 'Shadow weave' names a type of color-and-weave effect. It shares with the drafts in **Figure 6** the use of alternating colors in warp and weft to produce a visual pattern different from the interlacement. In the color-and-weave drawdown in **Figure 7a**, warp and weft colors alternate dark(D)/light(L). In **7b**, warp colors alternate D/L and weft colors alternate L/D. The warp drawdown in **7c** shows the structure produced by the drafts in **7a-b**. Compare the shadow weave structure in **7c** with the twill structure in **6a**. No float in **7c** is longer than *two* threads (two black vertical squares indicate a warp float, two white horizontal squares a weft float).

To design shadow weave, first draft two twills, one for dark threads and one for light threads. It is usually best to use the same twill for both. Begin the second twill on the number of shafts away from the first that is equal to half of the shafts available (the opposite number on the twill circle, see p. 17). Varying this number can produce overlong floats. If one 8-shaft twill begins on shaft 1, for example, begin the second twill four shafts away, on shaft 5. The twills in **8a-b** are used to derive the draft in **7a**. The twill for dark begins on shaft 4; the twill for light begins on shaft 2.

The design is most satisfying if the draft is symmetrical. To provide symmetry *and* maintain one-and-one color alternation, add (**8d**) or subtract (**8c**) a thread from one of the twills at each shared 'turning point' — a point where the twill reverses. Write the complete draft, alternating ends of each color.

8. Drafting shadow weave

a. Write a twill threading for dark warp ends.
b. Write the same twill threading for light warp ends, but begin the twill on a different shaft.
c. Subtract a thread, or
d. add a thread from one of the twills at every turning point.
e. Write the complete draft by alternating an end from one draft with an end from the other.

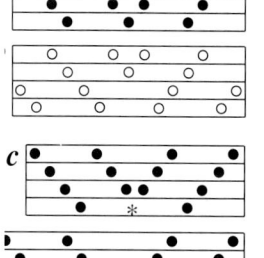

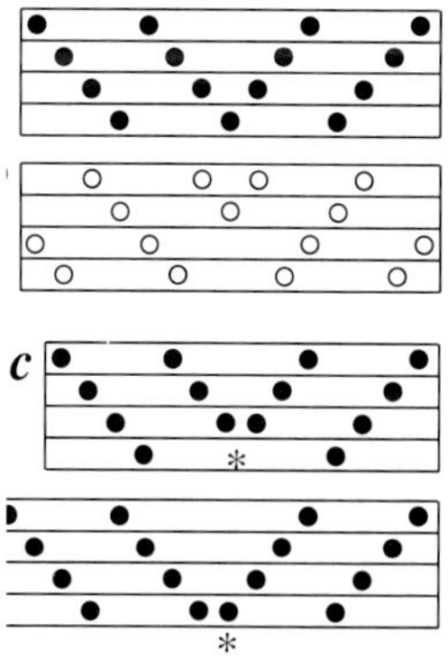

21

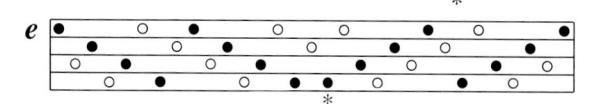

9. 8-shaft shadow weave threading

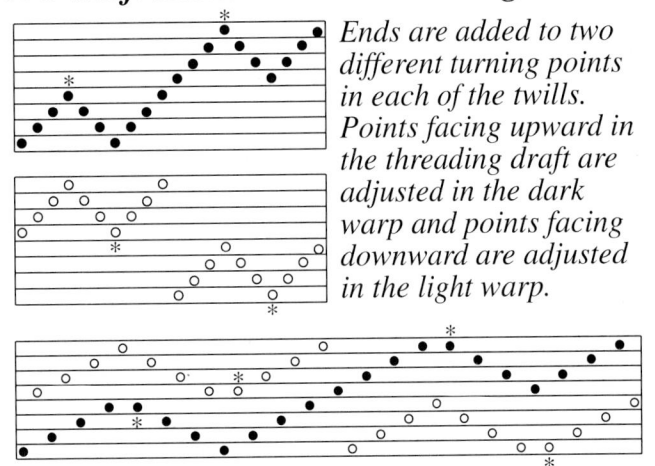

Ends are added to two different turning points in each of the twills. Points facing upward in the threading draft are adjusted in the dark warp and points facing downward are adjusted in the light warp.

10a. Shadow weave structure

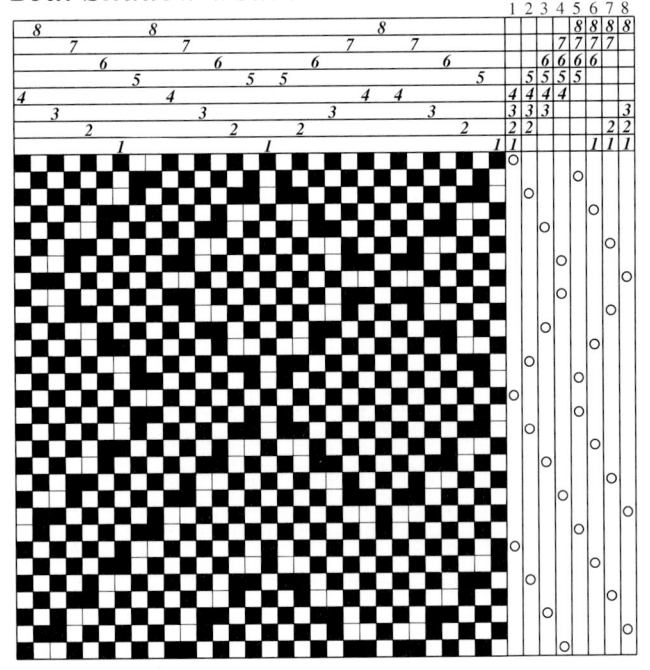

Two twill drafts are used to derive an 8-shaft threading in **Figure 9**. The two twills share four turning points. Ends are added to two turning points in the light twill and two turning points in the dark twill to insure a symmetrical shadow-weave draft.

The warp drawdown in **Figure 10a** shows the structure of a part of the threading and treadling repeat. Notice the predominance of plain-weave interlacement. Notice also that the two-thread warp and weft floats emphasize the design outlines. Compare the structural drawdown with the corresponding highlighted portion of the design in the color-and-weave drawdown in **10b**.

To see how the plain-weave structure occurs, examine the relationship between the tie-up, threading, and treadling sequences in **10a**. Half of the shafts are raised in each pick. Each pick is followed by a lift of the *opposite* shafts. Plain weave is automatically produced since in the threading, combinations of consecutive shafts in one twill alternate with consecutive shafts in the other twill. Two-thread floats are caused where adjacent ends rise, one from each twill. Notice, for example, in pick 2, shafts 5 and 8 both rise; in pick 3, 2 and 5 both rise, etc.

10b. Shadow weave dark/light alternate in warp and weft

10c. Shadow weave dark/light warp; light/dark weft

The Princess: satin

Imagine a cone of mulberry silk. As you turn the cone, it reflects light brilliantly. You decide to weave a silk blouse in plain weave, but as you watch the first inches grow, you realize that the brilliance is gone. Plain weave interlacement interrupts the reflection of light as the threads cross each other. Twill's longer floats provide more reflection, but diagonal lines compete for attention.

Very beautiful (though without much depth of character!) satin is the princess of weaves. Satin produces floats without strong diagonals.

Satin can be thought of as a small, very limited subset of twills. Satin is threaded in straight draw order: 1-2-3-4-5–n; n equals the number of shafts threaded. In the interlacement, each weft thread passes over or under every warp thread but one, and each warp thread passes over or under every weft thread but one.

The satin counter

Twills are characterized by a diagonal line that occurs because in each succeeding pick the warp end that interlaces with the weft is the *next* end in the threading sequence. In satin, the warp end that interlaces with the weft in each succeeding pick is *not* the next one. The second or third (or fourth, etc.) warp end *away* from the one raised in the previous row interlaces with each succeeding weft. In true satin the number of warp ends 'away' is the same for each pick. This number is called the satin 'counter' or 'distribution number.' This ordered scattering of the interlacement of warp and weft and the maximum, unbroken length of the warp or weft float produce the smooth, uninterrupted texture we associate with the word 'satin.'

Examine *Figure 11b*. In the first row, warp end 1 is raised. The weft passes over ends 2-5. In the second row, warp end 3 is raised. This end is *two* ends away from the previous end. In the third row, the raised end 5 is *two* ends removed from 3. In *11c*, each interlacing end is *three* ends away from the preceding end.

The order in which the warp ends are raised is the primary feature which distinguishes satin from twill. For this reason, satin is often called a 'rearranged' twill. Changing the order in one area — threading order, treadling order, or tie-up — can make a twill into a satin, or a satin into twill. Examine the effects of the tie-ups and treadling orders in *11b-11d*.

11. From 1/4 twill to 1/4 satin

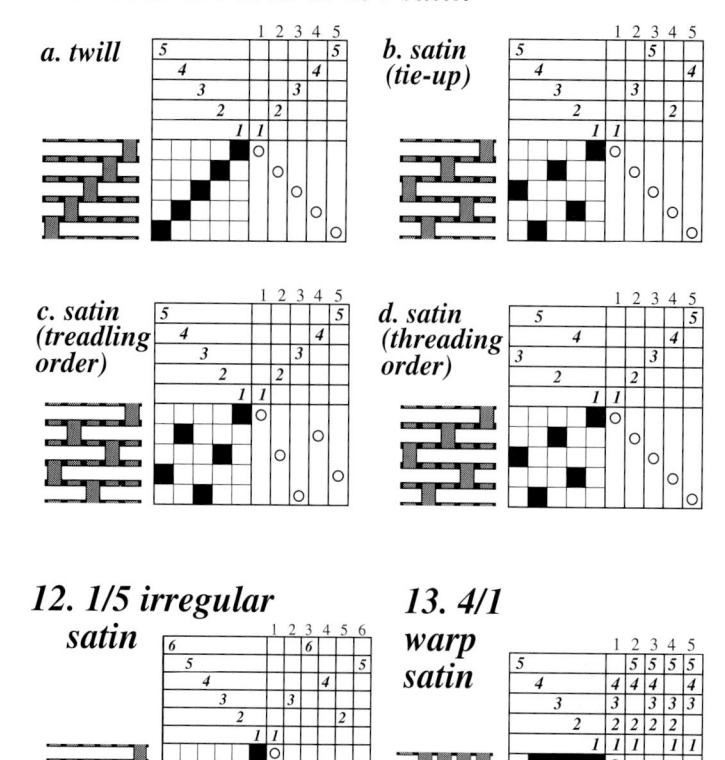

a. twill

b. satin (tie-up)

c. satin (treadling order)

d. satin (threading order)

12. 1/5 irregular satin

13. 4/1 warp satin

If you try to fill the squares for a 6-end satin so that each interlacing warp end is the same number of ends away from the previous interlacing warp end, you will discover that it cannot be done. Every possible counter causes some of the six ends to be darkened twice and some not at all. True satin cannot be woven on six shafts (or on three or four). Study *Figure 12*. Notice that in the second pick, the raised warp end is two ends away from the preceding end. In the third pick, however, end 6 is three ends away from the preceding end, end 3. This compromise produces a satin-like effect, but the overall surface texture is not regular as in true satin. All other numbers of shafts threaded in straight order (5, 7, 8, 9, 10, etc.) can produce true satin.

The satins in *Figures 11* and *12* are examples of *weft*-predominant (or weft-float) satin, which is sometimes called sateen. In each pick one warp end is raised and all others are covered by the weft. If all ends are raised *but* one, warp-predominant (warp-float) satin appears, see *Figure 13*. Weft satin occurs on the reverse side of the cloth wherever warp satin is on the face; warp satin occurs on the reverse of any area of weft satin. The more shafts used in the satin threading repeat and the closer the sett, the more the satin resembles that lustrous mulberry silk on the cone!

Lesson: Drafting Twills and Color-and-Weave

Draft regular twills and what you see is what you get: the fabric's design and the interlacement coincide. To show color-and-weave effects, warp and weft color must be represented in the drawdown instead of 'warp up' or 'warp down.' The process is a bit more tedious, but the results are an exciting surprise. Practice your skills on these twill and shadow weave drafts, and then design your own! (See answers, pp. 120-121.)

Twill drawdowns

For *Exercises 1* and *2*, prepare warp drawdowns. Treadling diagrams are not included; the drafts are woven 'as drawn in.' In other words, lift the treadle whose number corresponds to each thread in the threading diagram. Reading from right to left: begin with treadle 4, then 3, then 2, etc., in *1* and begin with 8, then 7, then 6, etc., in *2*. For *Exercise 2*, first construct a 3/2/2/1 twill tie-up. The first treadle must raise the first three shafts, leave two down, raise two, leave one down. Write the same interlacement on the second treadle, moving up one shaft.

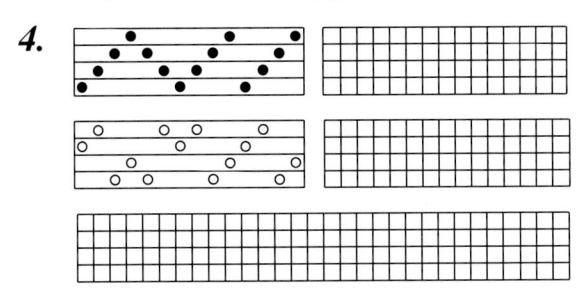

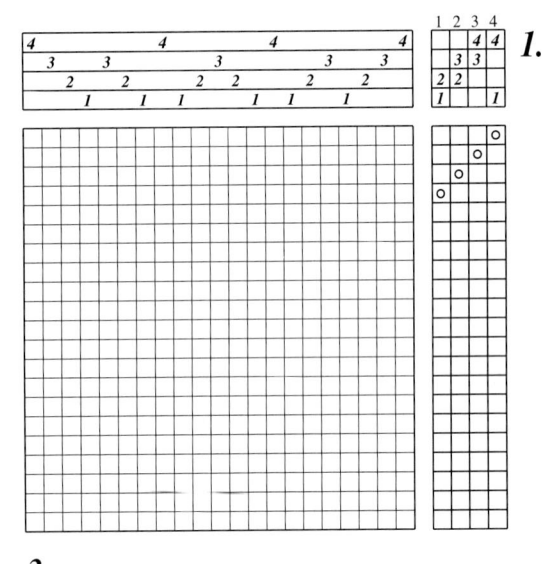

Exercise 4 gives two twill threadings; one begins on shaft 4 the other on shaft 2. Rewrite the threadings adding an end to one turning point in each draft, then combine both threadings for a shadow-weave draft.

In *Exercise 5*, fill in squares for a weft-predominant (1/7) satin on eight shafts. Hint: the number of 'ends away' (satin counter) cannot be 7 or 1 or else twill, not satin, is produced, nor can it share a divisor with eight (2, 4, or 6) or else the same end is lifted repeatedly. Choose 3 or 5.

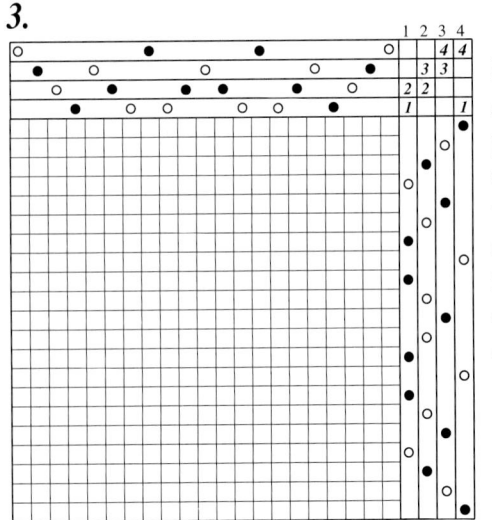

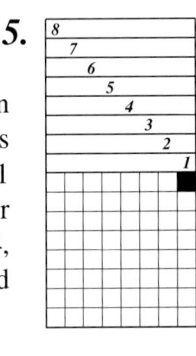

For *Exercise 3*, prepare a color-and-weave drawdown following directions on p. 16.

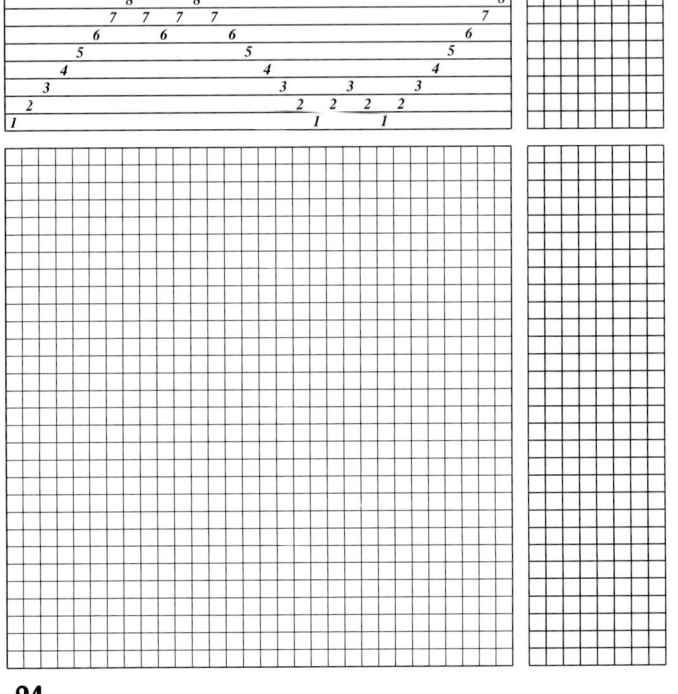

Part II
Blocks

Blocks can sometimes feel like stumbling blocks instead of the powerful design tools they really are. The block is the basic component of pattern in weaving. Warp and weft threads interlace in a particular way in one block and in another way in a different block so that we see one area as pattern and the other as background. In Chapter 3 you'll learn about blocks without reference to what the specific threads are doing. You'll learn to make designs composed of blocks in the form of profile drafts. In later chapters you'll learn how to translate your designs into actual weave structures.

Take a minute to look through Part III, pp. 58-110. Notice that the same design is produced in many different weave structures. Compare the fabric examples with the profile draft on page 58. Notice that each weave structure uses a different threading and treadling system to produce the same design. A different number of shafts may be required by different weave structures to produce the same design.

Now look at pages 26-27. 'Keys to Block Weaves' gives the basic information for weaving a particular profile design in a particular weave structure. You'll need more than just the chart to thread the loom and produce the cloth, however. You'll have to know how the structure works. Is it a supplementary-weft weave, for example, that requires a heavy pattern weft and a fine tabby weft? You'll also need to consider the desired weight and hand of the finished fabric in order to select appropriate materials and setts. Use the chart as a quick reference guide to block weaves. It shows at a glance how many shafts and treadles are required for each structure. After you've studied Chapters 4-9, the chart can serve as a review outline of the components of most unit weaves.

In Chapter 4 you'll learn to translate block designs into 4-shaft and 8-shaft overshot. Chapter 5 explains the concept of 'unit' weaves and gives the steps by which a profile draft is translated into a specific unit weave structure.

After you've read Chapter 3, complete the exercises and check your work. When you're sure you understand how to generate a profile drawdown, you'll enjoy designing original profile drafts.

Profile Drafts: Words to Know

as drawn in: the treadling sequence follows the same order as the threading sequence (synonym, 'tromp as writ.') For example, if the first warp end is threaded on shaft 1, the first weft pick is entered by depressing treadle 1. If the second warp end is threaded on shaft 4, the second pick is made with treadle 4. Blocks are also woven 'as drawn in' when they make pattern in the same order in which they are threaded. When used with blocks, 'as drawn in' is synonymous with 'star fashion.'

background: pattern motifs are formed on a background when warp and weft threads interlace in one way in the pattern area and in another way in the background area.

block: refers to the building blocks of a design. Groups of warp threads and weft threads that always weave pattern at the same time are in the same block. Any group of warp threads and weft threads that can weave pattern independently of other groups are in a separate block.

pattern: the design formed in a fabric either by color orders in warp and weft, or by weave structure, or by a combination of both. 'Pattern' is also used in contrast to 'background,' as in 'figure' vs. 'ground.'

profile draft: a graphed design. The *profile threading draft* consists of rows representing blocks: A, B, C, D, etc. The *profile drawdown* is the design that results when pattern is produced in the block(s) indicated by the *profile tie-up* and *profile treadling order*.

rose fashion: instead of weaving blocks as drawn in, pairs of blocks are exchanged in the treadling order. For example, if a motif is threaded ABA; it is woven BAB in a rose fashion treadling.

rosepath: a point twill extended one thread beyond the number of shafts available (1-2-3-4-1-4-3-2-1 or 4-3-2-1-4-1-2-3-4) that produces a diamond with a center 'goose-eye' when treadled as drawn in.

star fashion: blocks produce pattern in the same order in which they are threaded.

structure: the specific order in which warp ends and weft picks interlace to form a fabric.

thread-by-thread draft: a draft for weaving that shows the interlacement of individual threads. It consists of a threading draft, a tie-up, a treadling order, and a drawdown. The symbols, rows, and columns represent individual threads, shafts, or treadles.

tromp as writ: ('treadle as written') see 'as drawn in.'

Keys to Block Weaves

Threading keys

NON-UNIT WEAVES:	Block A	Block B	Block C	Block D
Spot Bronson	1-2-1-2	1-3-1-3	1-4-1-4	1-5-1-5
M's and O's (4-shaft)	1-2-1-2-3-4-3-4	1-3-1-3-2-4-2-4		
Overshot (4-shaft)	1-2	2-3	3-4	4-1
Overshot (8-shaft)	1-2	3-4	5-6	7-8
Crackle (4-shaft)	1-2-3-2	2-3-4-3	3-4-1-4	4-1-2-1

UNIT WEAVES:				
Bronson lace	1-3-1-3-1-2	1-4-1-4-1-2	1-5-1-5-1-2	1-6-1-6-1-2
Huck lace*	[2-3-2-3-2	1-4-1-4-1]	[2-5-2-5-2	1-6-1-6-1]
Turned twill	1-2-3-4	5-6-7-8	9-10-11-12	13-14-15-16
Damask (five-end units)	1-2-3-4-5	6-7-8-9-10	11-12-13-14-15	16-17-18-19-20

Two-tie unit weaves

	Block A	Block B	Block C	Block D
Summer and winter (1:1)	1-3-**2**-3	1-4-**2**-4	1-5-**2**-5	1-6-**2**-6
(1:2)	1-4-3-**2**-3-4	1-6-5-**2**-5-6	1-8-7-**2**-7-8	1-10-9-**2**-9-10
(1:3)	1-3-4-3-**2**-3-4-3	1-5-6-5-**2**-5-6-5	1-7-8-7-**2**-7-8-7	1-9-10-9-**2**-9-10-9
(1:4)	1-4-3-4-3-**2**-3-4-3-4	1-6-5-6-5-**2**-5-6-5-6	1-8-7-8-7-**2**-7-8-7-8	1-10-9-10-9-**2**-9-10-9-10
(2:4)	1-**2**-3-4-3-4	1-**2**-5-6-5-6	1-**2**-7-8-7-8	1-**2**-9-10-9-10
Double two-tie unit weave	1-3-**2**-4	1-5-**2**-6	1-7-**2**-8	1-9-**2**-10
'Even tied overshot'*	[2-3-**2**-3-**2**-3	1-4 1-4-1-4]	[2-5-**2**-5-**2**-5	1-6-1-6-1-6]
'Uneven tied overshot'*	[3-**2**-3-**2**-3	4-1-4-1-4]	[5-**2**-5-**2**-5	6-1-6-1-6]

Three-tie unit weaves

	Block A	Block B	Block C	Block D
'Half-satin'	1-4-**2**-4-**3**-4	1-5-**2**-5-**3**-5	1-6-**2**-6-**3**-6	1-7-**2**-7-**3**-7
Bergman	1-4-3-4-**2**-4-1-4- 3-4-1-4-**2**-4-3-4	1-5-3-5-**2**-5-1-5- 3-5-1-5-**2**-5-3-5	1-6-3-6-**2**-6-1-6- 3-6-1-6-**2**-6-3-6	1-7-**3**-7-**2**-7-1-7- 3-7-1-7-**2**-7-**3**-7

Patterned double weave	1-2-3-4 (DLDL)	5-6-7-8 (DLDL)	9-10-11-12 (DLDL)	13-14-15-16 (DLDL)

Lampas

	Block A	Block B	Block C	Block D
Beiderwand*	[**1**-3-4-3-4	**2**-5-6-5-6]	[**1**-7-8-7-8	**2**-9-10-9-10]
Twill/plain weave*	[**1**-5-6-**2**-5-6	**3**-7-8-**4**-7-8]	[**1**-9-10-**2**-9-10	**3**-11-12-**4**-11-12]

*For these weaves, the structural unit [in brackets] may contain more than one block; see related chapters for explanations.

Tie-up templates

Bronson lace
- □ lace
- ⊙ plain weave

Huck lace
plain weave — huck lace — huck texture
- warp floats
- weft floats

Turned twill
weft twill — warp twill — weft twill — warp twill

Damask
weft satin — warp satin

Two-tie unit weaves

Summer and winter
- □ float on the face
- ⊙⊙ float on the back

Extended summer and winter: 1:2, 1:3, 1:4, 2:4 two-tie weaves ('tied beiderwand,' paired-tie weaves, etc.)
- float on the face
- float on the back

Three-tie unit weaves
- pattern shafts
  - float on the face
  - float on the back
- tie-down shafts

Patterned double weave
- odd shafts on top
- even shafts on top

Lampas
main structure — secondary structure — for stitching — pattern templates

Sample 4-block tie-ups

4-block profile tie-up

Bronson lace — pattern = lace

Huck lace — pattern = lace

Turned twill — pattern = warp twill

Summer and winter — pattern = float on the face

Extended summer and winter — pattern = float on the face

'Half satin' — pattern = float on the face

Double weave — pattern = even shafts on top

Beiderwand
- main weave: plain weave
- secondary weave: plain weave
- pattern = main weave on top
- not stitched

Treadling keys

Bronson lace

Huck lace

Turned twill

Turned twill or damask

xN [o's   x's]

Summer and winter

xN   xN

Extended summer and winter

'Half satin'   'Bergman'

Double weave

Lampas
main structure — secondary structure

27

Chapter 3
Reading Profile Drafts

1. Four-shaft weave draft

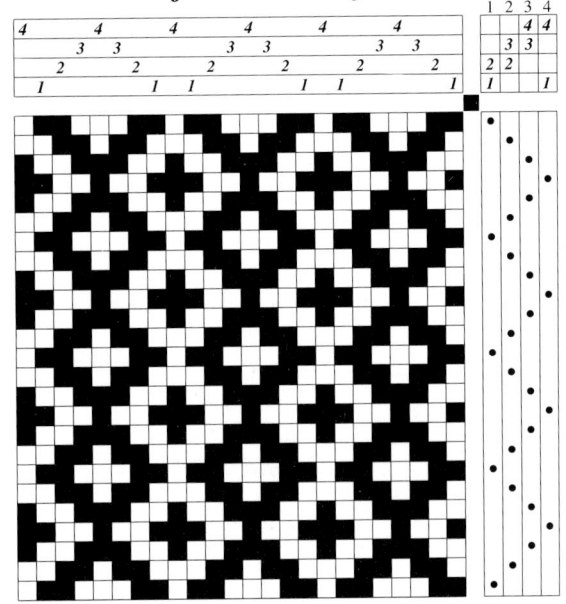

2. Four-block profile draft

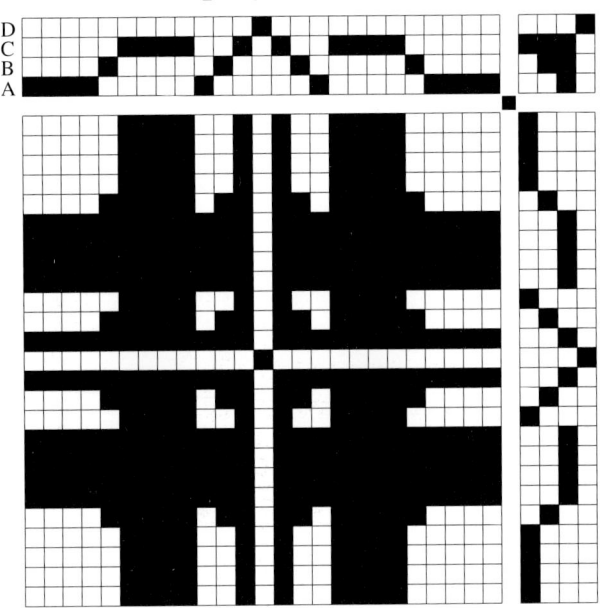

The weave draft: thread by thread

All of the drafts we have studied so far are 'thread-by-thread' drafts: they show individual warp threads and weft threads. In the thread-by-thread rosepath draft in *Figure 1*, for example, warp threads and weft threads pass over two and under two to create the diamond design. Each black square in the drawdown represents one visible warp thread and each white square represents one visible weft thread on the face of the cloth.

Examine the draft in *Figure 2*. The same four parts are arranged in the same way: threading, tie-up, treadling order, and drawdown. Notice, however, that in *Figure 2* four 'warp ends' are threaded consecutively on shaft 3 and as many as four 'picks' are woven successively in the same shed. The drawdown shows that warp ends on shaft 3 are raised for 12 picks in succession! These are all clues that this is *not* a thread-by-thread draft.

The profile draft: block by block

The draft in *Figure 2* is called a profile draft. The black squares in the profile threading and treadling diagrams represent *groups* of warp ends and *groups* of weft picks. Each group of warp ends can interlace with a group of picks in two *different* ways. A black square in the profile drawdown represents one of the ways and a white square represents the other way. We see a design because of the contrast between the two ways, one represented by black squares in the profile draft, the other represented by white squares. The area formed by the black squares is the 'pattern,' and the area formed by the white squares is the 'background.'

Figures 3a-d show four different weave structures producing the design in the profile drawdown at the top of the page. Study the cloth diagrams carefully and compare them to the profile drawdown. Notice that in *3a* and *3b* heavy pattern wefts float over warp ends in the areas in the highlighted squares. Compare the threads inside the squares with the threads outside to see how they interlace differently. In *3c*, for example, the threads inside the squares interlace in 3/1 twill; the threads outside of the squares interlace in 1/3 twill. In *3d*, two of the six picks form floats inside the squares; the threads outside of the squares weave plain weave.

Notice that each of the structures is threaded differently and that each of the tie-ups and treadling orders is different. These structures are called block weaves because they form blocks of pattern (the highlighted squares in the cloth diagrams). A design is first planned in profile draft form and then translated into a specific block weave. In this chapter we'll learn how to work with profile drafts without referring to specific weaves. In the following chapters we'll learn how to use a profile draft for each block weave.

3. One profile draft interpreted in four different weave structures

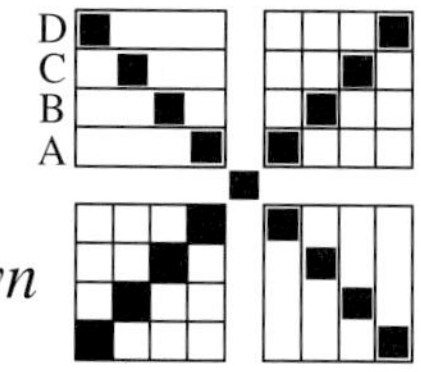

profile threading   profile tie-up

Compare the profile drawdown with the cloth diagrams in a-d.

profile drawdown   profile treadling

a. Summer and winter
Pattern: the supplementary weft floats over three warp ends, under one.
Background: the supplementary weft floats under three warp ends, over one.

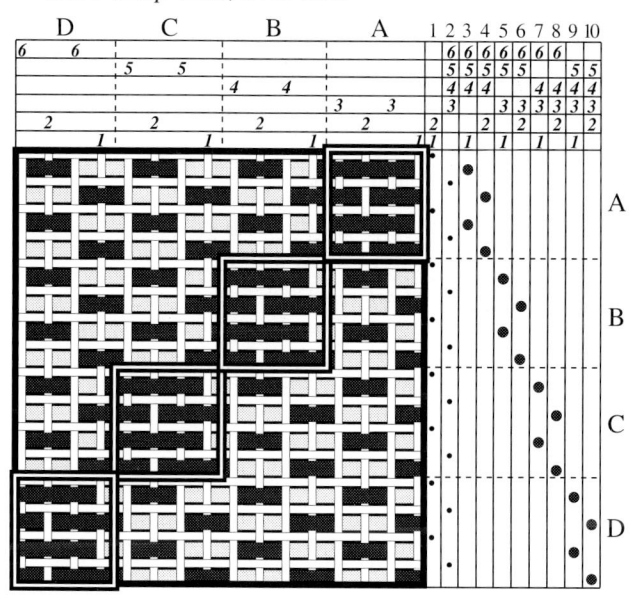

b. Overshot
Pattern: the supplementary weft floats over all of the ends in one block.
Background: the supplementary weft floats under all of the ends in one block and forms halftones in the other two blocks.

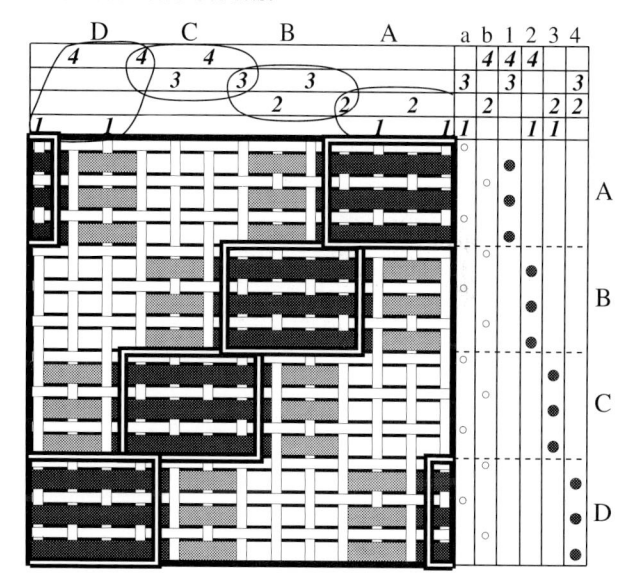

c. Turned twill
Pattern: 3/1 warp twill
Background: 1/3 weft twill

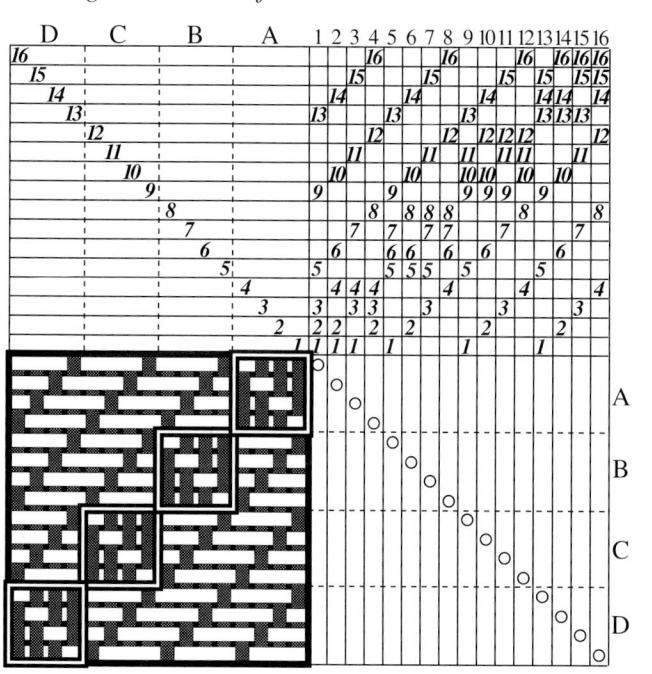

d. Bronson lace
Pattern: the second and fourth weft threads float over five ends and under one.
Background: plain weave

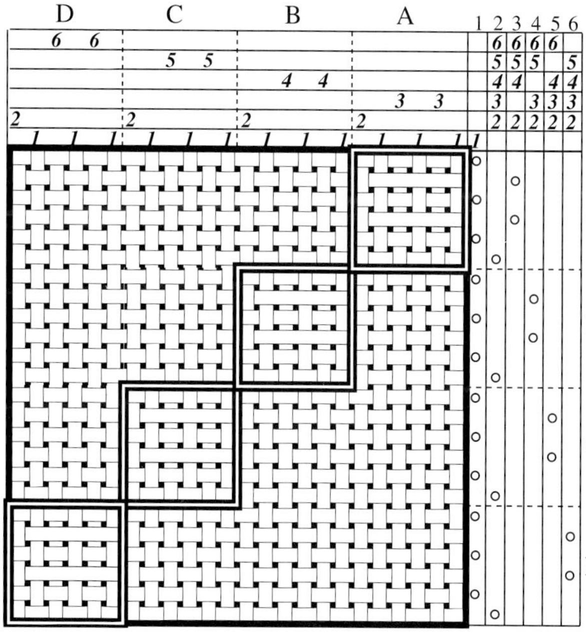

4a. Profile draft format

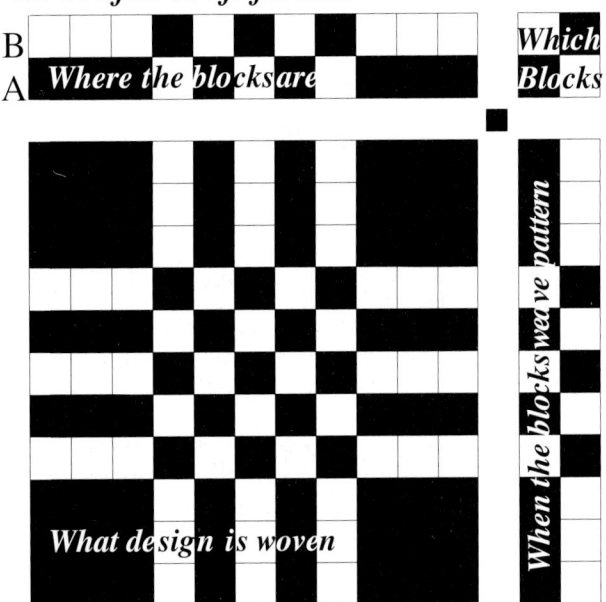

Where the blocks are — B, A
Which Blocks
When the blocks weave pattern
What design is woven

4b. Two-block profile draft

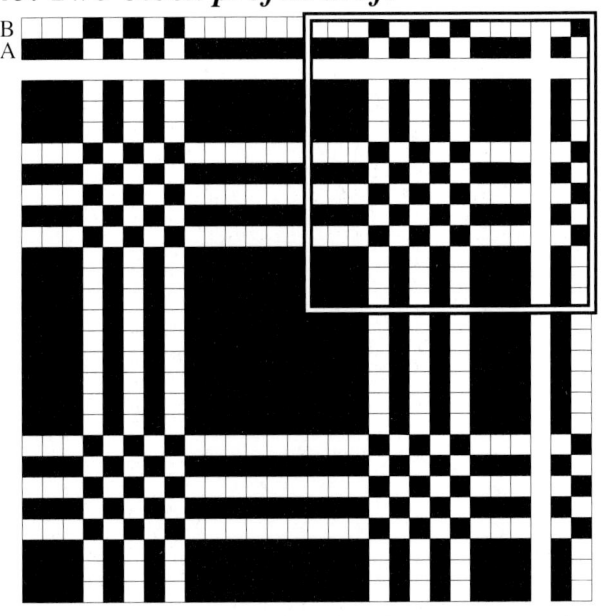

The profile threading tells <u>where</u> the blocks are, the profile tie-up tells <u>which</u> blocks weave pattern (black squares) and which weave background (white squares), the profile treadling tells <u>when</u> the blocks weave pattern, the profile drawdown shows <u>what</u> design is produced.

Write a profile draft exactly as you write a thread-by-thread draft. The threading rows represent blocks instead of shafts. Black squares in the profile drawdown represent pattern instead of raised warp threads; white squares represent background instead of weft threads.

The profile threading draft

Profile-draft rows are marked by letters that identify the blocks: A, B, C, etc. The first row in a profile draft is A. Each black square on the A row in the threading draft represents a group of warp ends that are threaded according to a formula determined by the selected weave structure. Turn back to **Figure 3** to see that the threading for Block A in summer and winter is 1-3-2-3; the threading for Block A in Bronson lace is 1-3-1-3-1-2. (Threading formulas for all of the common block weaves appear on p. 26.) Each square on the B row is threaded following the same formula but on different shafts so that the threads in Block B can make pattern while the threads in Block A make background or vice versa. Examine the threadings for the B block in **3a-d**. Now study the profile threading draft and see the enlarged section of the **Figure 4b** profile draft in **Figure 4a**: the profile threading draft shows *where* the blocks are located across the warp.

The profile tie-up

The profile tie-up shows *which* blocks make pattern. In **Figure 4a**, the first column in the profile tie-up, the column closest to the 'you are here' square, indicates that Block A (black square) makes pattern and Block B (white square) makes background. The second column shows that Block B makes pattern and Block A makes background.

Each column in the tie-up represents *more* than one treadle. Turn again to **Figure 3**: four treadles are used to weave pattern in Block A in **3c**. The number of treadles and the specific shafts lifted for each shed follow a formula determined by the selected weave structure. For the first column in **Figure 4a** the shafts must be tied to treadles so that the threads in Block A weave pattern and the threads in Block B weave background.

The profile treadling order

The profile treadling order tells *when* the blocks marked in the profile tie-up make pattern. Follow the treadling order in **Figure 4a**. The first row in the profile treadling (closest to the 'you are here' square) indicates that Block A makes pattern, Block B makes background. The next two rows are the same. In the fourth row, Block B makes pattern, Block A makes background. Each square in the treadling diagram represents a group of picks determined by the weave structure: eight picks in summer and winter, four in turned twill, six in Bronson lace (see **3a, 3c, 3d**). Read the complete profile treadling order in **4b**.

30

5. Three-block profile draft with four different profile tie-ups

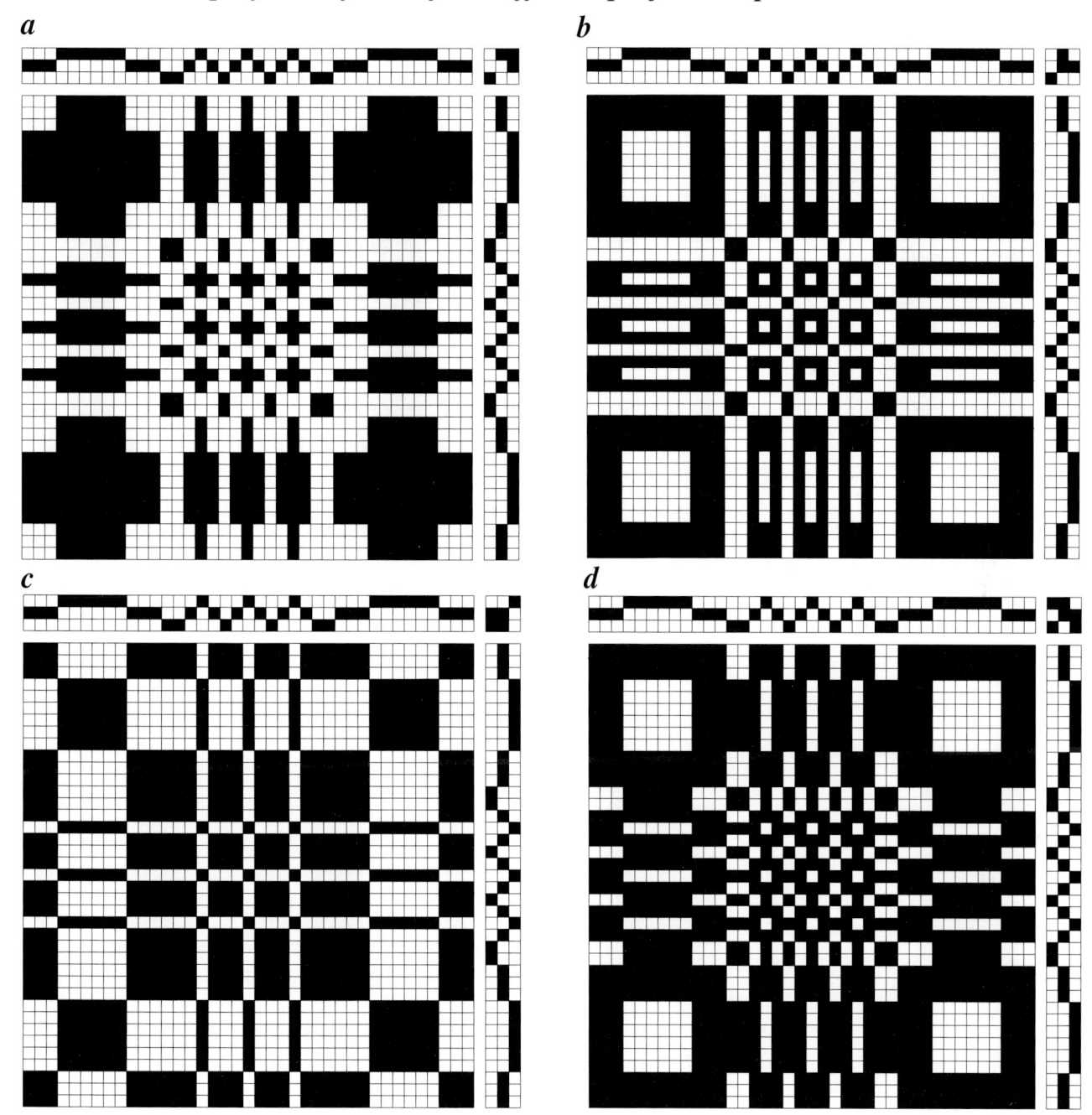

a

b

c

d

Combining blocks

Study the 3-block profile draft in *Figure 5a*. An important aid to working with profile drafts is *to memorize* that the bottom row of a profile threading draft is always Block A, the second row Block B, the third row Block C, etc., so that it is not necessary to write letters on the draft. Very often the letters cause unnecessary confusion. With that in mind, identify the blocks in the three profile threading rows in *Figures 5a-5d*.

Next comes a harder task. In *Figure 5a*, which block makes pattern first? If you said Block A, you looked first at the tie-up instead of the profile treadling order. Always look first at the mark in the treadling diagram closest to the tie-up — exactly where you would look for the first pick in a thread-by-thread draft — and then to the tie-up. In *5a*, Block C makes pattern first.

Before following the treadling sequence further, examine the profile tie-up in *5a*. The first column in the tie-up tells us that pattern is woven in Block A, background in B and C. The second column in the tie-up indicates that pattern is woven in C, background in A and B. The third column shows pattern woven in B *and* C, background in A. (If you are having trouble at

6. Four-block profile drafts: blocks are combined in a, b, and c; in d, the blocks weave pattern independently.

a

b

c

d

this point, you might have forgotten that the columns in the tie-up are read *vertically* in the same way as treadles are read in a regular tie-up. Read the draft exactly as you would a thread-by-thread draft for three shafts.) Because the squares in the profile drawdown do not represent single threads but groups of threads *that are interlacing*, we can produce large areas of pattern or background without worrying about overlong floats. Consequently any of the blocks can produce pattern or background together. Notice that combinations of blocks weave pattern in *Figures 5a-5d* and *6a-6c*.

Notice also that the profile treadling orders in the drafts in *Figures 5* and *6* are identical to the profile threading orders. An amazing variety of designs can be generated by changing *only* the profile tie-up. Changes in profile treadling order also produce changes in the design.

Varying combinations of blocks in profile tie-ups is a rich area for exploration. Computer programs can produce profile drawdown after drawdown with the click of a mouse or a single keystroke. What would have taken hours to draw by hand, takes only seconds!

DESIGNING WITH PROFILE DRAFTS

If we wove on jacquard looms and could control every warp thread independently, we could draw pictures in place of profile drawdowns. To transcend the limitations imposed by the number of shafts available, however, handweavers have developed ingenious techniques for creating complex designs. Even 2- and 3-block designs can look like a lot more.

Many designs owe their effectiveness to the use of symmetry. Look again at the treadling orders and drawdowns in *Figures 5* and *6*. Notice that the drawdowns are completely —'quadrilaterally'— symmetrical. Quadrilateral symmetry is guaranteed when the profile threading order and the profile treadling order are symmetrical and identical (no matter what the tie-up). If the profile threading and treadling orders are asymmetrical but identical, the design is bilaterally symmetrical along the diagonal if blocks are not combined in the tie-up, see *Figure 11*, p. 35.

Blocks woven 'as drawn in'

When the threading order and the treadling order of a thread-by-thread draft are identical, the draft is considered to be woven *as drawn in* (or *'trompt as writ'*): one weft is inserted in each shed formed by the treadle whose number corresponds to each succeeding shaft number in the threading. The draft in *Figure 1*, p. 28, for example, is woven as drawn in. 'As drawn in' and 'tromp as writ' are often given with a threading draft to save writing treadling instructions.

Identical threading and treadling orders in a profile draft do not indicate that the draft is woven literally 'as drawn in,' weft pick for warp end. A profile draft shows blocks, not individual threads. The *blocks* can be woven 'as drawn in,' however, if they produce pattern in the same order in which they are threaded.

Examine *Figure 7a*. In this 3-block draft, the blocks are woven as drawn in. Block C is the first block threaded (see the upper right-hand corner) and it is also the first block that produces pattern (see the top row of the profile drawdown). When instructed to weave 'as drawn in' using a profile draft, produce pattern in each successive threaded block until the block is 'square,' forming a diagonal line that connects a string of different-sized squares. Follow the diagonal line of black squares in *7a*: single squares appear for Blocks C-B-A-B-C. Next, Block A is threaded six times and treadled six times to produce a large square. Any profile threading draft can be woven in this manner without a profile treadling draft.

7a. Three-block profile draft: blocks woven as drawn in

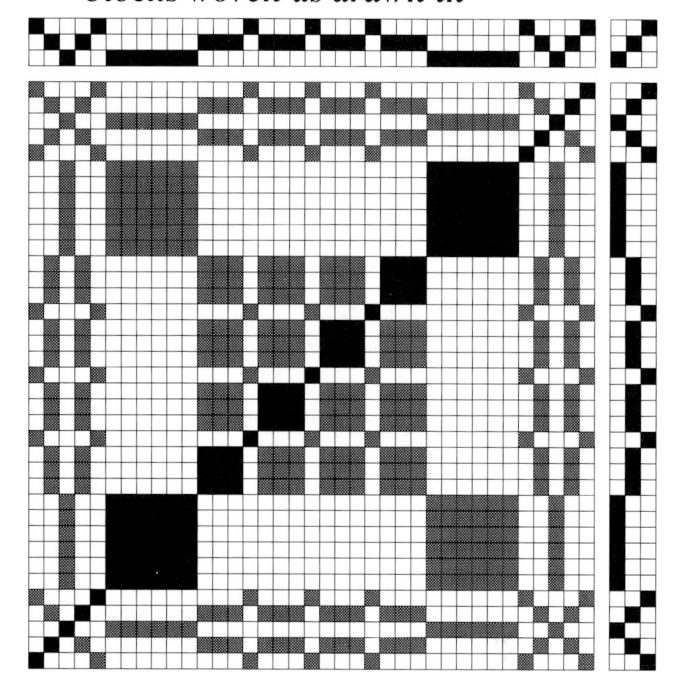

7b. Three-block profile draft: blocks B and C are combined

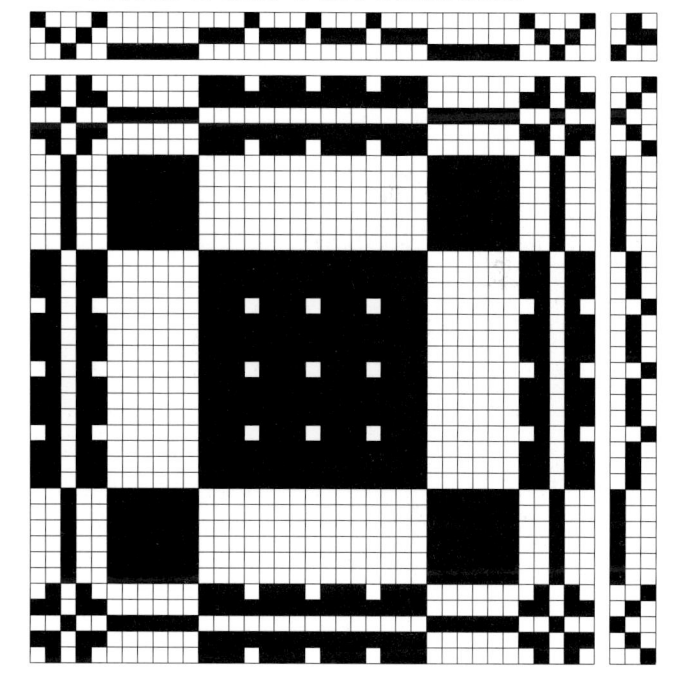

Blocks can only be woven 'as drawn in' if they produce pattern independently. The profile tie-ups in *6d* and *7a* show that each block weaves pattern independently; the treadling orders indicate that the blocks are woven as drawn in. Notice that blocks are combined in the profile tie-ups in *Figures 6a-c*, and *7b*. The drawdown in *7b* is symmetrical, but because Blocks B and C are combined in the tie-up, the blocks cannot be woven as drawn in.

8a. Blocks A, B, C, D woven as drawn in

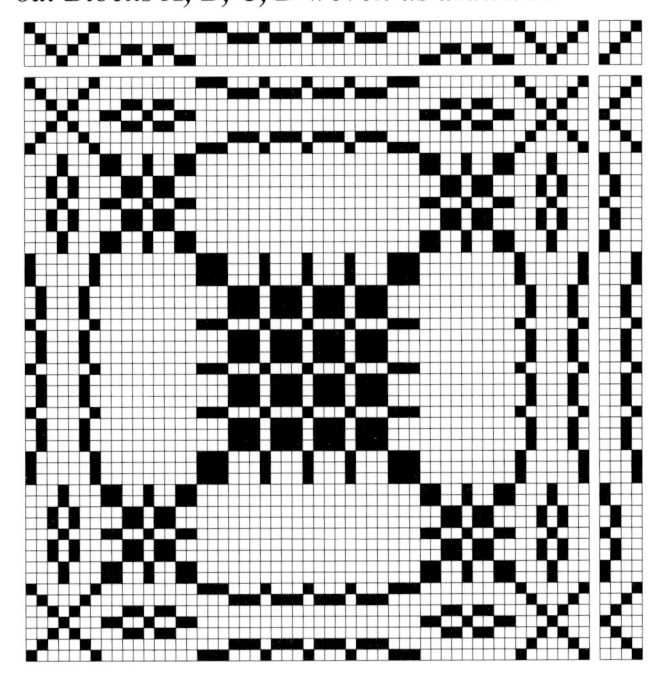

8b. Blocks A & B exchanged; C & D exchanged

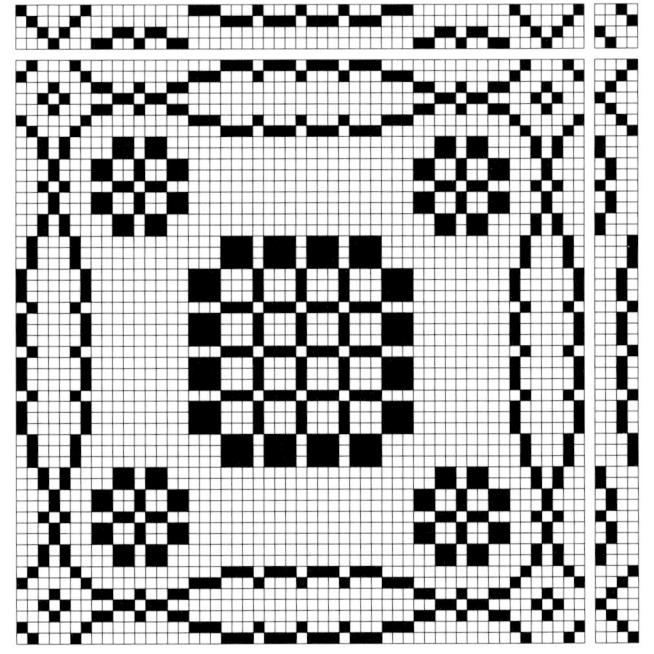

Star fashion vs. rose fashion

Compare the 4-block profile drafts in **Figures 8a** and **8b**. In both profile tie-ups, blocks produce pattern independently. The profile drawdown in **8a** shows a diagonal line of connected squares: the blocks are woven as drawn in. Notice the four motifs that flank the central table in **8a**. These are called 'star' motifs: two blocks (A and B in **8a**) are threaded in alternation a number of times (five times in **8a**, ABABA); the block in the center is narrower than the others. Since the blocks in a star are always woven as drawn in, 'star fashion' is a synonym for weaving blocks as drawn in. 'Star fashion' should not be used with a thread-by-thread draft to mean 'as drawn in' or 'tromp as writ.'

If the threading order of Blocks A and B (ABABA in **Figure 8**) is transposed in the treadling order to BABAB, a 'rose' motif is formed instead of a star. Compare the tie-ups in **8a** and **8b**. The tie-up in **8b** transposes Blocks A and B and Blocks C and D. Now compare the drawdowns in **8a** and **8b**. Where Block A produces pattern in **8a**, Block B produces pattern in **8b**; where Block B produces pattern in **8a**, Block A produces pattern in **8b**. The center motif in **8b** is produced from the exchange of blocks C and D.

This exchange of pairs of blocks in the tie-up produces a 'rose fashion' treadling order. A rose fashion treadling order can also be produced by exchanging treadling columns instead of blocks in the tie-up. Exchanging the first two treadling columns and the second two treadling columns in **8a** would also produce the same rose fashion motifs as in **8b**.

Both star-fashion and rose-fashion treadling orders produce symmetrical designs, but rose fashion treadling orders produce symmetry without diagonal lines. 'Rose fashion' is most successful with motifs containing two or three blocks. In a 4-block design made up of *two* 2-block motifs, one motif can be woven rose fashion and the other star fashion (see **8c**).

Design scope and complexity are increased when one 2-block motif is threaded ABABA and another is threaded BABAB (or CDCDC followed by DCDCD). When a star is woven in one of the motifs, a rose is

8c. A & B exchanged; C & D as drawn in

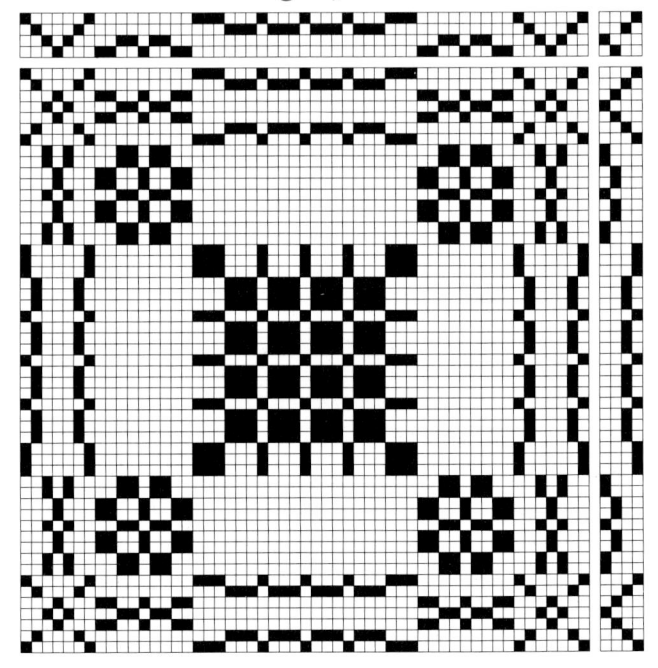

34

9. A & B; C & D exchanged in the threading

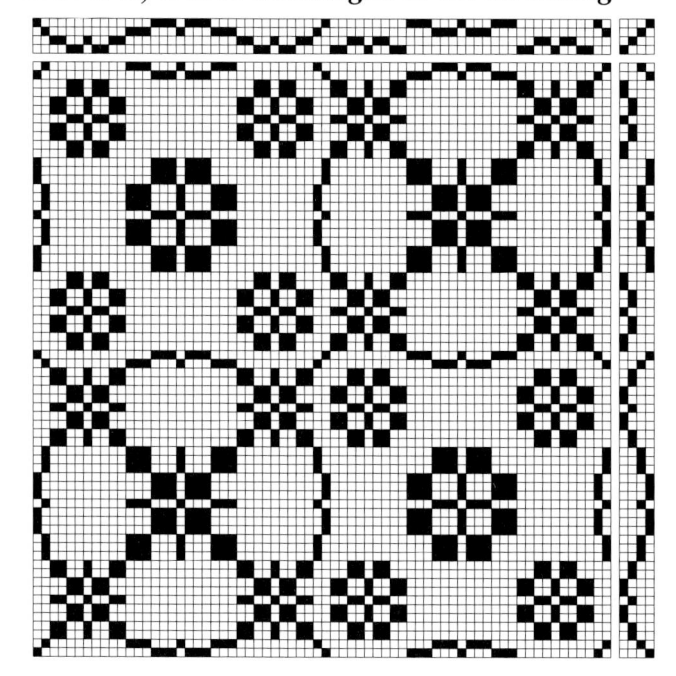

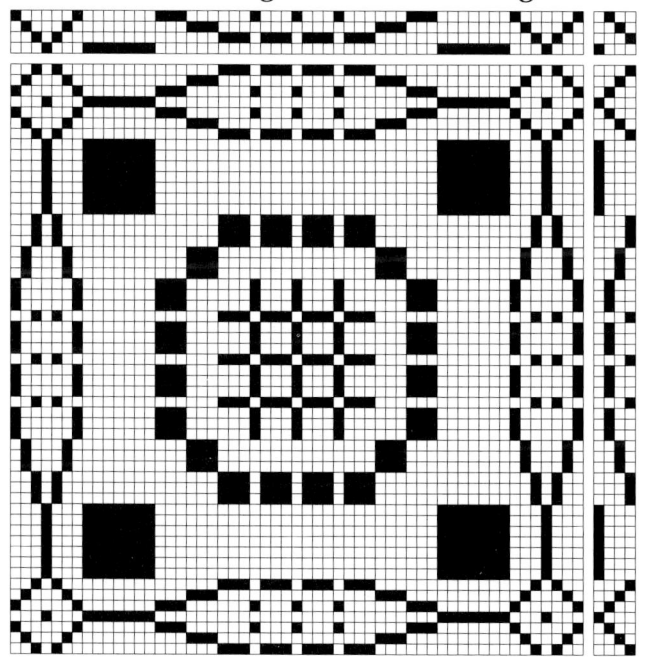

11. Asymmetrical threading and treadling

woven in the other, and vice versa; see *Figure 9*.

The rose fashion exchange is usually made between two blocks that make up one motif. If one motif is made up of B and C and the other of A and D, then the exchange is made between B and C, and/or A and D. In 3-block motifs, the *first* and *third* blocks are usually exchanged in the treadling order, while the second block is woven in the same order in which it is threaded. In the 3-block motif in *Figure 10*, B and D are exchanged in the treadling but C is woven in the same order in which it is threaded.

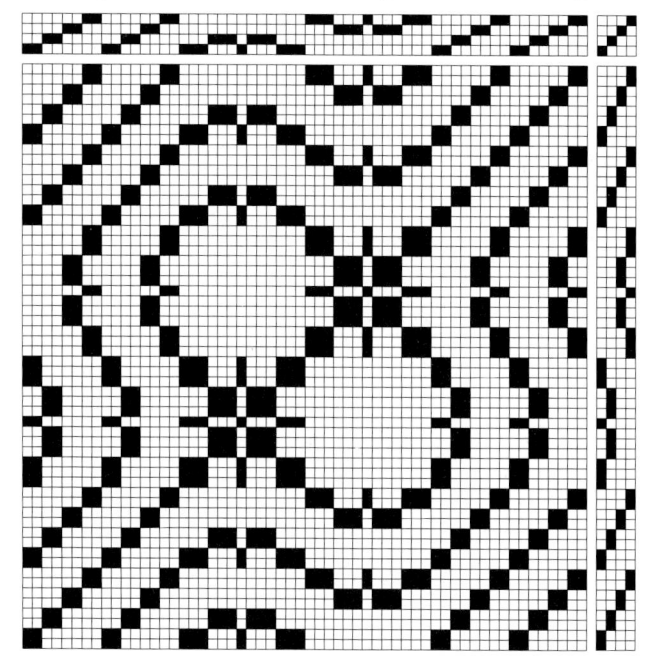

Asymmetrical threading and treadling orders

If the treadling and threading orders are the same but *asymmetrical*, the design is bilaterally symmetrical along the diagonal if the blocks weave pattern independently (*Figure 11*). This does not necessarily follow if blocks are combined in the tie-up. Asymmetrical treadling orders (*Figure 12*) offer endless possibilities for design variation. Threading and treadling orders can be asymmetrical and dissimilar, but such designs are not often successful when limited to very few blocks.

10. B & D exchanged in the treadling

12. Asymmetrical treadling

35

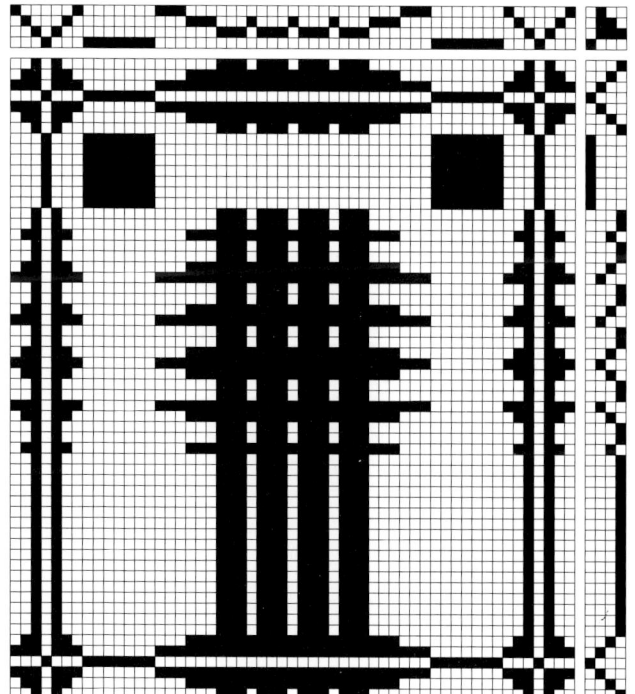

Lesson: Writing Profile Drafts

Enjoy designing original profile drafts. Test your understanding of profile drafting in these six exercises (see answers, p. 121). Then, on graph paper (pp. 128-129), prepare three additional profile drafts: one with symmetrical and identical threading and treadling orders, one with a rose fashion treadling order (use the threading profile draft in Exercise 2 or Exercise 3), and one with dissimilar and asymmetrical threading and treadling orders.

Basic profile draft

Complete the profile drawdown for the 2-block profile draft in ***Exercise 1***. To begin: look at the *first* square in the profile treadling sequence (remember the 'you are here' square). Which blocks are marked in the tie-up directly above this square? In ***Exercise 1***, Block A is marked in the tie-up above the first square in the treadling sequence. Block A weaves pattern for that row. Move across the horizontal row in the drawdown for that first treadling square, filling in the squares that appear under all Block A threading squares. Repeat this process for each row in the profile treadling diagram.

A profile tie-up can show any combination of blocks in any order; Block A does not necessarily produce pattern first. The *treadling diagram* tells the order in which the blocks make pattern, not the tie-up. Notice that with the tie-up and treadling order in ***Exercise 1***, blocks are woven as drawn in. Be sure to memorize that the bottom row in a profile threading draft is always A, the next row B, the next C, etc., so that you don't need to write these letters on the draft.

'As drawn in' or star fashion

Prepare a profile drawdown for the 4-block profile threading, tie-up, and treadling order in ***Exercise 2***. In this drawdown, as in ***Exercise 1***, the blocks make pattern in the same order in which they are threaded. In this draft, as in ***Exercise 1***, blocks are not combined in the tie-up (each block weaves pattern independently). The completed drawdown should show a diagonal line of different-sized squares, from the upper right corner of the drawdown to the bottom left corner.

The blocks in ***Exercise 3*** are also woven as drawn in. With this information, a profile tie-up and treadling order are not really necessary. Instead, follow the blocks in the threading. For example, the first block threaded is Block C; it is threaded one time. For the first row in the drawdown, fill in all squares under Block C. Next Block B is threaded one time, then Block A. Fill in one row for Block B and one row for Block A. Repeat these three rows. Block C is then threaded *three* times: fill in squares under Block C for three rows, then B for three rows, and A for three rows, etc.

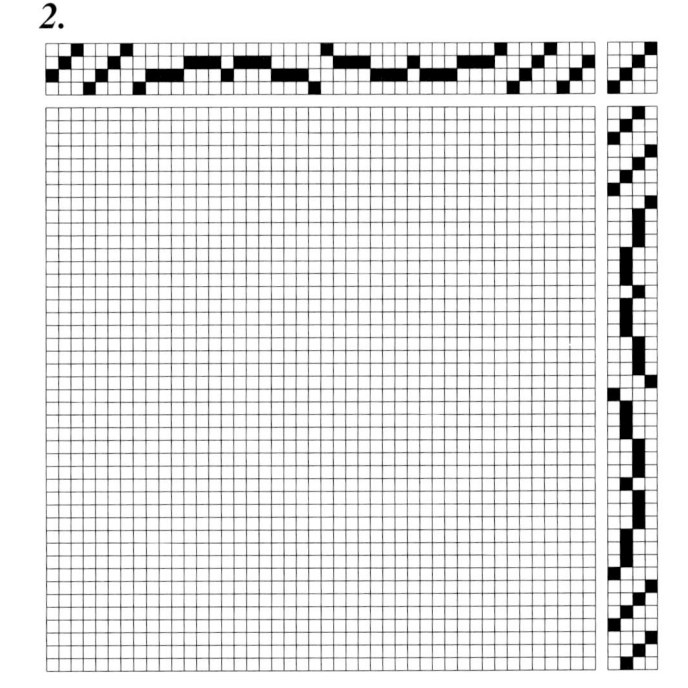

1.

2.

36

3.

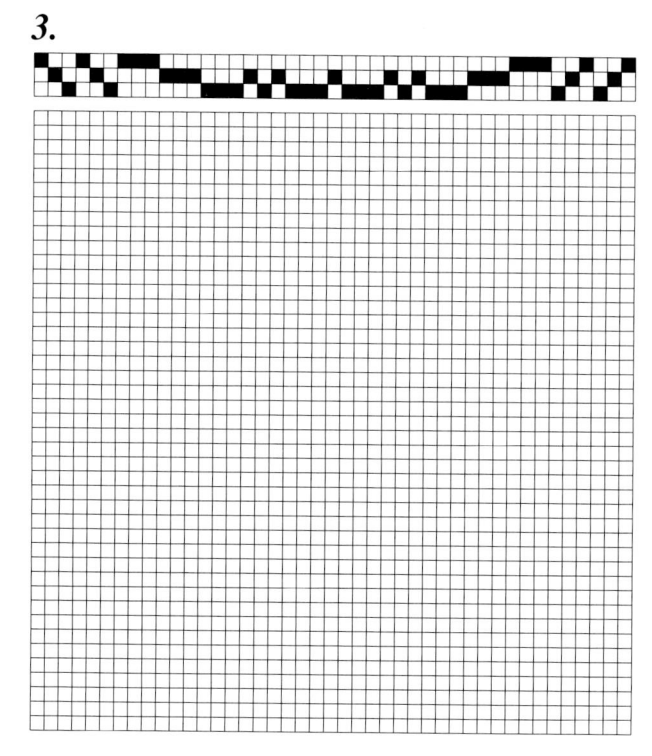

Combined blocks

Study the profile tie-up in *Exercise 4*. Remember that the bottom threading row represents Block A, the second row B, the third row C. Identify the block combinations that produce pattern according to the *Exercise 4* profile tie-up. If you identified them as B-and-C, A-and-B, and A, you are correct. Which block weaves pattern first? If you said A, you are ready to begin the drawdown. Fill in the squares for A for four rows. For the fifth row, darken squares for both A *and* B, etc. Follow the same process for *Exercise 5*.

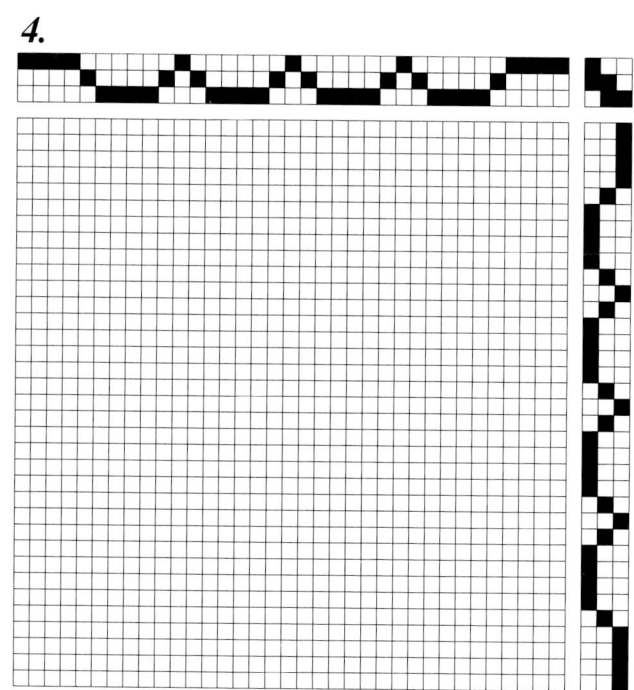

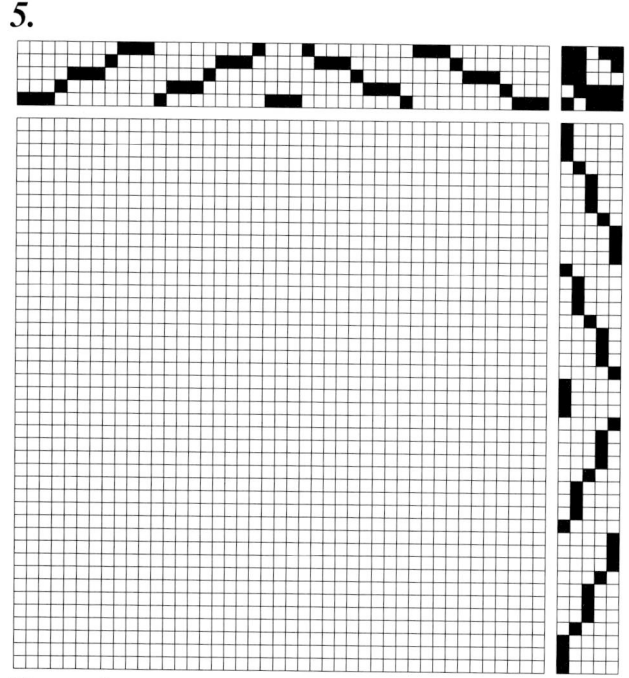

4.

5.

From bottom to top

Profile drafts are often written from bottom to top. Because a profile draft is a design and gives no information about real threads, you can turn it upside down if you are confused by an unaccustomed direction. It is a good test of your understanding, however, to see if you can complete a profile drawdown from bottom to top. Try the 5-block profile draft in *Exercise 6*. The bottom row of the profile threading draft is still Block A, the second row B, etc. Which block(s) weave pattern first? Check the first square in the treadling diagram next to the tie-up. It shows that Block E weaves pattern first, for one row. Block A weaves pattern next.

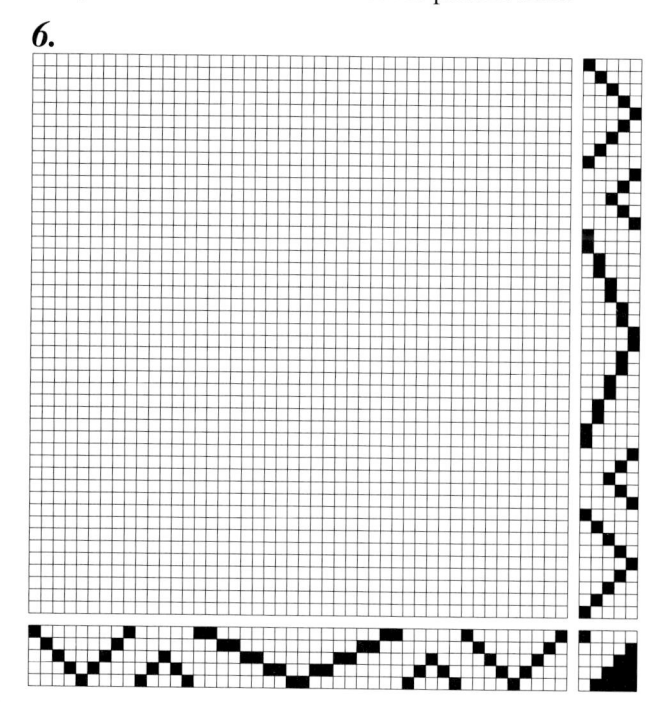

6.

Overshot: Words to Know

balanced draft: drafts for completely symmetrical overshot patterns are balanced when the threading draft is symmetrical. All blocks contain an even number of warp ends except turning blocks, which contain an odd number.

block weaves: weave structures in which blocks of pattern are formed because warp and weft threads interlace in one way in the pattern area and another way in the background area. Some block weaves are unit weaves, which form pattern and background with specific threading and treadling units. Overshot, which has no specific threading unit, is a block weave but not a unit weave.

blooming leaf: describes a leaf-like pattern in overshot in which blocks are threaded in one direction to the center, where the direction reverses on a turning block. Block sizes increase from very small at the outside edge to as large as the float permits in the center of each half of the design, then decrease in size until reaching the large center turning block.

compound elements: weaves with 'compound elements' are structures with more than one warp or more than one weft. There are two wefts in overshot: the function of one of the wefts is to weave a plain weave ground cloth. The function of the second weft is to float over and under the ground cloth to form pattern.

ground cloth: 'ground' indicates the cloth structure on which a supplementary pattern warp or weft floats. If the supplementary warp or weft is cut away, the ground structure remains intact. A plain weave ground cloth is formed in overshot, crackle, and in summer and winter and other tied unit weaves.

halftone: used to describe the blocks in overshot where the pattern weft weaves over and under alternate warp ends. The mix of warp and tabby weft color and pattern-weft color is close to 50/50, thus the name 'halftone.' Halftones in 4-shaft, 4-block overshot, in which blocks are threaded in succession, appear adjacent to blocks with pattern floats.

motif: usually refers to a figure within the complete design, such as a rose or a table in an overshot draft.

overshot: a supplementary-weft structure with a plain-weave ground cloth. The supplementary weft floats a) over an entire block, b) under an entire block, and c) over and under alternate ends in two blocks to form halftones. Since the pattern area is limited by float length (blocks cannot be combined in a draft) overshot is not a unit weave.

overshot on opposites: describes an overshot draft in which one block is threaded on one pair of shafts and another is threaded on the opposite pair: 1-2 and 3-4 in 2-block Monk's belt. The term is also used to describe overshot on eight shafts (or more) where Block A = 1-2, B = 3-4, C = 5-6, and D = 7-8, though none of these shafts is 'opposite' to another.

pattern weft: usually refers to a supplementary weft, also called 'extra' weft, that creates pattern by floating above groups of warp ends or creates background by floating beneath them, or vice versa.

pine: when the word 'pine' is included in the title of an overshot draft, as in 'Pine Cone' and 'Pine Bloom,' the draft is usually intended to be unbalanced since an unbalanced draft produces the one-directional scallops that imitate a pine cone.

rose: a 2-block motif threaded A-B-A-B-A but treadled B-A-B-A-B or threaded A-B-A-B-A-B-A but treadled B-A-B-A-B-A-B. The underlined blocks are two or three times larger than the blocks that are not underlined; see *Figure 4*, p. 41.

square the design: overshot drafts are usually intended to be symmetrical: the height of a motif measures the same as the width. The draft is woven to 'square' when the number of picks and appropriate sett and beat produce a perfectly symmetrical design.

star: a 2-block motif threaded A-B-A-B-A and treadled A-B-A-B-A or threaded A-B-A-B-A-B-A and treadled A-B-A-B-A-B-A. As with the rose, the underlined blocks are larger than the blocks that are not underlined. Both star and rose motifs can be produced on the same threading.

tabby weft: used to distinguish the weft that weaves a plain weave ground cloth from the pattern weft.

table: a central motif in an overshot draft usually formed by two or three blocks. Two of the blocks are repeated several times; one of the two repeated blocks is usually wider than the other.

turning blocks: in overshot, blocks are usually threaded in succession, moving in any direction (A-B-C-D or D-C-B-A), reversing directions at any time. When the direction changes, the block on which the draft pivots is a turning block: in A-B-C-D-C-B-A, D is a turning block; in D-A-B-C-B-A-D, C is a turning block.

Whig rose: a pattern in overshot with a table in the center flanked by four rose motifs. The design is treadled rose fashion, see p. 34. Patterns with 'rose' in the title are intended to be treadled rose fashion.

Chapter 4
Understanding Overshot

OVERSHOT: PATTERN PLUS

The familiar patterns of overshot — circles, roses, diamonds, stars — enchant many a beginning weaver. Overshot drafts, however, often intimidate even experienced weavers. Mastery of overshot is worth the effort, since it provides an astounding variety of patterning on only four shafts. A thorough understanding of overshot drafting methods is prerequisite to creating original patterns, designing unique borders, and miniaturizing, enlarging, or altering existing drafts.

A twill derivative

Overshot is often referred to as a derivative of twill. I have imagined that once upon a time a weaver, bored with the tiny floats of a 2/2 twill, wondered how to make them a bit more dramatic. Spreading the warp threads farther apart might make them longer, she thought, but the cloth could become unstable. How about alternating the twill weft with a tabby weft to improve the stability of the cloth — and — why not extend the threading in each twill pair so that instead of passing over only 1-2, the float covers 1-2-1-2, and instead of 2-3, the float covers 2-3-2-3. . . and so overshot was born.

Figure 1 shows four overshot blocks: A, B, C, D. Notice that a plain weave cloth is formed by the tabby weft (treadles *a* and *b*) alternating one-and-one with the pattern weft. Therefore, unlike twill, overshot is a structure with one warp and *two* wefts, see the middle column in 'The Family Tree of Weaves,' p. 2. The pattern weft in overshot is a 'supplementary' or 'extra' weft. It is not required for the stability of the cloth; if it is removed a stable plain weave cloth remains.

Each of the blocks weaving pattern in *Figure 1* is framed. In overshot, pattern occurs in a block when the pattern weft floats over all of the threads in the block. The pattern weft interlaces in a block adjacent to the one making pattern. The size of any threading block is therefore limited to the desirable length of a pattern-weft float. Since the pattern weft does not interlace in the block making pattern, overshot is not a unit weave. In unit weaves the complete interlacement characteristic of the structure takes place within each unit. A consequence is that with unit weaves, unlimited numbers of units in the same block can be threaded in succession.

1. Four-shaft overshot draft

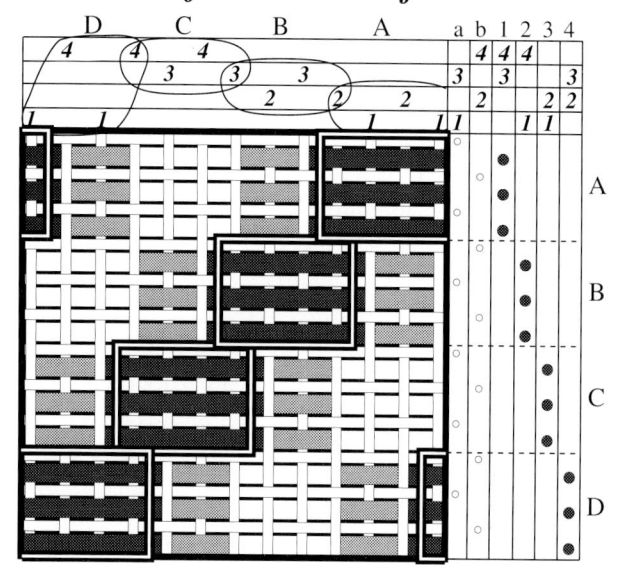

Characteristics of overshot

Follow the path of the first pattern pick in *Figure 1*. Shafts 3 and 4 are raised; shafts 1 and 2 are down. A pattern-weft float covers all of the warp threads in Block A because all four threads are down. Notice, however, Block D also includes warp threads on shaft 1 and Block B also includes warp threads on shaft 2. The pattern weft therefore passes over warp ends on shafts 1 and 2 in Blocks B and D (see light gray shading) but under threads on shafts 3 and 4. In Block C, the pattern weft passes under all four warp threads. The next two pattern picks are the same as the first.

The fourth pattern pick weaves pattern in Block B. Shafts 2 and 3 are down; shafts 1 and 4 are up. The pattern weft passes over all of the warp threads in Block B, under all of the warp threads in Block D, and over threads on 2 and 3 and under threads on 1 and 4 in Blocks A and C. Follow the pattern picks in the rest of the draft. Notice that for each, the weft passes *over* all of the warp threads in one of the blocks, *under* all of the warp threads in one of the blocks, and alternates *over and under* the warp threads in the remaining two 'halftone' blocks. Unlike unit weaves, in which one consistent interlacement appears in the pattern area and one consistent but different interlacement in the background, overshot produces a background mixed with halftone and 'float-on-the-back' blocks.

39

OVERSHOT THREADING DRAFTS

Weaving literature is sprinkled with a confusing variety of overshot drafting formats. Many of these formats have evolved as ways to abbreviate lengthy drafts and must be translated carefully to produce successful patterns. Some drafts do not include treadling instructions; the weaver is expected to use the threading draft to derive star or rose fashion treadling orders.

The twill circle and overshot blocks

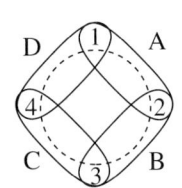

Blocks in overshot are usually threaded in succession. To understand what that means, examine a revised version of our twill circle. The numbers representing shafts 1 and 2 are circled to indicate Block A; 2 and 3 are Block B, 3 and 4 are Block C, and 4 and 1 are Block D. If Block A is threaded first and Block B second, the direction of the threading moves clockwise around the circle. If the threading changes directions to move counterclockwise, the block on which the threading pivots is called a turning block. For example, if Blocks A, B, C, B, A are threaded, C is a turning block. If Blocks A, B, A, B, A are threaded, the center three blocks, B, A, B, are turning blocks (turning blocks are underlined). If the threading skips to the opposite block in the circle, as from A to C, for example, the threading is said to be 'on opposites.' On-opposites threading drafts have some special characteristics that we will discuss later in this chapter.

2. Four blocks threaded in a point

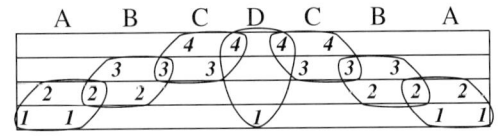

Because blocks are usually threaded in succession, Block B or Block D is adjacent to Block A; Block A or Block C is adjacent to B; Block B or Block D is adjacent to C; Block A or Block C is adjacent to B. Notice in *Figure 2* that adjacent blocks share threads on the same shafts. For example, Block B shares shaft 3 with Block C and shaft 2 with Block A. For this reason, if blocks are threaded in succession, halftone blocks always appear adjacent to pattern blocks. The effect of halftone blocks is to shadow the edges of the pattern motifs, see *Photo a*. Since the pattern weft always floats over one block, under one block, and alternately over and under warp threads in the remaining two blocks, halftones form fifty percent of an overshot fabric.

a. 4-shaft overshot, unbalanced draft

Identify the blocks.

It is not easy to recognize blocks and motifs in an overshot threading draft because the same shaft numbers appear in two different blocks. Such recognition is necessary for using overshot drafts in a creative way. Look again at *Figure 2*. Each block in the draft is circled, and the circles overlap each other. These circles give two important bits of information. They graphically identify the blocks and therefore tell something about the design. They also indicate the length of the pattern-weft float in each block. If shafts 1 and 2 are down, for example, a pattern-weft float covers four warp threads in Block A. If shafts 2 and 3 are down, a pattern-weft float covers four warp threads in Block B. The float in Block A covers the same warp end on shaft 2 that is covered by the float in Block B. When blocks are circled in an overshot draft, the circles always overlap to include that shared warp end.

3a. Circle the blocks.

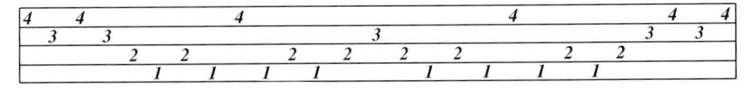

Study the overshot draft in *Figure 3a*. It looks a bit like a twill draft except that pairs of shafts are repeated in several places, 3-4, for example, and 1-2. To identify the blocks, circle all of the numbers belonging to a specific pair: 1-2, 2-3, 3-4, 4-1. Start at the right side of the *Figure 3a* draft. Draw the first circle around all four warp threads in the 3-4 pair. The next pair is 2-3.

40

3b. Identify the turning blocks.

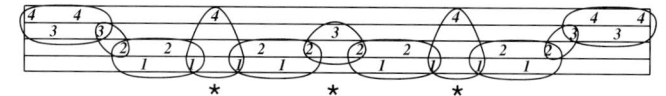

Even though this block contains only two threads, a float covers these two threads when shafts 2 and 3 are down: two threads constitute a threading block in overshot. The next circle encloses four warp threads on shafts 1 and 2. Complete the circles and check your work with *Figure 3b* (turning blocks are marked by *).

4. Threading for a rose or a star

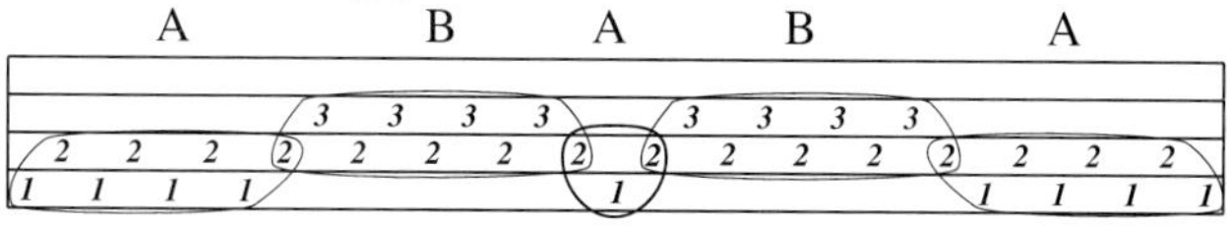

As you become familiar with overshot drafts, you'll begin to recognize recurring motifs. The draft in *Figure 4* produces either a rose or a star. Observe, too, that in overshot drafts, threads on even shafts always alternate with threads on odd shafts. Tabby sheds are formed by lifting shafts 1-3 and 2-4 alternately.

VARIATIONS IN DRAFTING FORMAT

Complete thread-by-thread drafts in overshot are often very long; a repeat may contain more than a hundred ends. The rose in *Figure 4*, for example, is likely to be only a small part of a complete threading repeat. Over time, many different ways of abbreviating overshot threading drafts have been devised. Unfortunately, translating an abbreviated draft into an effective thread-by-thread draft is not as straightforward as it looks.

5. Short draft

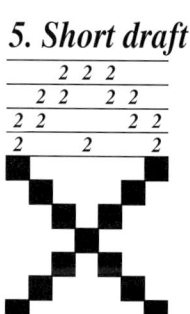

Figure 5 shows an abbreviated draft from Marguerite Davison's *A Handweaver's Source Book*. Each draft includes a drawdown of the pattern blocks. The drawdowns are misleading in that they do not show tabby picks, halftones, nor the overlapping of pattern-weft floats caused by shared threads in adjacent blocks.

In *Figure 5* a pair of numbers, one directly above the other, identifies the block and the number of times it is threaded. Read from right to left: a '2' appears on threading rows 1 and 2. This means that the A Block, on shafts 1 and 2, is threaded twice: 1-2-1-2. The next vertical column shows a '2' on threading row 2 and a '2' on threading row 3. Thread Block B twice: 2-3-2-3. An immediate problem arises: if the threading is written 1-2-1-2-2-3-2-3, two consecutive ends are threaded on shaft 2.

From short draft to thread-by-thread draft: Method 1

One solution is to reverse the threading order of the shafts in alternate pairs so that warp ends are never threaded on the same shaft consecutively: A is always 1-2, B is always 3-2, C is always 3-4, and D is always 1-4. The short draft from *Figure 5* is translated following this method in *Figure 6a*. The circles in this draft identify the four ends that are threaded following the 2/2 notation in the short draft.

6a. Reverse shaft order in alternate pairs.

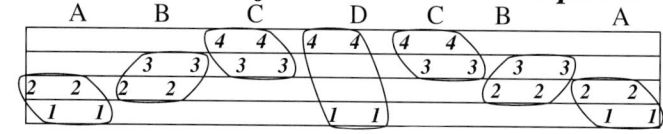

There are a number of advantages to this method. Threading can be done from the short draft alone once the correct order of the shafts in each block is memorized. Miniaturizing and enlarging drafts is a simple matter of changing the numbers that indicate how many times a block is threaded. The number of threads in a full repeat can be determined easily by adding all of the numbers, and the number of heddles required on each shaft is the total of the numbers on each threading row.

There is also a significant disadvantage. *Figure 6b* shows the same threading draft as *6a*, with the circles redrawn to show the true size of each block. Note that *six* ends are threaded in Block B on the right side of the motif, but only *four* ends in Block B on the left side. Six ends in Block C are threaded on the left, but four are threaded on the right. In fact, with this method, most pattern-weft floats pass over two more ends on one side of the motif than on the other. *Photo a, p. 40*, shows a threading draft derived with Method 1. Blocks on opposite sides of symmetrical motifs (see the center table and the roses) are different in width.

6b. Method 1 produces an unbalanced draft.

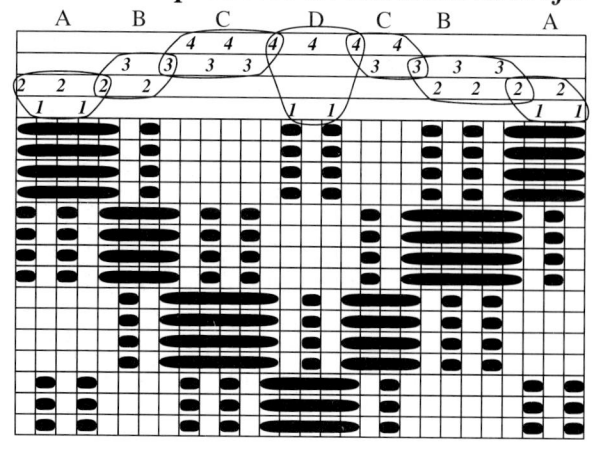

From short draft to thread-by-thread draft: Method 2

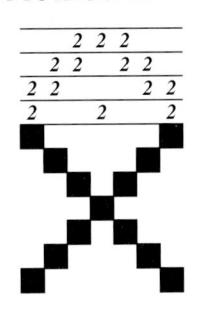

Writing symmetrical, or 'balanced,' overshot drafts requires memorizing one basic rule — and a little bit of practice. The rule is: count the last thread of one block as the first thread of the next. Look again at the short draft from *Figure 5*. Start as in Method 1 by threading Block A twice, 1-2-1-2. Now thread Block B, but count the last thread of A as the first thread of B, 2-3-2-3. Circle the blocks as you write, see *Figure 7*, *Step a*. After the D block, the draft reverses directions to Block C. Still following the rule, count the last thread of D as the first thread of C. But the last thread in D is on shaft 1 (see *7b*) and shaft 1 is not in the C block. You must either add a 4 or subtract the 1 so that the last thread in D is on shaft 4. Complete the rest of the draft as in *7e* or *7f*.

7. Steps for writing balanced drafts

To thread A-B-C-D-C-B-A:

a. Count the last thread of one block (2) as the first thread of the next.

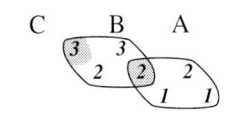

b. To go from D to C, The first thread of the C block must be 4, not 1. Add a 4 as in Step c, or subtract a 1 as in Step d.

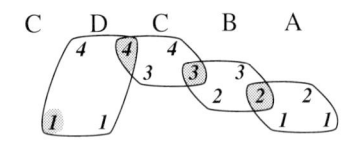

c. Add a 4 to produce the draft in e.

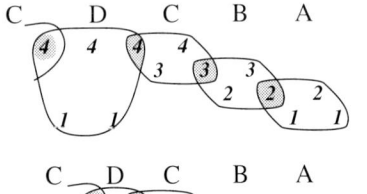

d. Subtract the 1 to produce the draft in f.

e. The completed draft with a 4 added in the turning block.

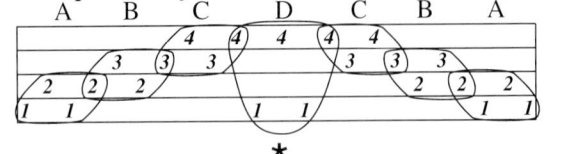

f. The completed draft with a 1 subtracted in the turning block.

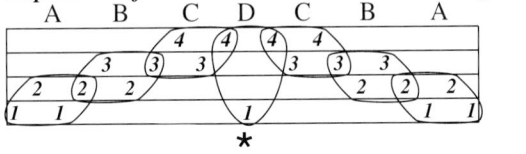

b. 4-shaft overshot, balanced draft

Study the threading drafts in *7e* and *7f*. Notice that both drafts are completely symmetrical; the center thread in *7e* is on shaft 4, and the center thread in *7f* is on shaft 1 (see *). Overshot threading drafts must be symmetrical in order to produce symmetrical motifs. Notice also that an even number of threads appears inside each circle except in Block D. In overshot drafts all blocks are threaded with an even number of threads except turning blocks, which have an odd number.

The pattern-weft drawdown in *Figure 8* shows the symmetrical blocks produced by the draft in *7f*. Compare *Figure 8* with *Figure 6b*. Next compare the motifs from a balanced draft in *Photo b* with the motifs from an unbalanced draft in *Photo a*, p. 40.

8. Method 2 produces a balanced draft.

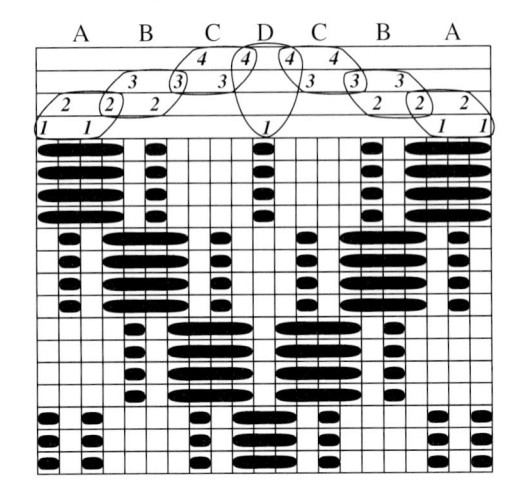

To balance or not to balance

With Method 2, a decision must be made at each turning block: whether to add a thread or to subtract a thread. The choice can be constant for an entire draft, i.e., add threads to all turning blocks or subtract threads from all turning blocks, or the choice can vary throughout the draft. Remember, however, that to produce symmetrical motifs, turning blocks in symmetrical positions must be treated the same way. Usually the choice to add or subtract depends on whether more or fewer threads are desired in a complete repeat.

A disadvantage to Method 2 is that the total number of warp ends in the thread-by-thread draft cannot be determined simply by counting the numbers written in the short draft. In the corresponding thread-by-thread draft, one thread must be subtracted each time the threading changes to a new block because of the 'shared' thread. An additional thread must also be added or subtracted for each turning block in the draft.

Balanced drafts are not necessarily 'correct' drafts. Many historical coverlets, if not most, are woven from unbalanced drafts. Some overshot drafts depend on a *lack* of symmetry for their effectiveness. Beware of balancing an overshot draft with 'pine' in its name, like 'Pine Bloom' or 'Pine Blossom,' for example. Such names usually indicate a design that is most effective if the draft is *unbalanced*, so that it can produce the one-directional scallops characteristic of pine cones. The goal is to know enough to *choose*, so that you can design a draft that does what you expect it to do.

Using other short draft forms

The short draft in *Figure 5* can be rewritten as a profile draft. If each square on the profile threading row is to equal four warp threads, the profile draft corresponding to *Figure 5* appears in *Figure 9*. The method for translating a profile draft into a thread-by-thread draft is the same as for the *Figure 5* short draft, with one extra step: choose how many threads each square in the profile threading draft represents. This number depends on the desired size of the smallest block and is limited by practical float length in the largest block and therefore varies according to the setts and materials used. The minimum size of a block is two threads. If each square is to represent two threads in *Figure 9*, the threading is 1-2-3-4-1-4-3-2-1, as in the reduced draft in *Figure 11a*.

9. Profile draft

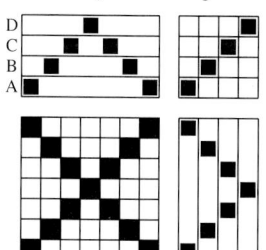

10. Thread overshot from a profile draft.

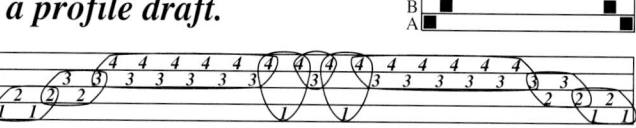

Study the profile threading draft in *Figure 10* and the corresponding thread-by-thread draft. Can you identify the turning blocks? Verify that a thread is subtracted from each turning block in the thread-by-thread draft. (The turning blocks in *Figure 10* are D-C-D.)

Since the width of a pattern area in overshot is limited to the length of a pattern-weft float, not all profile drafts can be used for overshot. No block can be repeated in the threading nor combined in the treadling beyond the practical limit of a pattern-weft float. Therefore, select profile drafts for overshot that do not show many consecutive squares on a profile threading row and those that show blocks producing pattern independently in the tie-up, as in *Figure 9*.

Reducing or enlarging overshot drafts

Once the blocks are circled in an overshot threading draft, reducing or enlarging the draft is a simple process. Any block size can be reduced by eliminating one or more *pairs* of threads. For example, *Figure 11a* shows a 21-thread draft in which one pair of warp threads is eliminated from each block to reduce the draft to 9 threads. In *Figure 11b*, one pair is added to each block to increase the draft to 35 warp threads. Threads can be added *and* subtracted in the same draft to alter proportions within a motif, change relative sizes of motifs, or to achieve other design goals.

11a. Reduce a draft: eliminate pairs.

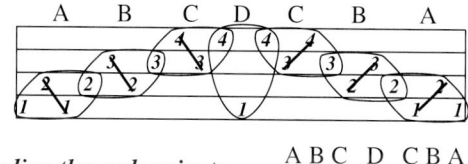

Draw a line through pairs to be eliminated. Rewrite the draft. Circle the blocks. Minimum block size is two threads.

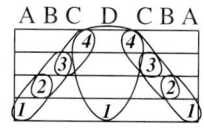

11b. Enlarge a draft: add pairs.

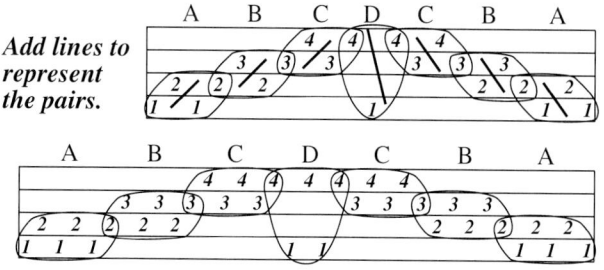

Add lines to represent the pairs.

43

12a. Blocks C and D alternate in the table.

12b. Two C-D pairs are added to the table.

Subtract or add pairs of blocks

Drafts can also be enlarged or reduced by adding or subtracting pairs of blocks. Compare the profile drafts in *12a-c*. In *12a* Blocks C and D are threaded nine times (D-C-<u>D-C</u>-<u>D-C</u>-D-C-D) to form the table motif. Removing two C-D pairs in the center of the table (see underlined pairs) reduces the size of the table (see *12c*). Adding two C-D pairs increases the size of the table: D-C-<u>D-C</u>-<u>D-C</u>-D-C-D-C-D-C-D (see *12b*).

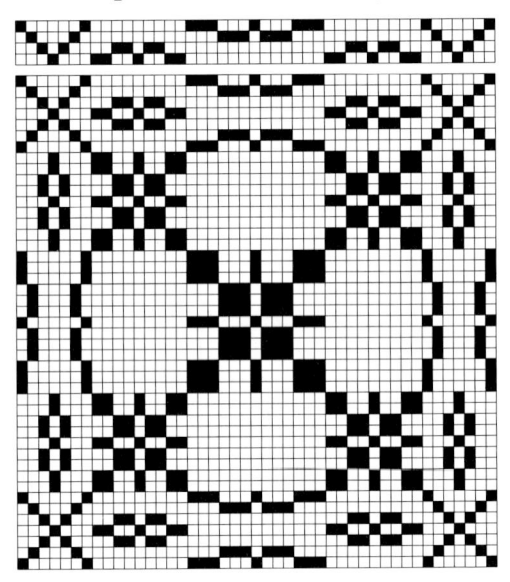

13. Steps for subtracting and adding blocks

Identify the pairs of blocks to be added or subtracted. Omit the last warp thread (on shaft 4) at one end of the sequence of added or subtracted blocks.

a.

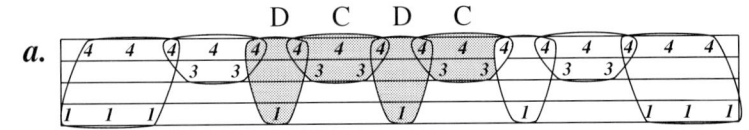

The shaded blocks have been subtracted from a, see also Figure 12c.

b.

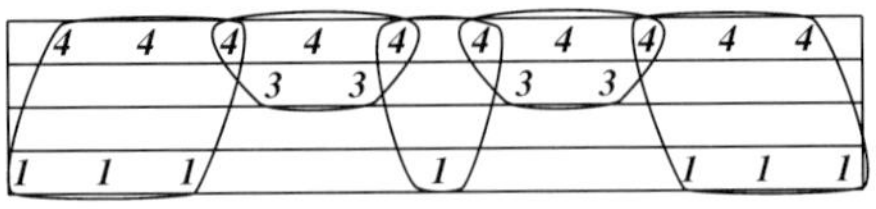

The shaded blocks have been added to a, see also Figure 12b.

c.

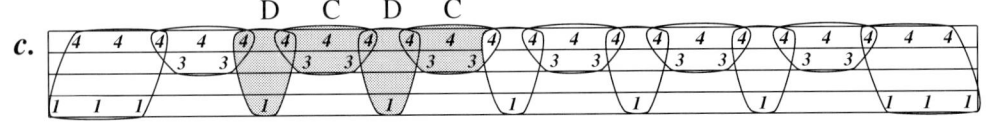

12c. Two C-D pairs are subtracted from the table.

To add or subtract blocks from a profile draft, simply add or subtract squares in the profile draft. To add or subtract blocks from a thread-by-thread draft, circle the blocks in the threading to determine the proportion and shape of each motif. When eliminating blocks, as from *13a* to *13b*, do not eliminate the last warp thread on one side of the threading (the warp end on shaft 4).

When adding blocks, as from *13a* to *13c*, do not duplicate the last warp thread on one side.

c. Overshot on opposites produces solid areas of halftones with 2-thread incidental floats.

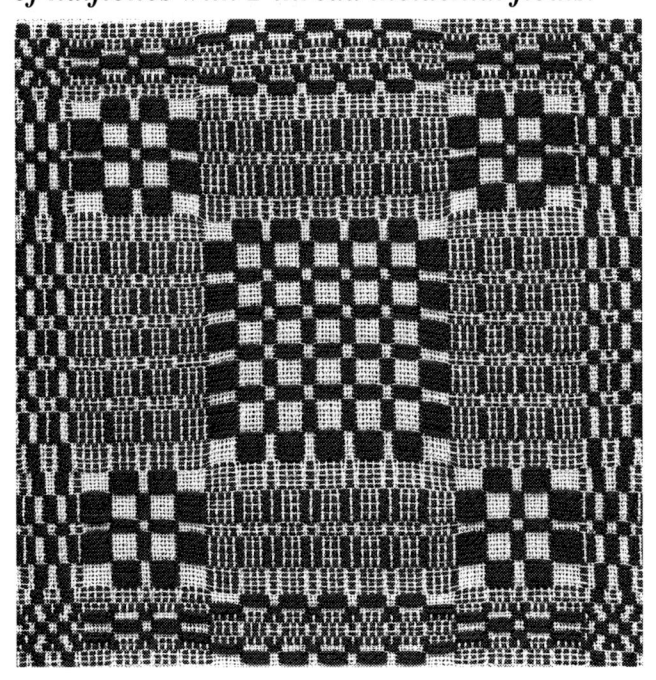

14. Four-shaft overshot on opposites: a 2-thread float occurs in halftone areas.

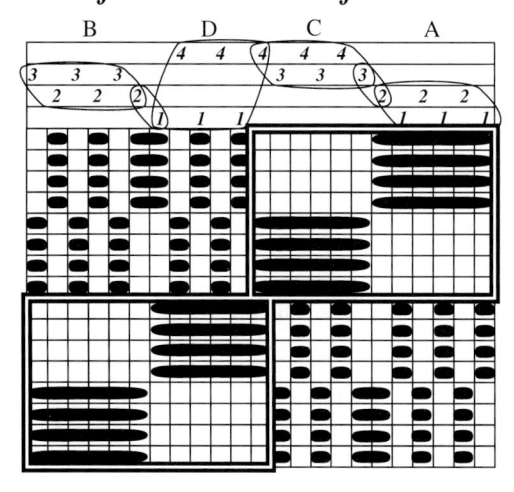

FOUR-SHAFT OVERSHOT ON OPPOSITES

Overshot drafts are 'on opposites' when Block A (1-2) is threaded next to C (3-4) and B (2-3) is threaded next to D (4-1) since these blocks are 'opposite' to each other on the twill circle. In 'on opposites' drafts A and C usually form one motif and B and D another, as in *Photo c*. The pattern weft passes over one block and under the other in one motif, and forms halftones in both of the blocks in the other motif.

Because the two blocks in each motif are threaded on independent shafts, no internal halftones blur the definition of the motif. Compare the roses and table in *Photo c* with the roses and table in *Photo b*, p. 42.

In the blocks producing halftones, however, incidental 2-thread floats occur that can detract from the smooth texture of the halftone background; see the halftones in *Photo c*. To understand how this happens, examine *Figure 14*. Blocks A and C form one 'motif.' Blocks B and D form a second motif (framed in the pattern-weft drawdown). When opposite blocks produce halftones, 2-thread incidental floats occur since warp ends on shafts 1 and 2 are threaded next to each other where Blocks B and D meet, and warp ends on shafts 2 and 3 are threaded next to each other where Blocks A and C meet. If the order of the pairs is reversed, incidental floats occur over 4-1 and 3-4 when the corresponding blocks produce pattern.

When only two blocks are threaded (1-2 and 3-4) as in Monk's belt, no halftones are produced.

EIGHT-SHAFT OVERSHOT 'ON OPPOSITES'

An 8-shaft overshot threading draft is said to be 'on opposites' when Block A is threaded on shafts 1-2; Block B, 3-4; Block C, 5-6; and Block D, 7-8, even though none of these shaft pairs is 'opposite' to the rest.

Study the 8-shaft draft in *Figure 15a*. The drawdown shows the pattern weft only. The four blocks are circled in the threading. The circles do not overlap since blocks do not share threads. Pattern is produced in the same way as in 4-shaft overshot: the two shafts of the designated pattern block are down for the pattern-weft pick (represented by ∎ in the tie-up). If shafts 1-2 are down to weave pattern in Block A, and all of the shafts in the other three blocks are raised to produce background, a float appears only in Block A. *No halftones are formed since no other block contains warp threads on the same shafts as Block A.* What a miracle! — that is, until you discover that what is not a halftone on the face is a l-o-o-ong float on the back.

15a. Eight-shaft overshot draft: no halftones

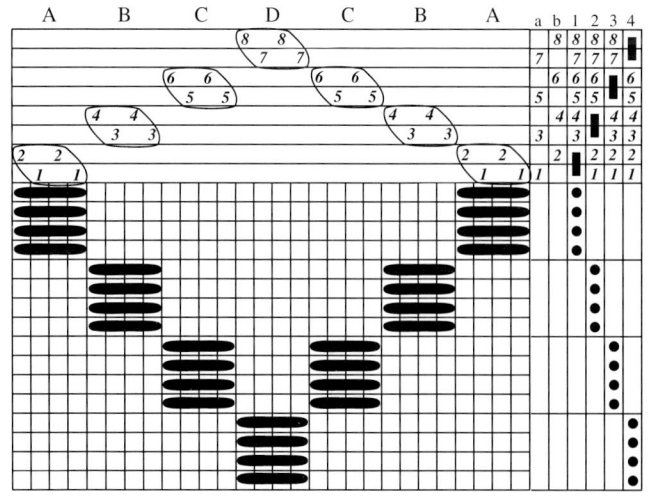

45

15b. Unbalanced draft; halftones in opposite blocks; A/C B/D; see Photo d

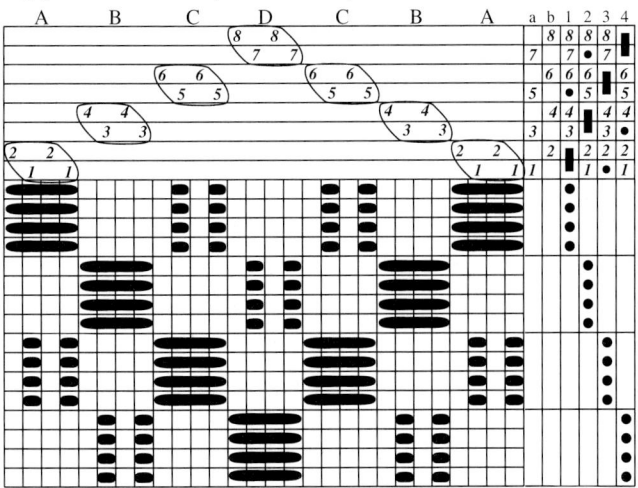

15c. Balanced draft; halftones in opposite blocks; A/C, B/D, see Photo e

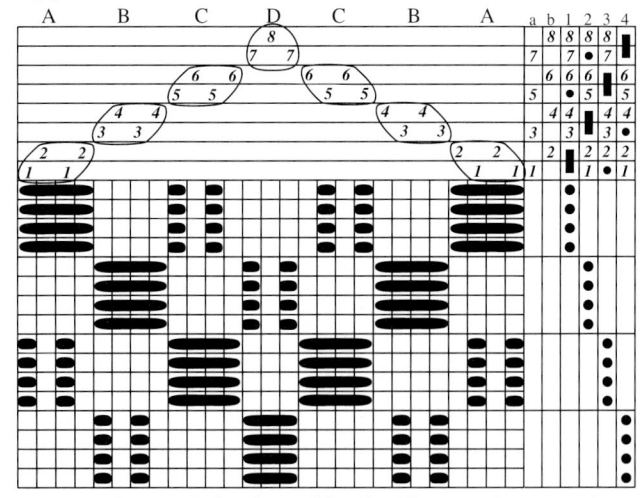

15d. Balanced draft; tabby halftones in 'opposite' blocks: A/C, B/D; see Photo f

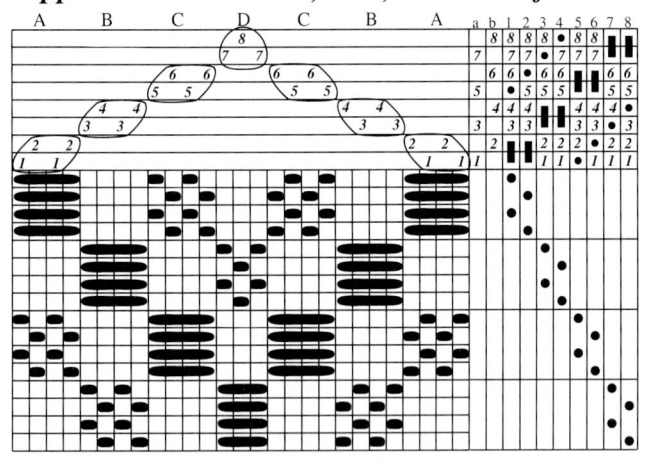

15e. Balanced draft; tabby halftones form stripes in D for A and B; in A for C and D, see Photo g

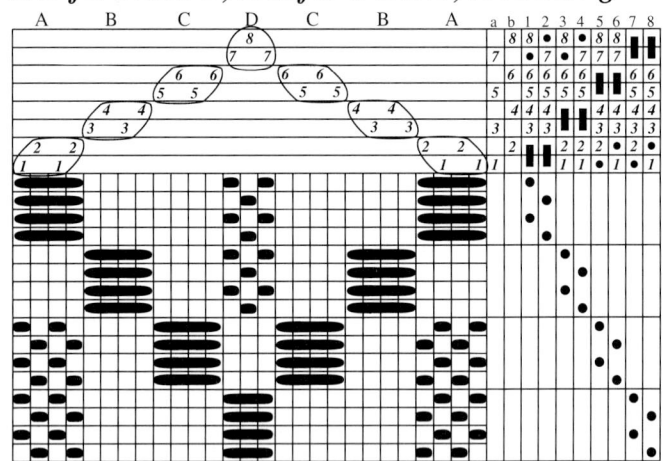

Designing with halftones

The real miracle is that halftones can be used to contribute to the total design effect in addition to performing the function of tying the pattern weft to the cloth. Remember that a halftone occurs in 4-shaft overshot because one shaft in each of the two halftone blocks is down for the pattern pick. To duplicate the 4-shaft halftone interlacement with an 8-shaft threading, we must leave one shaft down in a non-pattern block. However, we can choose *which* block.

In the first pattern pick in *Figure 15b*, shafts 1-2 are down to produce pattern in Block A, and shaft 5 is down to produce a halftone in Block C; see ● in the tie-up. If blocks are threaded in succession, Block C is never adjacent to Block A. Therefore a halftone never appears adjacent to a pattern float in A. This is also true when D is selected as the halftone block for B, when A is the halftone block for C, and when B is the halftone block for D. With the tie-up in *Figure 15b*, there is only one halftone block in each pattern row instead of two as in 4-shaft overshot. Twenty-five percent of the surface of the cloth is therefore halftone instead of fifty percent. Compare *Photo d*, p. 47, with *Photo b*, p. 42. Notice also that the pattern weft in **15b** passes under all of the warp threads in two of the four blocks. On the back of the fabric, a float shows over two blocks instead of over one as on the face. The positions of the halftones can be varied for design purposes; halftones form stripes in *Photo g*.

The threading draft in *Figure 15b* does not require balancing to ensure that float lengths are symmetrical. However, a slight lack of symmetry appears in the halftone blocks when the threading draft is not symmetrical. See if you can discover this asymmetry in the 'join' (the border that surrounds the roses and table) in the *Photo d* example. Balancing an 8-shaft draft is much easier than balancing a 4-shaft draft. Simply add or subtract a thread from all turning blocks and reverse the direction of the subsequent pairs (see **15c**). Always

d. Unbalanced draft; halftone is off-center in join; see right and left sides of draft

e. Balanced draft; halftones in join are symmetrical

f. Tabby halftones in opposite blocks; halftones contribute to the design

g. Tabby halftones form stripes; halftones form a secondary design

move from one block to the next on the adjacent shafts. To thread from Block D to Block C, for example, end Block D on shaft 7 and begin Block C on shaft 6; do not move from shaft 8 to shaft 5. Even shafts and odd shafts always alternate to form tabby.

Halftones can contribute to the overall design by more than just their location. Interesting effects can be also achieved by raising the two shafts in the halftone blocks alternately for the pattern picks. Examine the halftones in *Figure 15d*. When Block A weaves pattern, a halftone appears in Block C. In the first pattern pick, shaft 5 is down in C, but in the second pattern pick shaft 6 is down in C. The pattern weft forms tabby in the halftone block. Notice that 'tabby' halftones require twice as many pattern treadles as regular halftones.

47

h. Balanced draft; one pattern block, three halftone blocks; face

i. Balanced draft; one pattern block, three halftone blocks; back

In *Figure 15f*, *all* of the background blocks produce tabby halftones. Look closely at the tie-up in *15f*. Pattern treadles 1 and 2 are tied so that shafts 1 and 2 are down to weave pattern in Block A. Treadle 1 leaves odd shafts down in the other three blocks and treadle 2 leaves even shafts down in the other three blocks. Used in alternation, these two treadles produce tabby in all blocks but A. Treadles 3 and 4 produce tabby in all blocks but B, 5 and 6 in all blocks but C, and 7 and 8 in all blocks but D.

This variation of overshot provides an extremely durable cloth. The back side, which has no floats at all, is suitable for upholstery and has a damask-like appearance; see *Photos h* and *i*. A 5-block design can be woven on ten shafts.

15f. One block weaves pattern; three blocks weave tabby halftones, as in Photos h, i.

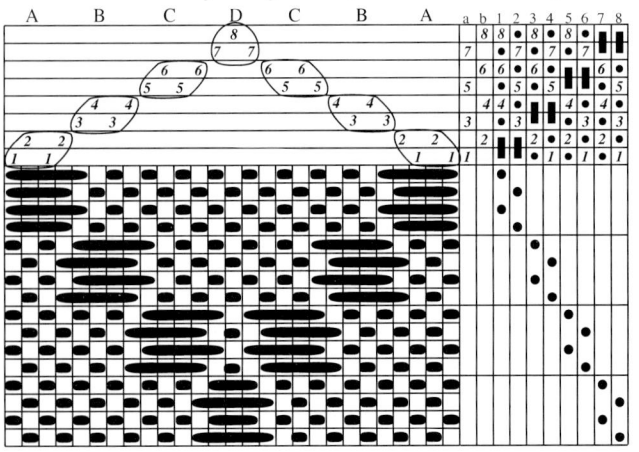

Other tie-up variations

Any 8-shaft, 4-block overshot threading can provide opportunity for designing with halftones. Once you've experimented with some of the possibilities, you are likely never to thread overshot on four shafts again. Should you wish for your 8-shaft draft to look as if it were woven on four shafts, use the tie-up in *Figure 16a*. Just as in 4-shaft overshot, halftones occur in the two blocks adjacent to the pattern block. On treadle 1, for example, shafts 1 and 2 are down to weave pattern in Block A, and shafts 3 and 8 are also down to form halftones in Blocks B and D. On treadle 2 shafts 3 and 4 are down to weave pattern in B, and 2 and 5 are also down to form halftones in A and C. The fabric in *Photo b*, p. 42, is woven on eight shafts using the tie-up in *16a*.

16a. Eight-shaft tie-up imitates 4-shaft overshot

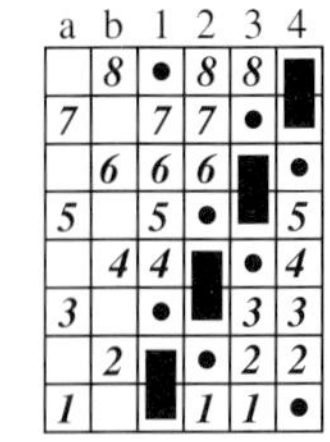

16b. Eight-shaft tie-up produces 4-block overshot on opposites

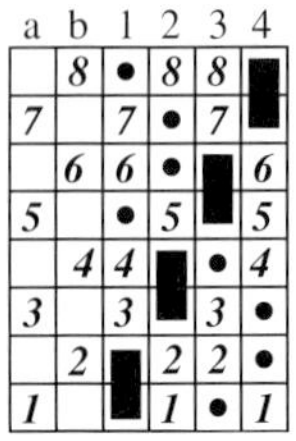

Four-shaft overshot on opposites can be imitated on an 8-shaft threading with the tie-up in *16b*. Blocks A and B produce one motif while C and D produce halftones with 2-thread incidental floats, and C and D produce a motif with halftones and incidentals in A and B.

OVERSHOT: FROM FOUR TO EIGHT

The best sources for 8-shaft overshot drafts are 4-block profile drafts and 4-shaft overshot drafts.

Thread from a 4-block profile draft.

17. Four-block profile

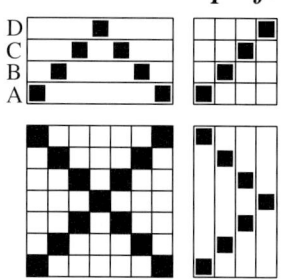

Derive an 8-shaft overshot draft from a profile draft in the same way as a 4-shaft overshot draft, with one exception: do not count the last thread of one block as the first thread of the next. Select profile drafts in which block width does not exceed practical float length. Thread all blocks with an even number of warp ends except turning blocks, which have an odd number.

To thread from a profile draft: assign a specific number of warp ends to equal one square in the profile threading, four in our example. Write the threading for each block; begin with A=1-2-1-2 in *Figure 17*. Odd shafts always alternate with even shafts. Move to an adjacent block by moving to an adjacent shaft. At the turning block, Block D, remove a thread on shaft 8 (as in *19*) or add a thread on shaft 7 so that the 6 in Block C follows the 7 in Block D. Circle the blocks. Note that the circles do not overlap, see *Figure 19*.

The total number of ends in a threading repeat can be deduced from the profile draft by counting all of the squares in the profile threading draft then multiplying by the number of threads assigned to each square. Count turning blocks. Subtract this number from the first total if you intend to subtract threads from turning blocks, and add it if you intend to add threads.

Thread from a 4-shaft overshot draft.

Circle the blocks in the 4-shaft draft as in *Figure 18*. The 8-shaft draft will have exactly the same num-

18. Four-shaft draft

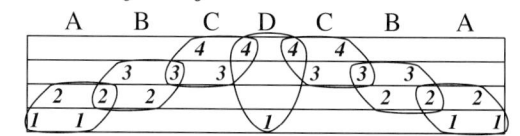

19. Eight-shaft threading for 17 and 18

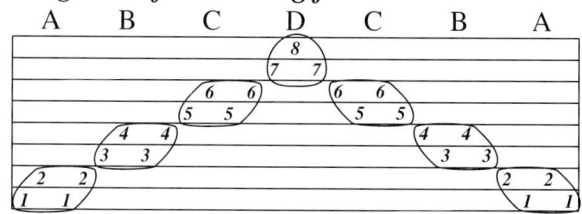

j. Balanced draft; blocks woven as drawn in

ber of ends within each of its circles. For example, replace 1-2-1-2 with 1-2-1-2; 2-3-2-3 with 3-4-3-4; 3-4-3-4 with 5-6-5-6, 4-1-4 with 7-8-7. Compare the circled numbers in *18* with those in *19*. An 8-shaft draft has more ends than its corresponding 4-shaft draft: an extra end for each circle in the draft.

OVERSHOT TREADLING ORDERS

Traditional overshot drafts are usually woven in one of two ways: 'rose fashion' or 'star fashion,' see pp. 34-35. To weave overshot star fashion, i.e., to weave the blocks as drawn in (see *Photo j*), select the pattern treadle that leaves warp threads down in the first block at one side of the warp. Weave pattern in that block until it is square. Put a pin in it to mark that it is the last block completed. Find the pattern treadle that leaves warp threads down in the block adjacent to the last block completed. Weave pattern in it until it is square. Move the pin to the new block. Proceed, moving the pin from block to block along the diagonal of squares until it reaches the opposite edge.

It is generally easiest to weave a draft rose fashion by studying the intended motifs and weaving pattern as necessary to produce them. When no drawdown or visual picture of the draft is included, determine the rose-fashion exchange of pairs from the blocks paired in the motifs (A/B and C/D in *Photos b-h*, for example). Then follow the threading draft: where one block is threaded, weave the other block.

Lesson: Drafting Overshot

Remember the excitement of your first overshot pattern pick? What a miracle! Then you tried to plan your first overshot project. What a mess! You wondered how anyone could look at an overshot threading draft and know what it represents. The key is in learning to identify the blocks. From that skill follows the ability to design original drafts, to adapt any draft to a desired size, and to extend 4-shaft overshot to more shafts.

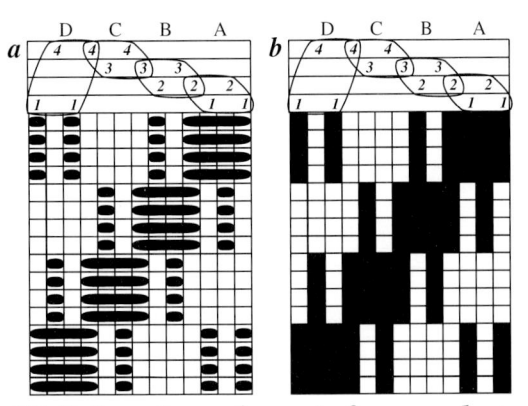

Weft drawdown formats for overshot

Because pattern in overshot is created by a weft float covering the warp threads in a block, overshot is usually drafted with a weft drawdown. The tabby picks are usually omitted in the drawdown for two reasons: a drawdown is unable to show the difference in size between the tabby and pattern picks, and because there is no need to diagram the tabby picks once it is determined that they alternate with the pattern picks to provide the plain weave cloth. In most overshot drawdowns, therefore, black squares represent the pattern weft and weaving instructions include 'use tabby' to indicate the tabby picks. It is even more representative of the cloth's appearance to draw weft threads rather than to fill in squares, compare *a* and *b*. For the following exercises use method *a*: draw the pattern weft so it looks like a weft thread.

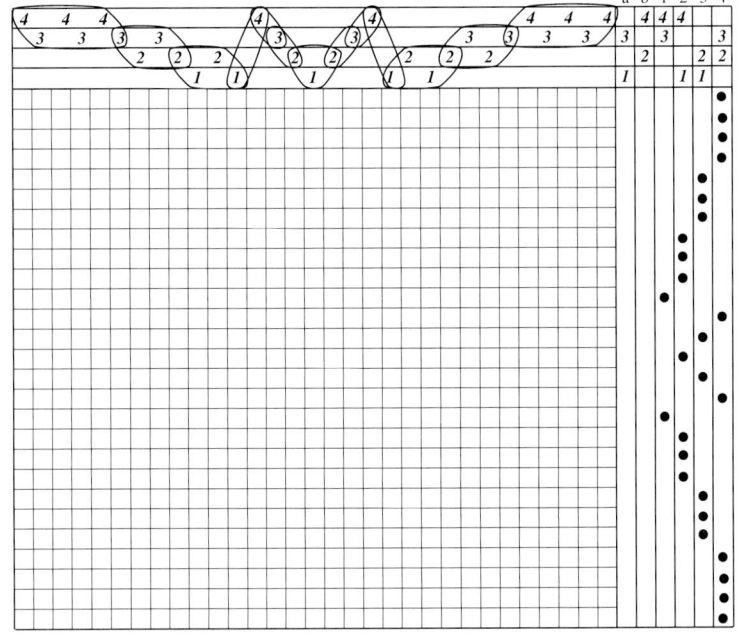

Complete the pattern-weft drawdown in **Exercise 1**. Remember that the pattern weft covers threads on shafts that are down. Compare the circled blocks in the draft with the length of the pattern floats.

Circle the blocks in **Exercise 2**. Read the draft from right to left, following the direction of the arrows. Remember that all circles overlap. Include in the circle all numbers of the same pair, no matter how many there are. (See answers, p. 122-123.)

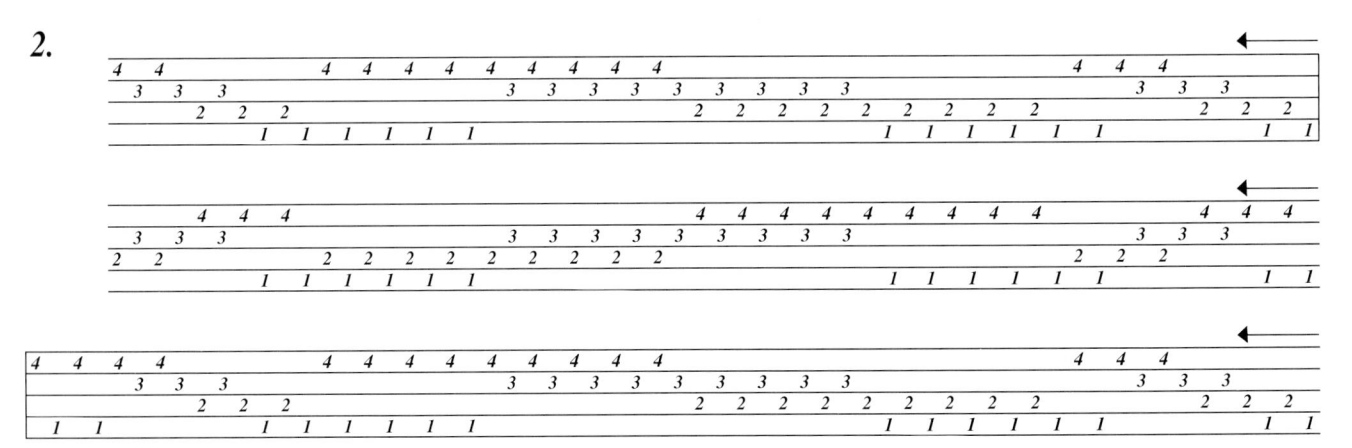

3.

```
2 2           4 4 4 4 4        4 4 4 4 4           2 2
 2   2        4   4      2     4   4      2   2     2
   2 2 2 2           2 2 2           2 2 2 2
   2 2   2   2 4   4   4 2   2 4   4   4 2   2   2 2
```

Translate this draft (Marguerite Davison's *A Handweaver's Source Book*, p. 187) into a balanced thread-by-thread draft for four shafts. Circle the blocks.

⟵

⟵

⟵

Circle the blocks in this 'Double Chariot Wheels' draft. Reduce the draft so that it contains fewer than 120 warp threads by eliminating pairs of warp threads and pairs of blocks: lightly draw a pencil line through all eliminated threads. Rewrite the draft on a separate sheet of paper.

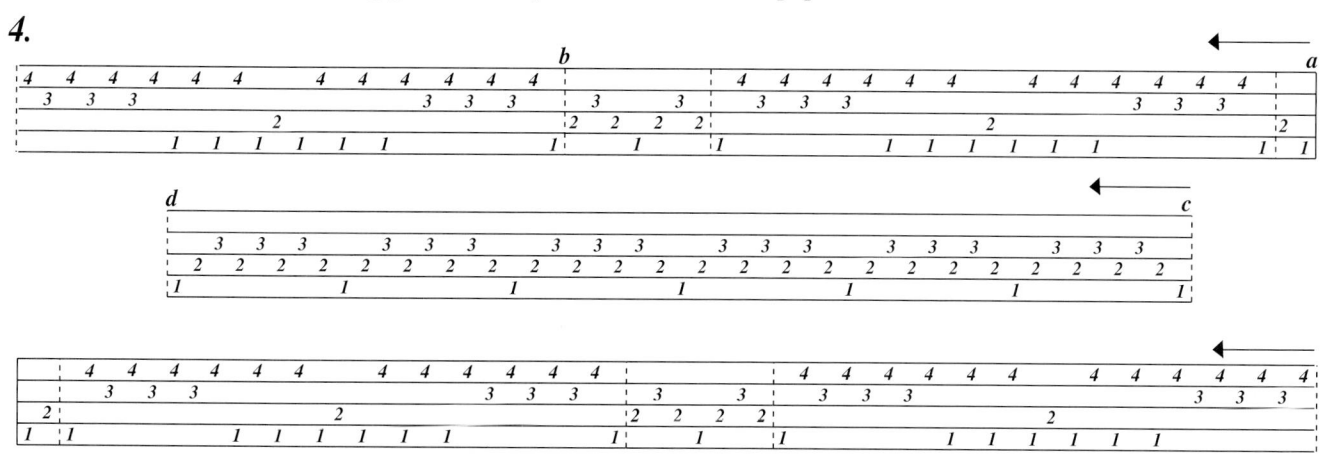

4.

⟵ *a*
b

⟵ *c*
d

⟵

To translate a 4-shaft overshot draft into an 8-shaft 'overshot-on-opposites' draft, first circle the blocks in the 4-shaft draft. To complete **Exercise 5**, transpose sections *a-b* and *c-d* in the original **Exercise 4** draft to eight shafts. Each circle in the 8-shaft draft contains the same number of ends as the corresponding circle in the 4-shaft draft, but the circles do not overlap. Check your work on p. 123.

5. *b* ⟵ *a*

d *c*

From Blocks to Units: Words to Know

background: in block weaves, background refers to the areas of the cloth that are not considered pattern. Usually warp and weft threads interlace in one way in the pattern area and in a different way in the background area. Background is not synonymous with ground (the structure on which a pattern weft or warp floats).

block vs. counterblock: refers to the two interlacements in a block weave without necessarily designating either interlacement as pattern or background. In most block weaves, the designation of one of the interlacements as pattern and the other as background is arbitrary.

combined blocks: when two or more blocks make pattern at the same time across the width of a fabric, blocks are said to be combined. The profile tie-up indicates the combined blocks.

pattern vs. design: 'pattern' is used to identify one interlacement when background names the other. 'Design' refers to the visual image created by the whole (though 'pattern' is often used as synonymous with 'design'). In weaving, 'pattern' is also used to identify a repeating motif or motifs, such as in an overall pattern. Pattern is sometimes misleadingly used to identify a draft for weaving much as instructions for sewing a garment are called a pattern.

turned twill: warp-predominant twill and weft-predominant twill form pattern and background on the same surface of the cloth. Three-end turned twill (2/1 and 1/2 twill) is sometimes called 'dimity,' and four-end turned twill (3/1 and 1/3 twill) is sometimes called 'twill diaper.' Weft-predominant or warp-predominant twills are sometimes called weft twills or warp twills. These terms are distinct from 'weft-faced' or 'warp-faced' twills, in which the warp is sett so closely that the weft doesn't show (or vice versa). Turned twill is sometimes called 'twill damask.'

unit: refers to the group of warp threads and weft threads that provide the two characteristic interlacements of the specific unit weave, one for pattern, one for background.

unit weaves: block weaves in which a specific number of warp threads and weft threads interlace in a specific way to produce either pattern or background *independently of* but *identically to* other groups. A threading formula – *the threading unit* – is substituted for one filled square of a profile threading draft; a treadling formula – the treadling unit – is substituted for one filled square of a profile treadling draft.

Chapter 5
From Blocks to Units

Your study group members are examining an intricately patterned table runner. Everyone but you seems to know right away that the design has six blocks. How do they know? What structure is it? How many shafts are required to weave it?

Sometimes weaving is like standing in a room full of windows that open on tantalizing vistas. You struggle to decide which vista to enter, only to discover that the door is locked. If a skeleton key could unlock all the doors, it would be unit weaves.

Recognizing blocks

Does the 2-block profile draft in **Figure 1** look familiar? To review: each row in the profile threading draft represents a block; each black square represents a group of warp threads. Each black square in the profile tie-up represents a group of treadles, and each black square in the profile treadling represents a group of weft picks. In the drawdown, each black square represents a group of warp threads *and* weft threads that interlace in one way, and each white square a group of warp threads *and* weft threads that interlace in a different way. Because the two interlacements are different, we see one as pattern against the other as background.

Study the drawdown in **Figure 1**. When Block A makes pattern, black squares appear in a horizontal row under all of the A threading squares. Whenever *one* of these squares is black, *all* of them are black.

1. Two-block profile draft

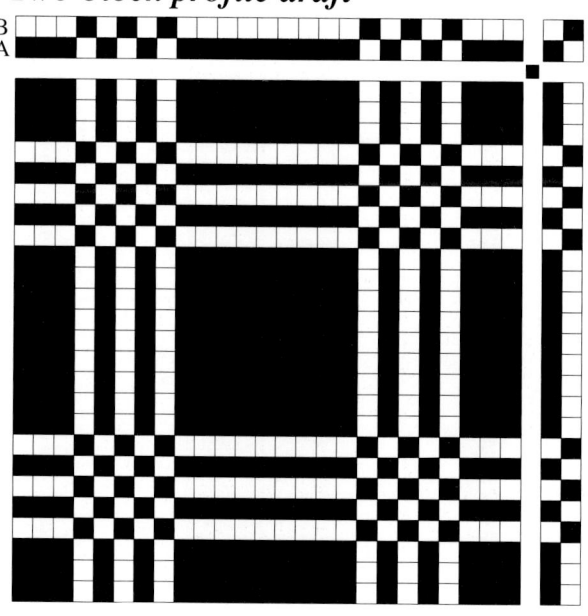

2. Profile drawdown: how many blocks?

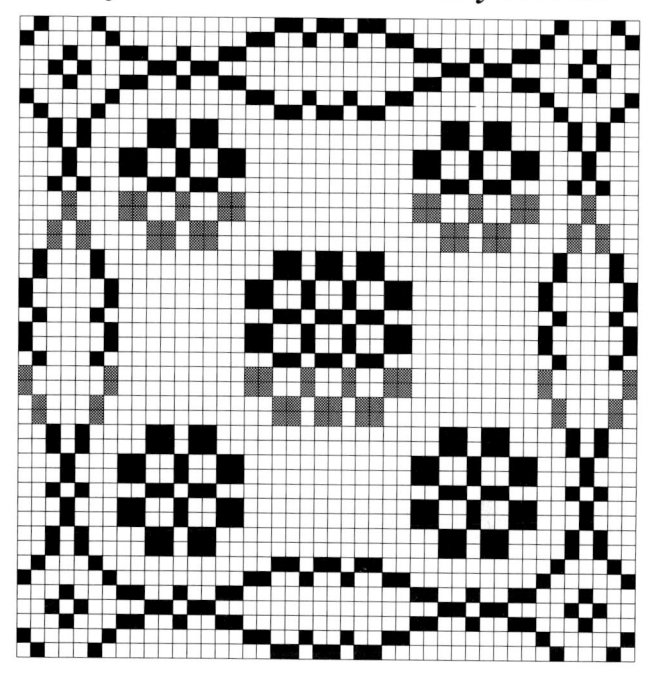

Whenever one of these squares is white, all of them are white. In the same way, when Block B makes pattern, black squares appear in a horizontal row under the B threading squares.

You can discover the blocks from the profile drawdown — without a profile threading draft. Examine the drawdown in **2**. It is easiest to find the blocks by looking at the major motifs. Start with the center motif. Notice the gray squares in the two horizontal rows that form the bottom of the motif. Note the corresponding squares in the same horizontal rows in each of the borders. Check the rest of the drawdown to see that when any one of these squares makes pattern, all of them make pattern: they are one block. Immediately above these two rows are two horizontal rows with a different set of gray squares; they are a second block. The rest of the motif repeats the same two blocks.

Now examine the roses above the center motif. The gray squares that form the bottom of the roses (and the other gray squares in the same horizontal rows) form a third block. Immediately above them is a different set of gray squares, a fourth block. The rest of the rose repeats the same two blocks. Examine the drawdown to verify that every horizontal row is exactly like one of the four we have already identified: this profile drawdown is comprised of four blocks.

53

3. Profile drawdown with combined blocks

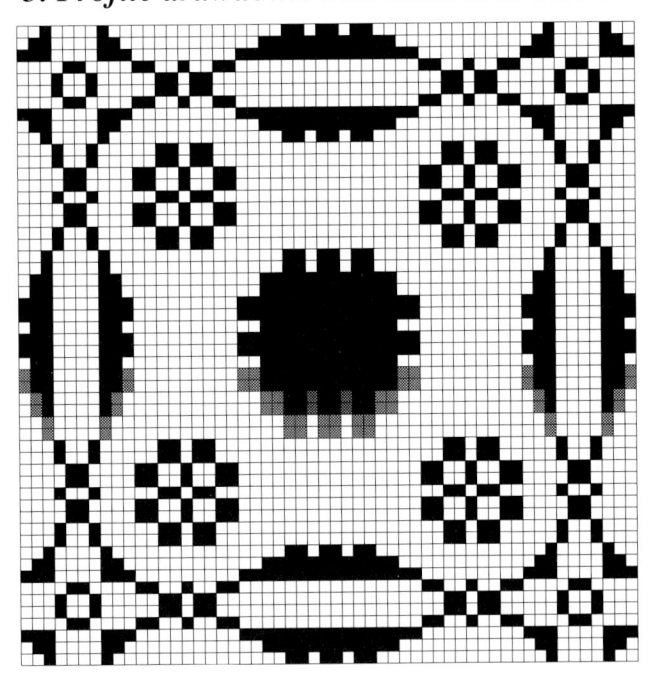

Recognizing combined blocks

It is a bit more difficult to identify blocks when they are combined in the profile drawdown, i.e., when two or more blocks make pattern together. Examine the profile drawdown in *Figure 3*. The rose is identical to the rose in *Figure 2*, a 2-block motif in which each of the blocks makes pattern independently. The center motif in *Figure 3*, however, unlike the center motif in *Figure 2*, shows more than one block making pattern at the same time.

The two horizontal rows of gray squares at the bottom of the center motif show pattern in one block. Verify that throughout the drawdown, whenever one of these squares makes pattern, all of them do. Now look at the next two horizontal rows above these rows. The same squares still make pattern as in the first two rows, but some new squares (gray in the drawdown) *also* make pattern: these new squares are a different block. In the next two horizontal rows above these two, *more* new squares (shaded gray in the drawdown) are added: these form a third block. Examine the rest of the snowball. Throughout the motif, pattern appears in either all three blocks combined, the first two blocks combined, or the first block alone.

Together, the snowball and rose motifs are made up of five blocks. To make sure that all of the blocks in the drawdown have been discovered, check to see that each horizontal row is exactly like one of the five we have already identified. If a black square were to appear in a different place, it would be in a sixth block.

MEET UNIT WEAVES

'Profile draft' and 'block' are terms that refer to pattern, not to structure. It is a weave structure, however, that enables us to see blocks of pattern in a fabric, just as black ink enables us to see blocks of pattern on white paper.

Unit weaves are the tool by which any profile draft can be translated into a weave structure. Limitations such as float length in non-unit weaves like overshot do not apply to unit weaves. Each black square in the profile drawdown represents a unit of warp and weft threads that interlace in a specific way. Each white square represents a unit of the same number of warp and weft threads that interlace in a way different enough that the two can be distinguished from each other. Every unit can interlace in either of the two ways; *all* of the interlacement required by the structure takes place *within* each unit. See 'Keys to Block Weaves, p. 26-27) for a list of unit weaves.

Now examine the units of 'turned twill' in *Figures 4b* and *4d*. Each unit consists of four warp threads and four weft threads. In some places, the units weave 3/1 (warp-predominant) twill and in other places they weave 1/3 (weft-predominant) twill. Compare the diagrams of the interlacements with the corresponding profile drawdowns in *4a* and *4c*. In *Figure 4*, a black square in the drawdown represents a unit of 3/1 twill, a white square represents a unit of 1/3 twill. This choice is arbitrary: either profile drawdown (*4a* or *4c*) can be used to represent either interlacement (*4b* or *4d*).

4. Black squares in the profile drawdowns represent 3/1 twill; white squares 1/3 twill.

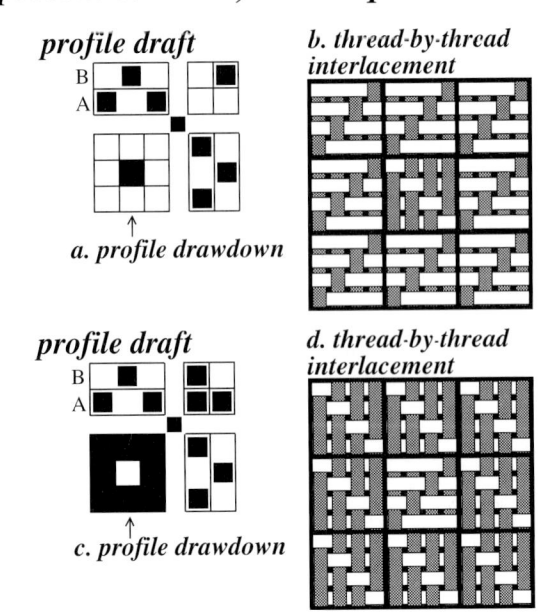

profile draft

a. profile drawdown

b. thread-by-thread interlacement

profile draft

c. profile drawdown

d. thread-by-thread interlacement

USING UNIT WEAVES

A unit weave is any weave structure that can be used — without limitations — to produce the design in a profile drawdown. The important requirement is that the unit must be capable of forming two different interlacements: one for pattern and the other for background. Units that always make pattern or background together are in the same block. Units in different blocks must be threaded on at least *some* different shafts in order to be able to produce the two interlacements independently as required by the profile draft.

Weavers often use the term 'unit' to refer to the threading unit alone, but the unit really includes all of the warp ends and weft picks that form the interlacement as, for example, each group of four warp threads and four weft threads in **4b** and **4d**. The complete unit is composed of both a threading unit and a treadling unit.

The first step to mastering unit weaves is to understand the connection between the profile draft and the actual interlacement. Next is to determine how to draft and weave units in a selected structure so that they produce the design in a selected profile draft. Before examining the unit weaves one by one, we'll follow the process of translating a profile draft into a thread-by-thread draft using turned twill as an example. Once you understand the process, you can apply it to any unit weave. To apply the process to a unit weave that is not described in this book, find a source that shows a draft of that unit weave with at least two blocks.

Draft two units.

To translate a specific profile draft into a specific unit weave, you must first understand how the threads in the unit interlace to make pattern and how they interlace to make background.

✍ **Prepare a thread-by-thread draft of the two interlacements.** Write one draft showing a unit of Block A forming one of the interlacements and another draft showing another unit of Block A forming the other interlacement. In our example, four threads weave 3/1 twill in **5a**, and four threads weave 1/3 twill in **5b**.

5. 3/1 twill (a) and 1/3 twill (b)

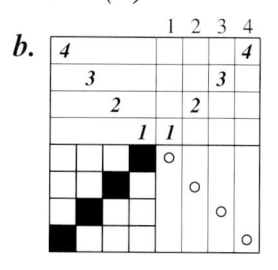

Draft two blocks.

If all the units across a warp are threaded in the same block, only one interlacement can be produced at a time, either 3/1 twill *or* 1/3 twill in our example. In order for one area to produce one interlacement at the same time as another area produces the other, a new block is required. To produce 3/1 twill *and* 1/3 twill in two different areas at the same time, we need four more shafts for Block B. In some unit weaves only one or two more shafts are required for each new block.

✍ **Prepare a thread-by-thread draft with one unit of Block A and one unit of Block B.** Copy the drawdown for one of the interlacements under the threading for Block A and the drawdown for the other interlacement under the threading for Block B (A = 3/1 twill in our example; B = 1/3 twill). Extend the drawdown to show the opposite interlacement in each block. In our example Block A weaves 1/3 twill in the second section of the drawdown, and Block B weaves 3/1 twill. To derive the tie-up and treadling order, examine each weft pick to see which shafts are raised. Place a weft symbol in the treadling column and above the weft symbol write the raised shafts in the corresponding tie-up column. *Figure 6* shows the completed 2-block draft.

6. Two blocks of turned twill

A = 3/1 twill
B = 1/3 twill

A = 1/3 twill
B = 3/1 twill

These steps provide the necessary information for translating a profile draft into a thread-by-thread draft in turned twill. To weave a 3-block design, for example, four more shafts are required. The new set of four shafts does exactly what the first two sets do in order to produce pattern or background, i.e., weave 3/1 twill or 1/3 twill. We'll use this information to derive the threading, treadling, and tie-up keys to substitute for the appropriate squares in the threading, treadling, and tie-up sections of a selected profile draft.

Thread from a profile threading draft.

✍ **Select an appropriate profile draft**, such as the 3-block profile draft in *Figure 7*. Look again at 'Keys for Block Weaves,' pp. 26-27. Note that while three blocks of turned twill require 12 shafts, three blocks of summer and winter require only five.

✍ **Substitute threading units for squares in the profile threading draft**. For turned twill, each square in the threading draft represents four ends: Block A = 1-2-3-4; Block B = 5-6-7-8; Block C = 9-10-11-12. Begin threading with the profile threading square closest to the tie-up. Remember that the bottom row of the threading profile draft is always Block A. In *Figure 7*, the first profile threading square is in the C row. Thread 9-10-11-12. The next square is also in the C row. Repeat 9-10-11-12 for that square and the next two squares. The fifth square is in the A row. Thread 1-2-3-4. The next square is in the B row, thread 5-6-7-8. Continue in this way across the profile threading draft. There are 51 squares in the threading row for 204 warp ends. Translating a profile threading draft into a real threading draft is the easiest part of the translation process. The only information required is the threading key for the specific unit weave. It is not necessary to write out the thread-by-thread draft; instead, thread directly from the profile draft alone.

Turn again to pp. 26-27. For summer and winter using the profile draft in *Figure 7*, thread 1-5-2-5 four times, then 1-3-2-3, 1-4-2-4, 1-5-2-5, etc. For Bronson lace, thread 1-5-1-5-1-2 four times, then 1-3-1-3-1-2, 1-4-1-4-1-2, 1-5-1-5-1-2, etc.

7. Three-block profile draft

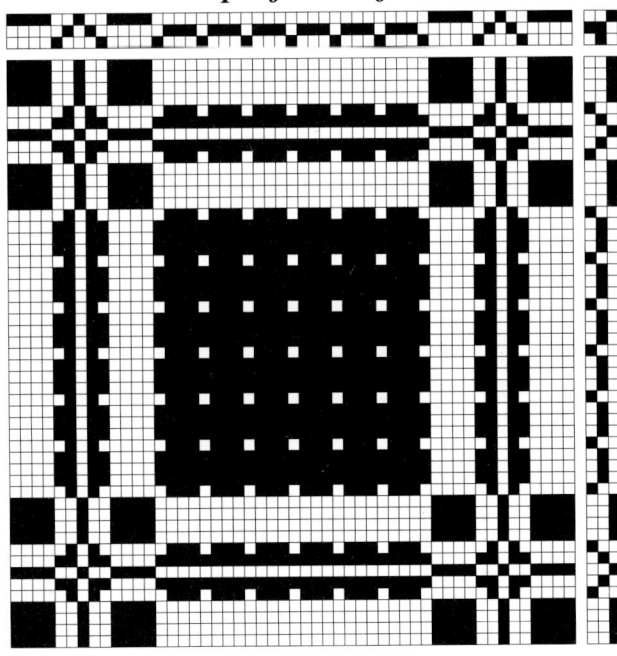

Derive the tie-up.

Tie-ups are not a major concern for the owner of a 4-shaft loom. A 'standard' tie-up, 1-2, 2-3, 3-4, 1-4, 1-3, 2-4 is satisfactory for most weaves, and a 'direct' tie-up (one shaft to each treadle) can be used for all of them. Unfortunately there is no standard tie-up for six or more shafts, nor do we have enough feet to lift the required shaft combinations using a direct tie-up. There isn't even a standard tie-up for each unit weave, as for summer and winter on eight shafts, for example. The tie-up for a unit weave depends on *two* factors: the specific unit weave and the specific profile draft. The profile tie-up tells which blocks must make pattern to produce the profile drawdown. The real tie-up for the treadles must provide the necessary sheds to weave pattern in those blocks and background in the others.

Examine the profile tie-up in *Figure 7*. Remember that a tie-up is read vertically. Block B weaves pattern alone in the first column, Blocks A and B weave pattern together in the second column, and Block C weaves pattern alone in the third column. We must tie up the actual treadles so that whatever weave structure we have selected can produce *a)* pattern in B, background in A and C; *b)* pattern in A and B, background in C; and *c)* pattern in C, background in A and B.

If we designate 3/1 twill as pattern and 1/3 twill as background, then for the first column in the profile tie-up, we must tie up four treadles so that shafts 1-4 (Block A) weave 1/3 twill; shafts 5-8 (Block B) weave 3/1 twill; shafts 9-12 (Block C) weave 1/3 twill. If we select a different unit weave, summer and winter, for example, the treadles must be tied to lift the combinations of shafts required by *that* weave structure. The process for determining the tie-up is the same for any weave structure, though the actual tie-up is different.

✍ **Derive the tie-up templates for each of the two interlacements**. The tie-up for two blocks of turned twill (from *Figure 6*) is rewritten in *Figure 8a*. With the first four treadles, 3/1 twill is produced in Block A and 1/3 twill is produced in Block B. With the second four treadles, 1/3 twill is produced in Block A and 3/1 twill in Block B. No matter what shaft numbers are given in the four-by-four square tie-up section, they appear in the same positions to produce 3/1 twill and in the same positions to produce 1/3 twill. Compare, for example, the positions of the numbers in the tie-up when A weaves 3/1 twill with their positions in B when B weaves 3/1 twill. In *Figure 8b* symbols replace the shaft numbers ('o' indicates shafts raised) to become a 4-shaft, 4-treadle template for producing 3/1 or 1/3 twill in *any* set of four shafts.

56

8. The tie-up templates

a. tie-up for two blocks of turned twill

1/3 twill / 3/1 twill / 3/1 twill / 1/3 twill

b. tie-up templates for turned twill

3/1 twill / 1/3 twill

Derive the tie-up by substituting one template for each black square in the profile tie-up and the other template for each white square. If 3/1 twill is pattern, the template for 3/1 twill is substituted for every black square in the profile tie-up and the template for 1/3 twill is substituted for every white square. Study *Figure 9*. For the first column in the profile tie-up, substitute a template for 3/1 twill in the tie-up for shafts 5-8 and templates for 1/3 twill in the tie-up for shafts 1-4 and 9-12. The first column in the profile tie-up becomes treadles 1-4. Follow the same steps for the second and third columns of the profile tie-up, treadles 5-12. Notice how the sections of 3/1 twill in the real tie-up correspond to the positions of the black squares in the profile tie-up. If you know what to look for, you can determine which blocks weave pattern in a treadle-by-treadle tie-up by identifying the templates. The templates for 3/1 twill are shaded gray in *Figure 9*. The tie-up for each unit weave can be derived in much the same way.

9. Substitute tie-up templates for squares in the profile tie-up.

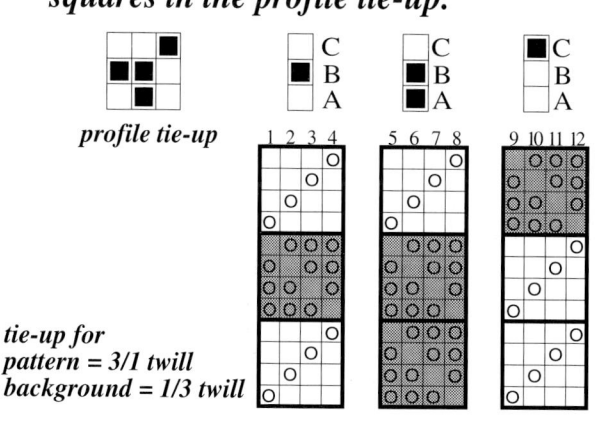

profile tie-up

tie-up for pattern = 3/1 twill background = 1/3 twill

Replace tie-up symbols with shaft numbers. Since o's in the tie-up indicate raised shafts, it is not really necessary to change them to numbers. To tie up a loom with 12 shafts, however, numbers are easier to read.

10. The tie-up

Weave following the profile treadling draft.

Substitute treadling units for squares on the profile treadling draft. Three treadling units (see *11a*) are used in the order given in the **Figure 7** profile treadling draft to produce the design (as in *11b*). For a square in the first (left) column of the treadling draft, weave four picks with treadles 1-4. For a square in the second column, weave four picks with treadles 5-8. For a square in the third column, weave four picks with treadles 9-12. For example, the first four squares in the treadling profile (from top to bottom) appear in the third column. Weave four picks with treadles 9-12 four times. The next square appears in the first column. Weave four picks with treadles 1-4; next weave four picks with treadles 5-8, etc. Use only the profile draft at the loom.

11a. Treadling units to substitute for profile treadling squares

profile tie-up from Figure 7

11b. Treadling for first nine squares of profile treadling draft

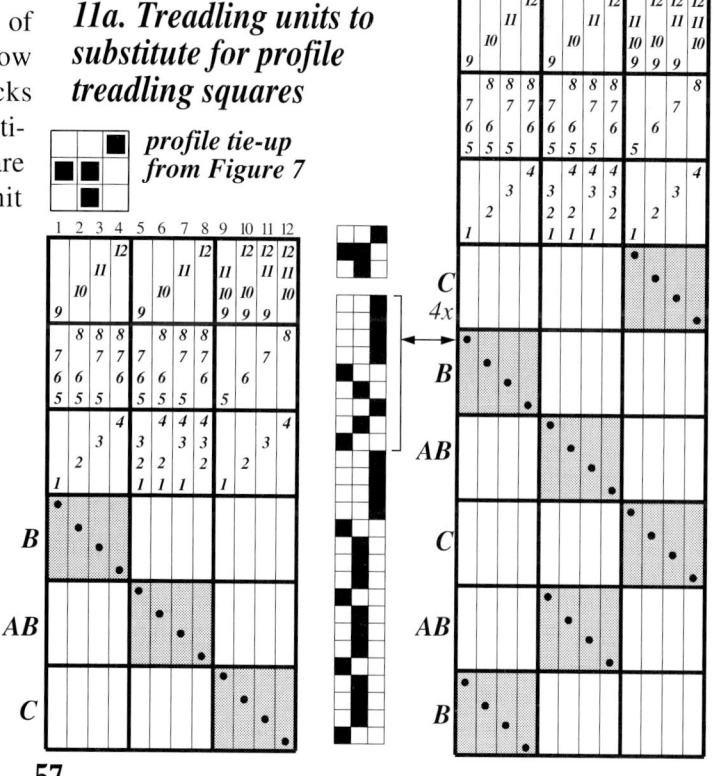

57

Part III
Unit Weaves

Introduction

In Chapter 5, we followed the process for translating profile drafts into thread-by-thread drafts using turned twill as an example. In Part III, we'll apply the same steps to many different unit weaves. As you've discovered, it's very easy to translate a profile threading draft into a real threading draft. Just look up the threading key in 'Keys to Block Weaves,' pp. 26-27, and substitute. To translate the profile tie-up into a real tie-up for the treadles, and the profile treadling draft into a pick-by-pick treadling order, you must know how the weave structure works. If you know what the threads do, then you know which shafts must be up and which must be down for the required picks (the tie-up) as well as the order in which each of the sheds must be made (the treadling order).

Before you start reading Chapter 6, leaf through the pages in Part III. Notice how the same design, the 4-block profile draft at the right (#58, from *Jacob Angstadt Designs*, see 'For Further Study,' p. 126) can be woven in many *different* weave structures: pattern and structure are different components of a fabric. Each weave structure has specific and distinct advantages. In some, the contrast between pattern and background is very strong, emphasizing the design and making possible maximum color contrast. In others, the contrast is weaker; parts of the background color appear in the pattern area and parts of the pattern color appear in the background. These structures are suitable for color blending and softer contrasts.

Unfortunately, the choice of weave structure is often limited by the number of shafts available. Examine once again 'Keys to Block Weaves.' See if you can extend the threading units in the different structures to more blocks. For example, if Block F in summer and winter is 1-8-2-8, what is Block G? By extending the threadings in this way you can determine how many shafts produce how many blocks in any unit weave.

If you study the text and complete the exercises, you'll be able to use any of the unit weaves in Part III to produce any profile design, provided you have a loom with enough shafts. Some of the weaves (marked with *) in 'Keys to Block Weaves' have special design limitations, which are explained in Part III.

4-block profile draft from Jacob Angstadt

Part III illustrates the steps for drafting and weaving this 4-block profile design in most of the unit weaves available to handweavers. Study the steps in order to understand how the tie-up templates and the treadling keys are derived for each weave. You'll then be able to use the templates for a profile design of your choice. If you want to use a unit weave that is not shown here, locate a 2-block draft of the weave in a weaving text or magazine, and follow the six steps to derive the required templates.

To understand a unit weave:
✍ Step 1. Draft two units.

✍ Step 2. Draft two blocks.

✍ Step 3. Derive tie-up templates and treadling keys.

To use the unit weave with a profile draft:
✍ Step 4. Substitute threading units for squares on the profile threading draft.

✍ Step 5. Substitute tie-up templates for squares in the profile tie-up.

✍ Step 6. Substitute treadling units for squares on the profile treadling draft.

Chapter 6
Understanding Lace Weaves

Lace Weaves: Words to Know

Bronson lace: a unit weave with (usually) six ends and six picks in a unit. Each unit can produce plain weave or 'lace.' To produce lace, two of the six weft picks float over (or under) five warp ends and are caught by the sixth warp end, and two of the six warp ends float over (or under) five weft picks and are caught by the sixth weft pick.

gauze: a lacy weave in which warp threads cross to the left or right of each other for one weft pick and then return to their original positions for a tabby pick. Crossings can be one over one, two over two, three over three (or more) or a combination of these.

huck and huck lace: a unit weave with at least six ends and picks in a unit. The threading and treadling units are divided into half-units, each with an odd number of ends and picks (3/3, 5/5, 7/7). Three interlacements are possible: *a)* plain weave, *b) huck texture*: warp or weft floats alternating with plain weave, *c) huck lace*: warp floats alternating with weft floats.

lace weaves: simple weaves, i.e., one warp and one weft, in which floats are caused by an interruption of plain weave interlacement. Lace weaves are distinguished from spot weaves by the holes or spaces that are designed to appear in the cloth.

leno: a lacy weave with areas of gauze (warp crossings) and areas of plain weave.

'pattern' shafts: the shafts in a Bronson or huck lace threading unit that control pattern by being raised to produce warp floats or lowered to produce weft floats. For example, in Bronson lace, Block A is threaded 1-3-1-3-1-2. Shaft 3 is the pattern shaft. Shafts 1 and 2 do not affect pattern and are raised alternately throughout.

spot weaves: simple weaves, i.e., one warp and one weft in which pattern is formed by 'spots' or floats on (usually) a plain weave background. A spot occurs when a warp or weft thread skips its plain weave interlacement; on one surface of the cloth a weft float occurs; on the other surface a warp float occurs. Block size is limited by the practical length of a float.

Weave structures that produce small, regularly spaced holes are called 'lace' weaves. Holes can also be formed by leaving spaces between pairs or groups of warp threads in the reed or between pairs or groups of weft picks during weaving. In lace weave structures, however, the specific interlacement causes warp threads or weft threads to slide together, leaving holes on either side of each group. Most of these weaves belong to the structural category 'spot' weaves, in which selected warp or weft threads weave plain weave in some areas, but in other areas skip their plain weave interlacement to form floats. Lace weaves are distinguished from other spot weaves by the holes formed by the grouping of threads.

Bronson lace and huck lace are great favorites of handweavers. In Bronson lace, a single warp thread separates each weft-float group from the next, or a single weft thread separates each warp-float group from the next. In huck lace, a weft-float group separates each warp-float group from the next and vice versa.

Bronson lace is an especially versatile pattern weave requiring only one shaft for each pattern block beyond shafts 1 and 2. The weaver with an 8-shaft loom, therefore, has six blocks available for pattern. Huck lace also provides six blocks of pattern *if* the blocks are threaded in straight or point order. When used with a profile draft in which blocks are *not* threaded in succession, *two* shafts beyond 1 and 2 are required for each block.

Gauze and leno are also techniques that produce holes in a fabric. One warp thread (or threads) of a pair crosses over an adjacent warp thread (or threads) for a pick, and then returns to its original position for the next pick. Spaces form between the pairs (or groups) of crossed warp ends. Gauze is entirely formed of alternate picks of crossed and uncrossed warp threads. In leno, areas of plain weave are mixed with warp crossings. Special heddles or pick-up techniques are required to produce the crossings.

Chapter 6 shows how to derive a thread-by-thread draft in weft-float Bronson lace and huck lace for a profile design. The same principles apply to warp-float Bronson lace. Non-unit weaves such as Swedish lace cannot be used for block designs without limitations.

DESIGNING BRONSON LACE

Remember that the important function of each unit in a unit weave is to provide two different interlacements. Either interlacement can be designated pattern, the other background.

Step 1 shows the two interlacements of Bronson lace: one unit of six warp threads and six weft threads produces plain weave in ***1a***, and the same unit produces floats, or 'lace,' in ***1b***.

Notice that five warp threads and five weft threads are grouped together in the photographed fabric at *b*. The sixth warp thread and the sixth weft thread are separated from the groups. When several units weave lace together, these separated threads form a '+,' the 'window pane' effect that characterizes Bronson lace.

Step 2 extends the threading to two blocks. In the first six picks Block A weaves lace and Block B weaves plain weave. In the second six picks Block B weaves lace and Block A weaves plain weave. The tie-up and treadling order show which shafts are raised for each pick. Each group of six picks comprises one treadling unit. Each treadling unit is equal to one square on the treadling profile draft just as each threading unit is equal to one square on the profile threading draft.

Study the tie-up and treadling order in ***Step 2***. Shafts 1 and 2 are lifted alternately throughout. Treadle 1 raises shaft 1 to form one of the tabby sheds. Treadle 2 raises shaft 2 and all of the other shafts for the alternate tabby shed. Now examine the part of the tie-up that determines where lace or plain weave appears, the *pattern section* of the tie-up, framed in ***Step 2***. Treadles 3 and 4 are often called the pattern treadles since they determine which blocks make pattern. Shafts 3 and 4 are often called the 'pattern' shafts. To weave plain weave in a block, the pattern shaft is raised with shaft 2 on the second and fourth picks, the 'pattern' picks. To weave lace in a block, the pattern shaft must be down on the second and fourth picks.

Tie-up templates showing the pattern shafts that are raised for plain weave or lowered for lace need only be derived for the pattern section of the tie-up. Shafts 1 and 2 and treadles 1 and 2 operate identically whether the unit weaves lace or plain weave. Study the templates in

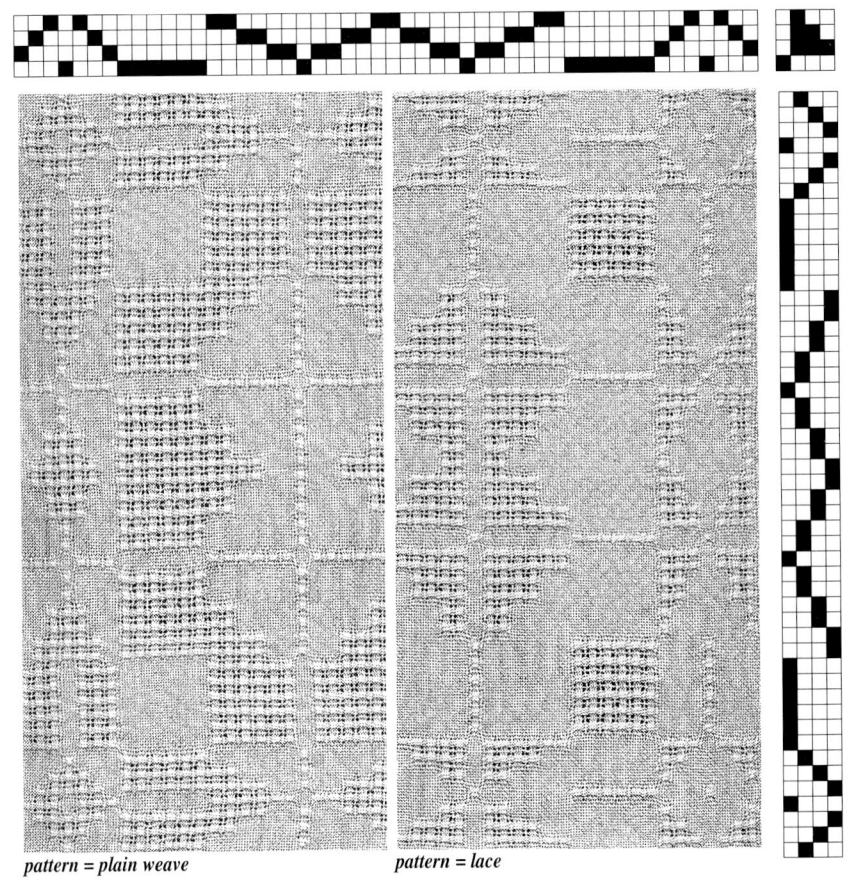

pattern = plain weave   *pattern = lace*

Step 3. A blank square indicates a lowered pattern shaft (for lace) in the tie-up. A square with 'o' indicates a raised pattern shaft (for plain weave) in the tie-up.

With this information we can translate the 4-block Angstadt profile draft into a thread-by-thread draft for Bronson lace. First substitute threading units for the corresponding squares on the profile threading draft as in ***Step 4***. Remember that there is no reason to write out the threading. Simply take the profile draft to the loom and make the substitutions there.

To derive the Bronson lace tie-up, first choose whether pattern is to be lace and background plain weave or vice versa. If pattern is lace (as in the right photo above), place blank squares in the pattern section of the real tie-up for every black square in the profile tie-up and squares with 'o' in the pattern section of the real tie-up for every blank square in the profile tie-up. If pattern is plain weave (as in the left photo above), place squares with 'o' in the pattern section of the real tie-up for every black square in the profile tie-up and blank squares for every blank square; see ***Step 5***.

Substitute the 6-pick treadling sequence for each corresponding square on the profile treadling draft as in ***Step 6***. There is no reason to write out the treadling sequence. Take the profile draft to the loom and make the substitutions there.

Step 1. Draft two units.

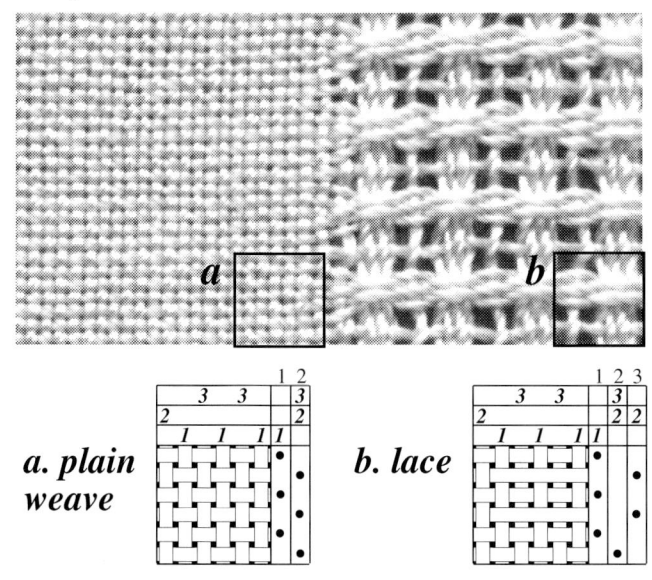

a. plain weave

b. lace

Step 2. Draft two blocks.

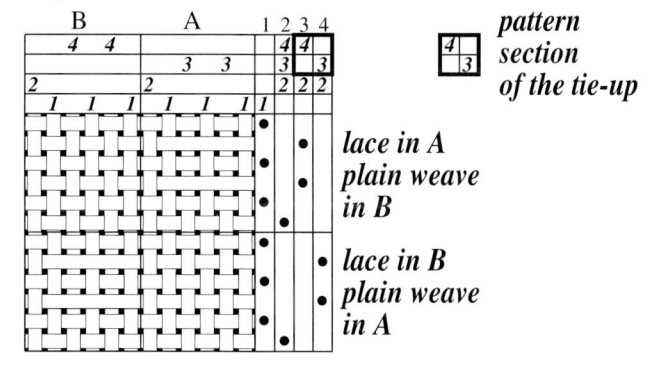

lace in A
plain weave in B

lace in B
plain weave in A

pattern section of the tie-up

Step 3. Derive the tie-up templates.

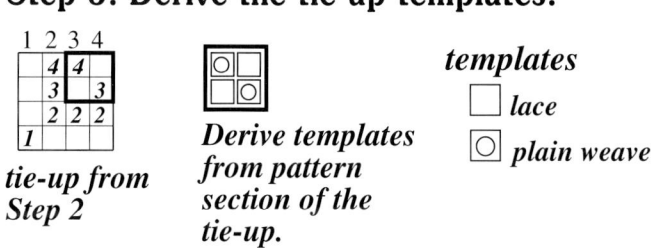

tie-up from Step 2

Derive templates from pattern section of the tie-up.

templates
☐ lace
◉ plain weave

Step 4. Substitute threading units for profile threading squares.

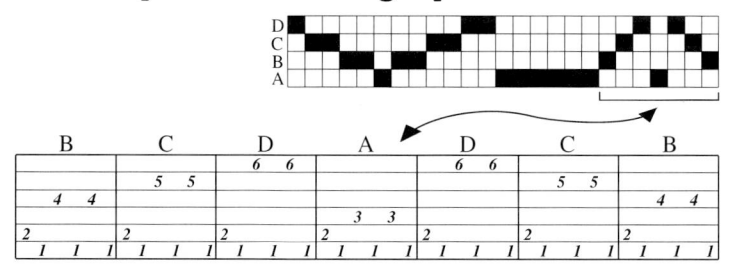

Step 5. Derive the tie-up.

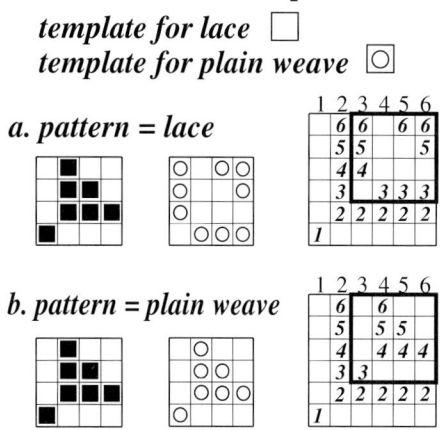

template for lace ☐
template for plain weave ◉

a. pattern = lace

b. pattern = plain weave

Substitute templates for lace or plain weave in the profile tie-up; place in the pattern section of the real tie-up.

Step 6. Substitute treadling units for profile treadling squares.

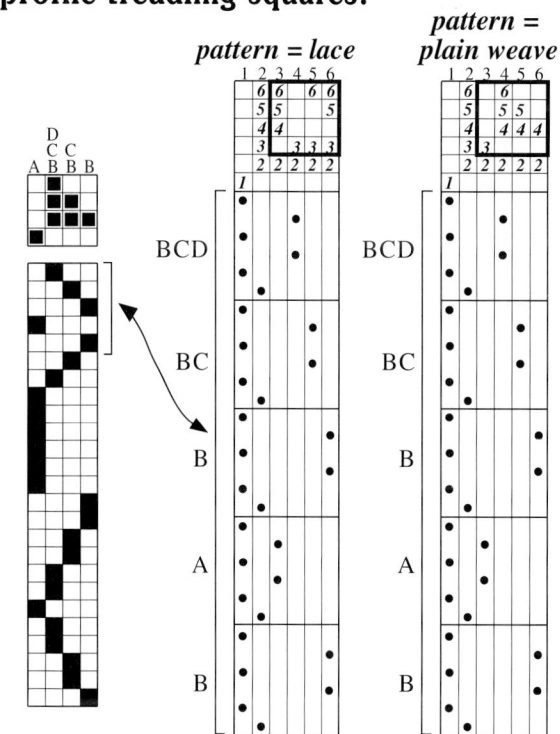

pattern = lace

pattern = plain weave

Bronson Lace Keys

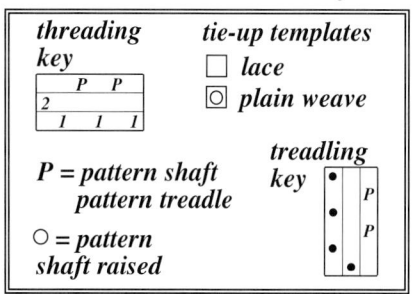

threading key

tie-up templates
☐ lace
◉ plain weave

P = pattern shaft
pattern treadle

○ = pattern shaft raised

treadling key

61

DESIGNING HUCK AND HUCK LACE

Huck is unusual among unit weaves in that the huck unit can produce four different interlacements. Each of the drafts in *Figures 1a-d* shows one full threading unit and one full treadling unit of huck. It is important to think of huck in terms of *half*-units. Each half-unit can produce plain weave or floats. (It's a bit of a puzzle why we don't call them *quarter*-units since there are actually four of them in a complete unit. It may be because we often talk about threading *or* treadling units rather than both together.) Units can produce plain weave/plain weave (*1a*), warp float/weft float (*1b*), warp float/plain weave (*1c*), or weft float/plain weave (*1d*). We usually think of these as *three* effective interlacements since warp floats and plain weave appear on the reverse of weft floats and plain weave.

Full units of huck have an even number of warp threads and an even number of weft threads; half-units have an odd number: three in 3-thread huck (*1e*), five in 5-thread huck (*1a-d*), and seven in 7-thread huck (*1f*). A unit can be as large as materials and sett permit. When warp and weft floats alternate, the structure is called huck lace. When warp floats or weft floats alternate with plain weave the structure is often called huck texture, or simply, huck.

Understand the structure

The first, third, and fifth *warp ends* in each half-unit of 5-thread huck, on shafts 1 and 2, always weave in plain weave order. The first, third, and fifth *weft picks* in each half-unit of 5-thread huck always weave in plain weave order. Warp floats occur when the second and fourth warp ends in each half-unit — the 'pattern' ends — are raised for all of the picks in the half-unit. Weft floats occur when these pattern ends are lowered for all of the picks in the half-unit. The pattern ends are threaded on shafts 3 in Block A and 4 in Block B in *Figure 1*.

The sequence for plain weave in the first treadling half-unit in *1a* is: even tabby (shafts 2-4), odd tabby (shafts 1-3), even tabby, odd tabby, even tabby. In the second half-unit, the sequence for plain weave is: odd tabby, even tabby, odd tabby, even tabby, odd tabby.

In the first treadling half-unit in *1b*, shaft 4 is raised for all five picks to produce warp floats, and shaft 3 is down for all five picks to produce weft floats. In the second treadling half-unit in *1b*, shaft 3 is raised for all five picks to produce warp floats, and shaft 4 is down for all five picks to produce weft floats. The pattern sections are outlined in the *Figure 1* tie-ups.

Only warp threads on even pattern shafts can produce warp floats in a treadling half-unit that begins

1. Huck interlacements

a. plain weave

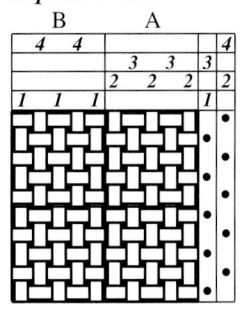

b. warp floats/weft floats

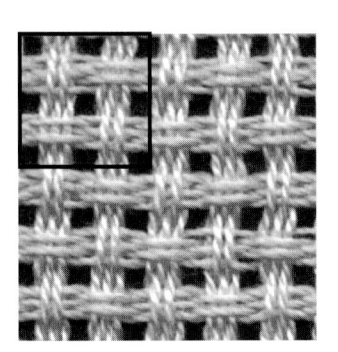

c. warp floats/plain weave

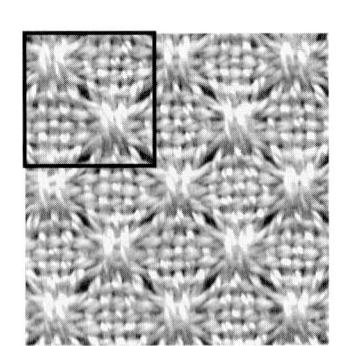

d. weft floats/plain weave

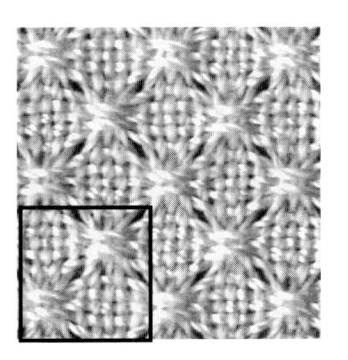

e. Three-thread huck

f. Seven-thread huck

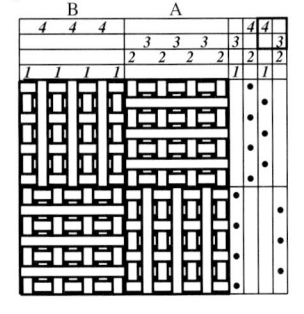

with the even tabby. Only warp threads on odd pattern shafts can produce warp floats in a treadling half-unit that begins with an odd tabby. Warp floats always alternate with plain weave or weft floats; adjacent half-units cannot produce the same type of float. In the first treadling half-unit in *Figures 1a-d*, shaft 4 can produce warp floats or plain weave; shaft 3 can produce weft floats or plain weave. In the second half-unit, shaft 3 can produce warp floats or plain weave and shaft 4 can produce weft floats or plain weave.

To produce warp floats in a half-unit: add its pattern shaft to the shafts that would be raised for tabby in the second and fourth picks. To produce weft floats in a half-unit: eliminate its pattern shafts from the shafts that would be raised for tabby in the second and fourth picks. Examine the tie-up in *1c*. In the second and fourth picks, shaft 4 is lifted *in addition to* 1 and 3 to produce warp floats. In the second half-unit shaft 3 is lifted *in addition to* 2 and 4 in the second and fourth picks to produce warp floats. In *1d*, shaft 3 is *subtracted from* the 1-3 tabby to produce weft floats in the first half-unit, and shaft 4 *is subtracted from* the 2-4 tabby to produce weft floats in the second half-unit.

Designing with huck

Since half-units can produce either floats or plain weave, each *half*-unit of huck can be thought of as forming a block of pattern. There are limitations, however. If, for example, the threads on 2-3-2-3-2 are considered Block A, what happens if Block A is threaded many times consecutively or treadled many times in succession? The practical limit of warp- or weft-float length prohibits the consecutive repetition of any half-unit. To preserve tabby, threads on even pattern shafts in one half-unit are always followed by threads on odd pattern shafts in the adjacent half-unit. Blocks are therefore usually threaded in alternating order on four shafts, ABAB; or when more shafts are available, in straight or point order, ABCDEF or ABCDEFEDCBA.

Huck designs can be planned with ease on special design paper (see p. 131). Study *Figure 2*. Each square in the design key represents one half-unit. The numbers above each column indicate the pattern shaft for that half-unit. The actual 8-shaft threading corresponding to the design key in *Figure 2b* is: 2-3-2-3-2, 1-4-1-4-1, 2-5-2-5-2, 1-6-1-6-1, 2-7-2-7-2, 1-8-1-8-1, 2-7-2-7-2, 1-6-1-6-1, 2-5-2-5-2, 1-4-1-4-1, 2-3-2-3-2.

Shade squares in the graph to indicate warp and weft floats. Squares with vertical lines can produce warp floats; squares with horizontal lines can produce weft floats. An unshaded square indicates plain weave.

2. Using huck design paper

Each square in the design key represents a half-unit. The numbers above the squares indicate the pattern shaft for the half-unit.

a. Shade squares for floats. Leave squares blank for plain weave.

b. Beside all rows in the design key: write shaft numbers for 2nd and 4th picks as if all blocks weave tabby (marked *).
1-3-5-7 in row 1: even, odd*, even, odd*, even (EOEOE);
2-4-6-8 in row 2: odd, even*, odd, even*, odd (OEOEO).

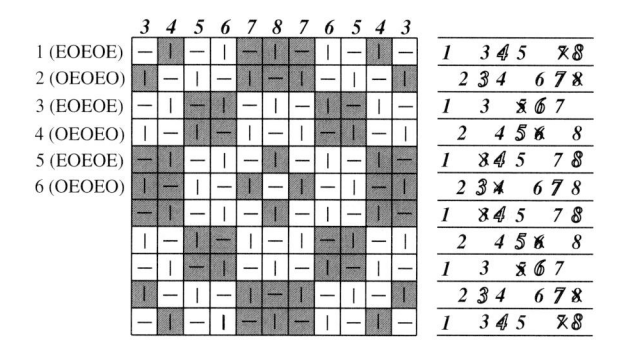

c. Add to these numbers the shaft numbers for warp floats (shaded verticals) and subtract shaft numbers for weft floats (shaded horizontals). For example: in row 1, tabby for second and fourth picks is 1-3-5-7. Add 4 and 8 (shaded verticals). Subtract 7 (shaded horizontal). The new numbers become the pattern treadle for this row, see treadle 1 in d.

d. tie-up

O = odd tabby
E = even tabby

Study *Figure 2b*. To translate the design key into a tie-up and treadling order, first write next to each design row the shaft numbers that produce tabby in the second and fourth picks. In row 1, for example, the even tabby starts the sequence (EOEOE); the second and fourth tabby picks are *odd*. Add to these numbers the shaft numbers for any shaded square with a vertical mark and *subtract* any shaded square with a horizontal mark (think of a horizontal mark as a minus sign). In row 1, add 4 and 8; subtract 7. In row 2, add 3 and 7, subtract 8. Rewrite these numbers as the pattern treadles in the tie-up as in *2d*. The shafts raised in the 5-pick sequence represented by row 1 are: 2-4-6-8(E), 1-3-4-5-8(O), 2-4-6-8(E), 1-3-4-5-8(O), 2-4-6-8(E); and for row 2: 1-3-5-7(O), 2-3-4-6-7(E), 1-3-5-7(O), 2-3-4-6-7(E), 1-3-5-7(O). Compare the design key in *Figure 3a* with the drawdown in *3b* and the woven cloth in *3c*.

63

3a. Design key

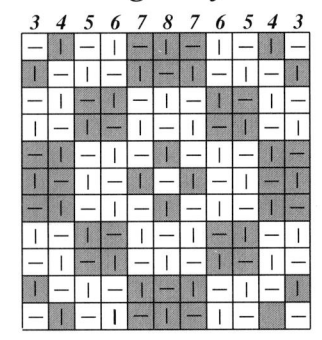

3b. Huck lace drawdown

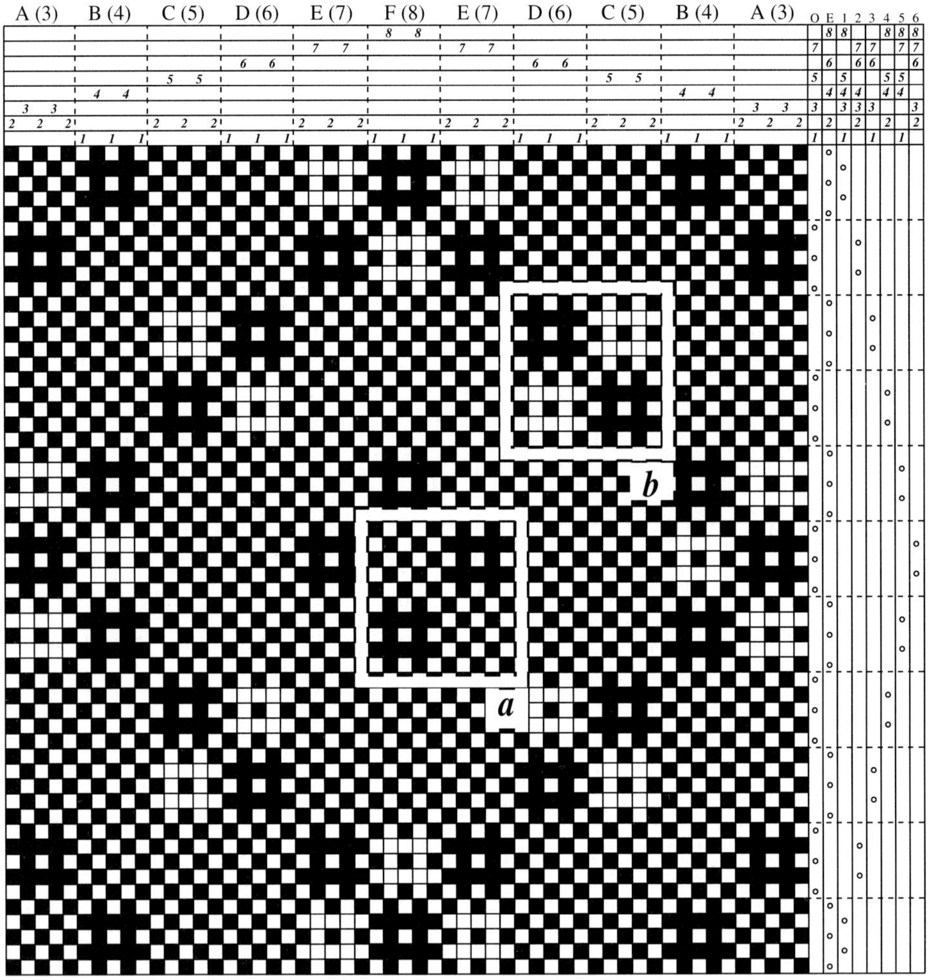

Huck drawdowns

Figure 3b shows a warp drawdown: black squares represent raised warp threads; white squares represent weft threads passing over warp threads. The framed section of cloth at *a* in *3c* shows huck texture, warp floats alternating with plain weave. The frame at *b* shows huck lace, warp floats alternating with weft floats. Both frames enclose full units of huck.

Once you understand how to use the design key, you'll never need to prepare a thread-by-thread drawdown.

3c. Huck lace fabric

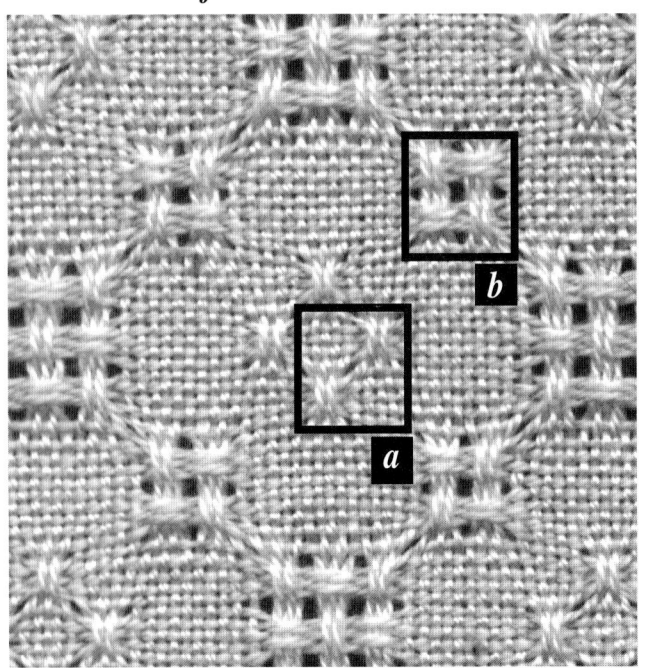

Huck and profile drafts

As a unit weave, huck can be used with profile drafts. Remember that unit weaves must provide two different interlacements, one for pattern and one for background. All of the interlacements made by the structure take place within the unit, and all units weave identically to produce either pattern or background. To meet this requirement, full units of huck must be substituted for each square on the profile threading draft. Therefore, in 5-thread huck, Block A is 2-3-2-3-2-1-4-1-4-1; Block B: 2-5-2-5-2-1-6-1-6-1; Block C: 2-7-2-7-2-1-8-1-8-1, etc. Unfortunately, twice as many pattern shafts are required when using huck with profile drafts as when blocks are threaded in succession. To understand why this is so, imagine what would happen if Block A = 2-3-2-3-2 and the profile draft calls for several squares of Block A threaded in succession!

Huck differs from most unit weaves in that three interlacements, rather than two, are possible: *a*) warp floats alternating with weft floats; *b*) warp or weft floats alternating with plain weave; and *c*) plain

64

Deriving huck tie-ups for profile drafts

If, for example, on the second and fourth picks in 5-thread huck, all odd shafts or all even shafts are raised, plain weave is produced in all blocks. The tie-ups on p. 66 show shaded squares in the pattern section for the shafts that produce plain weave when raised. If the symbol indicating a raised shaft does not appear in a shaded square, a weft float is produced (the pattern shaft has been subtracted from the plain weave shed). If a symbol appears in a square that is not shaded, the corresponding shaft produces a warp float.

Three-thread huck and seven-thread huck use the same tie-ups, but treadling half-units contain three or seven picks respectively.

pattern = lace   *pattern = plain weave*

weave. The greatest contrast is provided when warp and weft floats form one interlacement and plain weave forms the other. In the left photo above, pattern is lace and background is plain weave. In the right photo, pattern is plain weave and background is lace.

Study **Steps 1-6**, pp. 65-66. The complete process for drafting and weaving the 4-block profile draft is shown with warp and weft floats as one interlacement and plain weave as the other, but tie-up templates are included for the third huck interlacement (warp or weft floats alternating with plain weave).

Step 1 shows two units of 5-thread huck, and **Step 2** extends the two units to two blocks. The tie-up templates for each block are two-by-two squares that are placed in the pattern section of the complete tie-up. Note that shafts 1 and 2 and treadles 1 and 2 do not affect the pattern. The pattern shafts for each block weave either in plain weave order or are added to, or subtracted from, the second and fourth plain weave sheds (in 5-thread huck) to produce warp or weft floats respectively.

Step 1. Draft two units.

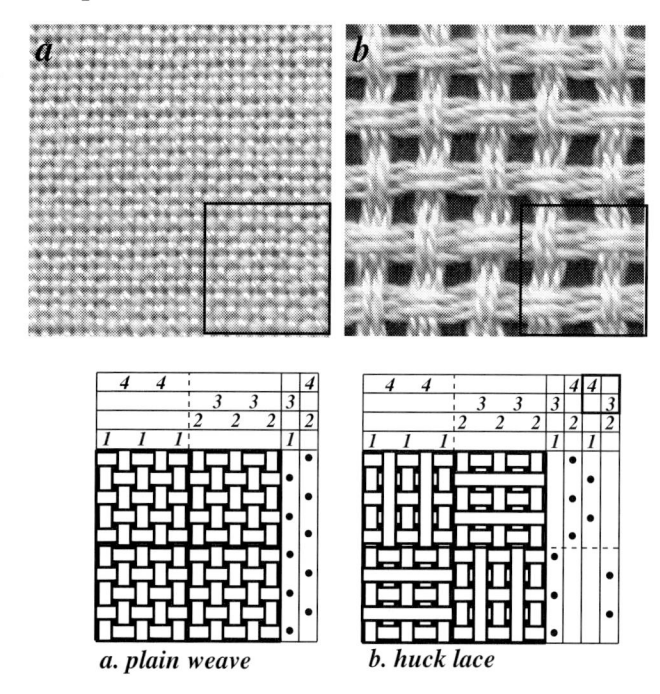

a. plain weave   *b. huck lace*

65

Step 2. Draft two blocks.

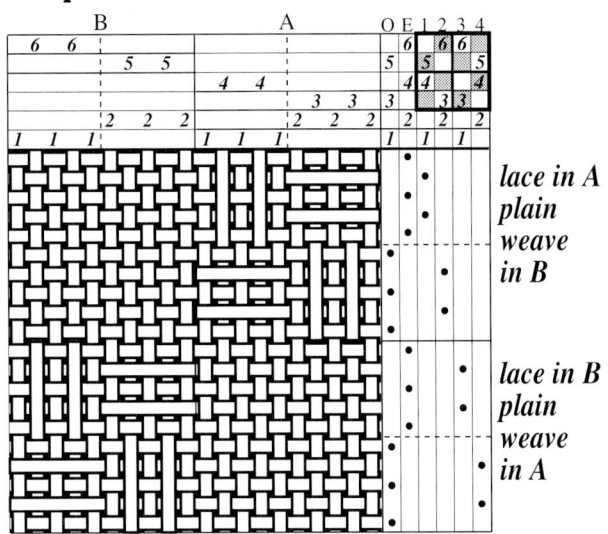

lace in A
plain weave in B

lace in B
plain weave in A

Step 3. Derive the tie-up templates.

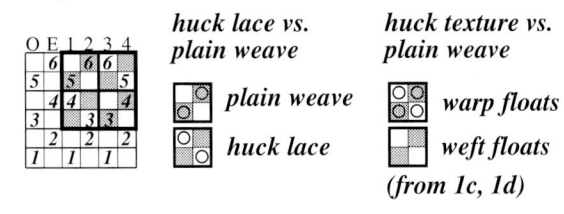

huck lace vs. plain weave

huck texture vs. plain weave

▢ plain weave
▢ huck lace

▢ warp floats
▢ weft floats
(from 1c, 1d)

Step 5. Derive the tie-up.

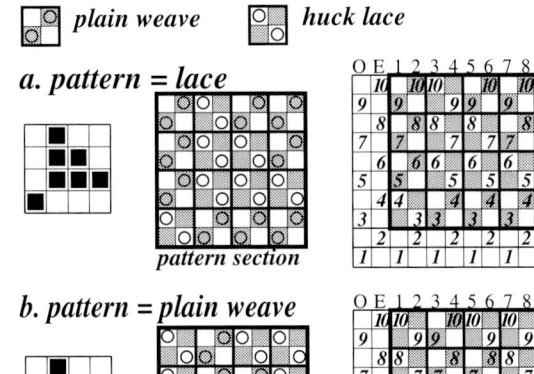

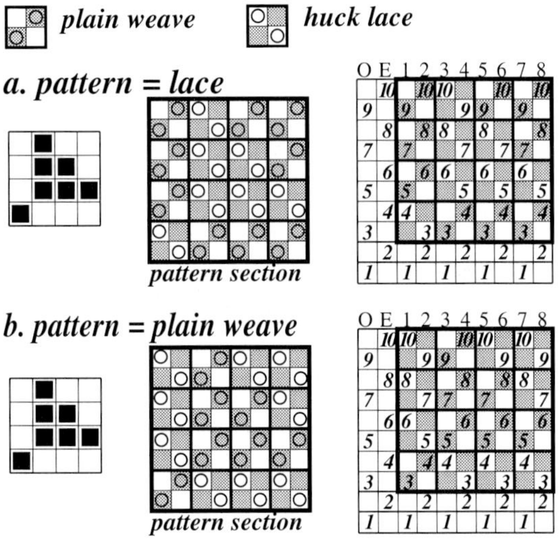

▢ plain weave   ▢ huck lace

a. pattern = lace

pattern section

b. pattern = plain weave

pattern section

Step 4. Substitute threading units for profile threading squares.

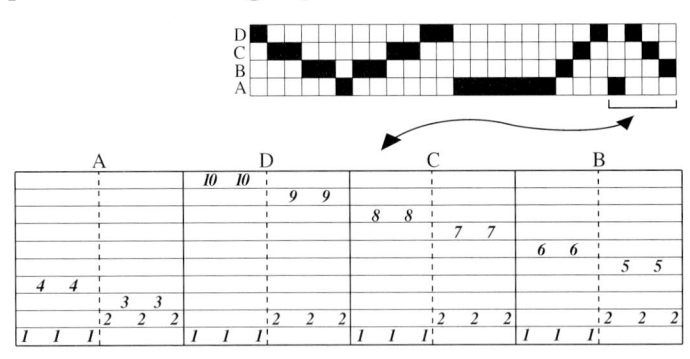

Note: A close examination of the huck fabric, p. 65, reveals that in symmetrical positions on opposite sides of motifs, warp floats appear on one side and weft floats on the other. If a perfectly symmetrical draft is desired, depart slightly from the unit weave concept and add half-units at all turning blocks. For example, for the fourth square in the profile draft above, thread Block A 2-3-2-3-2-1-4-1-4-1-2-3-2-3-2. The next block (D) begins with the half-unit that includes 1 and an even pattern shaft (1-10-1-10-1 2-9-2-9-2).

Huck Keys

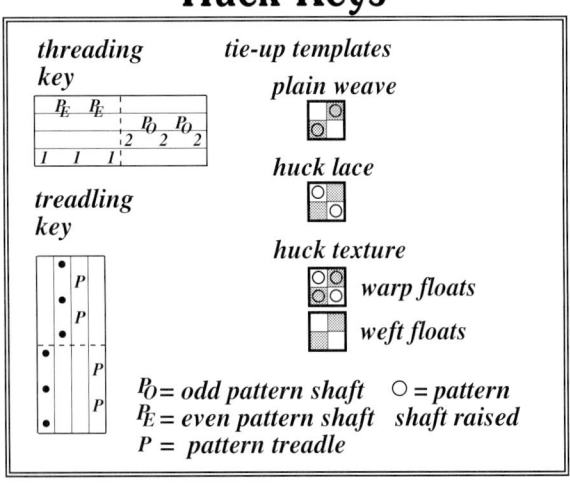

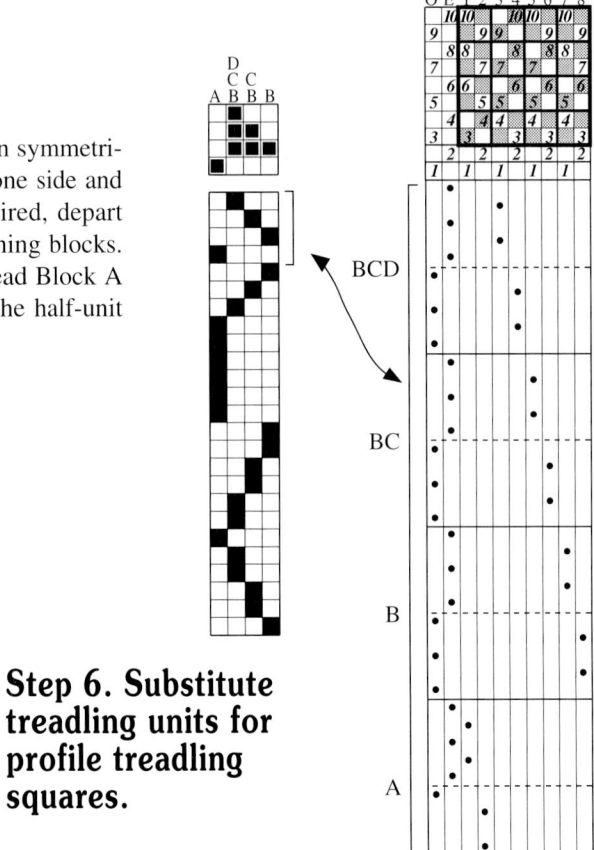

threading key

tie-up templates

plain weave

huck lace

huck texture
▢ warp floats
▢ weft floats

treadling key

P_O = odd pattern shaft   ○ = pattern shaft raised
P_E = even pattern shaft
P = pattern treadle

BCD
BC
B
A

Step 6. Substitute treadling units for profile treadling squares.

Lesson: Drafting Lace

Lace weaves look more complicated than they are. They weave quickly with one shuttle and adapt to a multitude of fibers and uses. An 8-shaft loom provides six blocks of Bronson lace and six blocks of huck lace if the huck half-units are threaded in straight or point order.

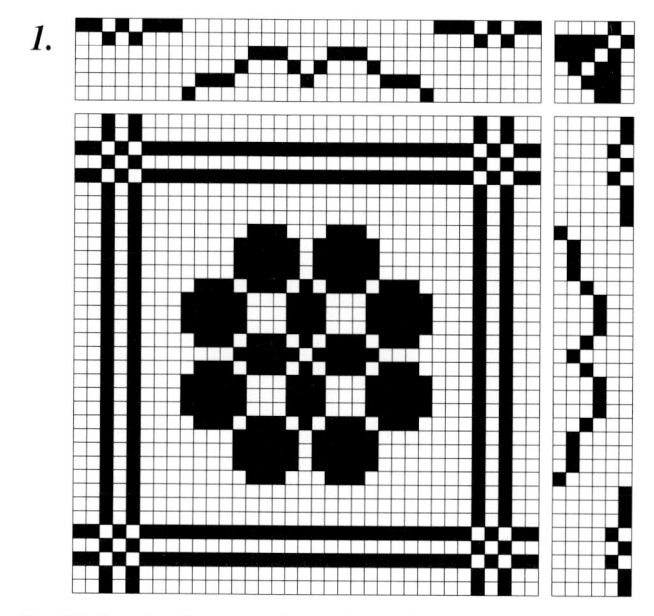

1.

2.

1a. Write the Bronson lace threading units for the first 12 squares in the profile threading draft in **1**.

1-8-1-8-1-2 _____ _____ _____
_____ _____ _____ _____
_____ _____ _____ _____

Fill in the template symbols (from p. 61) for pattern = lace; background = plain weave in *1b*. Change the symbols to shaft numbers and place the template in the treadle tie-up at *1c* (see answers, p. 122).

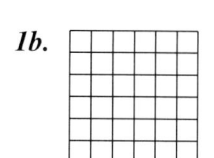

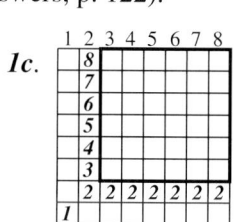

1b.   **1c.**

1d. Write treadle numbers for the first 10 treadling units.

1-8-1-8-1-2 _____ _____ _____
_____ _____ _____ _____
_____ _____ _____ _____

2a. Write the huck lace threading units for the first nine squares in the profile draft in **2**.

2-7-2-7-2-1-8-1-8-1 _____ _____
_____ _____ _____
_____ _____ _____

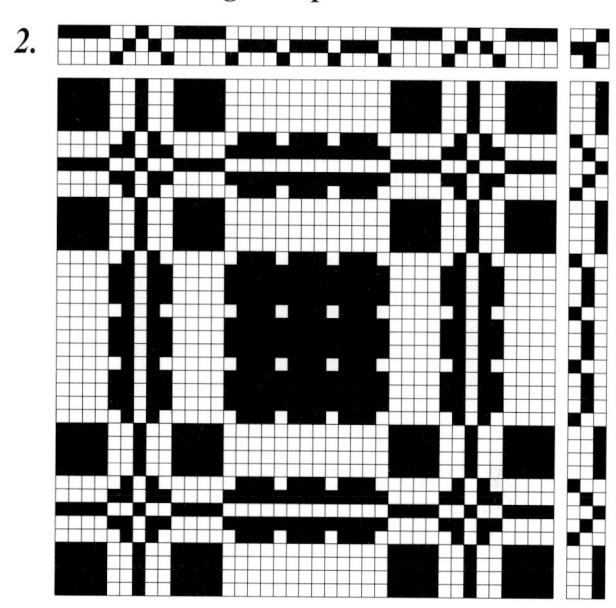

2b. Write the huck tie-up by placing shaft numbers in the positions indicated by the templates for pattern in lace; background in plain weave.

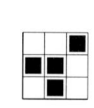

plain weave

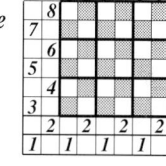

huck lace

3. Translate the design key below into a tie-up for huck lace. For example, for row 1: add 5 and 7; subtract 6 and 8.

Design key

	pattern treadles
(OEOEO)	2 4 6 8
(EOEOE)	1 3 5 7
(OEOEO)	2 4 6 8
(EOEOE)	1 3 5 7
(OEOEO)	2 4 6 8
(EOEOE)	1 3 5 7
	2 4 6 8
	1 3 5 7
	2 4 6 8
	1 3 5 7
	2 4 6 8

Add for warp floats (shaded verticals). Subtract for weft floats (shaded horizontals). Rewrite new numbers as treadles in the tie-up.

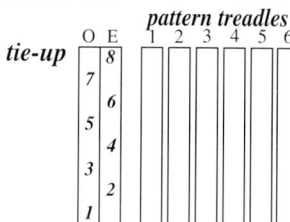

tie-up

67

Damask: Words to Know

clean cut: describes the sharp, straight edges where pattern meets background in turned twills and turned satins. Every warp and weft must interlace (exchange faces) at the design's edge to produce a clean cut.

counterchanged: when an interlacement appears on the face of the cloth at the same time as its reverse appears on the face. For example, in 4-end turned twill, units weaving 3/1 twill appear on the face with units of 1/3 twill. On the reverse side of each interlacement is the other interlacement.

cross twill: used in Swedish texts to describe a twill in which diagonals *within* the treadling or threading repeat move in opposite directions.

damask: turned satin; a simple weave in which areas of warp-predominant and weft-predominant satin appear on the *same surface* across the width and length of the cloth. In some sources turned twill is also considered damask.

damask diaper: turned satin in a pattern of small checks or small repeating block designs.

distribution factor: see satin counter.

double damask: describes damask with reciprocal complementary wefts of two different colors that produce a weft-effect satin on both sides of the cloth. The two wefts (i.e., the two colors) exchange faces in pattern and background areas. Also sometimes used to describe damask with a weft to warp ratio of 2:1.

dräll damask: damask patterning less elaborate than jacquard damasks but often containing many blocks such as a shaft drawloom produces. The edges of the design show a small step that includes a unit or half-unit of the satin structure. In jacquard damasks the design edges can show smooth curves.

dräll weaves: a Swedish term used to describe turned twills and satins in block designs simple enough to be produced on a regular shaft loom.

drawloom: a loom with two harnesses. The front harness is a set of shafts that weaves the structure. The back harness creates the pattern with either a set of shafts (shaft draw system) or with drawcords attached to individual pattern heddles (figure harness).

halb-dräll weaves: weaves in which patterning is formed with supplementary weft floats such as overshot or summer and winter. In dräll weaves, each new block requires a new set of shafts. In halb-dräll weaves, blocks share shafts.

interruption factor: see satin counter.

satin: simple weave (one warp and one weft) with warp floats on one face and weft floats on the other. The interlacement order is regular but dispersed: no adjacent warp threads interlace in adjacent picks. The interlacement is single: warp threads and weft threads pass over or under every thread but one in the repeat. The warp thread that interlaces in each successive pick is the same number of warp threads away from the warp thread that interlaced in the preceding pick. If it is not, the satin is *irregular*, as in 6-thread satin.

satin counter: indicates the number of warp threads away each interlacing warp thread is from the one that interlaced in the preceding pick; also called the satin distribution factor, interruption factor, or satin interval. For example, in 5-thread satin, when a lift of shaft 1 is followed by a lift of shaft 3, the counter is 2.

turned: describes unit weaves in which one of the two interlacements is identical to the other interlacement turned 90°, as in turned satin (warp-float satin becomes weft-float satin if turned 90°) and turned twills (1/3 twill becomes 3/1 twill if turned 90°).

turned satin: damask; warp-predominant satin and weft-predominant satin appear on the same surface of the cloth to create pattern and background.

twill damask: used in Sweden to identify turned twills with elaborate patterning such as can be produced by a drawloom.

twill diaper: turned or counterchanged twill; usually identifies turned 4-thread twills in which the designs are checks, stripes, or very simple block patterns.

warp-predominant satins or twills: describes satins or twills in which the warp predominates, as in 3/1 twill, 4/1 satin, etc.; also called warp-float, warp-effect, or warp-emphasis satins or twills; or warp satins or warp twills.

weft-predominant satins or twills: describes satins or twills in which the weft predominates; also called weft-float, weft-effect, weft-emphasis satins or twills; or weft satin, weft twill.

warp-faced: the warp completely hides the weft on the surface of the cloth. 'Warp-faced' is used misleadingly in some sources as a synonym for 'warp-predominant.'

weft-faced: the weft completely hides the warp on the surface of the cloth; sometimes used misleadingly as a synonym for 'weft-predominant.'

Chapter 7
Understanding Damask

1. Satin interlacement orders
a. 1/4 satin

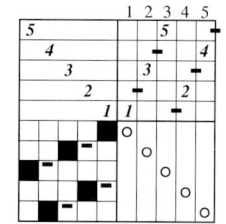

a. skip 1; counter 2.
b. skip 2; counter 3.
c. irregular satin: no counter.
■ indicates skips over shafts in the tie-up and over threads in the drawdown.

b. 1/7 satin

c. 1/5 irregular satin

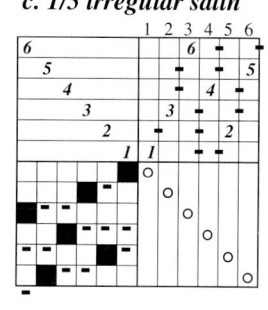

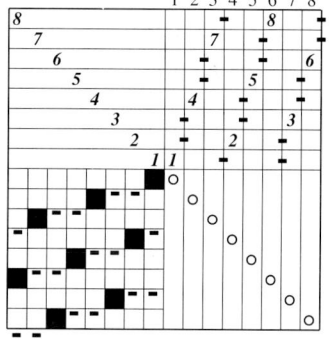

2. Turned twills and turned satins

a. turned twill

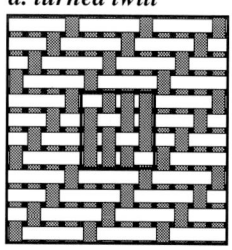

b. turned broken twill

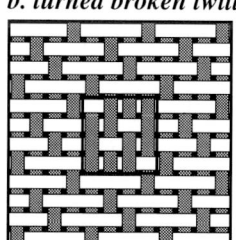

c. 5-thread unit: clean cut

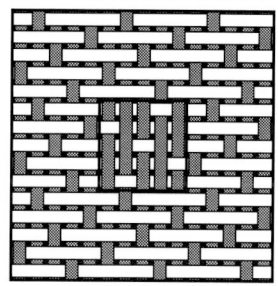

d. 5-thread unit: jagged cut

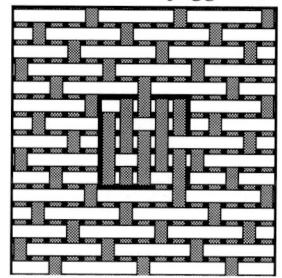

f. 6-thread unit: clean cut

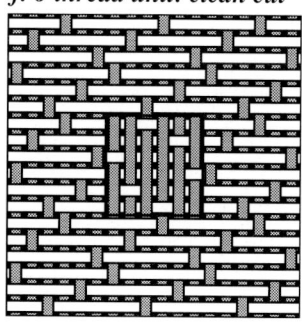

e. 8-thread unit: clean cut

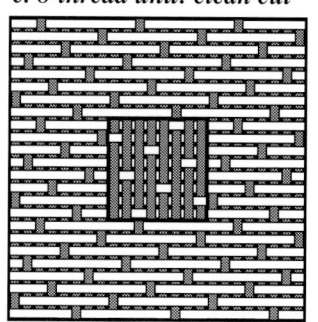

RULES FOR SATINS AND DAMASKS

Take a few minutes to review the short section on satin, p. 23. Satin units are usually threaded in straight-draw order beginning with shaft 1 and ending with the last shaft in the unit. The warp thread that interlaces with each weft thread is a certain number of warp threads away from the warp thread that interlaced in the preceding pick. This number is called the 'counter.' For example, in the first pick in *Figure 1a*, the warp thread on shaft 1 is raised. In the second pick, the warp thread on shaft 3 is raised. The warp thread on shaft 2 is skipped; the thread on shaft 3 is two threads away from 1. The counter is therefore 2. *Figure 1a* shows a true 5-thread satin: in each successive pick, the interlacement skips the same number of warp threads from the warp thread raised in the preceding pick.

Now study *Figure 1b*. The counter in the 8-thread satin in *Figure 1b* is 3: each successive interlacing warp thread is three threads away from the preceding interlacing warp thread.

The satin counter

The satin counter cannot be 1, or the interlacement forms a twill. It cannot be one fewer than the number in the unit (5-1=4), or the interlacement forms a twill in the opposite direction. The counter cannot share a divisor with the number in the unit, or some warp threads interlace more than once and others not at all. If a counter of 2 is used in *Figure 1b*, for example, only four warp threads in the unit interlace: 1, 3, 5, 7; 1, 3, 5, 7; etc.

Now look at *Figure 1c*. Following the rules, the counter cannot be 1 or 5. The remaining numbers 2, 3, and 4 share a divisor (2 and 3) with 6. There is no satin counter for a 6-thread unit nor for a 4-thread unit; the compromise in *Figure 1c* is an 'irregular' satin.

Satin into damask

The satins in *Figure 1* are *weft-predominant, or weft-float,* satins: in each pick *one* warp thread is lifted and all others are covered by the weft. If all warp threads in the unit are lifted *except* one, *warp-float* satin appears. Weft-float satin occurs on the reverse side of the cloth wherever warp-float satin is on the face, and warp-float satin occurs on the reverse side of any area of weft-float satin.

69

3a. Steps for deriving clean-cut damask tie-up templates with even-thread satin units

a. Write shaft numbers in tie-up grid using a satin counter: 3 or 5 for 8-thread satin.
b. Rearrange the treadles so that the sum of the shaft numbers in the center pair equals one more than the total number of shafts in the satin: for 8-thread satin: 8+1 or 7+2 = 9.
c. Replace shaft numbers with o's for the weft-float satin tie-up template.
d. Fill warp-satin tie-up grid with x's (for shafts to go down) in mirror-image positions to o's.
e. Fill in blank squares with o's (o = up) and erase x's (blank = down) for warp-float tie-up template.

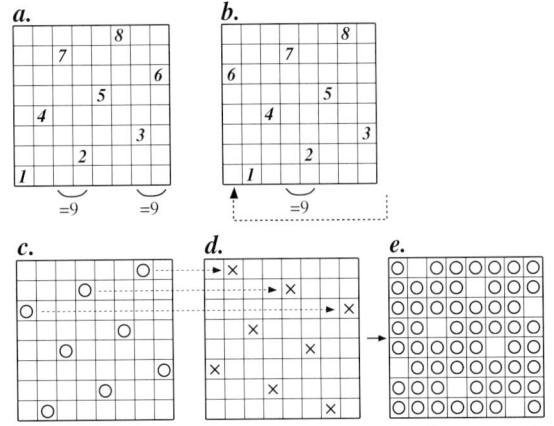

weft-float template   warp-float template

3b. Steps for deriving clean-cut damask tie-up templates with odd-thread satin units

a. Write shaft numbers in tie-up grid using a satin counter: 2 or 3 for 5-thread satin.
b. Rearrange the treadles so that the shaft number in the center treadle is the middle number of the total number of shafts in the satin: for 5-thread satin, 3 is the middle number.
c. Replace shaft numbers with o's for the weft-float satin tie-up template.
d. Fill warp-satin tie-up grid with x's (for shafts to go down) in mirror-image positions to o's.
e. Fill in blank squares with o's (o = up) and erase x's (blank = down) for warp-float tie-up template.

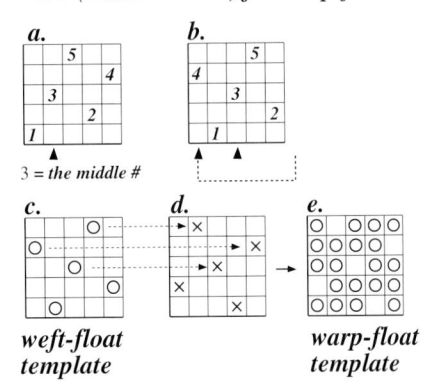

3 = the middle #

weft-float template   warp-float template

In damask, i.e., turned satin, both warp-float and weft-float satin appear on the same surface of the cloth to form pattern and background, as in the examples in *Figure 2*, p. 69. When warp and weft colors are different, strong contrast occurs between pattern and background areas. When warp and weft colors are the same, pattern is still visible because of the difference in reflected light from the opposing directions of the yarns in the two satins.

A disadvantage of damask for the handweaver is that each new block requires a new set of shafts. To weave damask based on 5-thread satin, for example, 10 shafts are required for two blocks, 15 for three. For damask based on 8-thread satin, 16 shafts are required for two blocks. Turned 4-thread twill (*2a*) on the other hand, provides four blocks on 16 shafts. Turned 4-thread broken twill (*2b*), sometimes called 'false damask,' shares with turned satin the characteristic of disrupting the twill diagonal for a smoother texture. In some sources turned twill and turned broken twill are classified as damask, and in others they are called 'twill damask' as opposed to 'satin damask.'

The clean cut

Damask designs are most effective when adjacent pattern and background areas (warp-float satin and weft-float satin) *cut* cleanly; i.e., every warp float is cut by a weft thread and every weft float cut by a warp thread at the design's edge. Examine *Figure 2a-f*. In all of the examples except *2d*, the four edges of the warp-float pattern block in the center are *cut* in the adjacent background blocks — warp threads by weft threads and weft threads by warp threads.

When warp threads and weft threads do not interlace at the block interchange, design edges can be messy or indistinct, and warp threads in designs with straight vertical lines can slide into the weft-float area and vice versa. *Figure 2d* shows a 5-thread satin warp-float unit with uncut edges on three sides.

The clean-cut warranty is provided by the damask tie-up when: *a)* the tie-up template for warp-float satin is the mirror-image reverse (see *e* in *3b*) of the tie-up template for weft-float satin; *b)* the templates are derived so that the sum of the shaft numbers tied to the two center weft-satin treadles for even-thread satin units is one more than the number of shafts used, and the shaft number tied to the center weft-satin treadle of a tie-up for uneven-thread satin units is the middle number of the number of shafts used. Fortunately, these rules are *much* simpler than they sound! Study the steps for deriving clean-cut tie-up templates in *3a-b*.

70

DESIGNING DAMASK

Review the steps for drafting turned twills (pp. 56-57). Follow the same steps for drafting damask.

✎ **Thread substituting the appropriate threading key** for each square in the profile threading draft. For example, for one square in Block A, thread: 1-2-3-4 for turned 4-thread twill, 1-2-3-4-5 for damask based on 5-thread satin, 1-2-3-4-5-6 for damask based on 6-thread (irregular) satin, and 1-2-3-4-5-6-7-8 for damask based on 8-thread satin, or choose units of seven, nine, ten, or more warp ends. Compare the 2-block profile threading draft and the 16-shaft threading draft in *Figure 4*. Unfortunately, so many shafts are required for designs of more than two blocks that most damasks are out of reach of the handweaver.

✎ **Derive the tie-up templates** following the process outlined on page 70 or select templates from p. 72. Two of several possible templates for damask based on 6-thread irregular satin, which do not follow the rules for deriving clean-cut templates, are given.

✎ **Substitute tie-up templates for squares in the profile tie-up.** Choose warp-float satin (or twill) for pattern and weft-float satin (or twill) for background, or vice versa. Compare the *Figure 4* treadle tie-up with the profile tie-up.

✎ **Weave by substituting the treadling key** that corresponds to each square in the profile treadling diagram. Compare the *Figure 4* treadling sequence with the profile treadling draft.

Half-units

In cases where full units of any even-numbered satin or twill (6, 8, 10, etc.) are too large for the desired scope of the design, half-units can be drafted instead. When threading 8-thread satin, for example, for a square of Block A, thread the first half-unit of A (1-2-3-4). For the next square, thread a second half-unit, either of A (5-6-7-8) or of some other block, 13-14-15-16 of B, 21-22-23-24 of C, etc. Continue, alternating first half-units with second half-units of whatever blocks are designated by the profile draft. Follow the same rule in the treadling: always follow a first half-unit of treadling with a second half-unit. Half-units form clean cuts, see *Figures 5-6*, if tie-ups are derived as in *Figure 3a*. For half-units of 6-thread irregular satin, use the 6-shaft clean-cut tie-up template, p. 72. Block numbers are not increased by drafting half-units unless they are threaded in straight or point order, providing small 4-block diamond or diagonal designs as in *Figure 6*.

4. Damask based on 8-thread satin: 16 shafts, two blocks

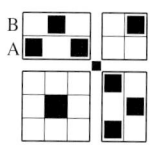

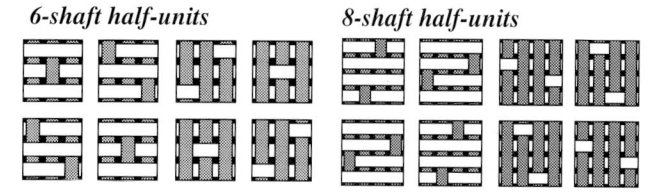

5. Half-units
6-shaft half-units   *8-shaft half-units*

6. Half-units threaded in succession

71

Damask Keys

turned twill: 4-thread units

turned broken twill: 4-thread units

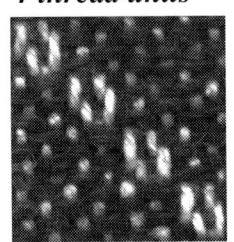

turned satin: 5-thread unit; no clean cut on right side or top

turned irregular satin: 6-thread unit

turned twill: 4-thread unit
threading — weft twill
treadling — warp twill

turned broken twill: 4-thread unit
threading — weft twill
treadling — warp twill

6-thread unit: clean cut
threading — weft satin
treadling — warp satin

6-thread unit: not clean cut
threading — weft satin
treadling — warp satin

5-thread unit
threading — weft satin
treadling — warp satin

8-thread unit
threading — weft satin
treadling — warp satin

P_N = shafts for unit
○ = shafts raised

Step 1. Draft two blocks.

6-thread units

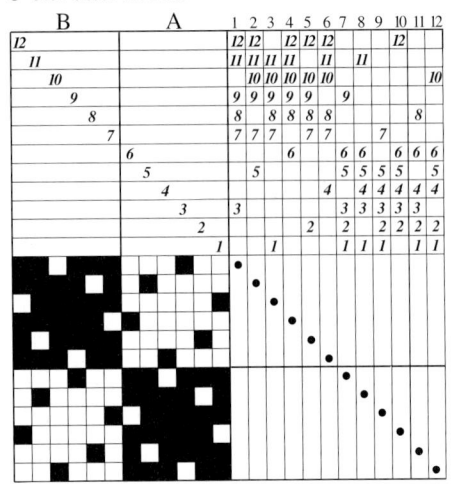

5-thread units

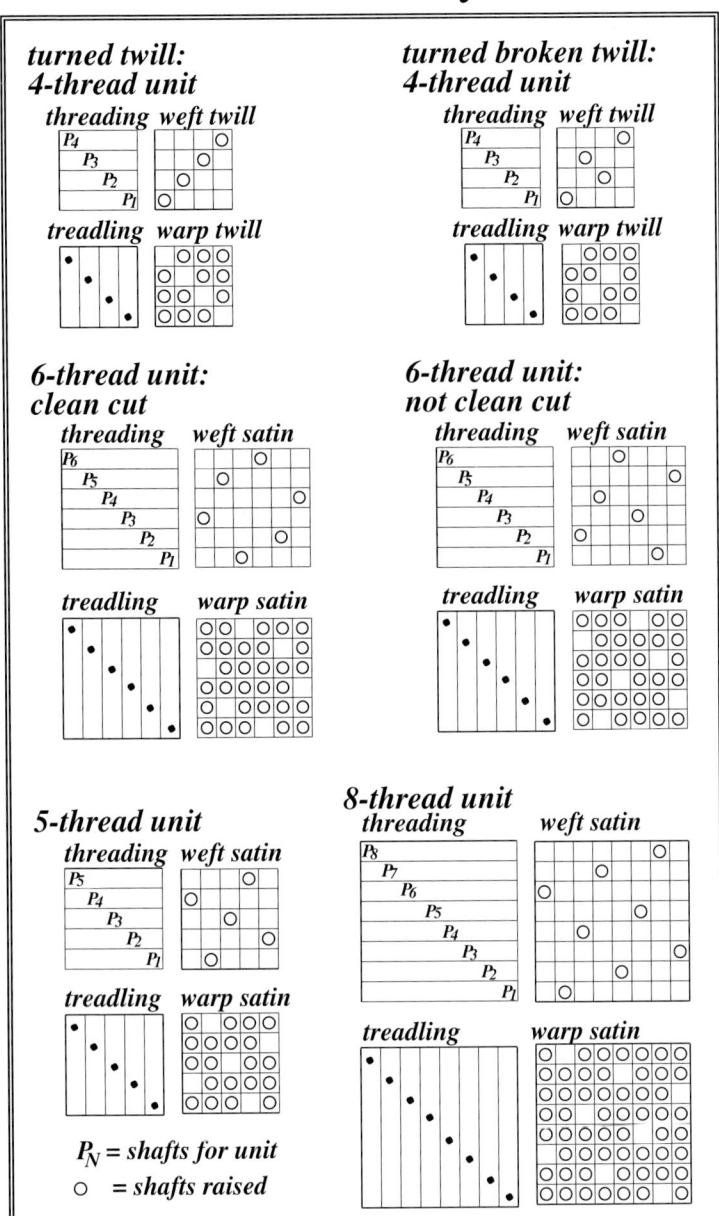

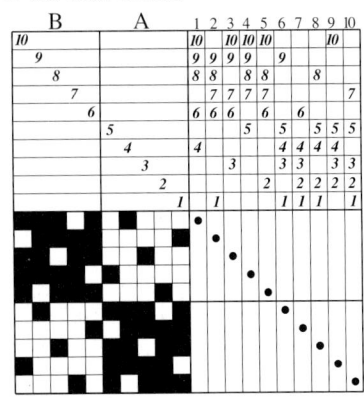

Step 2a. Substitute threading units for profile threading squares.

4-thread units for turned twill

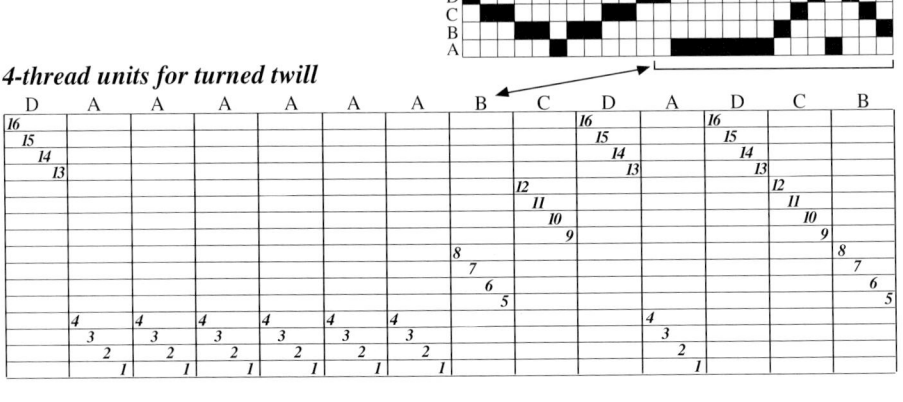

72

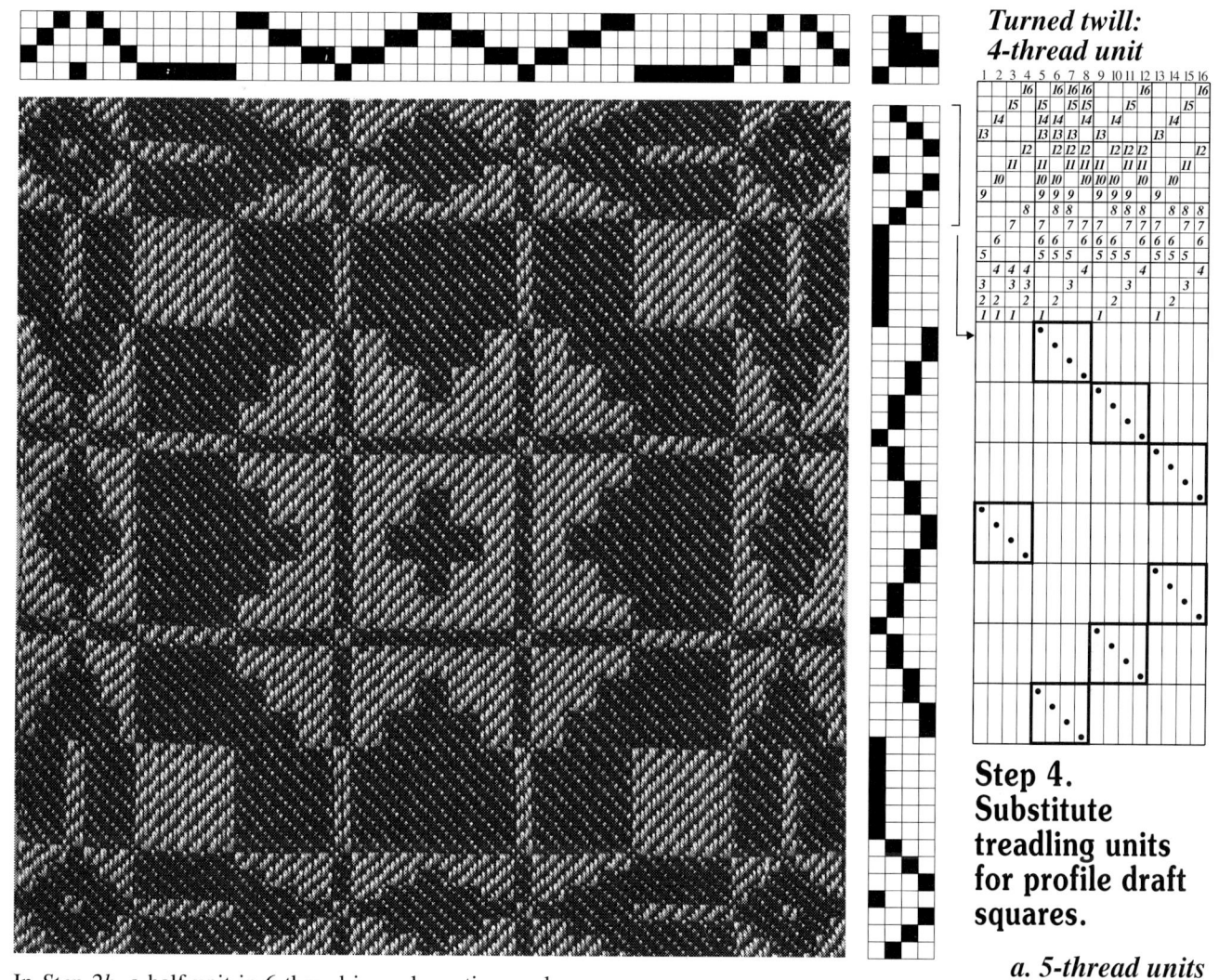

In *Step 2b*, a half-unit in 6-thread irregular satin equals one square in the profile threading draft. Use tie-up *b* in *Step 3*. Always follow a first half-unit in the treadling with a second half-unit. For example, treadles 1-2-3 can be followed by 4-5-6, 10-11-12, 16-17-18, or 22-23-24 — all second half-units.

Step 3. Derive the tie-up.

Turned twill: 4-thread unit

Step 4. Substitute treadling units for profile draft squares.

Step 2b. For smaller design scope, substitute half-units for profile squares.

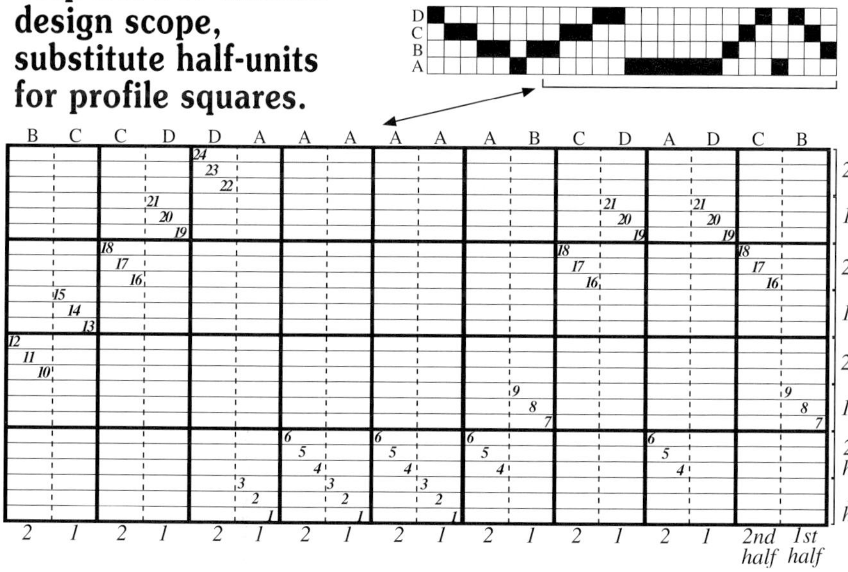

a. 5-thread units

b. 6-thread units

73

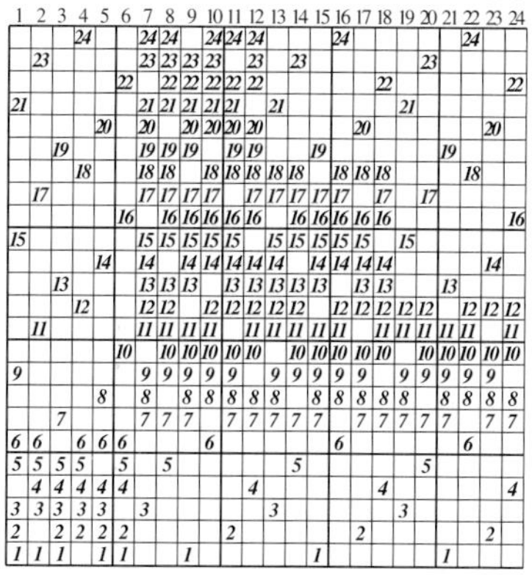

Lesson: Drafting Damask

Old jacquard linen damask tablecloths delight every weaver's eye, even though such elaborate patterning is far out of reach. The closest a handweaver can come with an 8-shaft loom is two blocks of turned twill; and with a 10-shaft loom, two blocks of turned 5-thread satin. Even so, damask is easy to understand and draft. Complete these exercises and dream of 24 shafts!

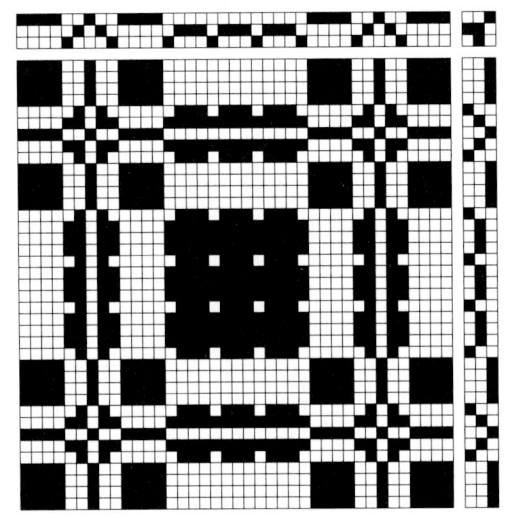

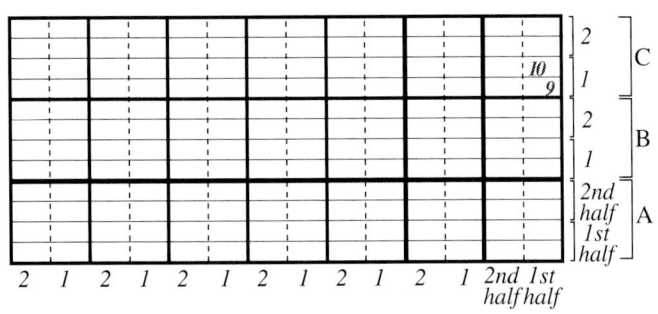

1. Fill in the threading diagram to correspond with the first 14 squares of the profile threading draft using half-units of 4-thread turned twill (see p. 73; answers p. 123).

2. Write the threading for the first 9 squares of the profile draft in 4-thread turned twill.

9-10-11-12 _____ _____ _____ _____

_____ _____ _____ _____

Translate the profile tie-up into a treadle tie-up for:
3a. turned 4-thread twill;
3b. turned 4-thread broken twill;
3c. turned 5-thread satin.

Fill in the **4a** treadling diagram to correspond with the first seven squares in the profile treadling draft.

3a.

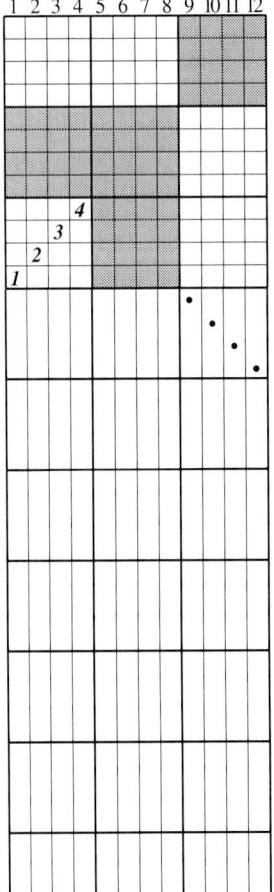

3b.

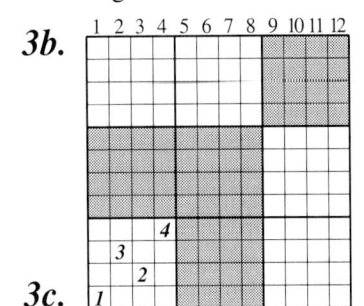

3c.

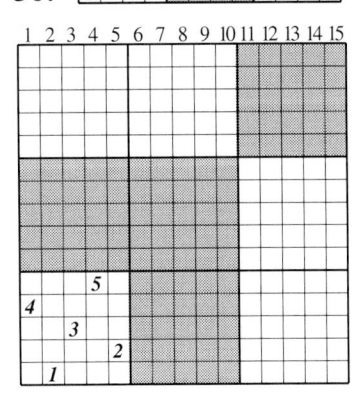

4. Follow the steps to derive templates for 8-shaft damask. Compare your work with **Figure 3a**, p. 70.

  a. Write shaft numbers in tie-up grid using a satin counter of 5.
  b. Rearrange the treadles so that the sum of the shaft numbers in the center pair = 9 (8+1 or 7+2).
  c. Replace shaft numbers with o's for the weft-float satin tie-up template.
  d. Fill warp-satin tie-up grid with x's (for shafts to go down) in mirror-image positions to o's.
  e. Fill in blank squares with o's (o = up) and erase x's (blank = down) for warp-float tie-up template.

a.   b.

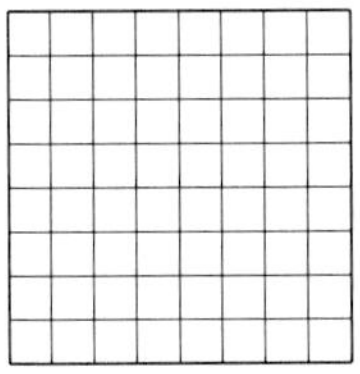

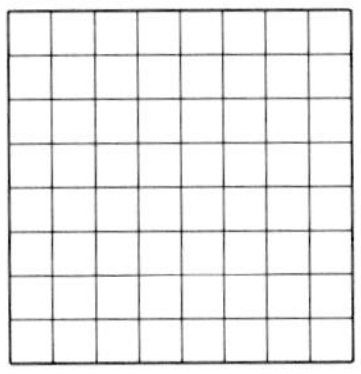

c.   d.   e.

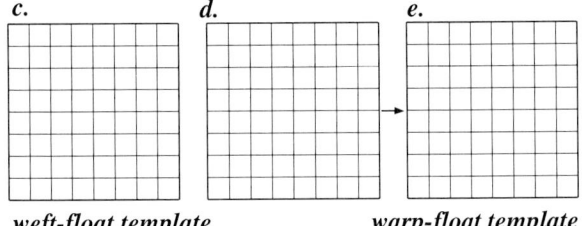

weft-float template   *warp-float template*

74

Tied Unit Weaves: Words to Know

Bateman weaves: 1-, 2-, or 3-tie block weaves. Tie-down ends are threaded at the beginning of the 'unit' (park weaves: 1; boulevard weaves: 1-2-1; chevron weaves: 1-2-3-2-1) followed by the pattern ends in straight or point twill order. In most of the threading variations, pattern ends in one block share shafts with pattern ends in one or more other blocks (these are block weaves but not unit weaves); in other variations blocks are threaded on independent shafts (these are unit weaves). The ground structure is plain weave. The lifting orders of tie-down ends and pattern ends can be varied for a multitude of effects.

Bergman: a 3-tie unit weave named for Margaret Bergman, who introduced it. The ratio of tie-down ends to pattern ends is 1:1; tie-down ends are threaded in 'rosepath' order (1-3-2-1-3-1-2-3) and alternate with pattern ends; there are 16 ends in a structural unit; each block requires one pattern shaft; ground structure is plain weave. A = 1-4-3-4-2-4-1-4-3-4-1-4-2-4-3-4.

crackle: a supplementary-weft structure with a plain-weave ground cloth. The pattern weft forms 3-thread floats on the face or on the back to produce pattern or background. Four shafts provide four blocks in which: *a)* one block shows floats on the face, one shows floats on the back, and two show halftones; or *b)* two blocks show floats on the face and two show floats on the back. Since blocks cannot weave pattern or background independently, crackle is not a unit weave.

double two-tie unit weave: a two-tie unit weave with four warp ends in a unit; the ratio of tie-down ends to pattern ends is 1:1; two pattern shafts (hence the 'double') are required for each block; the ground cloth is plain weave. Each block can produce three textures independently: pattern, background, or halftone. This threading is primarily used to combine different weaves in one fabric or to expand twill designs and is rarely used as a tied unit weave. A = 1-3-2-4.

extended summer and winter: 2-tie unit weaves in which one tie-down end is threaded at the beginning of the first half-unit and the other at the beginning of the second half-unit (as in summer and winter). There are six or more ends in a threading unit; the ratio of tie-down ends to pattern ends is 1:2 or 1:3 or 1:4 or more; two pattern shafts are required for each block; the tie-down ends interlace with the pattern weft in plain weave order; the ground cloth is plain weave. A = 1-4-3-2-3-4 or 1-4-3-4-2-4-3-4, etc.

four-tie unit weaves (also called Quigley weaves after Joyce Quigley, who introduced them). Usually the ratio of tie-down ends to pattern ends is 1:1 (i.e., tie-down ends alternate with pattern ends); tie-down ends are threaded in straight or point order; there are 8 or more ends in a unit; tie-down ends are raised in twill order; the ground cloth is plain weave. A = 1-5-2-5-3-5-4-5 or 1-5-2-5-3-5-4-5-3-5-2-5-1-5.

ground: refers to the cloth structure on which a pattern warp or pattern weft floats, as in overshot, crackle, and all tied unit weaves. 'Ground' is a structural term, not a pattern term, even though it is used as a pattern term in fields of study other than textiles to distinguish 'figure vs. ground.' In textile terminology 'pattern vs. background' makes that distinction. The ground warp and ground weft weave the ground cloth.

'half dukagang': a 2-tie unit weave. The ratio of tie-down ends to pattern ends is 1:2 or 1:3 or 1:4 (or more); one tie-down end is threaded at the beginning of the first half-unit, the other at the beginning of the second half-unit; there are six or more ends in a unit; the first tie-down end is raised and the second remains down for every pattern-weft pick. A = 1-4-3-2-3-4 or 1-4-3-4-2-4-3-4, etc.

'half satin': a 3-tie unit weave. The ratio of tie-down ends to pattern ends is 1:1; there are six ends in a unit; tie-down ends alternate with pattern ends in the threading; tie-down ends interlace with the pattern weft in twill order. A = 1-4-2-4-3-4.

Landes hybrid (named for 18th century weaver): a 2-tie weave, sometimes drafted as a unit weave, sometimes drafted with blocks sharing shafts. Usually, one tie-down end is threaded in the first half of the threading unit and the other in the second half. One tie-down end is raised for the first half of the treadling unit and the other for the second half. The ratio of tie-down ends to pattern ends is 1:2 or more, with six or more ends in a unit. Tie-down ends can be threaded at the beginning or the middle of the half-unit; when they are in the middle of a 3-thread half-unit, the weave is also tied overshot.

one-tie unit weave: one tie-down end is threaded in each unit. A 1-tie weave allows a pattern weft to float in some areas (pattern shaft and tie shaft down) and to form halftones in others (pattern shaft up, tie shaft down). Summer and winter has sometimes been called a 1-tie unit weave when shaft 1 is up and 2 down for all pattern picks, but shaft 2 ties the float to the bottom of the cloth.

'paired-tie' weaves ('tied Latvian,' 'tied Lithuanian,' or, from Lithuania, 'perverai,' or 'dimai'): 2-tie unit weaves with a ratio of tie-down ends to pattern ends of 2:4, 2:5, 2:6, etc. Two pattern shafts are required for each block; the ground cloth is plain weave. The tie-down ends are paired at the beginning of the unit. In the most common Lithuanian version, tie shaft 1 is raised and tie shaft 2 lowered for all the pattern picks, and in the most common Latvian version the tie-down ends are lifted alternately for the pattern picks. The ground cloth is plain weave. A = 1-2-3-4-3-4.

pattern weft: a supplementary weft that floats on the surface of the cloth to form pattern and on the back to form background or vice versa.

pattern (warp) ends: in a tied unit weave, the warp ends that determine whether a pattern-weft float shows on the face of the cloth or on the back by being raised or lowered for the pattern-weft pick.

pattern shafts: the shafts on which the 'pattern' ends are threaded.

single two-tie unit weave: a unit weave that requires one pattern shaft ('single') for each block and two tie-down shafts (i.e., summer and winter).

star and diamond weaves: see tied overshot.

summer and winter: a 2-tie unit weave. Ratio of tie-down ends to pattern ends is 1:1; there are four ends in each unit; each block requires one pattern shaft; the first tie-down end is threaded at the beginning of the first half-unit, and the second tie-down end at the beginning of the second half-unit; tie-down ends alternate with pattern ends; tie-down ends interlace with the pattern weft in plain weave order; the ground cloth is plain weave. A = 1-3-2-3.

summer and winter polychrome: Instead of one pattern weft, two or more are are inserted as one structural pattern pick: each appears on the face in selected areas as required by the pattern, the other(s) on the back.

supplementary weft: a structurally non-essential weft, i.e., the pattern weft in overshot and tied unit weaves.

taqueté: a weft-faced, complementary-weft structure woven on a summer and winter threading in which two or more heavy wefts, each a different color, form one structural pick. Each color floats on the face in selected areas while the other(s) float on the back; they interlace with ends on shafts 1 and 2 in alternate order. Syn. 'weft-faced compound tabby' and 'summer and winter polychrome without a tabby.'

tie, to tie: when a tie-down end is raised and the pattern weft passes under it but over the other ends of the unit, it is 'tied' by the tie-down end to the top surface of the cloth. When a tie-down end is lowered and the pattern weft passes over it but under the other ends of the unit, it is 'tied' by the tie-down end to the bottom surface of the cloth.

'tied Lithuanian': see 'paired-tie' weaves.

tied overshot (also called star and diamond weave): a 2-tie unit weave. Each threading unit contains two half-units (half-units of 'even' tied overshot have an even number of ends and half-units of 'uneven' tied overshot have an uneven number of ends). In the pattern area the pattern weft floats over one half-unit and forms a halftone in the other. In the background area the pattern weft floats under a half-unit and forms a halftone in the other. Each half-unit of treadling reverses the halftone/float position of the preceding half-unit. The ratio of tie-down ends to pattern ends is 1:1; there are at least six ends in a full unit. Usually, a tie-down end on shaft 1 alternates with a pattern end on an even pattern shaft in the first half-unit. A tie-down end on shaft 2 alternates with a pattern end on an odd pattern shaft in the second half-unit. One tie-down end is lifted for one half-unit of treadling, the other for the next half-unit of treadling. One structural unit usually contains two blocks: A = 3-1-3-1-3; B = 4-2-4-2-4; blocks are usually threaded in point or straight order.

tie-down (warp) end: a warp end within the threading unit that ties the pattern-weft float to the ground cloth and also weaves the ground cloth with the pattern ends. 'Tie-down' is sometimes used to identify the thread on shaft 2 that stops the weft float in Bronson lace. Since this float is not a supplementary weft but instead an integral part of the cloth, 'tie-down' does not describe its function.

tied unit weaves: unit weaves in which a supplementary pattern weft is tied to the cloth by designated warp threads called the 'tie-down ends' or 'tie threads.' Each threading unit consists of tie-down ends and pattern ends. The tie-down ends are threaded on the same shafts throughout (shafts 1, 2, 3, 4 respectively for 1-, 2-, 3-, and 4-tie weaves). The pattern ends are threaded on different shafts in each block. Tied unit weaves differ from each other in: a) the ratio of tie-down ends to pattern ends; b) the number of ends in the unit; c) the number of pattern shafts required for each block; d) the position of the tie-down ends in the unit; and e) the order in which the tie-down ends are raised to tie the pattern-weft float.

Chapter 8
Understanding Tied Unit Weaves

MORE FOR LESS

When Harriet Tidball's *Summer and Winter and Other Two-Tie Unit Weaves* was first printed in 1966, summer and winter was one of the few unit weaves familiar to most handweavers. Moreover, 'other two-tie unit weaves' are not explored in the monograph beyond a few threading systems. Tidball's *The Handloom Weaves* (1957) remained until recently the primary source for information about 2-, 3-, and 4-tie weaves. Two factors have led to the explosion of interest in these weaves: the expanded use of looms with eight or more shafts and the trend toward weaving with finer threads.

As a name for this structural category, 'tied unit weaves' is a bit awkward, since it is not unit weaves but supplementary-weft floats that are tied. 'Tied-float weaves,' as they are called in Latvia, is more descriptively accurate, though it lacks reference to the 'unit' aspect of the structures.

Tied unit weaves bring the most pattern potential to the handweaver for the lowest cost in numbers of shafts of any of the unit weaves. Tied unit weaves also provide a wide range of textures to combine with fiber and color in an astounding variety of ways.

How to recognize a tied unit weave

As is required of every unit weave, each threading and treadling unit in a tied unit weave can form at least two different interlacements, one to show pattern, the other to show background. All tied unit weaves share several specific additional characteristics:

♦ Each threading unit contains designated warp threads that tie supplementary-weft floats to a ground cloth. These threads are called the 'tie threads' or the 'tie-down ends.' They also weave the ground cloth with the other threads in the unit. The tie-down ends are threaded on the same shafts in every unit, usually the first shafts, i.e., shafts 1 and 2 for 2-tie weaves. The number of shafts used for the tie-down ends is the number that identifies a 1-tie, 2-tie, 3-tie, etc., weave.

♦ In addition to the tie-down ends, every unit includes other warp threads that are called the 'pattern' ends. These ends are threaded on different shafts in each block (the 'pattern shafts') so that in some blocks the pattern weft floats over them while in other blocks it floats under them. The pattern ends also weave the ground cloth with the tie-down ends.

♦ Pattern picks alternate with ground picks in the treadling sequence.

♦ When the pattern end is down and the tie-down end is raised in a unit, the pattern weft is tied to the top of the cloth. When the pattern end is raised and the tie-down end is down in a unit, the float is tied to the bottom.

How to tell one from the other

In spite of exotically different names like Quigley, half satin, tied Lithuanian, and Bergman, tied unit weaves all follow the same basic threading and weaving principles. They differ in small and very specific ways. Their names are unrelated to each other because they evolved in diverse places long before the name 'tied unit weaves' was coined.

Tied unit weaves differ from each other in the following ways:

♦ **the ratio of tie-down ends to pattern ends**

Summer and winter, for example, has a ratio of one tie-down end to one pattern end, or 1:1 (see *Figure 1*).

♦ **the number of warp ends in the unit**

There are four ends in a summer and winter unit.

♦ **the number of pattern shafts required for each block**

Summer and winter is the most shaft-efficient of all tied unit weaves. Two shafts are required for the tie-down ends. Each block requires one additional shaft for the pattern ends.

♦ **the position of the tie-down ends in the unit**

The tie-down ends in summer and winter alternate with the pattern ends in the threading. Another feature to notice about the summer and winter threading unit is that the tie-down end on shaft 1 is the first thread in the first half of the unit, and the tie-down end on shaft two is the first thread in the second half of the unit.

1. Summer and winter

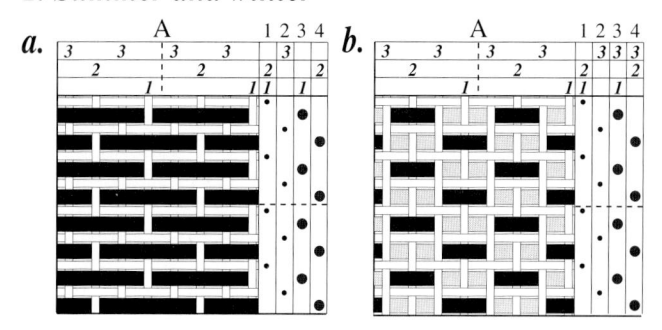

♦ **the order in which the tie-down ends are raised to tie the pattern-weft float**

The tie-down ends in summer and winter are usually raised in alternate (plain weave) order to interlace with the pattern weft. Follow the pattern-weft picks in *Figure 2a*. The pattern weft is tied alternately by shafts 1 and 2 so that the 3-thread floats are arranged in a brick-like fashion.

Summer and winter texture can be varied by using other lifting orders of the tie-down ends for the pattern picks: 2-1-1-2, 1-2-2-1 or 1-1-1-1. The first produces a small pattern of x's, and the second a small pattern of o's, see *Figures 2b-2c*. The third produces vertical lines, see the lower left quadrant in the fabric, p. 80.

♦ **the structure of the ground cloth**

In most tied unit weaves (and in all of those included in this chapter) the ground cloth is plain weave. Although a twill or satin ground cloth is also possible, additional shafts are almost always required to produce them. The cost in shafts is not worth the result, since the background structure is disturbed by the specks of pattern weft passing over tie-down ends. Plain weave is an appropriate choice, providing a dull-textured background for a shiny and/or differently-colored pattern weft.

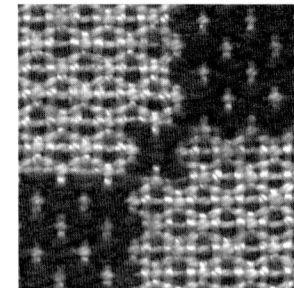

DRAFTING TIED UNIT WEAVES

The steps for translating a profile draft into a thread-by-thread draft are the same for all of the tied unit weaves except tied overshot, which requires some special design considerations. Follow the process first for summer and winter, and then apply the same steps to a variety of other tied unit weaves.

Step 1. Draft two units.

First draft two units, one that forms pattern and one that forms background, as in *Figure 1a-b*, p. 77. Remember either interlacement can be pattern and the other background. Since in summer and winter, the back side of the pattern-float area is structurally identical to the front side of the non-float area and vice versa, the fabric can be woven either way and used either way. Usually, it is advisable to

2a. Summer and winter: tie-down ends alternate

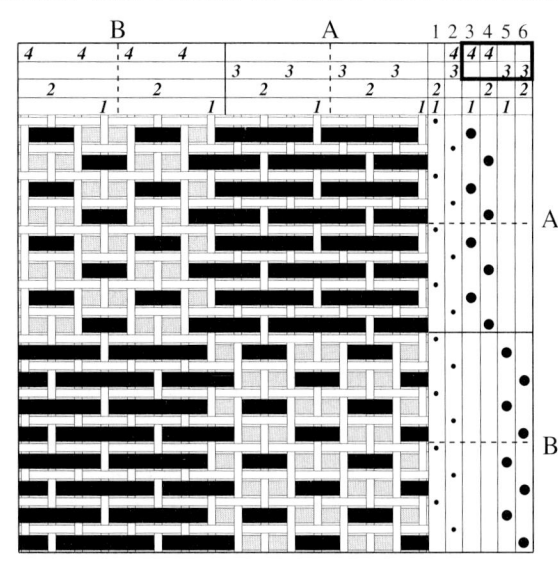

2b. Summer and winter: 2-1-1-2 tie-down order

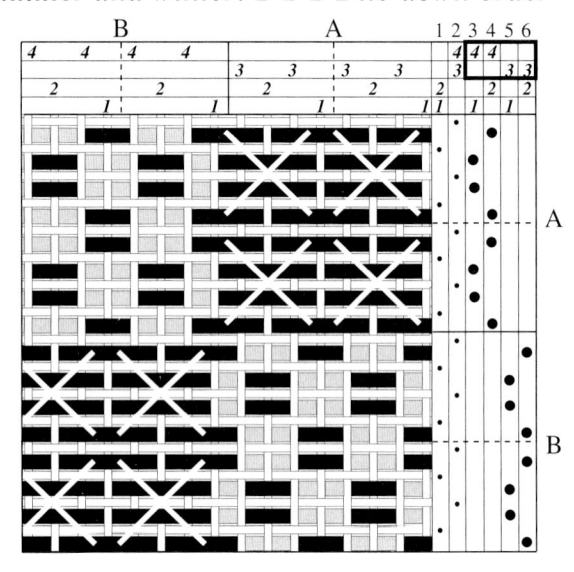

2c. Summer and winter: 1-2-2-1 tie-down order

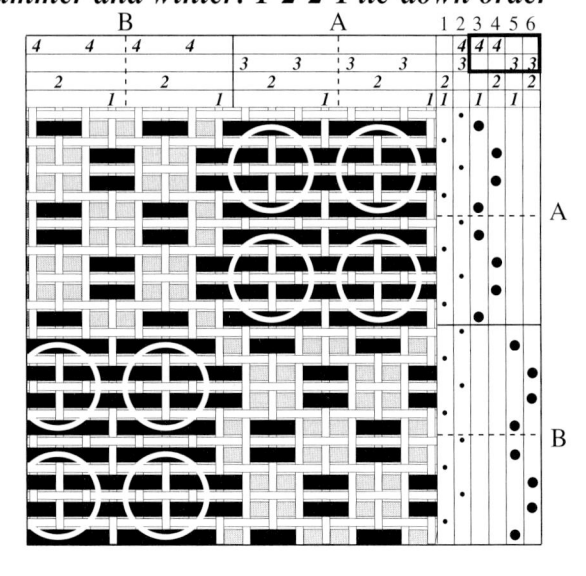

weave summer and winter with the side facing up that requires the raising of the fewest shafts.

Two units of pattern and two units of background are drafted in *Figures 1a-b*, p. 77. Although only one unit of each is essential for understanding the structure, two units give a clearer picture of the 3-thread floats. The number of pattern picks in a treadling unit is theoretically eight: to provide 50/50 plain weave with the four warp threads in the unit, four tabby weft picks and four pattern picks are required, but setts and materials sometimes require a different number to square.

A special miracle results from summer and winter's one-and-one alternation of tie-down and pattern ends: the pattern ends in each block are raised and lowered together for both the tabby sheds *and* the pattern sheds. They can therefore be threaded on the same shaft. Tied unit weaves that alternate tie-down ends and pattern ends require only one shaft for each block.

Step 2. Draft two blocks.

Each of the drafts in *Figure 2* extends the summer and winter units to two blocks. The same sheds are used in all three drafts; only their order differs. Examine the tie-ups in *Figure 2*. In all three drafts, to show pattern in Block A, tie-down shafts 1 and 2 are raised alternately with pattern shaft 4. To show pattern in Block B, tie-down shafts 1 and 2 are raised alternately with pattern shaft 3.

The transposed order of the tabby sheds in *2b* and *2c* forms a small + of warp and tabby weft in the centers of the x's or o's when the tie-down ends are raised in alternate pairs (see photos in *2a-c*). If the opposite tabby order is used, the + forms on the other side of the cloth.

Step 3. Derive the tie-up templates.

With the information in **Step 2**, we can derive the summer and winter tie-up templates. Tabby requires two treadles, one to raise shafts 1 and 2 and one to raise all of the pattern shafts. Two treadles are required for each block combination in the profile tie-up: one to raise the corresponding pattern shafts with tie-shaft 1 and the other to raise the same pattern shafts with tie-shaft 2. Pattern shafts are raised when no float is desired in a block (fill in a square for that shaft on each of the two treadles); pattern shafts are down when a float is desired (leave a blank square for that shaft on each of the two treadles).

Tie-up templates for summer and winter therefore consist of two adjacent squares that are placed in the pattern section (framed in *Figure 3*) of the tie-up for each shaft: two blank squares for pattern shafts in blocks where floats appear, two filled-in squares for pattern shafts in the blocks where floats do not appear.

3. Summer and winter tie-up templates

Treadles 3, 4: float on the face in A; float on the back in B.
Treadles 5, 6: float on the face in B; float on the back in A.

template for float on the face
template for float on the back

Step 4. Derive the tie-up

In *Figures 4a-b*, tie-up templates are substituted for each square of our 4-block profile tie-up. The set of templates is then placed in the pattern section of the treadle tie-up. The tie-up in *4a* produces floats in the pattern blocks, the tie-up in *4b* produces floats in the background blocks. Either tie-up can be used and the cloth reversed if the opposite interlacements are desired for pattern/background. An advantage to *4b* is that fewer shafts are raised. Note that eight pattern treadles are required for a four block profile. Six blocks would require 12 pattern treadles on an 8-shaft loom. When there are not enough treadles to execute a full tie-up, skeleton tie-ups are used instead.

To weave with the skeleton tie-ups in *Figures 4c* and *4d*, for example, depress treadles 3 *and* 5 to place the pattern-weft pick in the same shed that is formed by treadle 3 in *Figure 4a*. For the pattern pick corresponding to treadle 4 in *4a*, depress both treadles 4 and 5. Your tie-down foot and your tabby foot will learn their roles and require little thought from you!

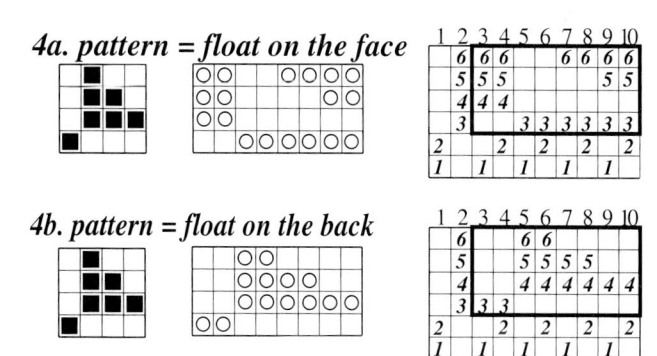

4a. pattern = float on the face

4b. pattern = float on the back

4c. skeleton tie-ups for jack looms

4d. skeleton tie-ups for countermarch looms, see pp. 10-11.

Summer and Winter Keys

Variations in summer and winter tie-down lifting orders: upper left 1-2-1-2; upper right 1-2-2-1, lower left 1-1-1-1; lower right 2-1-1-2.

Step 6. Substitute treadling units for profile treadling-draft squares.

Step 5. Substitute threading units for profile-draft squares.

EXTENDED SUMMER AND WINTER UNITS

Look again at 'Keys to Block Weaves,' pp. 26-27. Threadings with a ratio of tie-down ends (see bold type in 'Keys') to pattern ends of 1:2, 1:3, 1:4 (or more) are close summer and winter relatives. In all the first tie-down end is placed at the beginning of the first half of the unit, and the second tie-down end at the beginning of the second half.

When the tie-down ends are raised in alternation for the pattern-weft pick and the ground cloth is plain weave, the interlacement is identical to summer and winter except that the tie-down ends are farther apart and the pattern-weft float therefore longer. Unfortunately, adding threads between the tie-down ends requires an additional pattern shaft for each block in order to form plain weave sheds.

These members of the summer and winter family are called 'tied beiderwand' in some sources. Beiderwand, however, as we'll see in Chapter 11, is a double weave, not a tied unit weave.

To derive a thread-by-thread draft for extended summer and winter follow the same steps as for summer and winter except: *a)* substitute the extended threading unit for squares in the profile threading draft such as the 1:2 unit in **Step 2**, p. 81, and *b)* use tie-up templates with two pattern shafts per block as in **Step 3**.

Select the ratio of tie-down ends to pattern ends that provides a suitable float length for the design, materials, and intended use of the fabric.

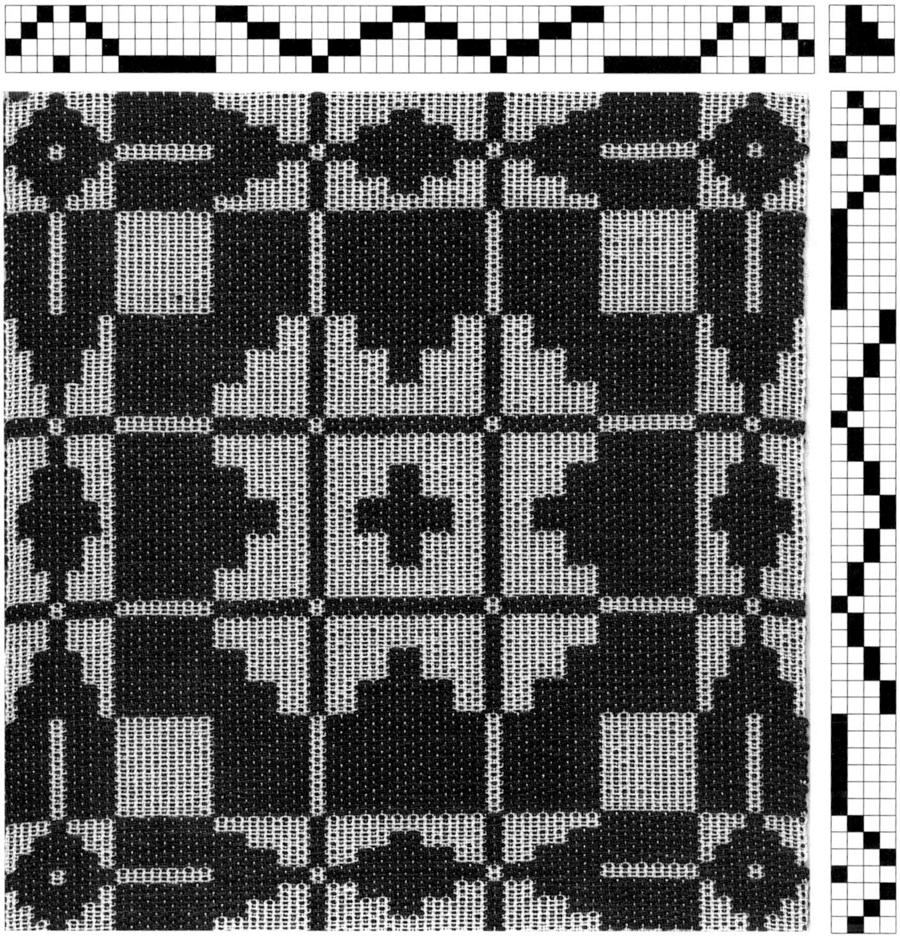

Keys for Extended Summer and Winter

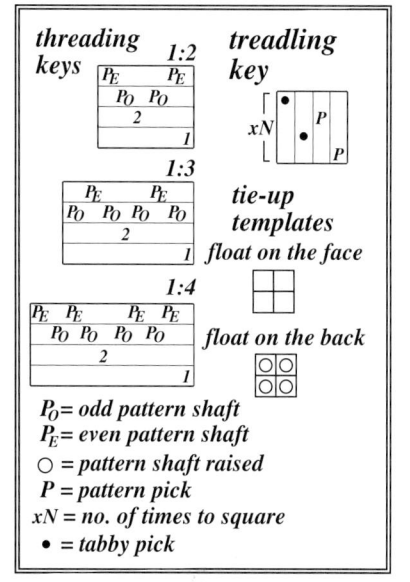

threading keys

1:2

P_E	P_E
P_O	P_O
2	
	1

1:3

P_E		P_E	
P_O	P_O	P_O	P_O
2			
			1

1:4

P_E	P_E		P_E	P_E
P_O	P_O		P_O	P_O
2				
				1

treadling key

xN [• P •] P

tie-up templates
float on the face
float on the back

P_O = odd pattern shaft
P_E = even pattern shaft
○ = pattern shaft raised
P = pattern pick
xN = no. of times to square
• = tabby pick

1:2 summer and winter

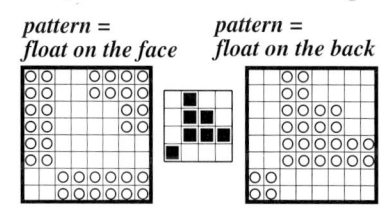

Step 1. Draft two blocks.

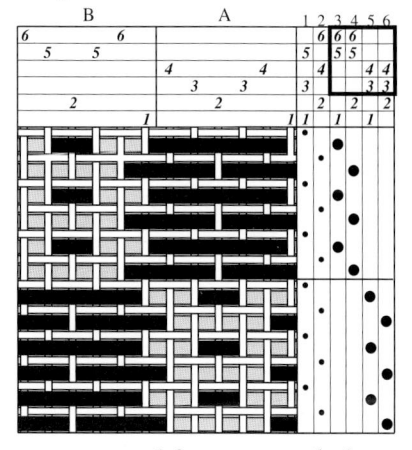

1:2 summer and winter

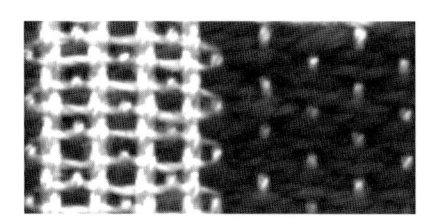

1:2 summer and winter

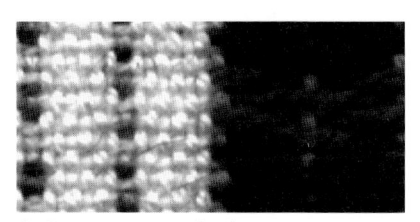

1:6 summer and winter

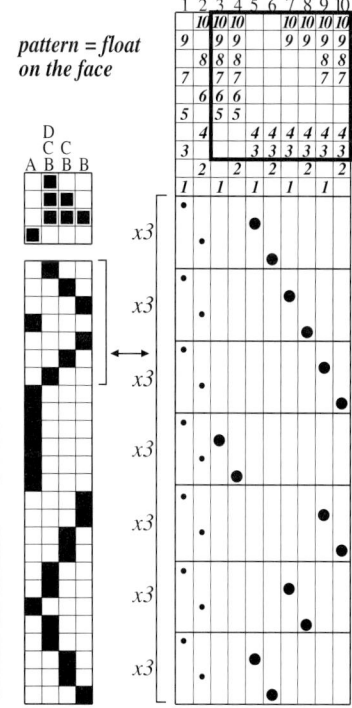

Step 2. Substitute threading units for profile squares.

Step 3. Derive the tie-up.

pattern = float on the face

pattern = float on the back

Step 4. Substitute treadling units for profile squares.

pattern = float on the face

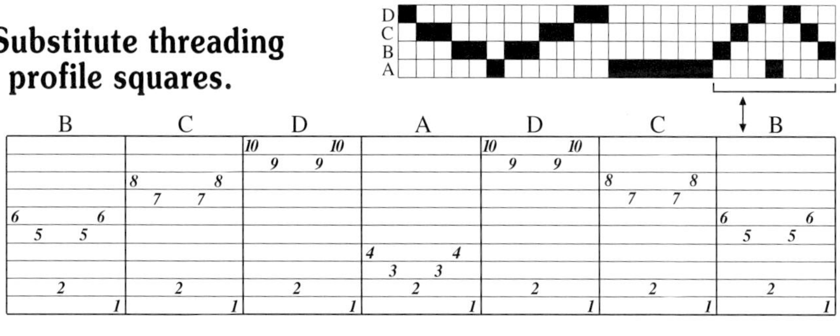

OTHER TWO-TIE UNIT WEAVES

Changing the lifting orders of the tie-down ends or placing them in different positions in the threading unit creates new textures. 'Half dukagang' (*7*) uses the same threading as in **Step 1**, p. 81, but tie-down shaft 1 is raised and 2 lowered for all pattern picks.

'Landes Hybrid' is also threaded with the same units as extended summer and winter (see *9*), but one tie-down shaft is raised for all the pattern picks in the first half of the treadling unit and the other tie-down shaft is raised for all the pattern picks in the second half of the treadling unit (*10a*).

The two tie-down ends appear at the beginning of each threading unit in the 'paired-tie' drafts in *8a-b*; in *8a* they are raised in alternate order, in *8b* shaft 1 is raised and 2 lowered for all pattern picks.

'Landes Hybrid' 1:5

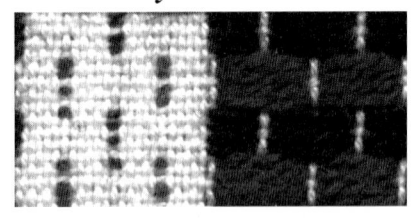

9. 'Landes Hybrid' 1:2

'Landes Hybrid' Keys

threading keys

P_O = odd pattern shaft
P_E = even pattern shaft
P = pattern pick
O = pattern shaft raised

tie-up templates
float on the face
float on the back

treadling key

xN = no. of times to square
• = tabby pick

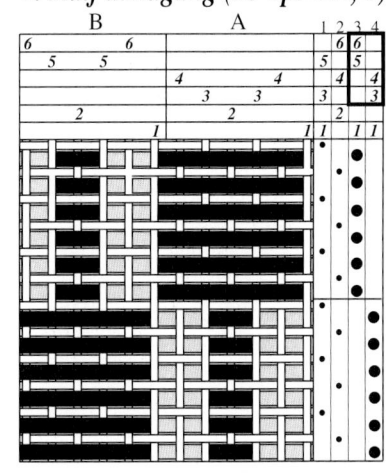

8a. Paired-tie weave (tie-up 10b)

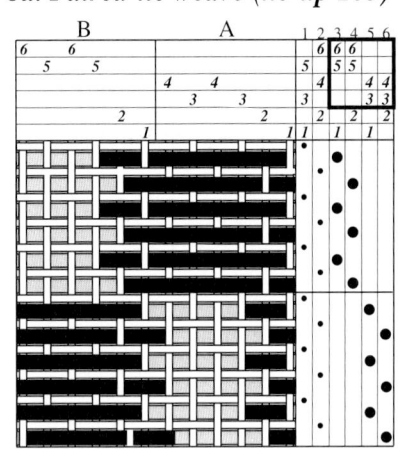

8b. Paired-tie weave (tie-up 10c)

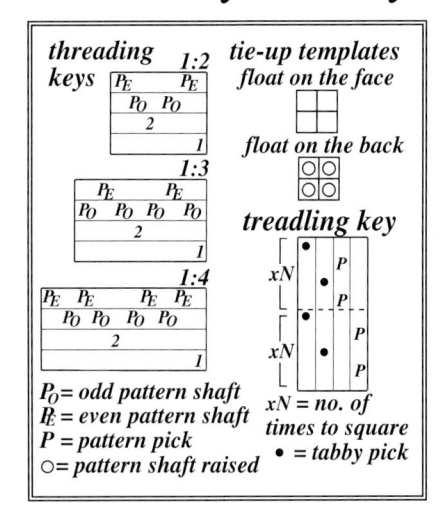

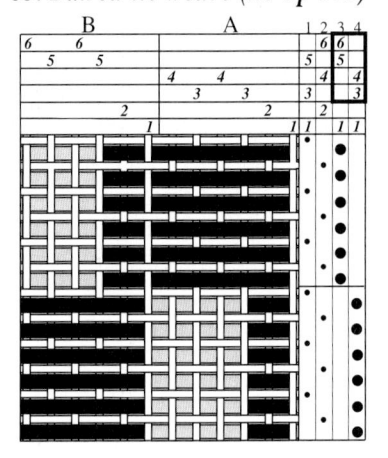

7. Half dukagang (tie-ups 10c, d)

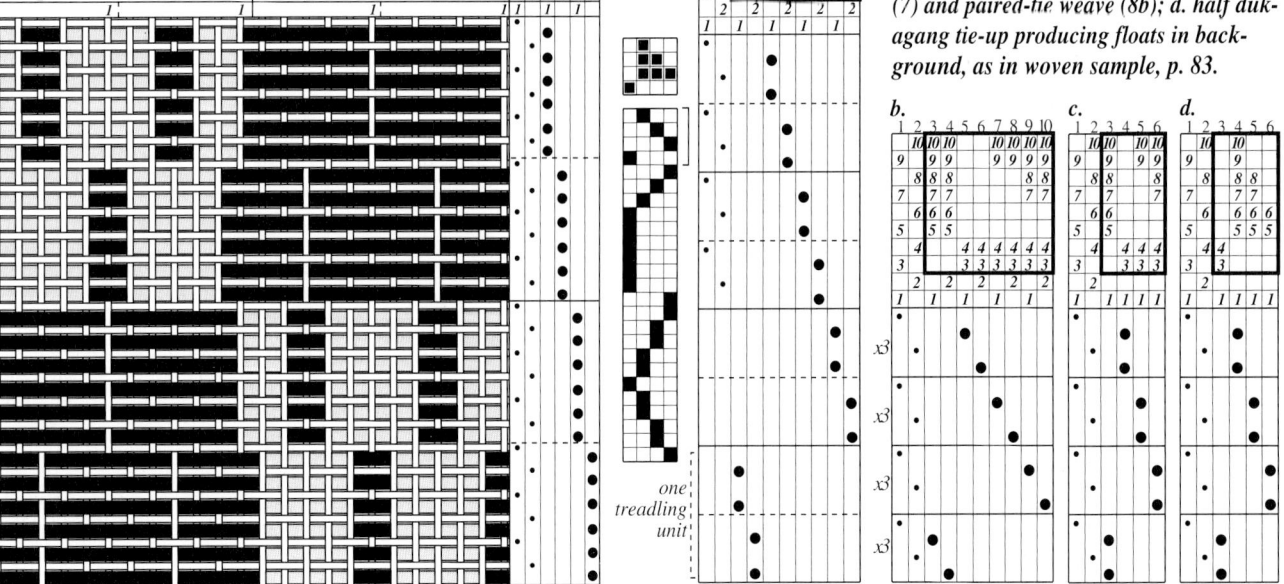

10. 2-tie treadling variations

a. Landes hybrid: square each half-unit before changing pattern treadles. For b-d repeat treadling units 3x or until square:
b. Paired tie weave (8a); c. half dukagang (7) and paired-tie weave (8b); d. half dukagang tie-up producing floats in background, as in woven sample, p. 83.

pattern = float on the face

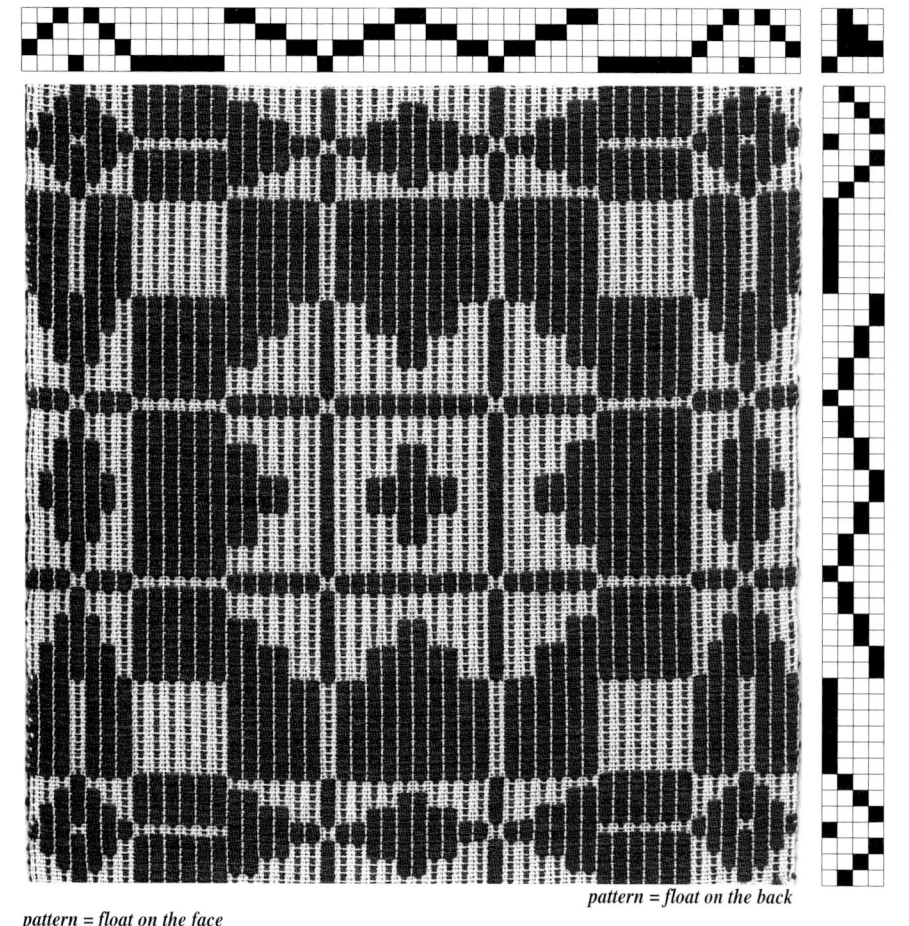

pattern = float on the back

'Half Dukagang' Keys

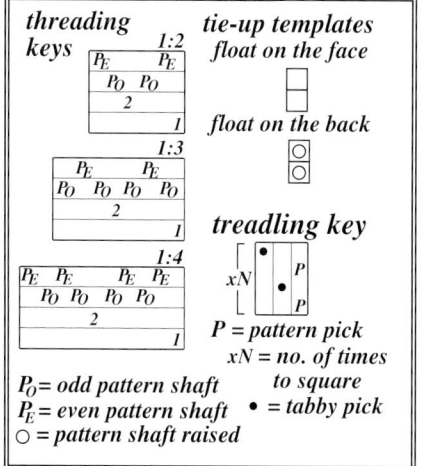

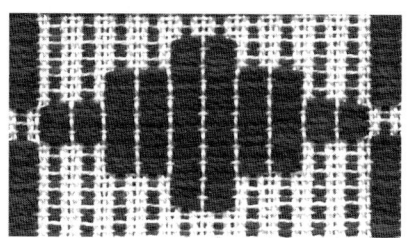

threading keys

1:2
P_E		P_E	
P_O		P_O	
	2		
			1

1:3
P_E			P_E		
P_O	P_O		P_O	P_O	
		2			
					1

1:4
P_E		P_E		P_E		P_E	
P_O	P_O	P_O	P_O				
			2				
							1

tie-up templates
float on the face

float on the back

treadling key

xN — with • and P marks
P = pattern pick
xN = no. of times to square
• = tabby pick

P_O = odd pattern shaft
P_E = even pattern shaft
○ = pattern shaft raised

Keys for 'Paired-tie' Weaves

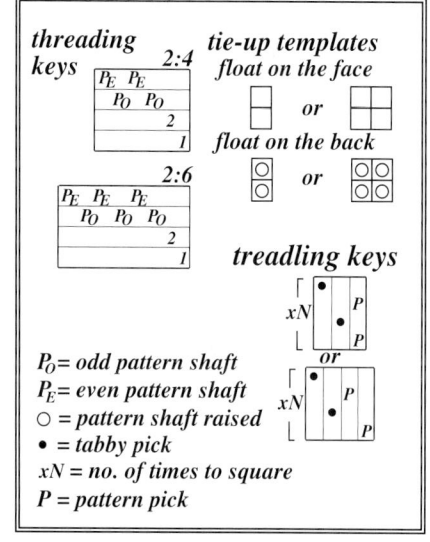

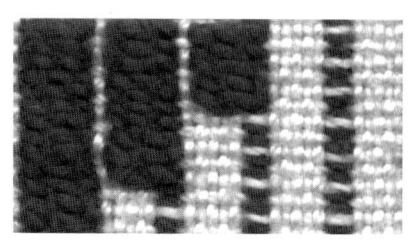

threading keys

2:4
P_E		P_E	
P_O	P_O		
	2		
			1

2:6
P_E		P_E		P_E	
P_O	P_O	P_O			
		2			
					1

tie-up templates
float on the face or
float on the back or

treadling keys

xN — P, P
or
xN — P, P

P_O = odd pattern shaft
P_E = even pattern shaft
○ = pattern shaft raised
• = tabby pick
xN = no. of times to square
P = pattern pick

2:4 paired-tie weave

83

TIED OVERSHOT

Also called star and diamond weave, this special two-tie unit weave forms halftones very like the halftones in overshot.

The threading order

The 2-tie unit weaves we've examined so far vary the summer and winter unit by *a)* extending its length; *b)* changing the position of the tie-down ends in the threading unit; and/or *c)* changing the lifting order of the tie-down ends in the treadling unit. Two-tie overshot extends the summer and winter unit in a fourth way, by repeating the pair of ends — tie-down and pattern — within each half-unit. The threading in **Figure 11a** is sometimes called 'even-tied' overshot because there is an even number of ends in the half-unit, and the threading in **Figure 11b** 'uneven' tied overshot because there is an uneven number of ends in the half-unit. Half-units are marked by dashed lines and full units by solid lines in the threading drafts.

The treadling order

The basic principles of the interlacement are the same as for other 2-tie weaves. All of the ends in the unit weave the ground cloth. The tie-down ends are raised and lowered in a designated order to tie the floats. The pattern shafts are raised or lowered so that the float appears on the back or the face of the cloth respectively. In tied overshot, one of the tie-down ends is raised for all of the picks in one half-unit of treadling and the other is raised for all of the picks in the second half to form overshot-like halftones.

Examine the drafts in **Figures 11a** and **11b**. Plain weave sheds in **11a** are formed by tie shafts against pattern shafts and in **11b** by even shafts against odd shafts. For the pattern-weft picks in the first half-unit (*a* in both drafts), tie-down ends on shaft 1 are raised and tie-down ends on shaft 2 are down. Pattern ends on shaft 3 are down so that the pattern weft passes over them, and pattern ends on 4, 5, and 6 are raised so that the pattern weft passes under them. A halftone forms in C, since tie shaft 2 is down and pattern shaft 5 is up.

In the second half-unit (*b*), shaft 2 is up and shaft 1 is down. A halftone forms in D where tie-down ends are down and pattern ends up *and* in A where tie-down ends are up and pattern ends down. In fact, halftones automatically appear in alternate blocks both in areas where pattern shafts are down (usually considered the pattern areas) and in areas where pattern shafts are up (usually considered the background areas) because of the alternately raised and lowered tie-down ends.

11a. Even 2-tie overshot: 6-thread half-unit

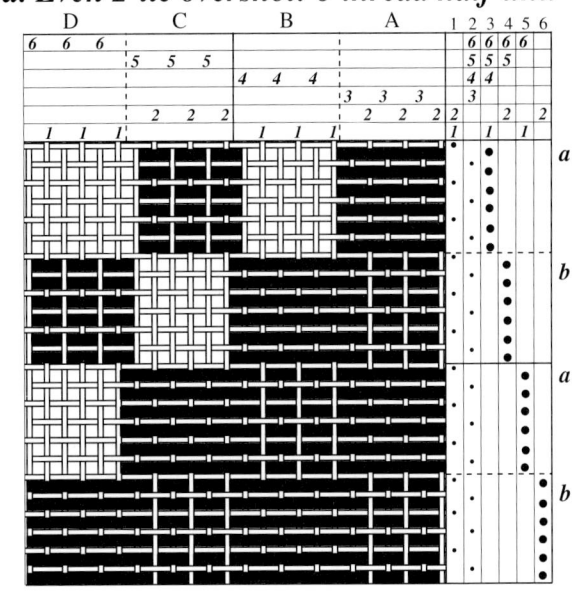

In **11a** and **11b** each half-unit forms a separate block (a float passes either over or under the *half* unit to form pattern or background). As in huck lace, one pattern shaft provides one block when blocks are threaded in straight or point order. When using a profile draft, however, a full unit must be substituted for each square in the profile threading, since both tie shafts must alternate regularly in the threading to guarantee the regular tying of the pattern-weft float.

A full unit of uneven-tied overshot requires two pattern shafts in order to form the plain weave ground sheds (A = 3-2-3-2-3-4-1-4-1-4 rather than 3-2-3-2-3-3-1-3-1-3), but a full unit of 'even-tied' overshot can be threaded with only one pattern shaft: 2-3-2-3-2-3-1-3-1-3-1-3. Even-tied overshot produces some irregularities that slightly offset its shaft efficiency, and both structures have design limitations when used with profile drafts.

11b. Uneven 2-tie overshot: 5-thread half-unit

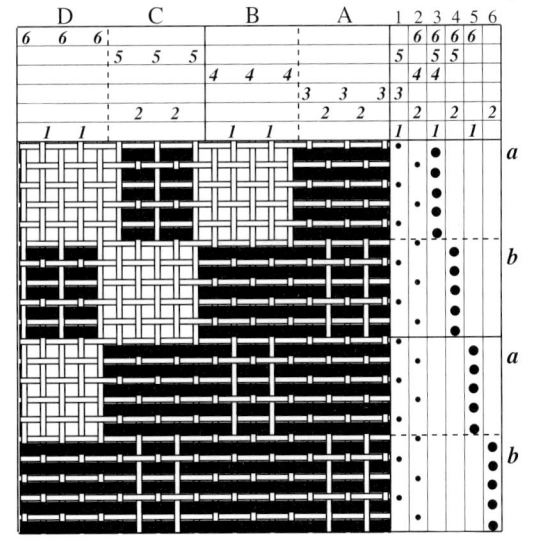

84

12. Half-units with an even number of ends show 2-thread incidental floats (* in b)

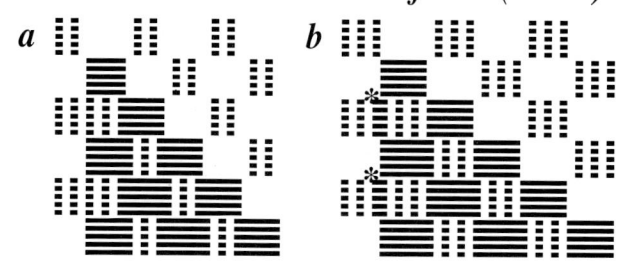

a *b*

13. Tie-shaft order affects design outlines

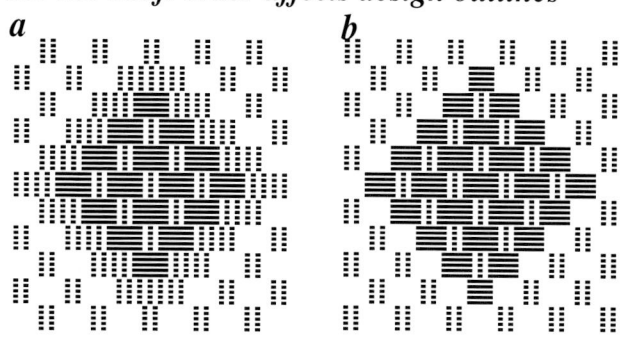

a *b*

Design considerations

In the pattern area, alternating halftones are produced by tie shafts that are up and pattern shafts that are down. In the background area, alternating halftones are produced by tie shafts that are down and pattern shafts that are up. Because halftones alternate throughout, only motifs that progress along a diagonal show well-defined outlines, hence stars and diamonds. Even-tied overshot has the additional drawback of producing 2-thread skips along the straight edges of one side of a motif, where a pattern shaft is down in the pattern area and an adjacent tie shaft is down in the background area (marked with * in *Figure 12b*).

An important factor influencing the outlines of motifs is the lifting order of the tie shafts, i.e., *which* tie shaft is lifted with *which* pattern shaft for the treadling half-unit. For example, a treadling half-unit with pattern shaft 3 down and tie shaft 2 down produces a float in the 3-2-3-2-3 threading half-unit. If the sequence begins with tie-shaft 1 down and 2 up, the same half-unit produces a halftone. Designs that progress along a diagonal can show outlines of floats or of halftones. *Figures 13a-b* show diamond motifs woven on the same uneven-tied threading of six blocks arranged in a point. The center block is threaded 8-1-8-1-8. If the diamond begins with shaft 8 down to form pattern but tie-shaft 1 is up, a halftone appears in the 8-1-8-1-8 block. At the same time halftones also appear in the adjacent 7-2-7-2-7 blocks since tie-shaft 2 is down and pattern shaft 7 is up to form background; see *13a*. If the same sequence begins with tie-shaft 1 and shaft 8 down (and 2 and 7 up), a pattern-weft float covers the 8-1-8-1-8 block but floats on the back in 7-2-7-2-7, as in *13b*.

Profile draft limitations

As a true unit weave, tied overshot's limitations are aesthetic not structural. Choose from four options when threading from a profile draft. For each square substitute: a) full units of uneven-tied overshot (3-2-3-2-3-4-1-4-1-4), as in *14a*; b) full units of 'even-tied' overshot, (2-3-2-3-2-3-1-3-1-3-1-3) *14b*; c) full units of uneven-tied overshot, subtracting or adding a half-unit at turning blocks to provide symmetry, *14c*; or d) full units of even-tied overshot, subtracting or adding a half-unit at turning blocks to provide symmetry, *14d*. When using profile drafts with single blocks threaded in isolation, plan to balance the draft for the most successful design.

14a. Uneven-tied: unit form (unbalanced)

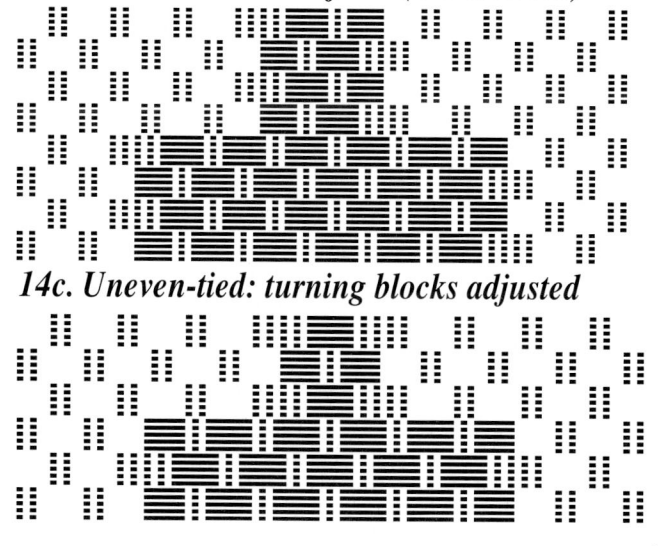

14b. Even-tied: unit form (unbalanced)

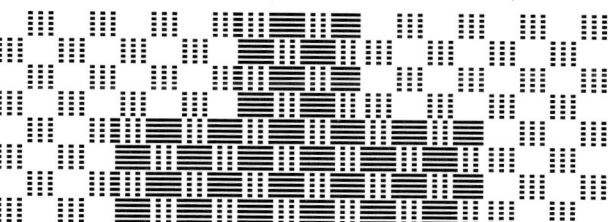

14c. Uneven-tied: turning blocks adjusted

14d. Even-tied: turning blocks adjusted

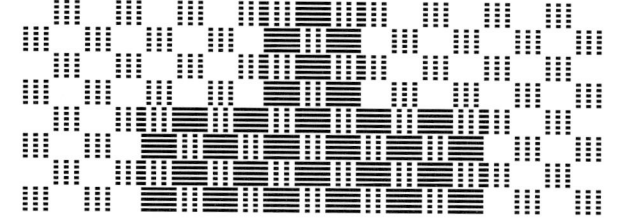

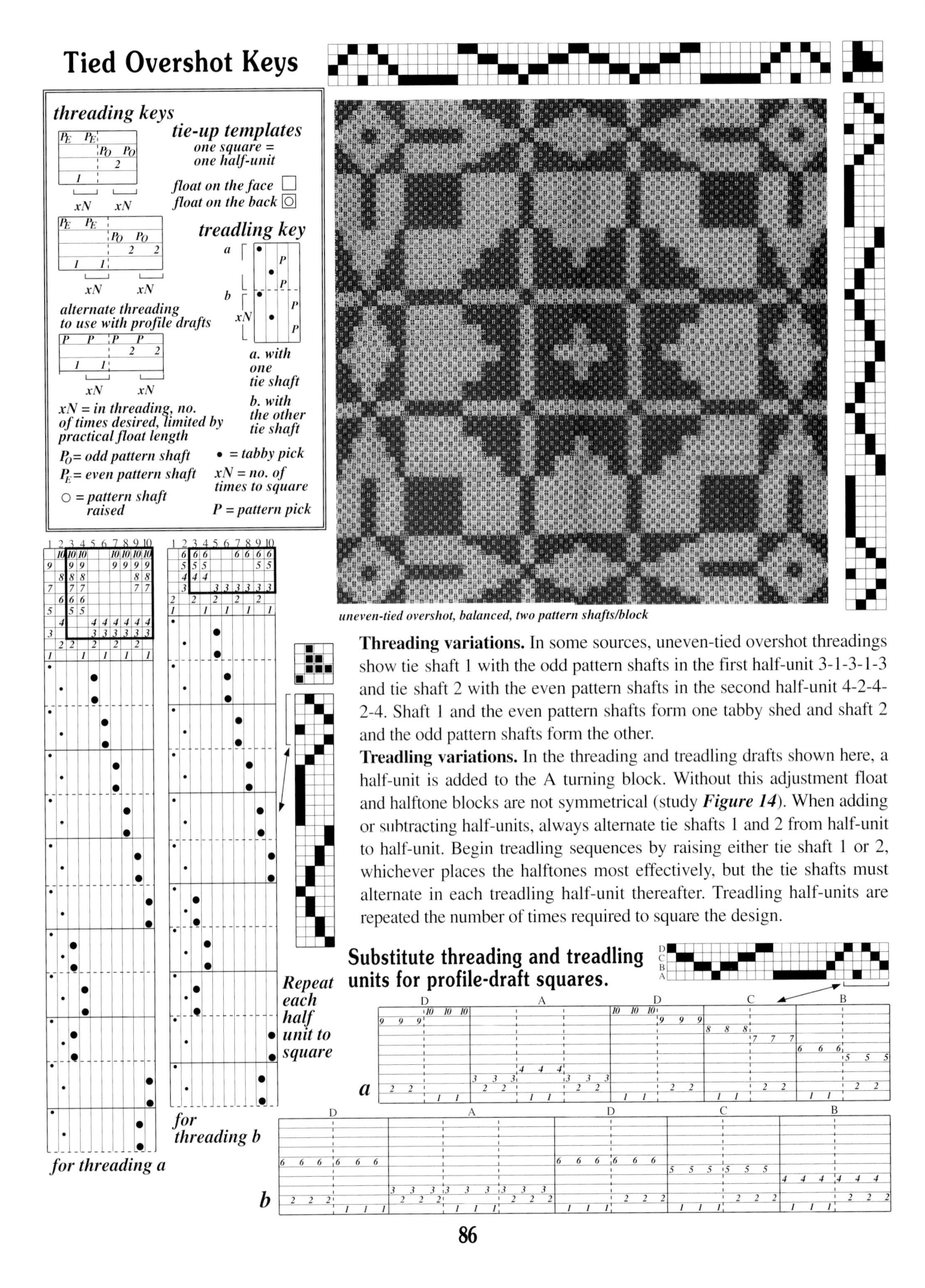

Tied Overshot Keys

threading keys

tie-up templates
one square = one half-unit

float on the face □
float on the back ◯

treadling key

a. with one tie shaft
b. with the other tie shaft

alternate threading to use with profile drafts

xN = in threading, no. of times desired, limited by practical float length

P_O = odd pattern shaft
P_E = even pattern shaft
◯ = pattern shaft raised

• = tabby pick
xN = no. of times to square
P = pattern pick

uneven-tied overshot, balanced, two pattern shafts/block

Threading variations. In some sources, uneven-tied overshot threadings show tie shaft 1 with the odd pattern shafts in the first half-unit 3-1-3-1-3 and tie shaft 2 with the even pattern shafts in the second half-unit 4-2-4-2-4. Shaft 1 and the even pattern shafts form one tabby shed and shaft 2 and the odd pattern shafts form the other.

Treadling variations. In the threading and treadling drafts shown here, a half-unit is added to the A turning block. Without this adjustment float and halftone blocks are not symmetrical (study *Figure 14*). When adding or subtracting half-units, always alternate tie shafts 1 and 2 from half-unit to half-unit. Begin treadling sequences by raising either tie shaft 1 or 2, whichever places the halftones most effectively, but the tie shafts must alternate in each treadling half-unit thereafter. Treadling half-units are repeated the number of times required to square the design.

Repeat each half unit to square

for threading a
for threading b

Substitute threading and treadling units for profile-draft squares.

a

b

15a. Tied overshot tie-ups for profile draft, p. 86; one unit = one block

**uneven-tied overshot
two pattern shafts/block**

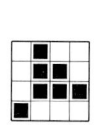

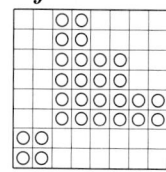

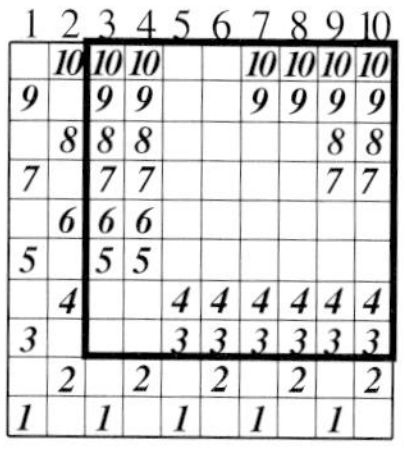

tie-down ends can be raised in opposite order

**even-tied overshot
one pattern shaft/block**

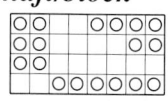

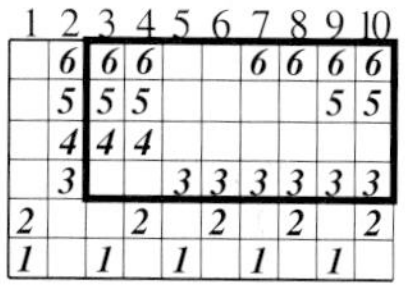

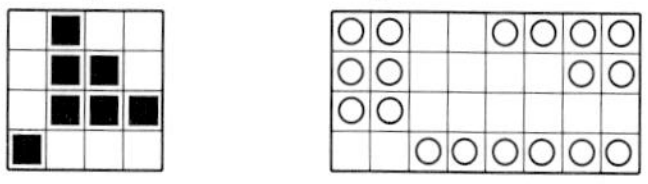

15b. Sample tie-ups for blocks threaded in a point; one half-unit = one block

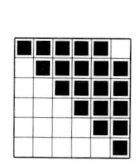

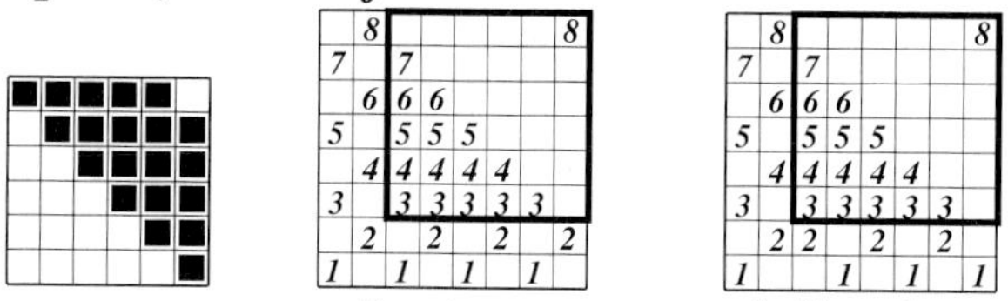

float in outline blocks

halftone in outline blocks

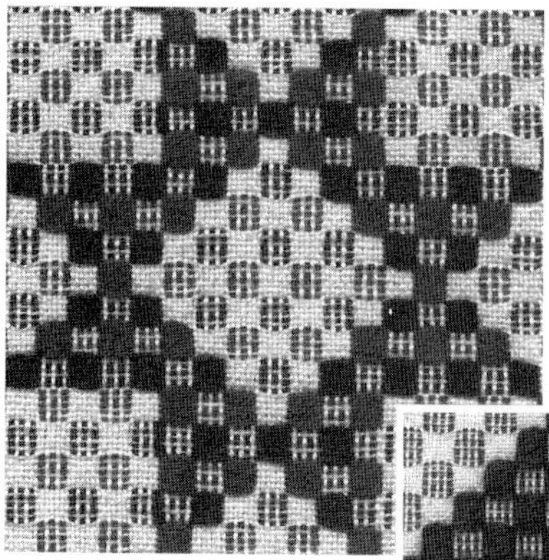

a. even-tied overshot
Blocks are threaded in a point; all blocks are the same size; 2-thread skips show on the left edge of the motif; 10 blocks (9 for star and 1 background, not shown); requires 12 shafts.

b. even-tied overshot
6 blocks; straight/point order; two block sizes (4, 8 threads); 2-thread skips; 8 shafts; tie-up in **15b**.

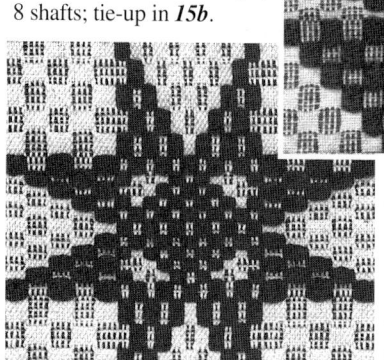

c. uneven-tied overshot
12 blocks threaded in straight and point order (background block not shown); two block sizes (5 and 9 threads); no skips; requires 14 shafts.

16. 3-tie and 4-tie units

a. half satin

b. Bergman

c. Quigley: tie-down ends threaded in straight order

d. Quigley: tie-down ends in point order

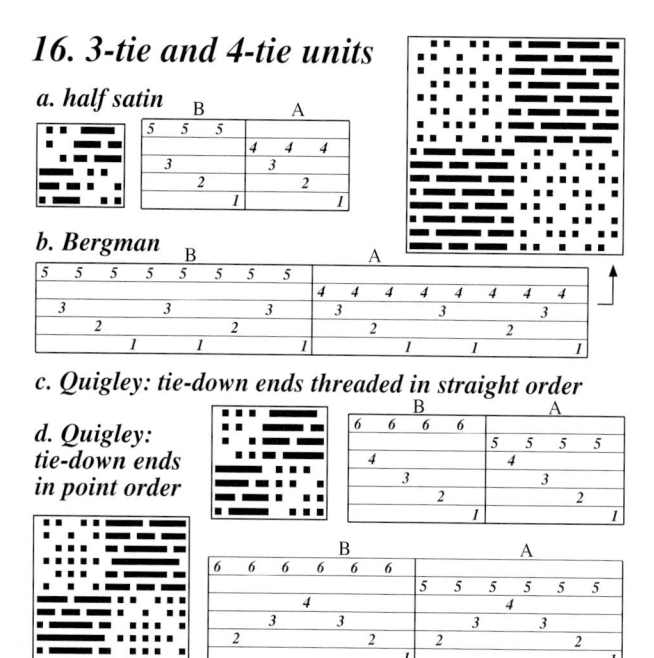

MORE THAN TWO TIES

Adding tie-down ends to the 2-tie threading unit increases the length of the pattern-weft float and provides new options for the threading and lifting orders of the tie-down ends; see **Figure 16**. As in summer and winter, tie-down ends alternate with pattern ends in the threading. Since tabby can therefore be formed by raising tie-down shafts against pattern shafts, only one pattern shaft is required for each block. Other variations of 3- and 4-tie threading orders than those given here are also possible. Lifting orders of tie-down ends can vary from 1/2, 1/3, 2/2 straight, point, broken, and rosepath twill orders. If five shafts are used for tie-down ends, they can be raised in satin order for the pattern picks (1-3-5-2-4). Tie-up templates and weaving principles for units with more than two ties are the same as for summer and winter.

As units become longer, minimum areas of pattern increase if one unit = one block. To reduce design size, blocks can be smaller than units. In **Figure 17**, one block equals a half-unit of Bergman, but any fraction can be designated. Whatever the threading and treadling orders of the pattern ends, always maintain the designated threading and lifting order of the tie-down ends.

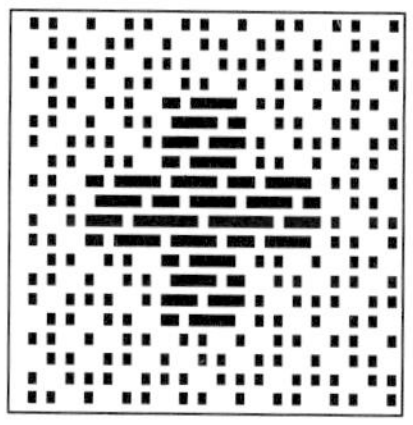

17. Bergman half-units

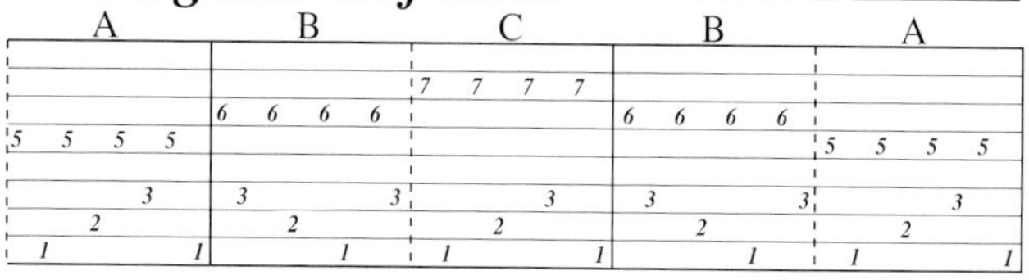

Keys for 3-tie Weaves

threading keys

a., b., c.

treadling keys

a., b., c.

*Tabby picks always alternate; next sequence begins with opposite tabby shed.

Treadling sequences show structural picks. Numbers of picks required to square the blocks vary, depending on setts and materials.

tie-up templates:
pattern shafts — tie shafts
- float on the face
- float on the back
- O = pattern shaft raised
- P = pattern pick   • = tabby pick

half satin

Bergman

Substitute treadling units.

full tie-up, half satin

skeleton tie-up

Derive the tie-up.

- float on the face
- float on the back
- tie-down ends

full tie-up   *skeleton tie-up*

To derive a skeleton tie-up for 3-tie and 4-tie weaves: use one treadle for each of the tie-shaft lifts, and one treadle for each pattern-shaft combination. To weave a pattern pick, depress one tie-down treadle and one pattern treadle together.

Substitute threading units.

half satin   C D A D C B

Bergman   C D A D C B

88

Keys for 4-tie Weaves

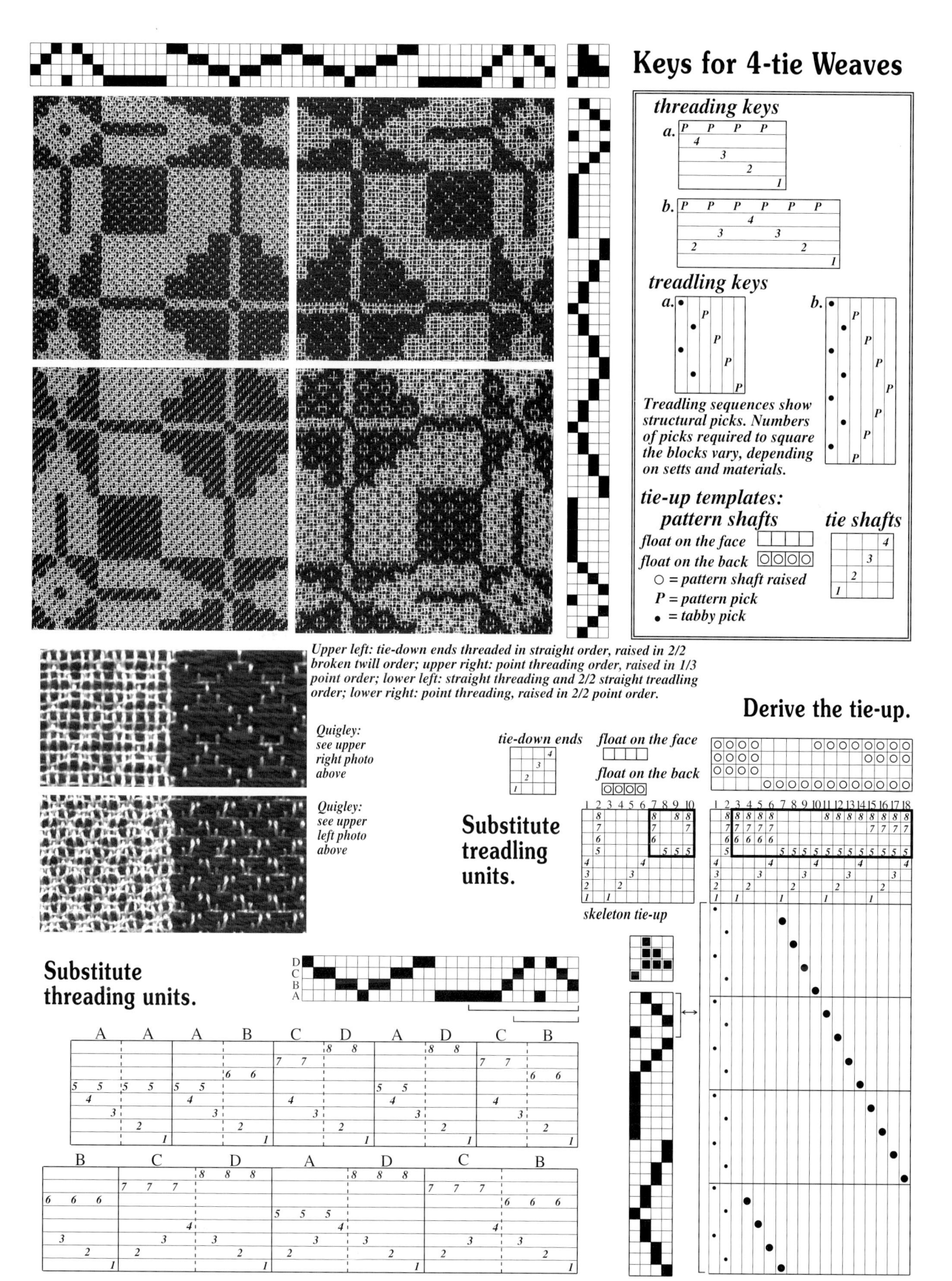

threading keys

treadling keys

Treadling sequences show structural picks. Numbers of picks required to square the blocks vary, depending on setts and materials.

tie-up templates: pattern shafts   **tie shafts**

float on the face
float on the back
○ = pattern shaft raised
P = pattern pick
• = tabby pick

Upper left: tie-down ends threaded in straight order, raised in 2/2 broken twill order; upper right: point threading order, raised in 1/3 point order; lower left: straight threading and 2/2 straight treadling order; lower right: point threading, raised in 2/2 point order.

Quigley: see upper right photo above

Quigley: see upper left photo above

tie-down ends   float on the face
float on the back

Substitute treadling units.

skeleton tie-up

Derive the tie-up.

Substitute threading units.

89

Double Summer and Winter Keys

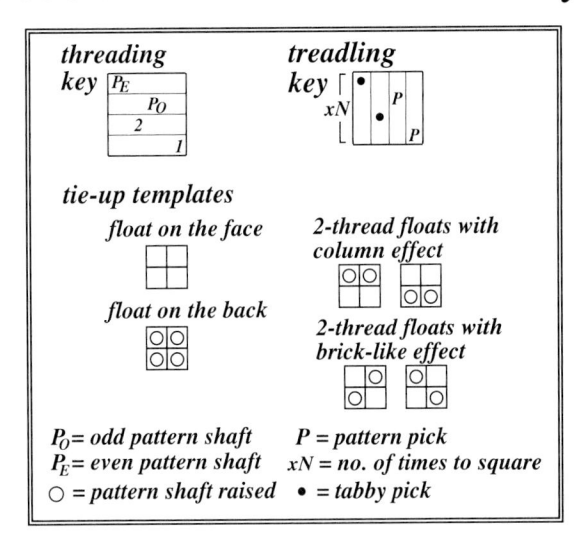

threading key
P_E
P_O
2
1

treadling key
xN
•
P
•
P

tie-up templates

float on the face — 2-thread floats with column effect

float on the back — 2-thread floats with brick-like effect

P_O = odd pattern shaft
P_E = even pattern shaft
○ = pattern shaft raised
P = pattern pick
xN = no. of times to square
• = tabby pick

18. Double summer and winter: four textures

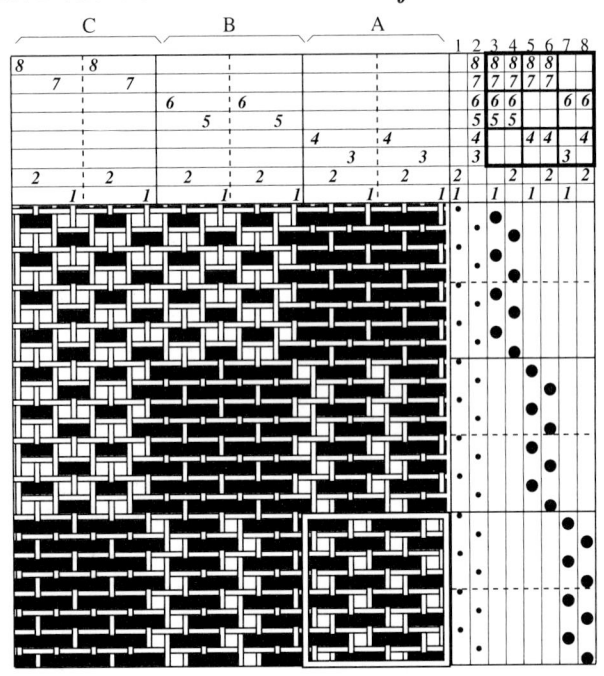

Dashed lines indicate units; solid lines indicate blocks.

A dark tabby weft emphasizes the vertical lines produced by the 2-thread pattern-weft floats in this double summer and winter sample.

DOUBLE TWO-TIE UNIT WEAVE

The 'double' in 'double two-tie unit weave' indicates a two-tie unit weave that requires *two* pattern shafts rather than *one* per block. Although there are many two-tie threading systems that fit this description, only one of them is given the name 'double two-tie unit weave' — A = 1-3-2-4, B = 1-5-2-6, C = 1-7-2-8, etc. — probably because the same threading was first known as 'double summer and winter.'

'Double Two-tie' as a tied unit weave

When used as a tied unit weave, each double two-tie unit can produce either of the two interlacements characteristic of summer and winter, or, when one pattern shaft in the unit is up and the other down for the pattern picks, any of several additional textures with 2-thread floats. Weavers appreciate the different blends of colors and fibers that these varied textures make possible. The variety provides little advantage when used with profile drafts, however, since only two interlacements are usually effective in portraying the design.

Templates for the pattern section of a double summer and winter tie-up are given in 'Keys.' Two units each of Blocks A, B, and C are drafted in *Figure 18*. The drawdown shows four different interlacements. Compare *Figure 18* with the woven sample. The sample does not include the interlacement in Block A that is framed in *Figure 18*.

Double two-tie twill blocks

'Double two-tie unit weave' is rarely used as a tied unit weave in spite of its name. Instead, this versatile threading system is used much more often to a) create fancy twills, or b) produce different interlacements in different blocks at the same time.

Figure 19 shows two units of Block A weaving 2/2 twill. The tie-up in *19a* produces a left twill; the tie-up in *19b* produces a right twill. Notice that only the order in which shafts 3 and 4 are raised (see gray squares in the drawups) affects the direction of the twill. Shafts 1 and 2 are raised in the same order (1-2-2-1) in both; their lifting order is called the 'base.' The lower tie-up template (black with white circles) represents the base. The upper template represents the lifting order of the pattern shafts within a 4-pick treadling unit. In double two-tie unit weaves, 'pattern' identifies the shafts that determine twill direction and distinguishes them from the base shafts, 1 and 2.

Right and left twills can also be produced with a 1-1-2-2 base, as in *Figure 20*. This is the most convenient base to use when designing double two tie twills.

19. 2/2 twills with a 1-2-2-1 base
drawup: left twill   drawup: right twill

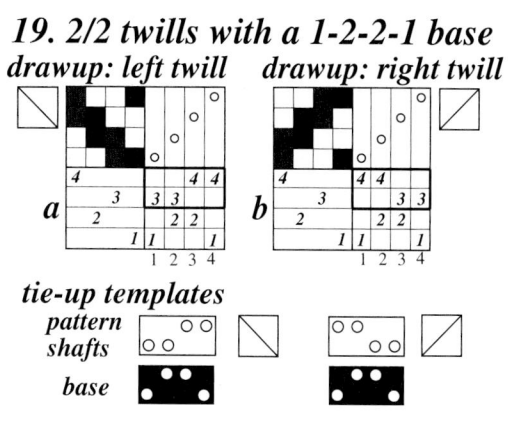

a   *b*

tie-up templates
pattern shafts
base

20. 2/2 twills with a 1-1-2-2 base
drawup: left twill   drawup: right twill

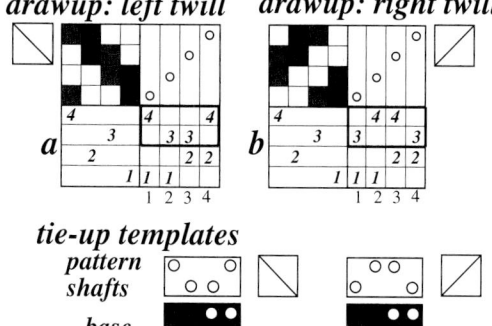

a   *b*

tie-up templates
pattern shafts
base

When more than one block is threaded, a right twill or a left twill can appear in each block independently of the others. In *Figure 21*, a key is used to design twill directions in Blocks A, B, and C for two treadling units. The template for the pattern shafts, shaped like a smile for a left twill or an eyebrow for a right twill, is substituted in the tie-up for the corresponding pair of pattern shafts. In the first four picks, Block A produces right twill, and B and C left twills. Find the symbol indicating twill direction in the design key for each block in treadling section I. Then find the corresponding template in the tie-up. Read the rows in the design key horizontally and read the tie-up templates vertically.

21. Derive the tie-up for twill blocks.
Substitute pattern shaft tie-up templates for design key squares to derive the tie-up.

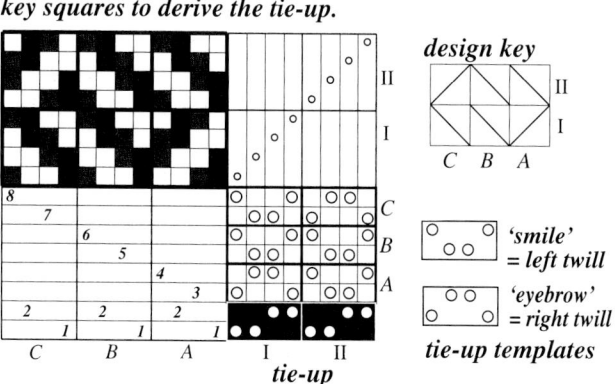

design key

'smile' = left twill
'eyebrow' = right twill
tie-up templates

tie-up

Keys for Double Two-tie Twill Blocks

Threading keys
a. Unit threadings: blocks produce right or left twills (or other structures) independently.

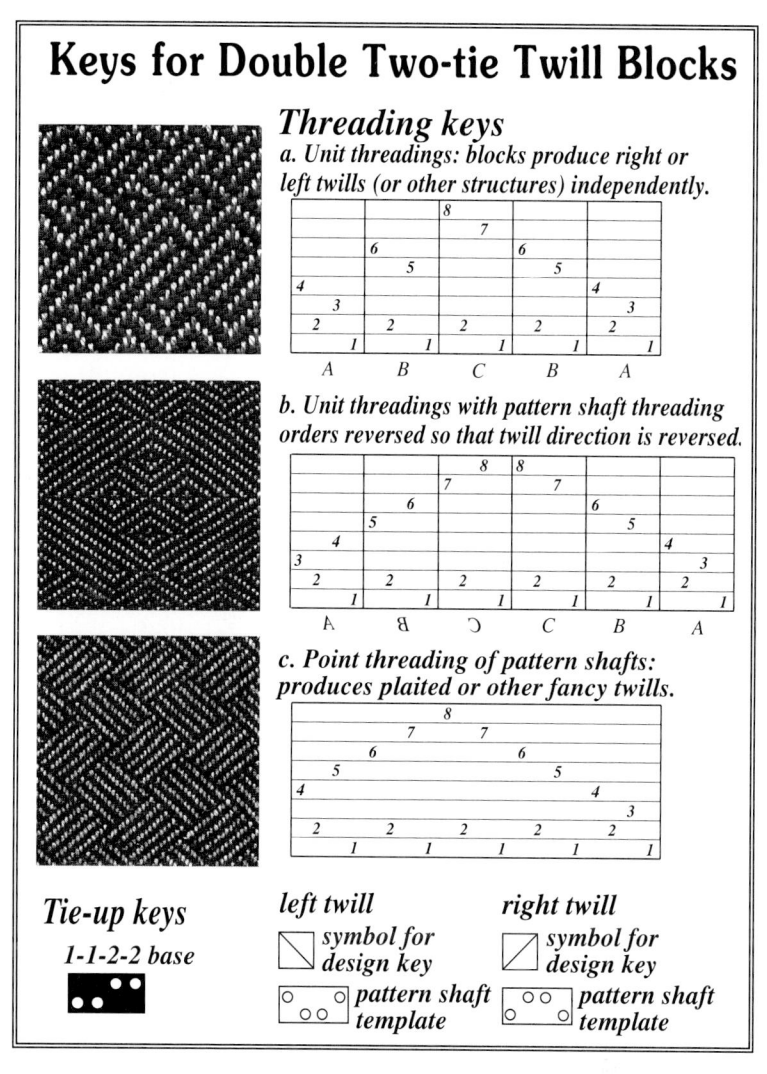

b. Unit threadings with pattern shaft threading orders reversed so that twill direction is reversed.

c. Point threading of pattern shafts: produces plaited or other fancy twills.

Tie-up keys
1-1-2-2 base

left twill — symbol for design key / pattern shaft template

right twill — symbol for design key / pattern shaft template

22. Design twill blocks with a design key.
Substitute pattern shaft tie-up templates for design key symbols to derive tie-ups.

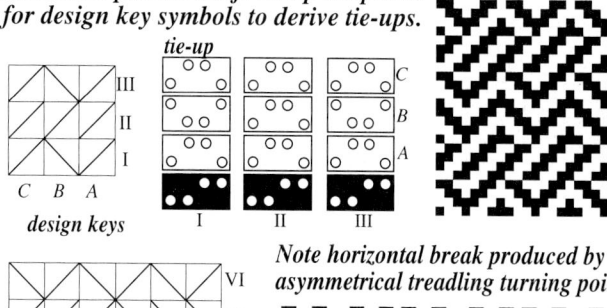

tie-up

design keys

Note horizontal break produced by asymmetrical treadling turning points.

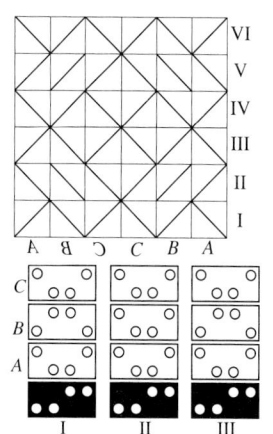

91

Design variations can be introduced in both threading and treadling orders. If the positions of the pattern shafts are reversed in a threading unit, twill direction is reversed. For example, if some units of Block A are threaded 1-4-2-3, instead of 1-3-2-4, any right twill in one unit is a left twill in the other and vice versa (compare threadings *a* and *b* in 'Keys,' p. 91). Design keys can be extended and varied vertically without limitation. A skeleton tie-up can provide all of the possible combinations of right and left twills for an 8-shaft unit threading.

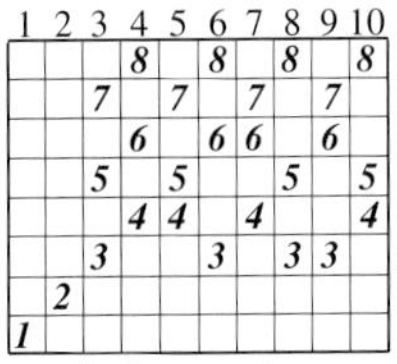

skeleton tie-up

Double two-tie plaited and other fancy twills

In the drafts produced with threadings *a* and *b* and the tie-up templates in 'Keys,' p. 91, changes in twill direction occur along vertical and horizontal lines between blocks. Changes can also be designed along diagonal lines to produce 'plaited' twills, using threading *c* in 'Keys' and the tie-up templates in **Figure 23**.

Examine the design key in **Figure 23**. Each square represents a half-unit of two warp threads and two weft threads. Black circles in the tie-up templates indicate the position *each pattern shaft* is tied in either a first half-unit *or* a second half-unit to produce a right twill or a left twill. One pattern shaft in a half-unit may be tied to weave twill in a different direction from the other pattern shaft. For example, to weave a left twill in a half-unit, the even pattern shaft (represented by a circle in the upper row of the template) is tied to the first treadle in the first half-unit or the last treadle in the second half-unit — its positions in the 'smile.' The odd pattern shaft (represented by a circle in the bottom row of the template) is tied to the second treadle in the first half-unit or the first treadle in the second half-unit — *its* positions in the 'smile.' The base for plaited-twill tie-ups is always 1-1-2-2. Compare the twill directions in the design key with the corresponding positions of the pattern shafts in the 12-treadle tie-up in **23**. Design possibilities abound, but since plaited twill tie-ups cannot be effectively abbreviated by skeleton tie-ups, a computer-aided dobby is almost a must.

Combining weave structures

With unit threadings, it is also possible for one block to produce a different weave structure from other blocks. The only limitation is that the base must be the same for all structures woven at the same time. **Figure 24** gives pattern shaft templates for structures that can be woven at the same time with several different bases.

23. Tie-up templates for plaited twills

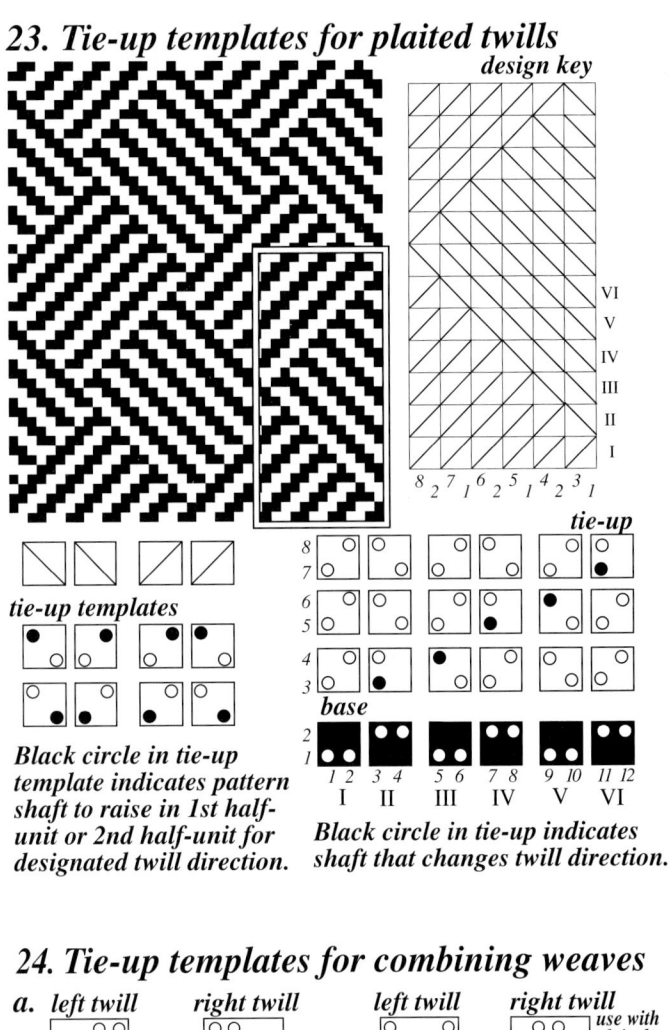

design key

tie-up templates

Black circle in tie-up template indicates pattern shaft to raise in 1st half-unit or 2nd half-unit for designated twill direction.

tie-up

base

Black circle in tie-up indicates shaft that changes twill direction.

24. Tie-up templates for combining weaves

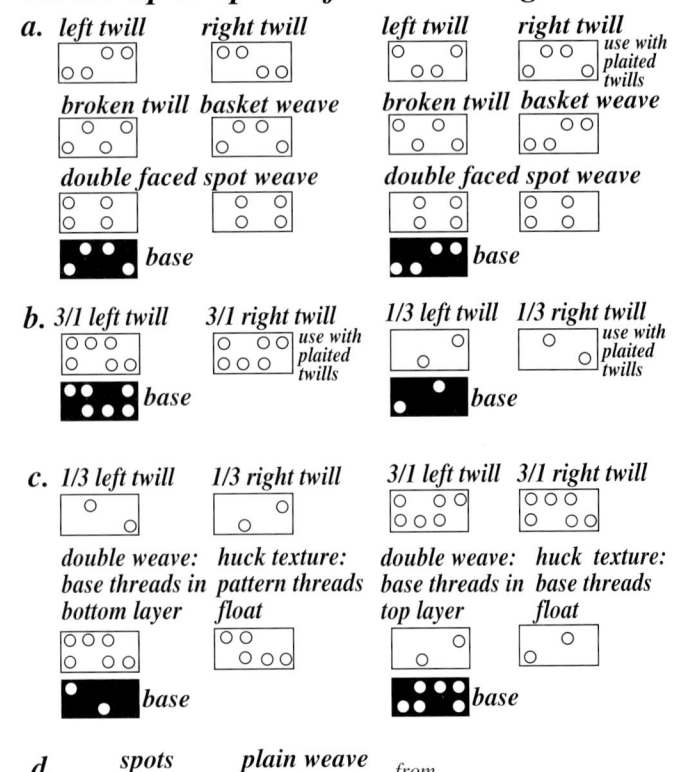

a. left twill   right twill   left twill   right twill *use with plaited twills*

broken twill   basket weave   broken twill   basket weave

double faced spot weave   double faced spot weave

base   base

b. 3/1 left twill   3/1 right twill *use with plaited twills*   1/3 left twill   1/3 right twill *use with plaited twills*

base   base

c. 1/3 left twill   1/3 right twill   3/1 left twill   3/1 right twill

double weave: base threads in bottom layer   huck texture: pattern threads float   double weave: base threads in top layer   huck texture: base threads float

base   base

d. spots   plain weave

base

from
Double Two-tie Unit Weaves
*Clotilde Barrett and Eunice Smith
Boulder, Colorado, 1983*

Lesson: Drafting Tied Unit Weaves

Tied unit weaves provide so many options they can be overwhelming. Once you see that most of them operate by the same simple and systematic principles, you'll find new freedom in choosing the one that's especially suited to your materials, fabric purpose, and loom. With finer materials, use higher ratios of pattern ends to tie-down ends for smoother textures in pattern and background. Practice drafting double two-tie twills with the special drawdown paper on p. 132. (See answers to exercises 1-4, p. 124.)

5-block profile draft

Derive the tie-up.

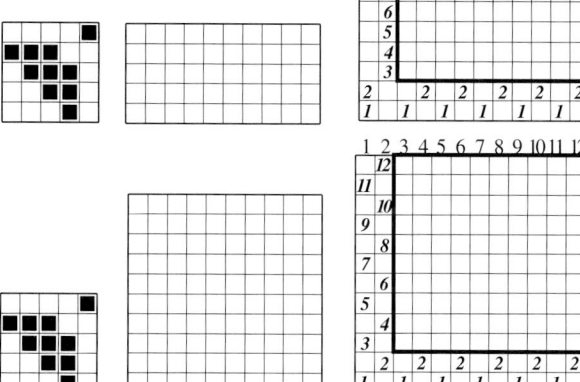

1. Fill in the templates for pattern = float; then write the full tie-ups. The upper tie-up is for summer and winter; the lower tie-up is for 2-tie unit weaves with two pattern shafts per block, such as extended summer and winter, paired-tie weaves, etc.

Substitute threading units or partial units as instructed for the first 12 squares in the 5-block profile threading draft.

2. 1:2 extended summer and winter, full units.
1-8-7-2-7-8 _____ _____

3. Quarter units of Bergman (each square on the profile threading draft represents two pattern ends and two tie-down ends):
1-6-3-6   2-8-1-8   3-8-1-8

4. Fill in the tie-up below for 'double two-tie' twill blocks (smile = left twill, eyebrow = right twill) and complete the drawup. The alternating 2-pick lifts of shafts 1 and 2 (the base) are already marked in the drawup.

Hint. Since numbers are easier to read than 'o's in the tie-up, use a separate piece of paper to draft the tie-up templates; then write shaft numbers in the exercise tie-up grid.

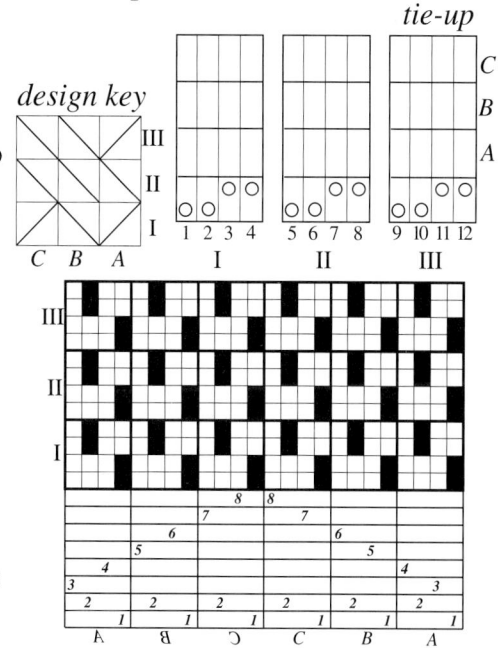

Double Weave: Words to Know

beiderwand: a lampas structure; see Chapter 11. The main and secondary weave structures are both plain weave. The ratio of secondary warp ends to main warp ends is 1:4; the ratio of secondary weft picks to main weft picks is 1:1. Two separate layers are formed in the areas where the main structure is on top. In traditional beiderwand, these areas are considered 'pattern.' In the background, the two structures are connected since the secondary weft floats over the main structure but interlaces underneath it with the secondary warp.

binder or binding warp: the secondary warp of lampas; see Chapter 11. The binder warp interlaces with the secondary (pattern) weft. 'Binding system' in some Scandinavian sources is synonymous with 'order of interlacement,' and in that context 'binder' refers to a warp thread that completes an interlacement.

compound sets of elements: two or more sets of weft threads or two or more sets of warp threads. The additional warp or weft set may be *supplementary* as in overshot and tied unit weaves or *complementary* as in Bedford cord and summer and winter polychrome, etc.

compound weaves: two or more weave structures (two separate warp-*and*-weft sets) that are connected in one of several ways to form one cloth.

double weave: a compound weave in which two sets of warp threads each weave with a respective set of weft threads. The two structures are usually connected to each other in one of several ways: *a)* the structures exchange layers from top to bottom or vice versa, *b)* the structures are 'stitched' together by warp threads or weft threads of one structure (or extra warp or weft threads) interlacing with weft threads or warp threads of the other; *c)* the warp of one structure interlaces with its weft on opposite sides of the other structure — or by a combination of these. 'Double weave' is also used to refer to the technique of weaving two layers even if they become a single structure after removed from the loom, as with fabrics woven 'double-width.'

patterned (layer-exchange) double weave: two equal and independent structures exchange layers across the width and length of the warp for the purpose of patterning; also called 'block double weave,' 'figured double weave,' or sometimes just 'double weave.' The fibers of one structure are usually a different color and/or material from the warp and weft of the other for strong contrast between pattern and background areas.

lampas: a double weave in which a main structure is patterned by the weft of a secondary structure. The two structures do not exchange layers. The main warp and weft can weave on the top (while the secondary structure weaves on the bottom), but only the secondary *weft* can pass above the main structure; the secondary *warp* always interlaces with the secondary weft beneath the main structure. Areas of free double cloth occur where the main structure is on top, or these areas can be stitched together for stability. The main and secondary structures can each be plain weave, twill, or satin. In most lampas fabrics other than beiderwand, areas where the secondary weft appears on the face of the cloth are considered the pattern areas; *synonym*, diasper, tissue.

matelassé: a double cloth with decorative stitching. Matelassé is distinguished from piqué by one or more of the following characteristics: matelassé is not always wadded; the face cloth is often twill or satin; the stitchers usually form small allover patterns; the stitchers are sometimes threaded in a ratio of 1:1 with the face warp; the back or stitcher warp is often held at the same tension as the face warp; matelassé is always a double cloth.

piqué: loom-produced quilted cloth. A face structure is stitched in selected areas by a bottom warp held at tighter tension than the face warp. The stitching warp threads pull the face cloth down, while the surrounding unstitched areas puff freely. The contrast between stitched and puffed areas is accentuated by an extra wadding weft that passes between the face and the stitcher warp in unstitched areas but lies flat below both face and stitchers in the stitched areas. Most piqués are double weaves: a back (or bottom) weft weaves with the stitcher (also called the back, or bottom) warp. When a back weft weaves with the stitcher warp, piqué is a double weave (also called 'fast-backed' piqué). When there is no back weft, piqué is a single structure with an extra (stitcher) warp and (stuffer) weft (also called 'loose-backed' piqué). The ratio of face warp and weft to back warp (and weft if there is one) is usually 2:1.

stitched double cloth: two independent structures are 'stitched' together when warp threads of one interlace with weft threads of the other, or when a supplementary warp or weft weaves with weft or warp threads of both structures. Stitching can be decorative or invisible.

Chapter 9
Understanding Patterned Double Weave

DOUBLE WEAVE

A double-weave fabric is made of two weave structures that cannot be separated from each other when the fabric is removed from the loom. The two structures are connected: by exchanging layers, by stitching, or by interweaving. This chapter explores double weaves in which layers are exchanged to create pattern; chapters 10 and 11 examine stitched double cloths and lampas.

Some confusion about the term 'double weave' comes from calling the technique that produces two layers of fabric 'double weave' even though not all cloths requiring the technique *are* double weaves. To weave two layers, the top layer is raised when the bottom layer is woven, and the bottom layer is lowered when the top layer is woven. Imagine a jack loom threaded as in *Figure 1*. In order to weave dark plain weave in the top layer, shafts 1 and 3 are raised alternately. The light layer is not raised and so remains underneath the dark layer. To weave light plain weave in the bottom layer, shafts 1 and 3 are raised, first with 2 and then with 4, so that the light weft weaves with its light warp threads underneath the dark layer. If this process is followed and the two shuttles are kept from interlocking at the selvedges, two completely separate single-layer plain-weave fabrics are formed.

If a single weft joins the layers at one selvedge but separates them at the other, however, the cloth unfolds off the loom to become a single-layer fabric double the width of the two layers on the loom, as in *Figure 2a*. Although double-weave technique is used to produce a double-width fabric, the fabric is not a double weave. Other shuttle numbers, orders, and paths in and out of the warp can produce other effects such as tubes, tubes within tubes, tubes with slits, pockets, etc. The fabrics are only double weaves if they show two connected structures when removed from the loom. A tube, for example, is not a double weave, since it shows one warp and one weft when it is off the loom. Note that to avoid an error when weaving tubes, one layer must have one warp thread fewer than the other (*Figure 2b-c*).

The same manipulation of layers on the loom that produces 'double weave' can be used to produce more layers: as each layer is woven, warp threads in the layers that are to be above it must be raised and those in the layers that are to be below it must be down.

1. Two layers: two weave structures

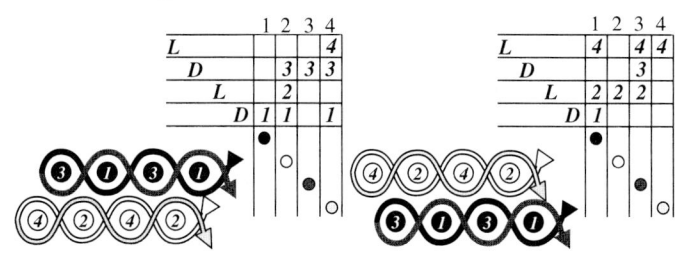

2. Double width: two layers, one weave structure

a. double width

b. double-woven tube: two threads weave in the same shed

c. double-woven tube: error is eliminated by removing a thread

3. Shuttle order produces slits in tube.

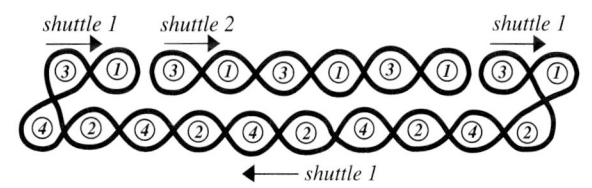

shuttle 1   shuttle 2   shuttle 1

← shuttle 1

4. Layers can be exchanged to create pattern and background.

95

Exchanging layers for pattern

Examine *Figure 4*, p 95. In the center of the cross section, two dark warp threads and two light warp threads change layers. As a result, on the top of the cloth an area composed of two light warp threads and two light weft threads appears surrounded by dark warp and weft threads. The bottom of the cloth shows the reverse interlacement: an area of dark plain weave is surrounded by light plain weave. Several important observations can be made: a) no light weft thread weaves with any dark warp thread or vice versa; b) when this fabric is removed from the loom, the two layers cannot be separated; c) there is a slight gap where the layers exchange on one side in the top layer and on the other side in the bottom layer, caused by the relative positions of the dark and light warp threads to each other.

This form of double weave, in which layers exchange for the purpose of patterning, meets the requirements of a unit weave. To produce pattern or background, each unit of four warp threads and four weft threads can form two interlacements: dark plain weave on top, light plain weave on the bottom, or light plain weave on top, dark plain weave on the bottom.

Examine the warp drawdown and warp cross section in *Figure 5*. Notice that a drawdown for double weave does not aid in understanding the interlacement in the same way that a cross section does, since the drawdown includes the lifts of the layers and does not distinguish them from the lifts of the warp threads that are actually interlacing. Follow the paths of the four weft threads in the cross section.

All of the information necessary for drafting double weave with profile drafts can be determined from the draft in *Figure 5*. Threads from the two plain weave structures alternate in the threading. In this draft, odds are dark and evens are light — the opposite arrangement can be chosen. (Consistently choosing the same arrangement, however, helps speed up the designing process when working with double weaves.) Whatever the color order selected, all of the blocks show the same color order in this form of double weave.

Now study the tie-up in *Figure 5*. The ties for shafts 1-4 produce dark on top in A. The ties for shafts 5-8 produce light on top in B. If the four shafts in A are raised in exactly the same order as the four shafts in B, A weaves light on top. If the four shafts in B are raised in exactly the same order as the four shafts in A, B weaves dark on top. The 4-shaft templates for light-on-top and dark-on-top are shown in *Figure 6*. In the templates, the symbols that indicate the layers that are raised rather than the threads that are interlacing are marked with a 'T.'

5. Draft two blocks.

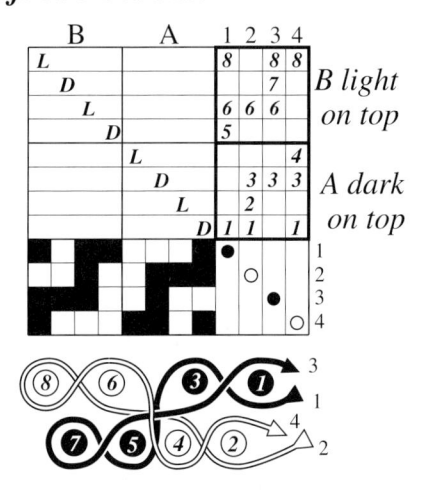

6. Derive the tie-up templates.

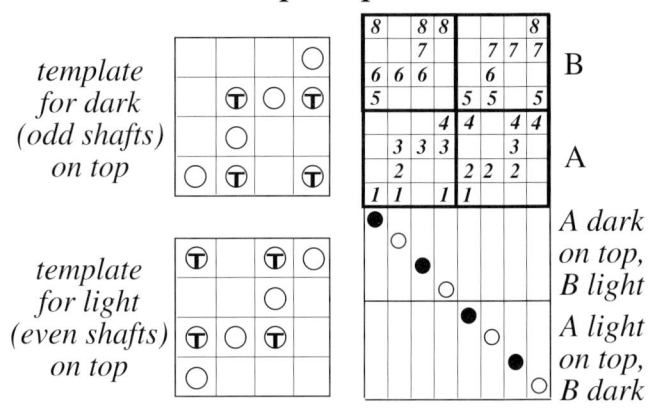

Note that the templates really indicate odd shafts or even shafts on top rather than dark or light. The color that appears on top is determined by whatever color is threaded on the designated shafts. In substituting tie-up templates for squares in the profile tie-up, first determine the pattern color and the background color; then substitute the templates that produce the pattern color on top for black squares in the profile tie-up and the templates that produce the background color on top for blank squares in the profile tie-up.

Now examine the treadling units. Weft threads from each structure alternate in the treadling just as warp threads from each structure alternate in the threading.

Usually the two structures in layer-exchange double weave are the same as each other and use the same fibers and setts. It is also possible, however, to draft one coarse weave and one fine weave by changing the ratio of one structure to the other from 1:1 to 1:2 or more. The two structures can be twill or satin, but numbers of required shafts multiply dramatically.

96

Keys for Patterned Double Weave

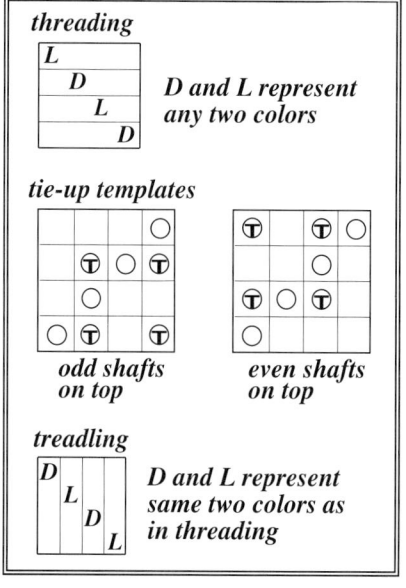

threading

L			
	D		
		L	
			D

D and L represent any two colors

tie-up templates

odd shafts on top   even shafts on top

treadling

D			
	L		
		D	
			L

D and L represent same two colors as in threading

Substitute threading units for squares in the profile threading draft.

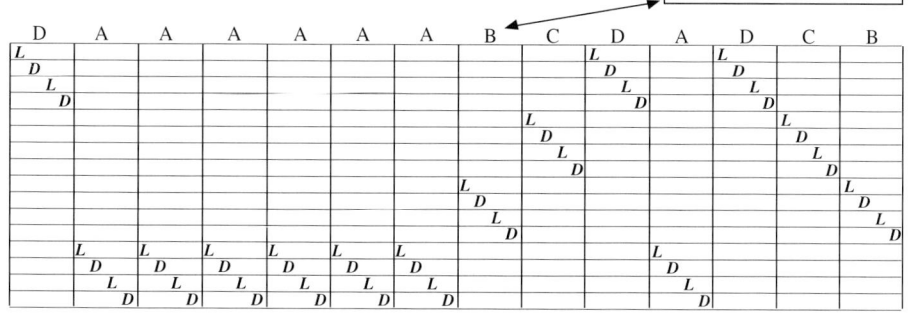

Substitute treadling units for squares in the profile treadling draft.

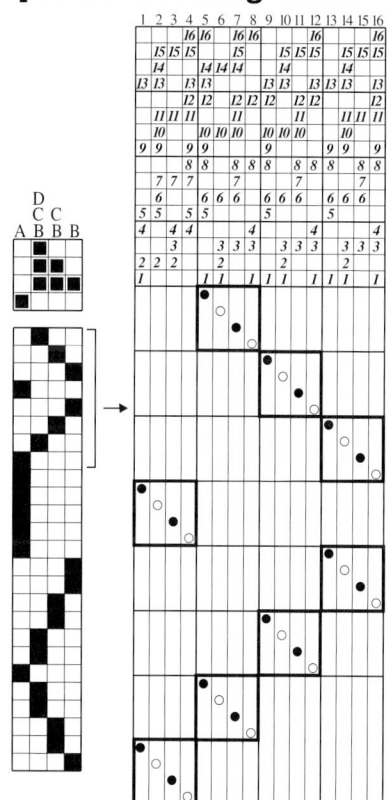

Derive the tie-up.

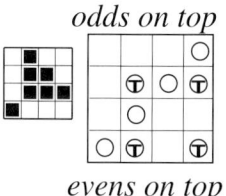

odds on top

evens on top

tie-up for even shafts on top (L) in pattern, odd shafts on top (D) in background

tie-up for odd shafts on top (D) in pattern, even shafts on top (L) in background

97

4-BLOCK DOUBLE WEAVE ON EIGHT SHAFTS

Examine the cross sections in **Figure 7**. Block A is threaded exactly as Block A in the 2-block draft in **Figure 5**, p. 96. Block C is threaded exactly as Block B in **Figure 5**. Two additional blocks can also be formed: Block B with shafts 3-4-5-6 and Block D with shafts 7-8-1-2. **Figure 7** shows the threading for B as 5-6-3-4 and for D as 1-2-7-8. Notice that each of the four blocks shares a pair of shafts with two other blocks (similarly to the way that each block shares shafts with two other blocks in 4-shaft overshot). As a result of these shared pairs, when dark weaves on top in A, the pair of warp ends shared with A in B (3, 4) and the pair of warp ends shared with A in D (1, 2) also produce dark on top. When at the same time light weaves on top in C, the pair of warp ends shared with C in D (7, 8) weave light on top and the pair of warp ends shared with C in B (5, 6) weave light on top. B and D therefore form halftones. B and D also form halftones when A weaves light on top and C weaves dark. When B or D weave dark or light on top, A and C form halftones because of their shared pairs of shafts with B and D.

Structural limitations of 4-block, 8-shaft double weave

Dark ends always alternate with light ends in the threading. Look again at the cross section and notice that dark plain weave (dark picks are isolated in **7a**) is produced by alternately raising shafts 1, 5 and 3, 7. Plain weave of the lights (**7b**) is produced by alternately raising shafts 2, 6 and 4, 8. To guarantee true plain weave, a thread on shaft 1 or 5 must therefore always alternate with a thread on 3 or 7 in the dark warp, and 2 or 6 alternate with 4 or 8 in the light warp.

To avoid errors in the plain weave sheds and also ensure that blocks on both sides of a symmetrical motif are the same size, follow the threading instructions in **Figure 10**. When blocks are threaded in succession (A next to B or D, B next to A or C, etc.) add a pair of transition threads before changing to a new block. After threading A as many times as the draft requires, for example, add 1-2; after B: 3-4; C: 5-6; D: 7-8. If A is threaded next to C, or B to D, do not add transition pairs.

Another adjustment is needed to ensure complete symmetry. Examine the threading drafts in **Figure 8**. In **8a** the threading moves up to D and down to C. Think of D as an up/down turning block. In **8b**, the threading moves down to A and up to B; A is a down/up turning block. Because of the positions of the shared pairs, down/up turning blocks contain four more threads than up/down turning blocks.

To balance, remove four threads from every down/up turning block in the threading draft. Compare the small turning blocks in the rose and table in **9a** (not adjusted) and **9b** (adjusted by removing four threads from the turning block in the rose).

Treadling units can be substituted without transition picks. In order to square the design, however, adjustments may be required. Change blocks at any time, but always use treadles in sequence: follow the second treadle in one group of four with the third treadle in the next group. Unfortunately, most 8-shaft floor looms are not equipped with enough treadles to accommodate even the skeleton tie-up indicated in **Figure 10**.

Note that as in 4-shaft overshot, only one block can produce pattern at a time. In every 4-pick sequence one block weaves light on top, the opposite block weaves dark on top, and two blocks form halftones.

7. Double weave that looks like overshot: dark, light, and halftone blocks

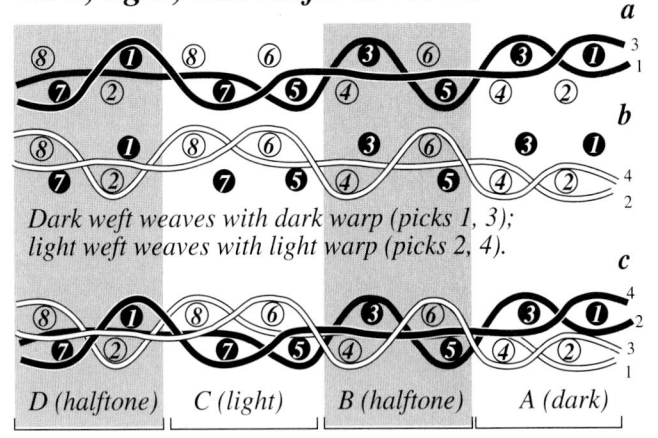

Dark weft weaves with dark warp (picks 1, 3); light weft weaves with light warp (picks 2, 4).

D (halftone)   C (light)   B (halftone)   A (dark)

tie-up for dark in A, light in C, halftones B, D

8. Remove four threads from down/up turning blocks for symmetrical block size.

a. up/down turning block with six threads

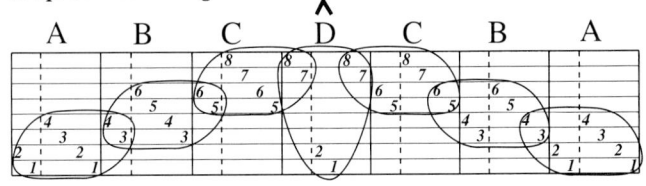

A   B   C   D   C   B   A

b. down/up turning block with ten threads

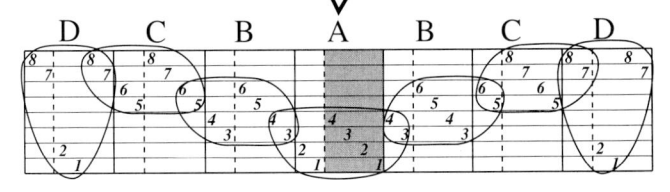

D   C   B   A   B   C   D

98

Compare the center block in the rose with the small blocks in the table in the fabric in 9a. Though drafted as the same size, the down/up turning block in the rose is wider than the up/down turning block in the table. In the fabric in 9b, four threads have been subtracted from the turning block in the rose as outlined in 8, to equalize the sizes of the small blocks.

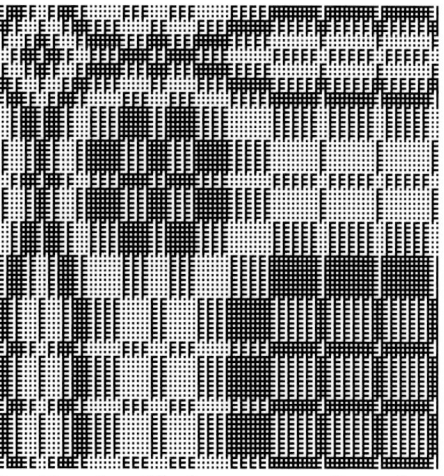

9a. Turning blocks are not adjusted.

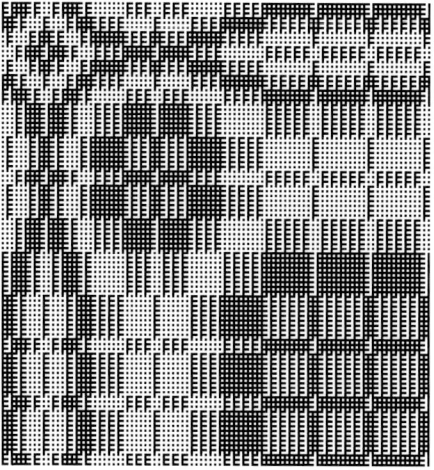

9b. Four threads are subtracted from the turning block in the rose.

Advantages

In spite of drafting limitations, an advantage to translating overshot drafts into this form of double weave is that block size is not restricted by float length. Interesting effects can be achieved by threading large areas of a single block to weave halftone or pattern. Furthermore (the one exception to the one-block-light, one-block-dark, two-blocks-halftone rule), all dark or all light can be woven on top at any time to produce horizontal areas of solid color.

Select a 4-block overshot or profile draft

Since the structure looks so much like overshot, overshot patterns are particularly successful. To change an overshot draft into a double weave draft, first write out the overshot draft. Circle the blocks to determine the order and relative size of each block.

Designate a number of double weave ends to substitute for overshot ends (this depends on the materials, sett, and scope of the design). Substitute the double weave 'units' shown in *Figure 10* and add the transition threads at every block change. For example, if four double-weave threads represent two overshot threads, for eight threads of Block A in overshot (1-2-1-2-1-2-1-2) thread 1-2-3-4-1-2-3-4-1-2-3-4-1-2-3-4-<u>1-2</u>.

To thread from a 4-block profile draft, select a draft that produces pattern in one block at a time. Let each square in the profile threading draft equal four threads. Add a transition pair when changing to a new block.

Note that this version of double weave is not a unit weave: blocks cannot produce pattern or background independently of other blocks.

10. Threading and treadling 'units' for 4-block, 8-shaft double weave

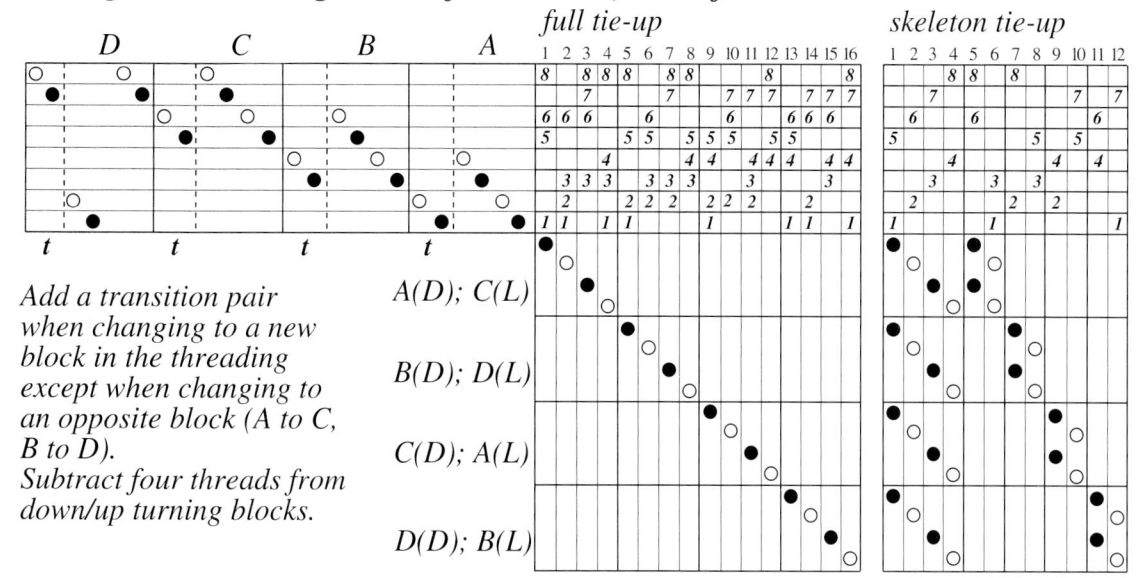

Add a transition pair when changing to a new block in the threading except when changing to an opposite block (A to C, B to D). Subtract four threads from down/up turning blocks.

To weave all light on top: use the skeleton tie-up and depress together treadles 1-2-4, 2, 2-3-4, 4.
To weave all dark on top: 1, 1-2-3, 3, 1-3-4.

Chapter 10
Understanding Stitched Double Cloth

STITCHING TWO LAYERS

Two layers of fabric can be 'stitched' together on the loom when warp ends of one layer weave with weft picks of the other, see *Figures 1* and *2*. (Almost every weaver discovers this truth quite by accident when trying to weave two layers that are completely separate!) Less often, fabrics are stitched together with an extra warp or weft, as in *Figure 2e*.

Stitching is usually intended to be invisible when it joins two structures in a reversible cloth or backs one structure with another. Stitching can also be used to decorate a cloth. The two different tensions of the back warp and the face warp in piqué cause indentations in the face structure that emphasize the decorative quality of the stitching. When decorative stitching is done with only one element, i.e., only warp threads or weft threads, the fabric is not a double weave but a single structure with a supplementary warp or weft.

HIDDEN STITCHING

Examine *Figure 1*. In a stitched double cloth, the layers do not change places. The upper layer is usually called the 'face,' and the lower layer the 'back.' When a warp or weft thread of one layer weaves in a shed of the other layer, stitching takes place. The thread stitching together two plain weave layers spans the same distance as the functional weft and is therefore fairly visible on the surface of the cloth.

Figure 2a shows two separate layers of 2/2 twill. Stitching can be done with either 'sinking' stitchers, *2b*, or 'rising' stitchers, *2c*, or both, *2d*. In *2b*, warp threads on shaft 7 are lowered for a back pick, and in *2c*, back warp threads on shaft 4 are raised for a face pick. When the face and back cloths are 2/2 twill, the stitching points can be disguised beneath floats on the face and above floats on the back. *Figure 3* shows the steps for designing hidden stitching. The final tie-ups #1 and #2 in *Figure 3* use both rising and sinking stitchers. When only one warp stitches, its take-up is greater than the non-stitching warp, and two warp beams or tensioning systems may be required.

Figure 2e shows two 2/2 twill layers stitched with an extra weft. An extra warp can be used in the same way, which saves time in the weaving, but more shafts and separate tensioning are usually required.

1. Stitching two plain-weave layers

face warp thread sinks to stitch

back warp thread rises to stitch

2. Invisible stitching: two layers of 2/2 twill
a. Two separate layers: not stitched

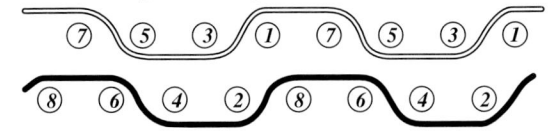

b. Back weft weaves with face warp.

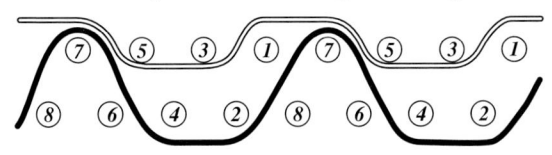

c. Face weft weaves with back warp.

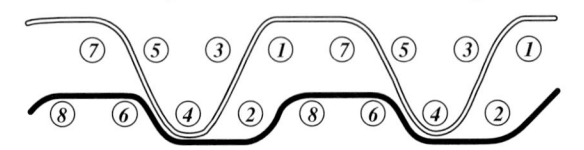

d. Face warp weaves with back weft; back warp weaves with face weft.

Face pick uses treadle 3, tie-up a, Figure 3.
Back pick uses treadle 2, tie-up a, Figure 3.

e. An extra weft weaves with both the face warp and the back warp.

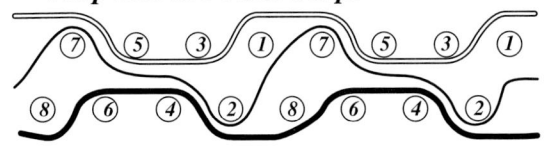

3. Designing hidden stitchers

a. Prepare a separate drawdown (or drawup) for each of the two structures, face and back. The shafts required by the new draft will be the sum of the shafts required by each: eight in our example.

b. Construct a grid for the drawdown (or drawup) of a full repeat of both structures. Warp threads and weft threads from each structure alternate one-and-one if the setts of the two cloths are the same. Another ratio can be chosen, such as 1:2, etc., if one cloth requires a finer sett than the other. Highlight or otherwise mark the warp threads and weft threads of the back layer. Back warp and weft threads are shaded gray here. The rows and columns are also marked 'B' for back and 'F' for face.

c. In the squares where face warp threads and face weft threads intersect, place the black squares from the face drawdown.

d. In the squares where back warp threads and back weft threads intersect, place the black squares from the back drawdown.

e. Fill in all the squares where a back weft thread intersects a face warp thread to show that the face thread is raised when the back weft weaves (shown as black squares with white dots here).

f. To stitch with 'risers' (back warp threads are raised for face weft picks): mark stitching points with an 'o' where a back warp thread can be raised between face warp threads that are up for successive face picks (see white lines). These stitchers will not show on the face of the cloth.

g. To stitch with 'sinkers' (face warp threads are down when a back pick is made): mark stitching points with an 'x' where a face thread can be lowered between back warp threads that are down for successive face picks (see dashed lines in the drawdown). These stitchers will not show on the back of the cloth.

h-i. To stitch with both risers and sinkers, mark stitching symbols from both *f* and *g*. Write the 8-shaft threading below the drawup. In *h*, the face is threaded on odd shafts and the back on even shafts. In *i*, the face is threaded on the first four shafts and the back on the second four.

j-k. To derive the tie-up, write the shaft numbers that are raised for each pick. Read the drawup from bottom to top. In *h*, for example, shafts 1, 2, and 3 are are raised on the first pick; see treadle 1. Next, shafts 1, 2, 3, 4, 5 are raised.

To weave, use the treadles in straight order, alternating a top weft with a bottom weft.

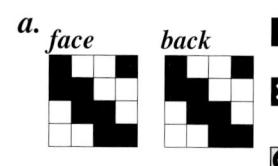

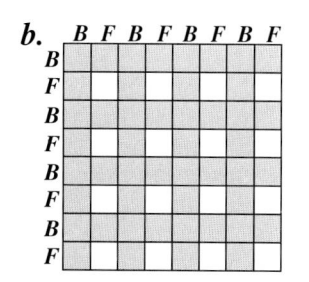

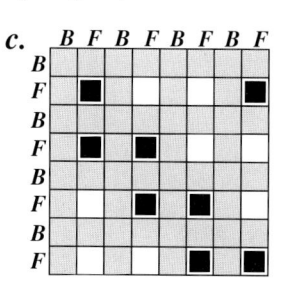

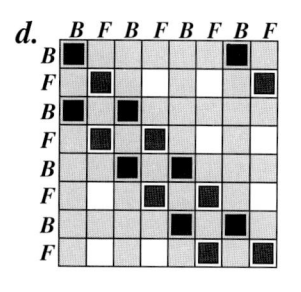

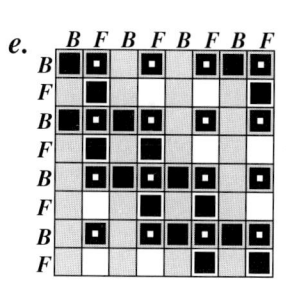

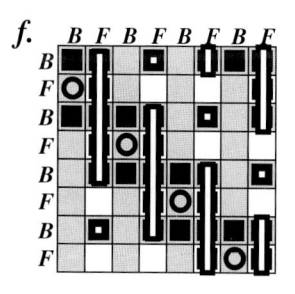

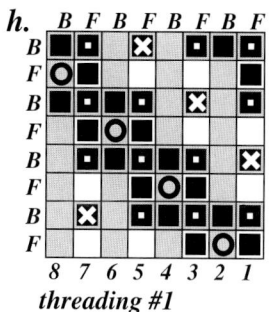

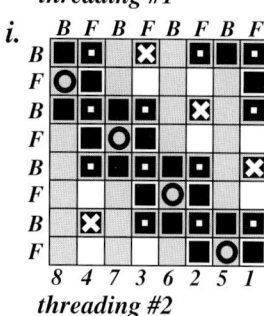

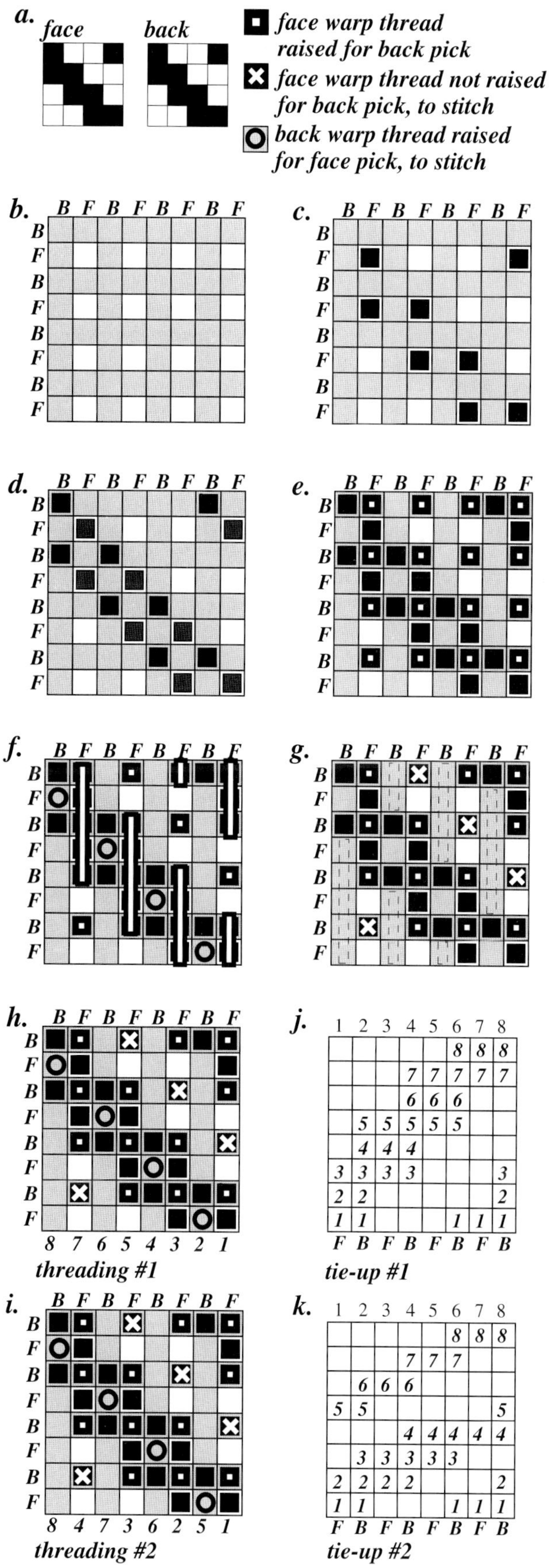

101

DECORATIVE STITCHING

Double cloths with decorative stitching are not usually reversible. The face structure is most often plain weave, though it can be any structure. Usually, the warp of the back structure patterns the face by stitching over it and is therefore called the 'stitcher' warp and its warp threads the 'stitchers.' The patterning options available to the stitchers are like the patterning options available to warp threads in a single cloth: they can be raised in twill order or in groups to form blocks of pattern.

Structural choices

The fabric structure and the design produced by the stitchers can be planned separately. Structural choices include: *a*) the face structure; *b*) the back structure; and *c*) the ratio of back warp and weft to face warp and weft. The fabric is woven following the same basic principle as all other double weaves: the top layer is raised when the bottom layer is woven; the bottom layer is down when the top layer is woven. To stitch, back warp threads are raised when face picks are woven. Since the stitchers are intended to show, they are often raised for two consecutive face picks.

Examine the drafts in *Figures 4* and *5*. Compare the shaded areas in the treadling with the shaded areas in the cross sections (read the treadling diagrams from top to bottom and the cross sections from bottom to top). The ratio of stitcher warp ends to face warp ends is 1:2. The use of two different tensions on the face warp and the stitcher warp produce a puffed face cloth in *Figures 5* and *6* called piqué. An extra stuffer (also called wadder) weft emphasizes the puffed areas.

If a back warp stitches over and under the face but does not weave with its own weft, the structure is not a double weave. The process for designing the stitcher pattern is the same for a single fabric stitched by an extra warp, a plain stitched double cloth as in *Photo b*, or a fabric produced with the special tension requirements of piqué.

Stitching choices

With two shafts available for stitching as in *Figures 4-5*, alternate stitchers can be raised or they can all be raised together, as in plain piqué. When more shafts are available, stitcher designs can be planned on special design paper (see p. 130).

When stitchers are threaded in succession, each one acts as a separate pattern element. To stitch in blocks, two stitcher shafts are required for each block (A = 1-3-2-1-4-2 when the ratio is 1:2). The design key in *Figure 8* shows a 3-block draft. Motifs are balanced if the draft is balanced; to balance, add half-units to turning blocks.

Pattern options for stitching a face cloth

a. no back weft; not a double cloth, back warp stitches in twill order.

b. double cloth, back warp stitches in twill order.

c. piqué, double cloth; back warp stitches in twill order.

d. piqué, double cloth; back warp stitches in blocks.

Types of piqué

e. plain piqué: stitchers form ribs; this example is not a double cloth since there is no back weft.

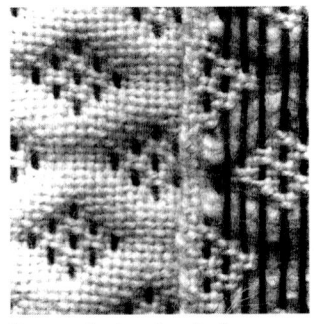

f. waved piqué: stitchers form a diamond; stuffer is inserted between diamonds; this example is not a double cloth; there is no back weft.

g. waved piqué: stitchers form a diamond; this example is a double cloth since there is a back weft.

h. figured piqué: stuffer is inserted for every stitcher lift; this example is a double cloth; there is a back weft.

102

4. Stitched double cloth: ratio of back warp/weft to face warp/weft is 1:2

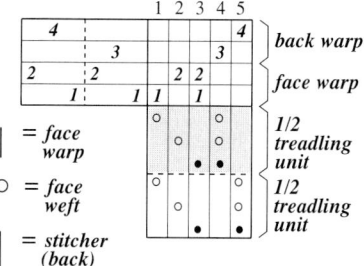

|| = face warp
○ = face weft
| = stitcher (back) warp
• = back weft

The shaded areas in the treadling diagrams produce the shaded areas in the cross sections. Read treadling diagrams from top to bottom and cross sections from bottom to top.

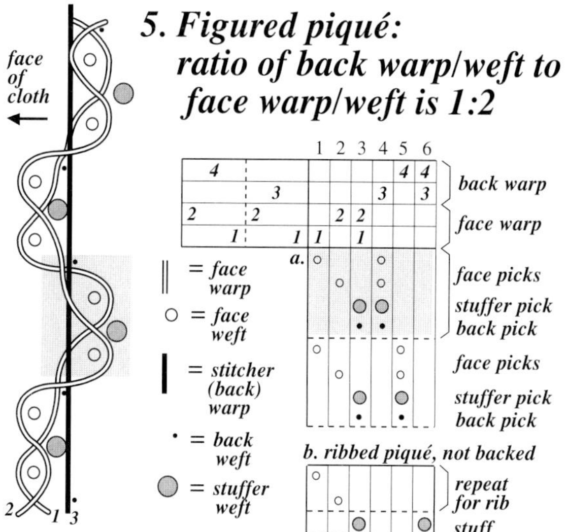

5. Figured piqué: ratio of back warp/weft to face warp/weft is 1:2

|| = face warp
○ = face weft
| = stitcher (back) warp
• = back weft
● = stuffer weft

Most 4-shaft piqué is ribbed as shown in sequence b.

b. ribbed piqué, not backed

The design paper

Each square in the design paper represents a stitcher.

In alternate sequences alternate stitchers (marked in the grid with a +) can stitch over the face.

Each design-paper row represents a designated number of face picks (two in Figures 4-6), back picks (one in Figures 4-6), and one stuffer pick in figured piqué (Figure 5).

Shaded squares can represent stitchers raised for face picks (in Figures 6-7) or not raised for face picks (8).

Stitched double cloths can be treated as unit weaves. Let each square in the profile threading draft represent two stitcher shafts and accompanying face threads. Odd and even stitchers alternate to form the back cloth.

6. Waved piqué

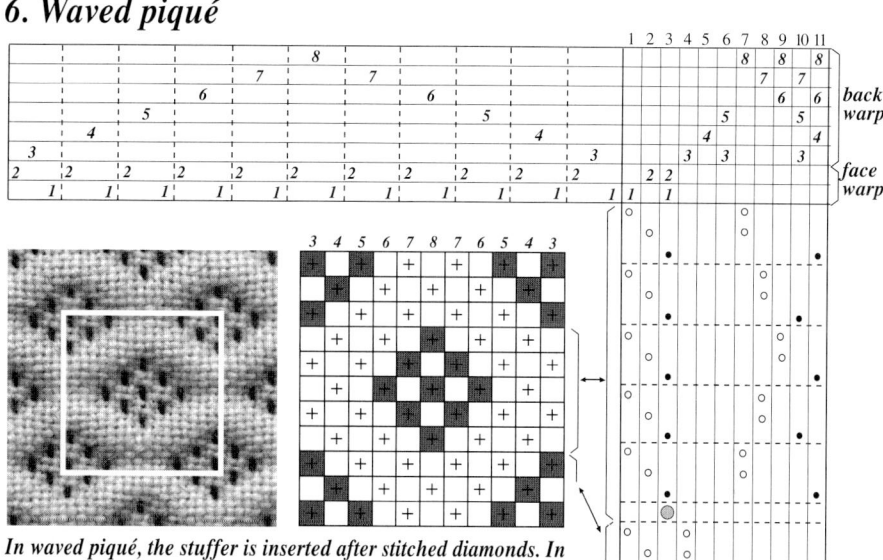

In waved piqué, the stuffer is inserted after stitched diamonds. In figured piqué, the stuffer is inserted in each 3- or 4-pick sequence.

7. Twill stitcher design

8. Blocks are unstitched, background stitched, as in Photo d.

A = 1-3-2-1-4-2; B = 1-5-2-1-6-2; C = 1-7-2-1-8-2

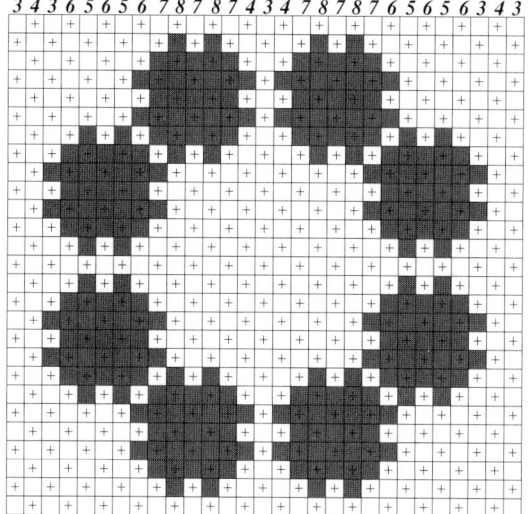

Stitched Double Cloth Keys

threading keys

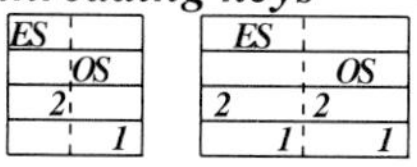

tie-up template
▣ = for raised stitcher shaft

OS = odd stitcher
ES = even stitcher

treadling keys 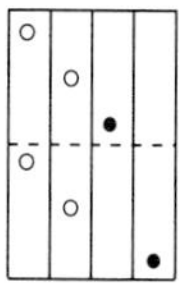
○ = face weft
• = back weft
● = stuffer weft

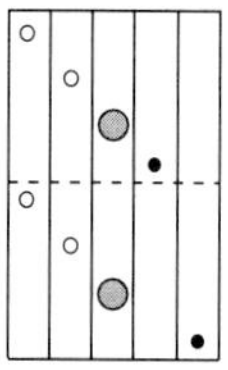

figured piqué

103

Chapter 11
Understanding Lampas

CHARACTERISTICS OF LAMPAS

Like layer-exchange double weave, lampas is a unit weave that creates strong contrast between pattern and background areas. Compare the layer-exchange double-weave fabric, p. 97, with the lampas fabric, p. 107.

Structural differences between the two types of double weave become apparent with a comparison of the backs of the two fabrics. The layer-exchange double-weave fabric is 'structurally reversible'; the interlacement on the reverse of the pattern area is identical to the interlacement on the face of the background area, and vice versa. Lampas fabrics are not structurally reversible; the interlacement on the reverse of the pattern area is *not* identical to the interlacement on the face of the background area. Compare the interlacements on the faces and backs of the two lampas fabrics in *Photos a* and *b*, p. 105. Now compare the cross section in *Figure 5*, p. 96, with the cross sections in *Figures 1b* and *2b*, p. 105. In the layer-exchange double weave cross section, both warp threads *and* weft threads of the dark and light structures completely change layers: the dark structure appears on top in Block A and on the bottom in Block B; the light structure appears on top in Block B and on the bottom in Block A. Notice that in the cross sections in *Figures 1b* and *2b*, only the dark *weft* changes faces. It weaves on top in Block A and on the bottom in Block B. Its warp, however, remains below the light warp and weft in both blocks. Imagine that you are looking at the cloths represented by the two cross sections. On the face, Block A shows all dark, Block B all light. On the back, however, though Block B shows all dark, the light plain weave structure in Block A is interrupted by the interlacement of the heavy dark weft with its warp.

A drawdown is particularly ineffective in portraying lampas since it does not portray the differences between the sizes of the fibers in the two structures. The dark weft threads in the fourth picks are shaded gray in the drawdowns and cross sections as points of comparison.

The two structures

The most important difference between lampas and layer-exchange double weave can be discovered in the threading. In *Figure 1a*, the dark warp is threaded on shafts 1 and 2 in Block A *and* on 1 and 2 in Block B. In *Figure 2a*, the dark warp is threaded on 1-2-3-4 in A *and* on 1-2-3-4 in B. For the light warp, however, Block A = 3-4; B = 5-6 in *Figure 1*, and A = 5-6; B = 7-8 in *Figure 2*. One of the two structures in lampas is threaded on the same set of shafts throughout. The other structure requires an independent set of shafts for each block of pattern.

Because the two structures in a lampas fabric are not co-equal and interchangeable as they are in layer-exchange double weave, they have different names to distinguish between them. In most sources, the structure that is shown as light in *Figures 1* and *2* is called the main weave or sometimes the ground weave. The structure that is shown as dark in *Figures 1* and *2* is called the secondary weave or less often the pattern weave. The warp of the secondary structure is sometimes called the binder warp and its weft the pattern weft. The main weave is so named because it is a sturdy (usually 50/50) weave that could stand alone as a viable fabric if the secondary weave were removed just as a ground cloth of a tied unit weave could stand alone if the supplementary weft were removed. The secondary weave, however, without the main weave, is not a viable fabric. Its warp threads are spaced too far apart in relation to the density of its weft threads.

Think of lampas fabrics as consisting of a main weave patterned by a secondary weave, similar to the way a ground weave is patterned by a supplementary weft. The secondary weave can be thought of as a supplementary *weave*.

Characteristics of the main weave

As in layer-exchange double weave, either of the two structures can be plain weave, twill, or satin. The main weave forms the greatest contrast to the secondary weave if it is a warp-emphasis structure such as warp-float satin, but since each new block of the main weave requires an additional set of shafts (two for plain weave, four for 4-thread twill, five for 5-thread satin, etc.), plain weave is the most common option for the handweaver. The main structure (light in these examples) is plain weave in *Photos a-h*, and 2/2 twill in *Photo i*. The same fiber is used for both the warp and weft of the main weave. The main weave is sett and sleyed in the reed almost as if the secondary structure did not exist.

*1a. Lampas: ratio secondary warp ends to main warp ends 1:4
secondary structure: plain weave; main structure: plain weave*

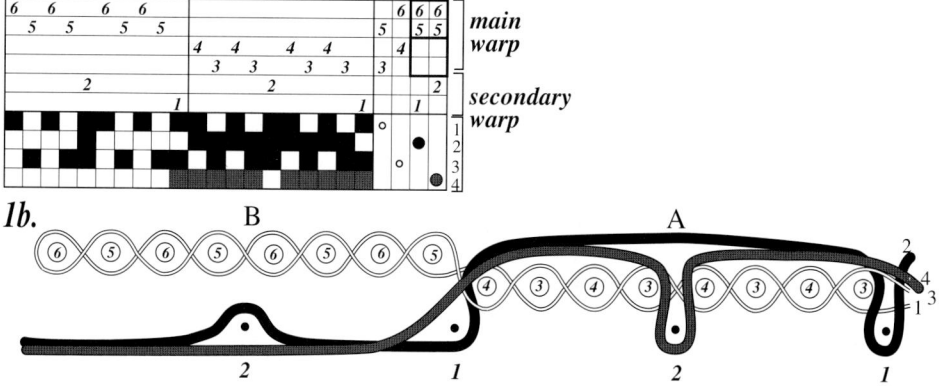

a. 1:4 lampas, face

plain weave   plain weave

1b.

b. 1:4 lampas, back

*2a. Lampas: ratio secondary warp ends to main warp ends 1:2
secondary structure: twill; main structure: plain weave*

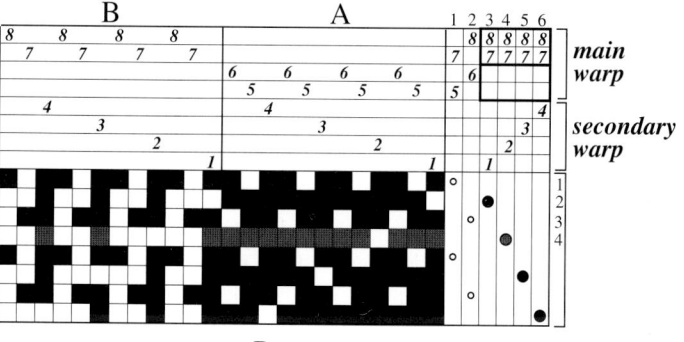

c. 1:2 lampas, face

plain weave   twill

d. 1:2 lampas, back

2b.

Characteristics of the secondary weave

The goal of the secondary weave is for its weft to cover the main weave in either pattern or background areas. To this end the weft of the secondary weave is much heavier than its warp and also heavier than the warp and weft of the main weave. The warp of the secondary weave invisibly secures the secondary weft. It is usually finer than the warp and weft of the main weave.

The size of the fiber chosen as the secondary weft is the most important factor in determining how far apart the secondary warp threads are sett. The secondary weft cannot span a greater distance across the main weave than the practical length of a float relative to its thickness. The selected sett for the secondary weave in relation to the main weave is reflected in the ratio of secondary warp ends to main warp ends. In *Figure 1* the ratio of secondary warp ends to main warp ends is 1:4; in *Figure 2* it is 1:2. The greater the ratio, the longer and smoother the float.

Choices

Lampas fabrics can vary from each other in the structure of the main weave, the structure of the secondary weave, and the ratio of secondary warp ends to main weave warp ends. Each of these choices can be made almost independently of the other. The two structures are connected only by the behavior of the secondary weft: it weaves with its warp either over (if main-weave warp threads are down) or under (if main-weave warp threads are raised) the main weave. The sheds of the main weave are always formed above the secondary structure; secondary warp ends are down when main weave picks are woven. Study the tie-ups in *Figures 1-2*. Main-weave picks are made by alternately raising 3, 5 and 4, 6 in *1* and 5, 7 and 6, 8 in *2*. The secondary weft joins the two structures in Block A where shafts 3 and 4 are down in *Figure 1* and shafts 5 and 6 are down in *Figure 2*. In Block B, main weave warp ends are raised, forming free double cloth.

105

3. Lampas: ratio 1:4, both structures plain weave

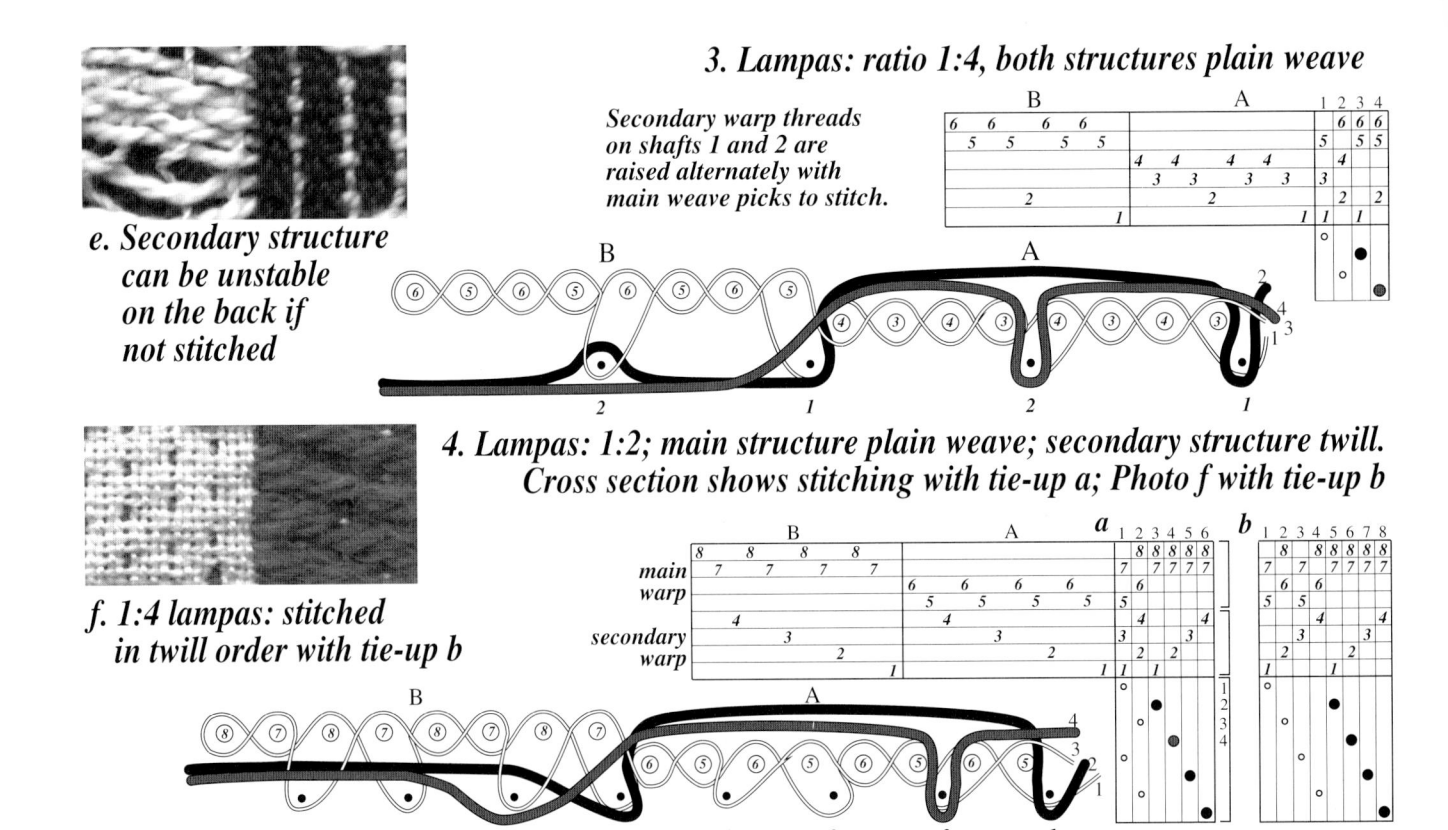

Secondary warp threads on shafts 1 and 2 are raised alternately with main weave picks to stitch.

e. Secondary structure can be unstable on the back if not stitched

4. Lampas: 1:2; main structure plain weave; secondary structure twill.
Cross section shows stitching with tie-up a; Photo f with tie-up b

f. 1:4 lampas: stitched in twill order with tie-up b

One more choice: stitch for stability

Since free double cloth is formed in areas where the main structure weaves on top, the secondary structure, if these areas are extensive, can become unstable, as in *Photo e*. (In the fabric in *Photo e*, the main structure is dark, and the secondary structure, distinguished by its heavy weft, is light.) This instability can be unsuitable for fabrics used for upholstery, bedcoverings, or clothing. A solution is to stitch together the layers in these areas. The drafts in *Figures 3* and *4* show how stitching can be achieved: warp threads from the secondary (bottom) structure weave with weft threads of the main (top) structure. In *Figure 3*, shafts 1 and 2 are raised alternately with main-weave picks. In *Figure 4*, the cross section and tie-up *a* show shafts 1, 3 and 2, 4 raised alternately with main-weave picks. In *Photo f*, the four warp threads of the secondary structure stitch in twill order with tie-up *b*. *Photo i* shows a twill/twill lampas (12 shafts are required for two blocks) with stitching in twill order. The stitchers are almost completely hidden by the twill main weave. A stitched lampas can always be recognized by its tie-up: main weave picks include lifts of the secondary warp.

A 1:4 lampas with two *unstitched* plain weave structures is called 'beiderwand' in Germany.

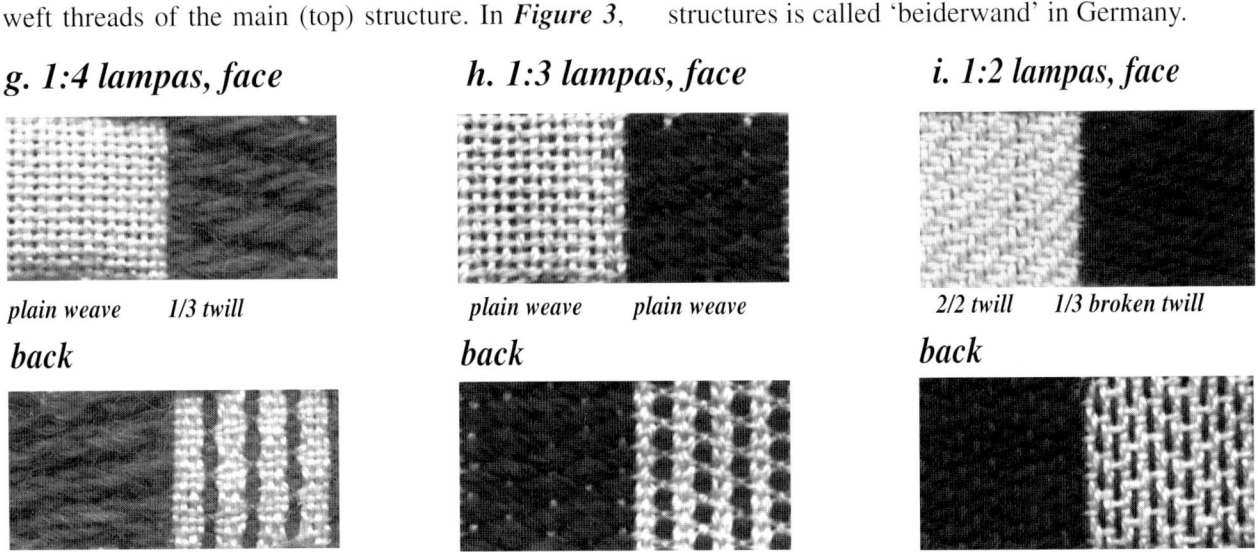

g. 1:4 lampas, face

plain weave   1/3 twill

h. 1:3 lampas, face

plain weave   plain weave

i. 1:2 lampas, face

2/2 twill   1/3 broken twill

back

back

back

106

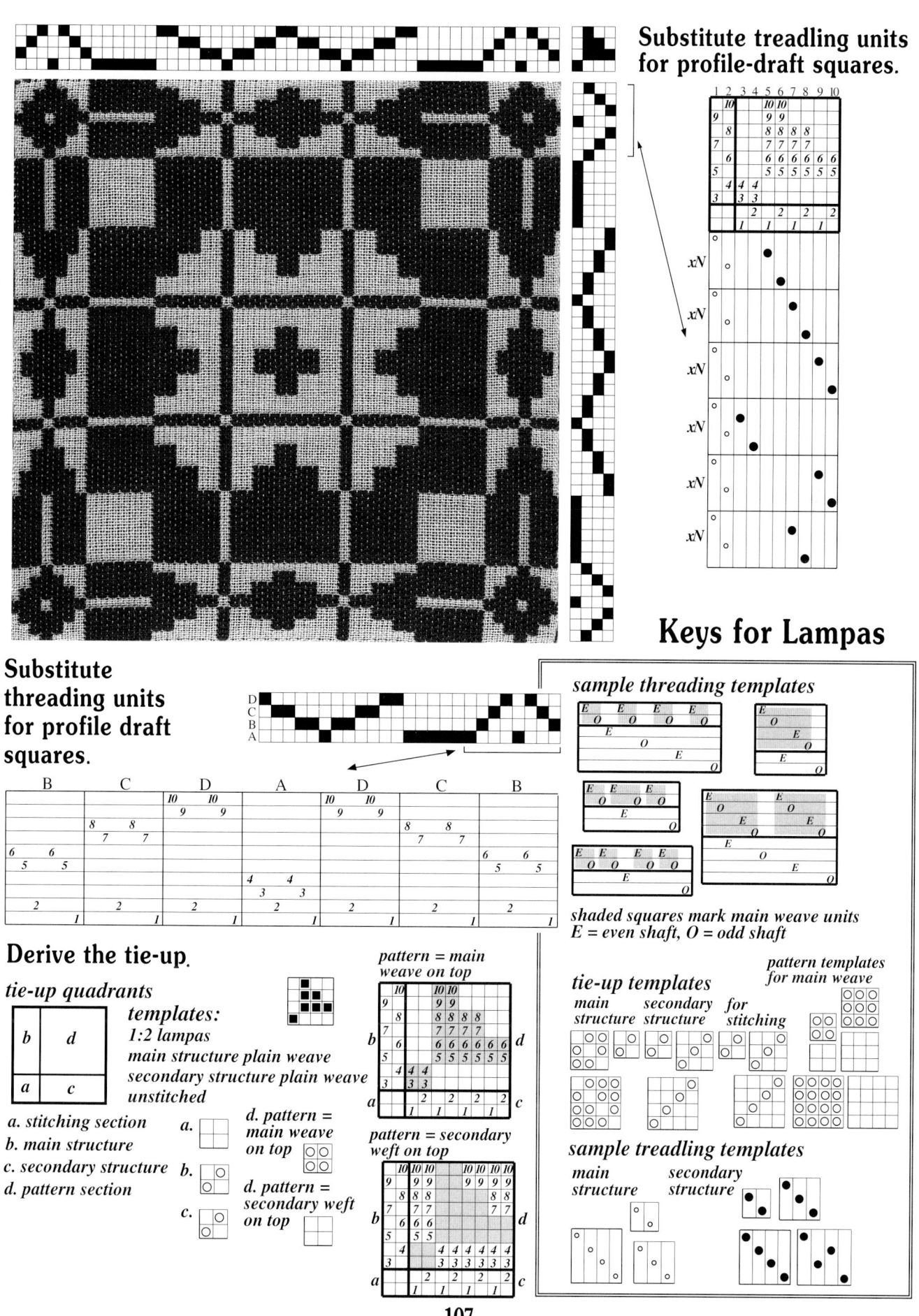

Substitute treadling units for profile-draft squares.

Substitute threading units for profile draft squares.

Derive the tie-up.

tie-up quadrants

b	d
a	c

templates:
1:2 lampas
main structure plain weave
secondary structure plain weave
unstitched

a. stitching section
b. main structure
c. secondary structure
d. pattern section

a.

b.

c.

d. pattern = main weave on top

d. pattern = secondary weft on top

pattern = main weave on top

pattern = secondary weft on top

Keys for Lampas

sample threading templates

shaded squares mark main weave units
E = even shaft, O = odd shaft

tie-up templates

main structure   secondary structure   for stitching

pattern templates for main weave

sample treadling templates

main structure   secondary structure

107

Lesson: Drafting Double Weave

When two weaves are joined in a single fabric, the whole is greater than the sum of its parts. With double weave, create pattern, make three-dimensional objects, form slits and tubes and pockets, insulate clothing, quilt together stuffed layers, and more. The secret to double weave on the loom is to raise the warp of the top layer when weaving with the weft in the bottom layer. Disobey that principle, and you'll 'stitch,' whether by intention or by accident!

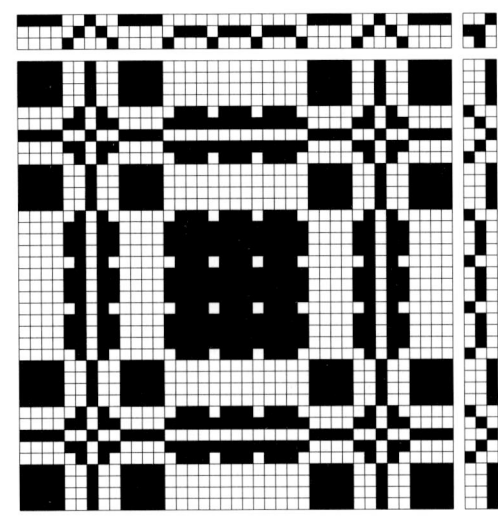

1d. Write the threading in layer-exchange patterned double weave for the first 9 squares of the 3-block profile draft so that dark threads are on odd shafts and light threads are on even shafts.

9(D)10(L)11(D)12(L) _____ _____

_____ _____

_____

2. Compare the cross section in **2a** with treadles 1 and 3 in the **1b** tie-up. Then in **2b** draw the two dark weft picks made with treadles 5 and 7 from the **1b** tie-up, and in **2c** draw the two dark weft picks made by treadles 9 and 11. Write the appropriate shaft number in each of the circles representing the warp threads.

1a. Write a layer-exchange double-weave tie-up for the 3-block profile draft so that pattern = even shafts on top.

1b. Write a layer-exchange double-weave tie-up for the 3-block profile draft so that pattern = odd shafts on top.

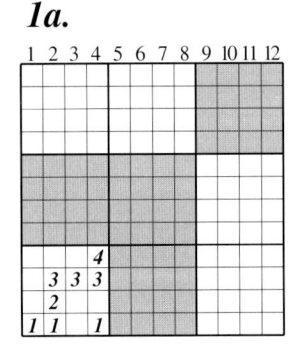

1c. Fill in the treadling units for the first seven squares in the profile treadling diagram.

See answers, pp. 124–125.

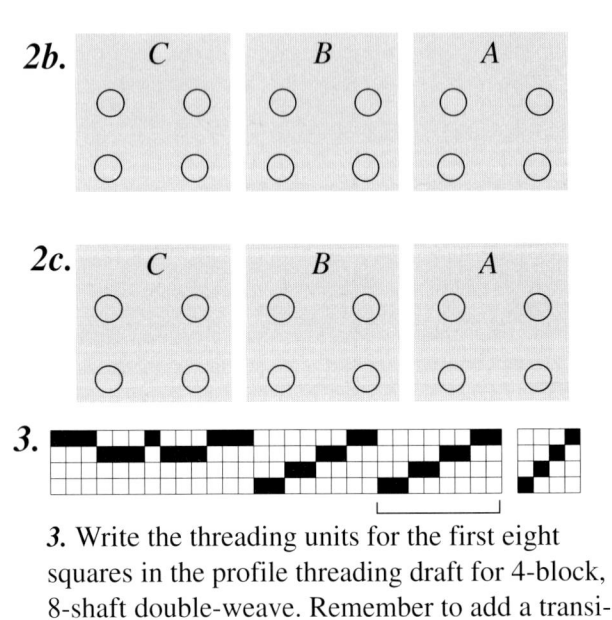

3. Write the threading units for the first eight squares in the profile threading draft for 4-block, 8-shaft double-weave. Remember to add a transition pair when changing to a new block.

_____ 7-8-1-2 _____ 7-8-1-2 ___ 7-8 ___

_____ _____

_____ _____

_____ _____

4. Stitched double cloth

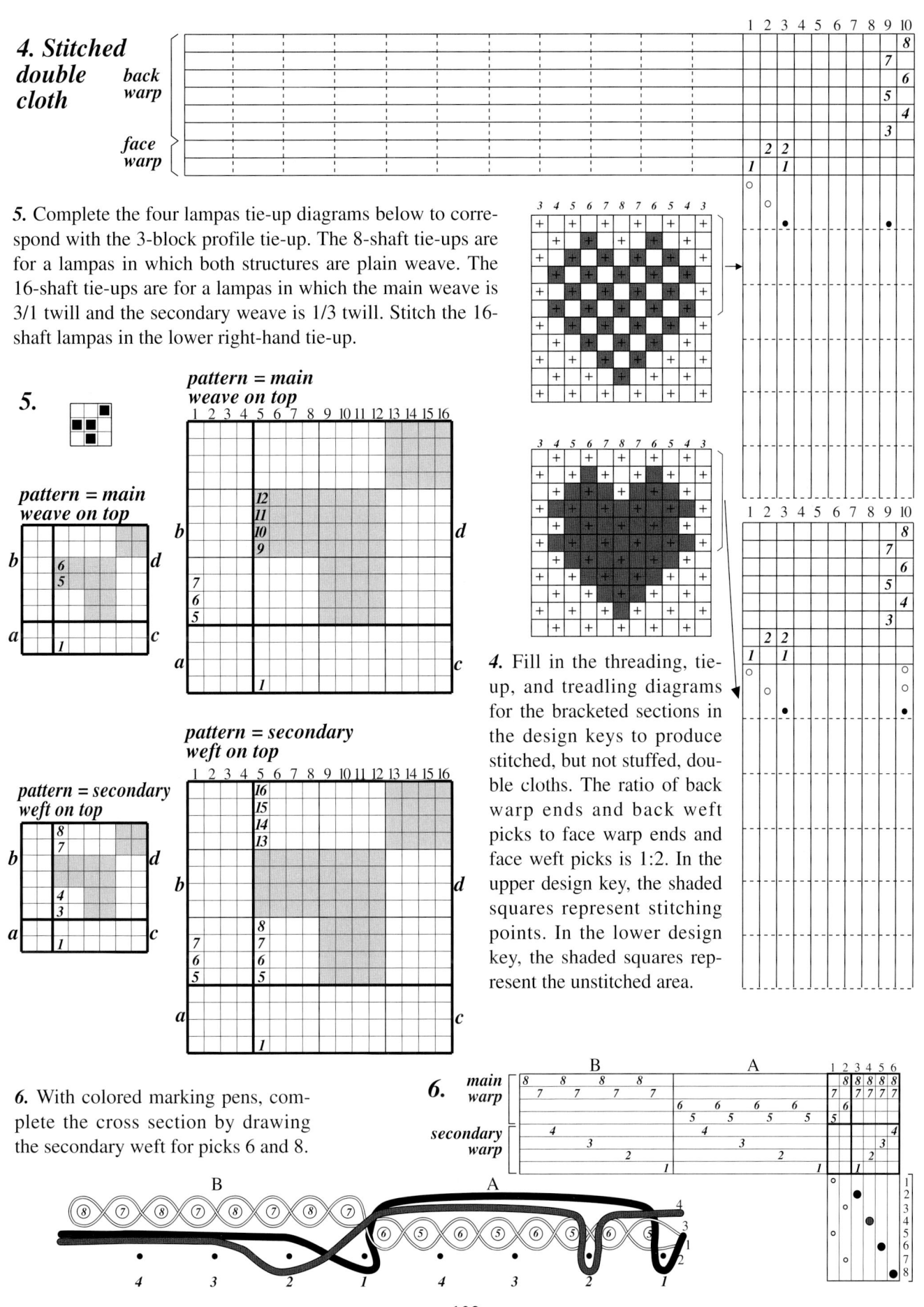

back warp

face warp

5. Complete the four lampas tie-up diagrams below to correspond with the 3-block profile tie-up. The 8-shaft tie-ups are for a lampas in which both structures are plain weave. The 16-shaft tie-ups are for a lampas in which the main weave is 3/1 twill and the secondary weave is 1/3 twill. Stitch the 16-shaft lampas in the lower right-hand tie-up.

5.

pattern = main weave on top

pattern = main weave on top

pattern = secondary weft on top

pattern = secondary weft on top

4. Fill in the threading, tie-up, and treadling diagrams for the bracketed sections in the design keys to produce stitched, but not stuffed, double cloths. The ratio of back warp ends and back weft picks to face warp ends and face weft picks is 1:2. In the upper design key, the shaded squares represent stitching points. In the lower design key, the shaded squares represent the unstitched area.

6. With colored marking pens, complete the cross section by drawing the secondary weft for picks 6 and 8.

6. *main warp*

secondary warp

109

Extra Words to Know

blended drafts: two or more threading drafts are blended when a single draft is devised that can produce each of the original drafts. For example, a threading for overshot can be blended with a threading for spot Bronson, and either overshot or spot Bronson can be woven on the same threading.

complementary warps or wefts: two or more co-equal sets of warp threads that are both necessary to complete the interlacement with one set of weft threads, or two or more co-equal sets of weft threads that are both necessary to complete the interlacement with one set of warp threads.

digitizing: reducing a threading profile to one that uses fewer horizontal rows and therefore fewer blocks or shafts by joining squares in adjacent rows into the same number of squares on one row. For example, the number of rows is reduced by half if every square on rows 1 and 2 in the original draft is placed on row 1 in the digitized draft, and every square on 3 and 4 on 2, etc.

double-faced: usually refers to warp-faced or weft-faced fabrics in which two complementary warps or wefts form identical structures on both sides of the cloth.

fabric analysis: the process of deriving a threading, tie-up, and treadling sequence from the interlacement itself. A drawdown is usually prepared from 'picking' the fabric to determine the warp threads raised for each successive pick in the repeat.

harmonics: parallel or incidental curves appearing in a pattern drawdown when a pattern line has been reduced by telescoping.

initial: a threading group like a threading unit but not necessarily independent that is used to build a threading grid (network).

network: a grid formed of initials repeated horizontally and vertically on which threading and treadling sequences are plotted.

network drafting: plotting a threading and treadling sequence on a grid built of regularly repeating initials. The resulting fabrics usually show large, complex, often curvy designs in which 'pattern' and 'background' areas are not clearly distinct.

opphämta: a Swedish term for a supplementary-weft structure with a plain-weave ground cloth in which the pattern weft floats either over all of the ends or under all of the ends in each block. Since the pattern area is limited by float length, opphämta is not a unit weave.

pattern line: a continuous, usually curved line drawn on a network that becomes the basis for generating a threading and/or treadling draft.

samitum: see weft-faced compound twill.

supplementary warp or weft: a set of warp threads or weft threads or both added to a structure usually to form pattern, as in overshot. Supplementary wefts or warps can also float between two structures to stuff, as in piqué, or to stitch two structures together.

taqueté: see weft-faced compound tabby; synonym summer and winter polychrome.

telescoping: reducing a threading profile to one that uses fewer horizontal rows and therefore fewer blocks or shafts by returning to the first row to thread segments that extend beyond the rows available. For example, to telescope an 8-row profile with squares drafted in sequence 1-2-3-4-5-6-7-8 to four rows, draft 1-2-3-4-1-2-3-4.

turned draft: a complete thread-by-thread draft is rotated 90º so that warp becomes weft, shafts become treadles, and threading sequence becomes treadling sequence.

velvet: a supplementary warp forms pile loops on a plain weave ground cloth. To form the pile loops, the pile warp and the ground warp are differently tensioned. Rods are inserted in the pile loops and secured by successive ground picks. Pile length is determined by the size of the rods. The loops can be cut to make cut velvet.

warp-faced compound tabby: a warp-faced pattern weave with two or more complementary warps, one of which appears on the face while the other(s) are on the back. Even picks separate the warps to determine the color on the face. Odd picks bind the warps in alternate ('tabby') order, thus the name warp-faced compound tabby. Warps bound in twill order are called warp-faced compound twill.

weft-faced compound tabby: a weft-faced pattern weave with two or more complementary wefts. Even warp ends separate the wefts so that one color is on the surface of the cloth and the other(s) on the back. Odd warp ends bind the wefts in alternate (tabby) order, thus the name weft-faced compound tabby, also called taqueté and summer and winter polychrome. If complementary wefts are bound in twill order, the structure is weft-faced compound twill, synonym, samitum.

Part IV Extras

Some special drafting techniques can lead to a rich supply of new ideas and unique variations of old ones. Gain in this section the basic skills you'll need for continued exploration in several areas. When you reach the end of 'Extras,' consult 'For Further Study' for in-depth sources to turn to next. 'Extra Words to Know' includes some structural terms that are not related to the drafting techniques explored in this book, but that might be helpful as you choose your next focus for study.

Chapter 12
Understanding Turned Drafts

TO TURN OR NOT TO TURN

If you were asked to analyze a piece of fabric with four raw edges, nothing but custom is a clue as to which way is warp way and which is weft way. All interlacements can be produced either way, although not all effects such as stitching or stuffing or forming pile are equally successful or efficient both ways.

When a draft is 'turned,' it is rotated 90° so that warp threads become weft threads and weft threads become warp threads. The original threading sequence becomes the treadling sequence in the new draft, and the original treadling sequence becomes the new threading sequence. The number of shafts threaded in the original draft therefore becomes the number of treadles in the new draft and vice versa. The draft in *Figure 1*, for example, requires six shafts and four treadles. Turned, the same interlacement requires four shafts and six treadles; see *Figure 2*. Oho! you say. I can weave 6-shaft drafts on my 4-shaft loom, and tossing this book aside, you run to find all the wonderful new things you can do. You'll be right back, because unfortunately there are very few drafts that require fewer treadles than shafts or they would have been turned ere now.

So why turn a draft? One of the slower and more awkward operations in the process of weaving is managing two shuttles. Imagine the speed gained if you could turn two-shuttle weaves into one-shuttle weaves. You can do that if you 'turn the draft.'

Steps for turning a draft

Rotate the draft 90°. In the new drawdown, black squares now represent weft threads. To prevent the new draft from weaving the cloth upside down, rewrite the tie-up, placing shaft numbers in blank squares (where the o's appear in *Figure 2*). Erase the old shaft numbers so that the corresponding squares are blank.

1. 6-shaft, 4-treadle plaited twill
warp drawdown

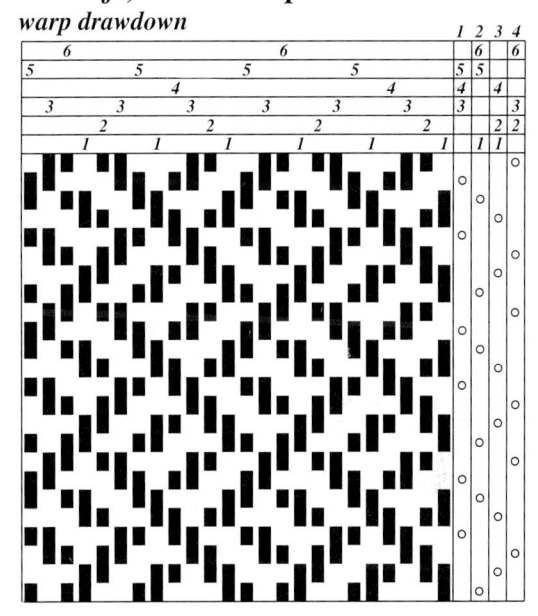

2. 4-shaft, 6-treadle plaited twill
weft drawdown

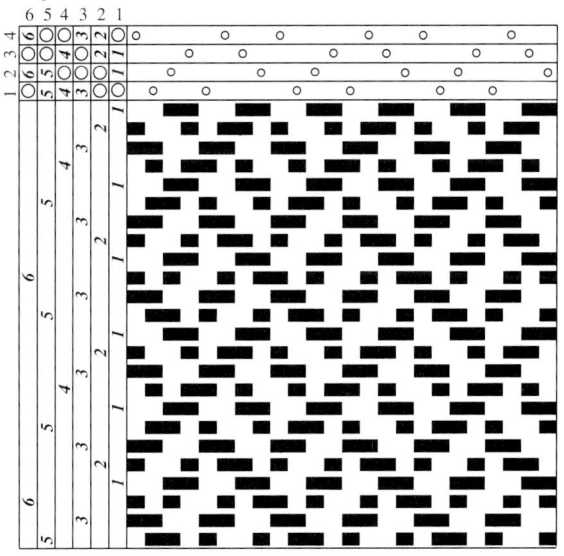

111

Turn two shuttles into one

In *Figure 3*, a supplementary weft forms pattern in Blocks A, B, and C successively. Notice that the pattern weft is not tied; it either floats on the face or on the back of the cloth. The *Figure 3* draft is rotated 90° to become *Figure 4*. The supplementary weft is now a supplementary warp. Symbols for rising shafts are placed in the blank squares in the tie-up and the tie-up is rewritten with the new numbers. Follow the treadling sequence to see how the single ground weft weaves plain weave with the ground warp either over or under the supplementary warp.

A supplementary-warp float is tied to the top of the cloth whenever the weaver desires if its shaft is lowered. It is tied to the bottom of the cloth if its shaft is raised. With the threading in *Figure 4*, the supplementary warp threads can be tied all at the same time or in different blocks at different times, since shafts 3, 4, and 5 can be raised together or separately. In *Figures 5* and *6*, where the number of blocks is an even number, the supplementary warp can be tied in alternate blocks to form uneven-tied overshot and 'Landes hybrid'; compare *Figures 5* and *6* with *Figure 9*, p. 82, and *Figure 11a*, p. 84. With a 'double two-tie threading,' as in *Figures 7* and *8*, supplementary warp threads can be tied in alternate order to produce summer and winter and its many extensions.

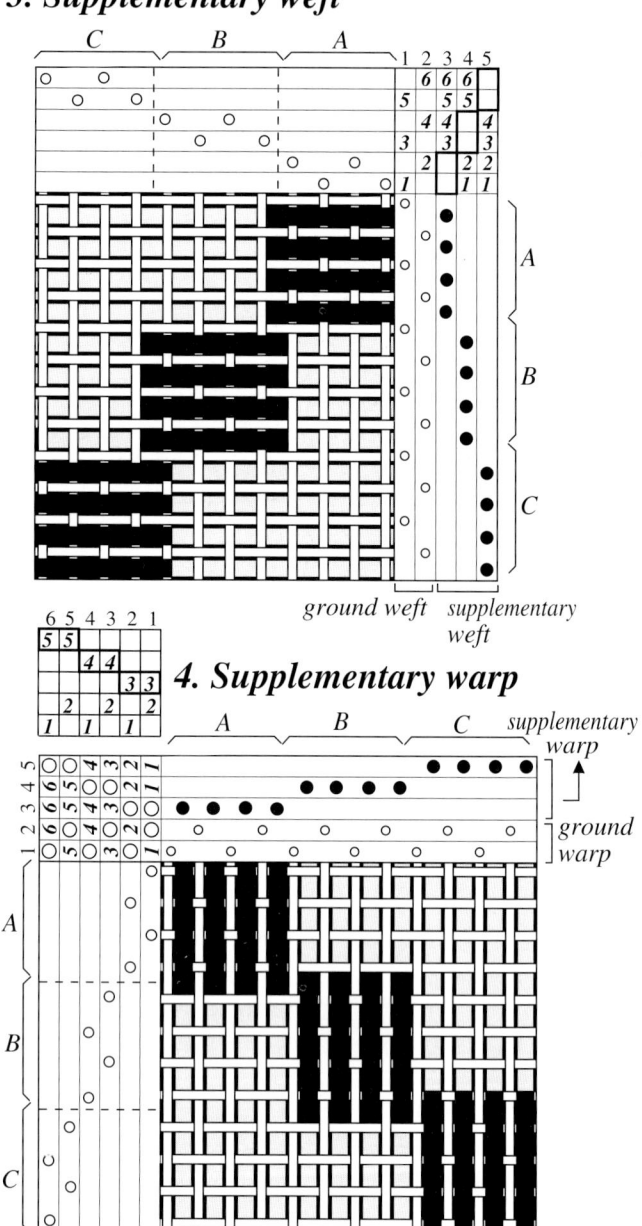

Ratios of tie-down ends to pattern ends in supplementary-weft structures become ratios of tie-down picks to pattern picks in supplementary-warp structures. Float length is no longer dependent on the width

Supplementary Warp Keys for Two-tie Weaves

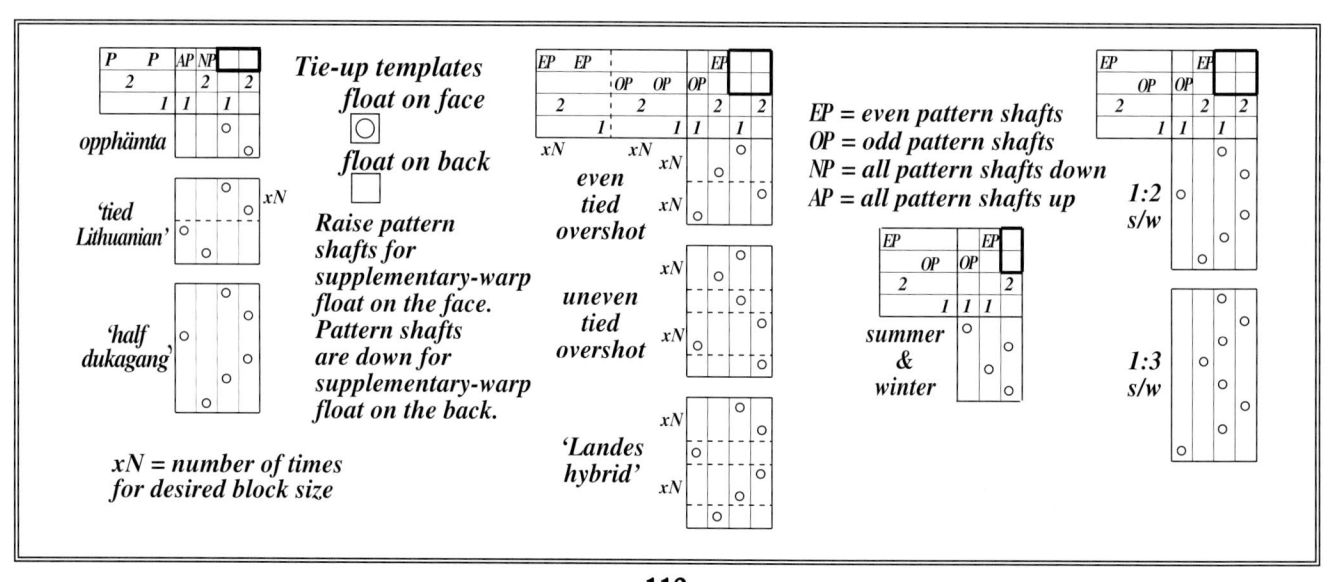

3. Supplementary weft

4. Supplementary warp

EP = even pattern shafts
OP = odd pattern shafts
NP = all pattern shafts down
AP = all pattern shafts up

xN = number of times for desired block size

112

5. Uneven-tied overshot

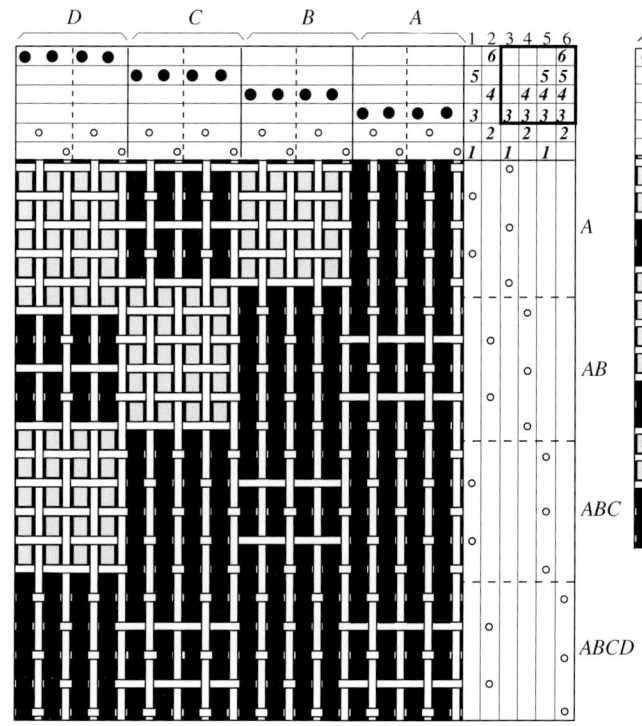

of the threading unit but instead on the length of the treadling unit, which can be changed as desired during weaving. See 'Supplementary Warp Keys' for the tie-up templates and treadling sequences for two-tie unit weaves. Note that if the 'double two-tie' threading system is used (A = 1-3-2-4, B = 1-5-2-6, etc.), all of them can be woven on the same warp.

7. Summer and winter

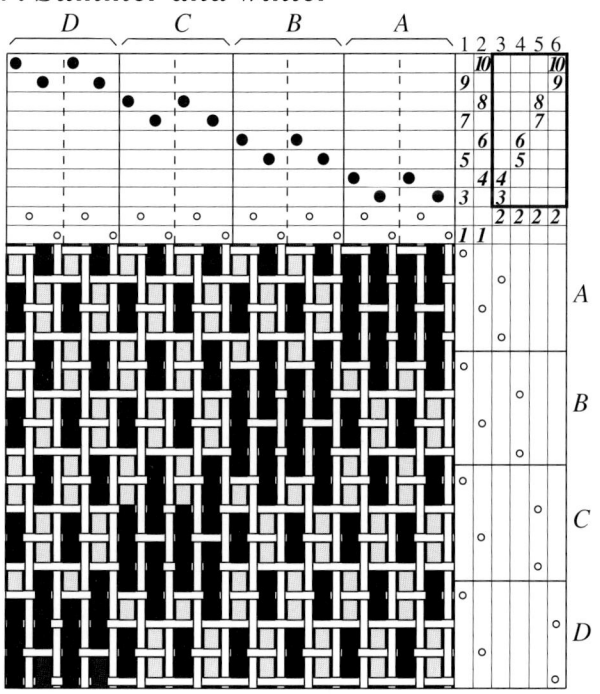

6. 'Landes hybrid'

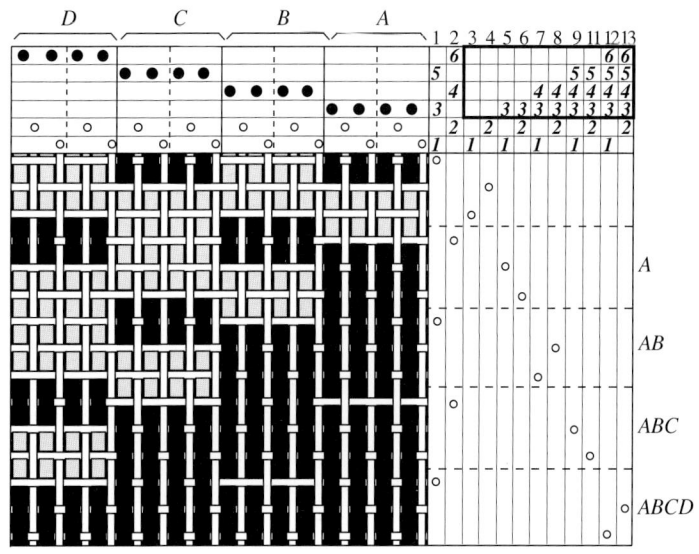

For best results when threading Landes hybrid and tied overshot as supplementary warp structures, choose profile drafts in which blocks are threaded in succession and designs that progress along the diagonal. Halftones are usually most effective when they appear in alternate blocks.

8. 1:2 extended summer and winter

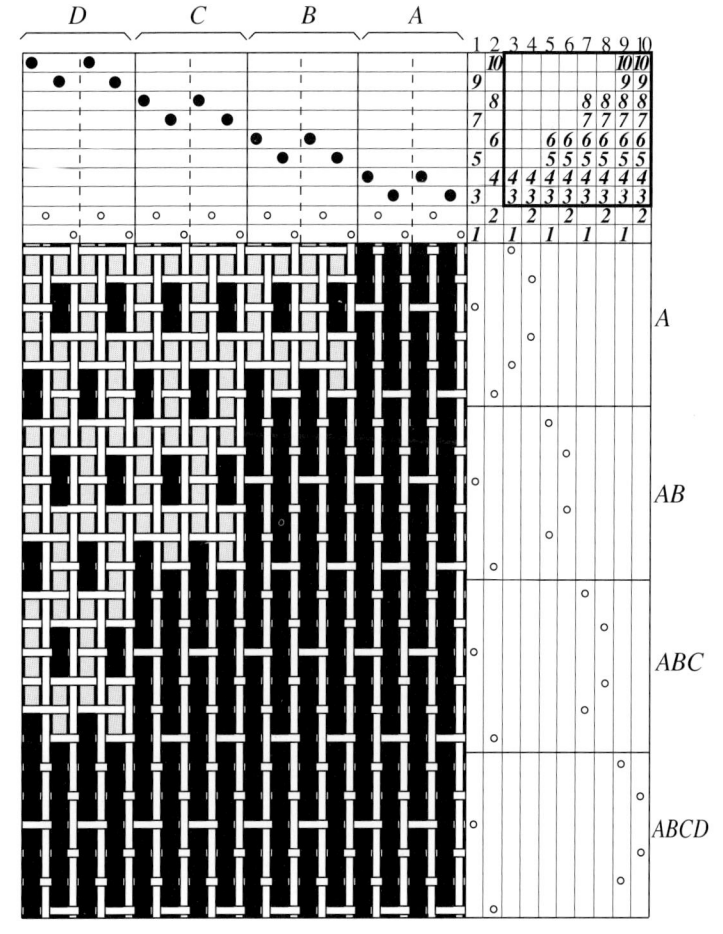

Chapter 13
Understanding Blended Drafts

TWO FOR ONE

Blended drafts are almost more appreciated for their gift of surprise than for their great usefulness. Even so, they belong in every weaver's bag of tricks. Two or more threading drafts are 'blended' when a single, new threading draft is written that can produce all of the interlacements of the original drafts. With a blended draft, for example, two completely different overshot patterns can be woven on the same warp, or a lacy area, a plain weave area, and an overshot border can all be a part of a single garment fabric. The possibilities are limited by the number of shafts and treadles that may be required by the new draft. If the drafts share characteristics, such as the regular alternation of even shafts and odd shafts, the cost is minimized, but even so, blending two 4-shaft drafts usually requires at least eight shafts, and blending three or more drafts can require more shafts than the sum of the shafts required by each of the original weaves. Experiment with blending drafts the next time you're stuck in a traffic jam.

Step 1

Write the threadings to be blended in a horizontal row, one above the other. Adjust them so that they contain the same number of ends. Either draft can be repeated more than one time, but the total number of ends to be blended must be the same for both. *Figure 1* shows two overshot drafts from Josephine Estes, *Miniature Patterns for Hand Weaving*, that have been adjusted so that they each have 68 ends.

Step 2

Each number in the top row forms a pair with the number directly below it. Each pair is given a number to represent a shaft in the new blended threading. This shaft can be raised or lowered in the same order as *either* of the shafts in the original drafts. Remember that the pair always begins with a shaft number from the upper draft and ends with a shaft number from the lower draft; 1-2 is a different pair than 2-1, for example. To blend three drafts, the order of the shaft numbers in the three drafts must also be maintained: upper, middle, lower.

Study *Figure 2*. Begin at the right: the first pair is (upper) 1 (lower) 2. Let 1 represent the pair 1-2. The next pair is (upper) 2 (lower) 3. Let 2 represent the number 2-3. Continue, assigning new numbers to each new pair, and the same numbers to like pairs. Write the complete blended draft as in *Figure 2b*.

1. Align the original threading drafts.

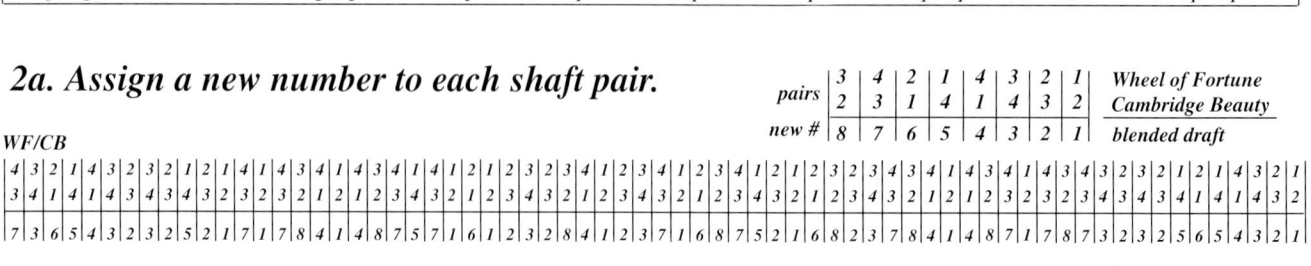

Wheel of Fortune

Cambridge Beauty

2a. Assign a new number to each shaft pair.

2b. Write the new draft.

3. Derive the tie-up

a. Align the pairs vertically with the new numbers.

WF - CB = blended draft

WF	-	CB	=	new
1	-	2	=	1
2	-	*3*	=	2
3	-	*4*	=	3
4	-	1	=	4
1	-	*4*	=	5
2	-	1	=	6
4	-	*3*	=	7
3	-	2	=	8

original tie-up Wheel of Fortune

original tie-up Cambridge Beauty

b. For each treadle in the original tie-ups, locate and substitute the new shaft numbers for the original numbers.

new tie-up for Wheel of Fortune

old #	new #
3 4	3 4 7 8
1 4	1 4 5 7
1 2	1 2 5 6
2 3	2 3 6 8
1 3	1 3 5 8
2 4	2 4 6 7

new tie-up for Cambridge Beauty

old #	new #
3 4	2 3 5 7
1 4	3 4 5 6
1 2	1 4 6 8
2 3	1 2 7 8
1 3	2 4 6 7
2 4	1 3 5 8

c. Write the complete new tie-up. The sheds for plain weave are the same for both drafts.

WF 1 2 3 4   CB 5 6 7 8   tabby 9 10

Step 3

To derive a new tie-up that can produce both of the original interlacements, first write the original tie-ups as in *Figure 3a*. Place the pairs from *Figure 2* in columns and align them vertically with the blended-draft numbers. Replace the shaft numbers in the original tie-ups with the blended-draft numbers. For example, to determine the ties to the new treadle to raise threads on shafts 3 and 4 in the Wheel of Fortune draft, find the new numbers for every 3 and 4 (underlined) in the Wheel of Fortune column. These are 3, 4, 7, and 8. To determine the ties to the first treadle in the Cambridge Beauty draft, find the new numbers for every 3 and 4 (underlined) in the Cambridge Beauty column: these are 2-3-5-7.

Step 4

Weave by following the treadling sequences of the original drafts to produce either of the original interlacements. Additional experimentation using treadles from both drafts can lead to interesting often asymmetrical new designs. The top weft drawdown in *Figure 4* shows Wheel of Fortune, the middle Cambridge Beauty, and the bottom is the result of mixing pattern treadles from both drafts in twill order.

4. Use either of the original treadling sequences as well as experimenting with blends of both.

Chapter 14
Understanding Network Drafting

NEW TRENDS IN HANDWEAVING

Mary Atwater's generation of handweavers prepared all of their drafts for weaving by hand. In the last ten years, many weavers have come to depend on the computer. We don't always understand the relationship between those seductive screen textiles and real fibers, but few of us would accept a total return to graph paper and colored pencils. One interesting way of generating drafts for weaving would surely not have developed without the use of the computer: network drafting. The use of 'network' in this context is not related to computer networking, but rather to something much more simple: a threading and treadling grid. Introduced by Oliver Masson and François Roussel in their book *Shaft Weaving and Graph Design* and explained by Alice Schlein in a series of articles (see 'For Further Study'), the process of network drafting produces large-scale designs without the chunky look of block weaves in addition to infinite potential variation on a single threading through changes in tie-ups and dobby peg plans. This chapter is merely an introduction; if you're intrigued, consult the sources in 'For Further Study' and join the explorers in this handweaving frontier.

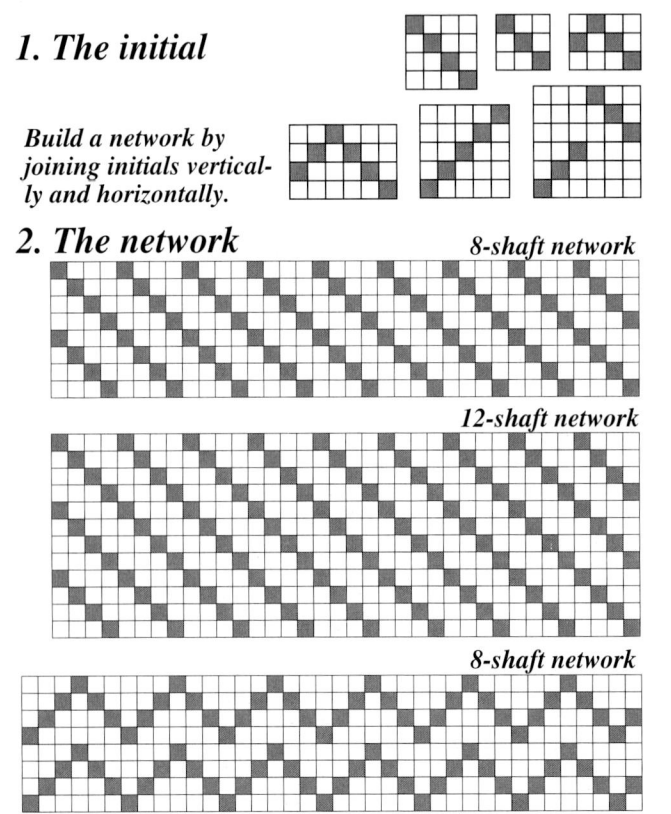

1. The initial

Build a network by joining initials vertically and horizontally.

2. The network

8-shaft network

12-shaft network

8-shaft network

From initial to network

The essential ingredient in network drafting is the network: the grid used as the base for plotting the threading and treadling orders. There are other ways to generate large-scale unblocky designs, but the network grid is specific to this technique. The network ensures that sufficient interlacement takes place with the expansive threading and treadling repeats the system generates.

The building block of the network is called the 'initial,' see *Figure 1*. The orders of the shaded squares in the initials in *Figure 1* suggest twill, and indeed most of the structures produced by networking are 'irregular' or 'fancy' twills: structures with one warp and one weft in which single threads form the smallest pattern element (as in the drawdowns in *Figures 4-5*). Network drafting can also be used for other structures than twill. It can be used to generate the threading for the pattern shafts in a tied unit weave, for example, for the main weave of a lampas, for the stitchers in piqué. The same network used for 4-thread turned twill can be used for layer-exchange patterned double weave. When used for unit weaves such as these, the network acts to ensure that the 'units' are divided properly, similarly to the way we thread half-units (a first half is always followed by a second half), except that the fractions can be as small as single threads.

Each network is made up of initials joined horizontally and vertically. The number that can be joined vertically is limited by the number of shafts available. The horizontal number is limited only by the number of warp ends. Note that the grids themselves cannot be used as threadings since each warp end is 'threaded' on more than one shaft. The rule of network drafting is that the threading must fall on shaded squares in the grid.

The networked threading drafts in *Figures 4-5* are derived from a 'pattern' line. The pattern line forms a base line for the threading, which looks a bit like quills extending from the back of a porcupine in attack mode. The pattern line can be drawn freehand on the network or designed first on graph paper without being restricted to the number of rows in the network. Such a pattern line is then reduced, usually to the number of rows that does not extend beyond the bottom row of the top initial in the network. For an 8-shaft grid of 4-row initials, the pattern line is five rows high (as in *4a*); for a 12-shaft grid, nine rows high, for a 16-shaft grid, 13 rows high.

REDUCING THE PATTERN LINE

Since the number of rows in a pattern line is limited by the shafts available, two techniques can be used for reducing fancy lines to the desired number of rows: *telescoping and digitizing*. Even if you never use network drafting, these techniques are useful for creating original block designs.

Telescoping

Number the rows of the pattern line from 1 to the number of rows in the reduced line, five in **Figure 3b**; repeat this sequence until you've reached the top row (see *a* in **Figure 3a**). Then draw the reduced line so that every square in a pattern-line row marked 1 is placed on row 1 in the reduced line, every square in a row marked 2 is on row 2, etc.; see **Figure 3b**. Telescoped pattern lines can be recognized by concentric lines called 'harmonics.'

Digitizing

Divide the pattern line into the number of sections corresponding to the number of rows in the reduced line. Rewrite the pattern line so that every square in section 1 is on row 1, in section 2 on row 2, etc., see **3c**.

3a. Draw a pattern line.

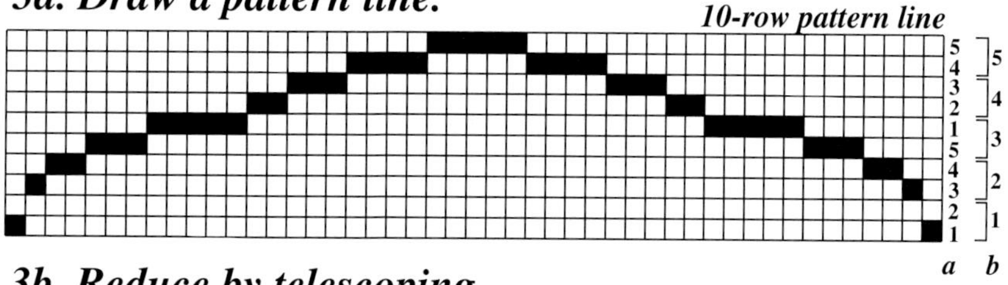

3b. Reduce by telescoping.

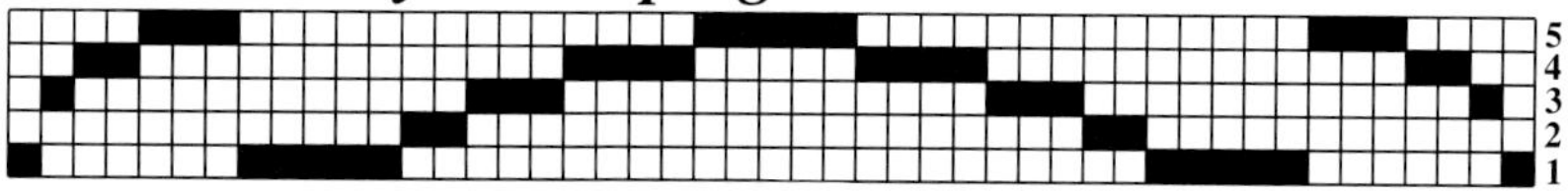

3c. Reduce by digitizing.

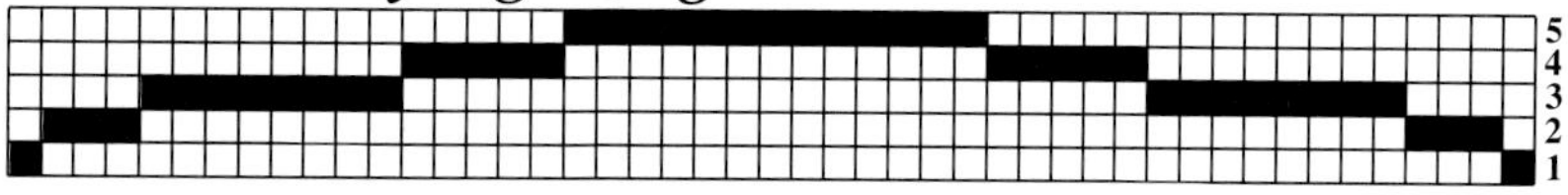

Derive the threading.

With a colored pencil, draw the pattern line on the network, with pattern line row 1 on row 1 of the network, as in **4a**. Mark with black ink every pattern-line square that falls on a shaded square in the network. Complete the threading by marking with black ink the nearest shaded square above the pattern line in every vertical column. If the pattern line reaches closer to the top of the network than the bottom row of the last initial, choose the nearest shaded square below the line or return to the bottom of the network and choose the next square up. Different choices produce different effects. Test for effectiveness with a good computer weaving program.

4a. The pattern line is drawn on the network as the base line for the threading

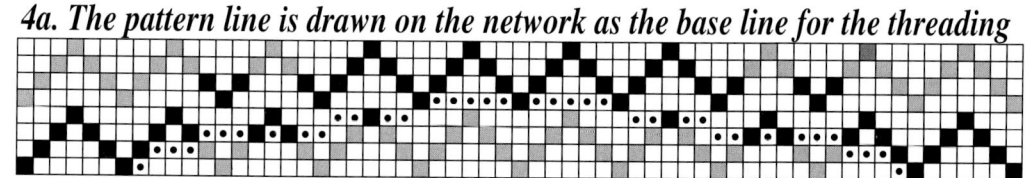

4b. Networked threading: regular twill tie-up

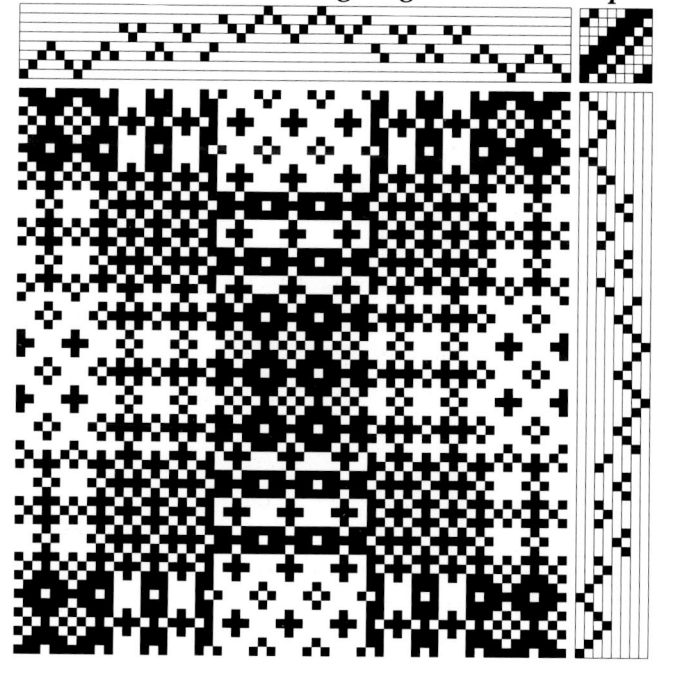

4c. Networked threading: turned twill tie-up

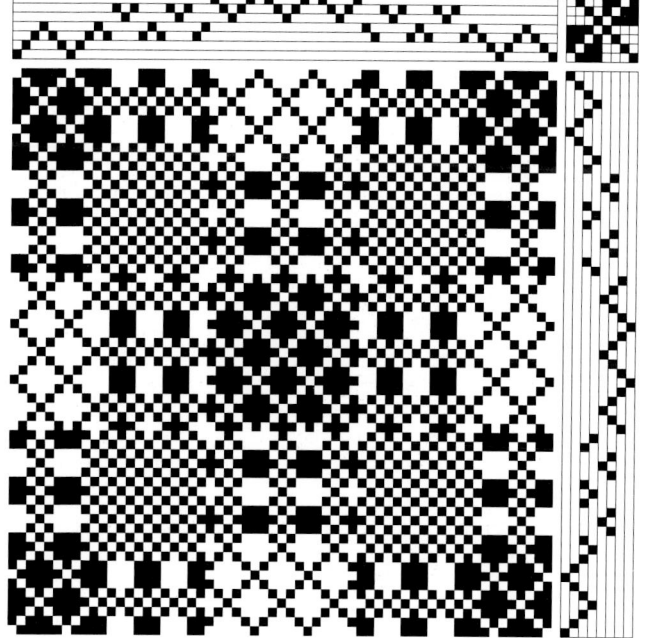

Derive the tie-up.

With a treadle loom, experiment with regular twill tie-ups and treadle as drawn in. Designs can be varied by 'flipping' the treadling order, see *Figure 5c*. Tie-ups can also be divided into sections, see the tie-up in *Figure 5d*. Different sections can produce different interlacements such as plain weave, 2/2 twill, broken twill, 3/1 twill, etc.

5a. Nine-row pattern line

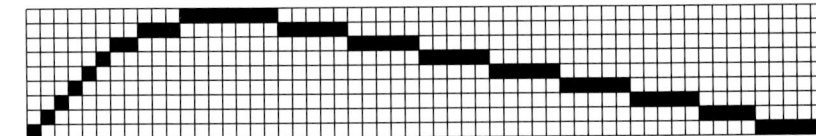

5b. The nine-row pattern line on a 12-row network

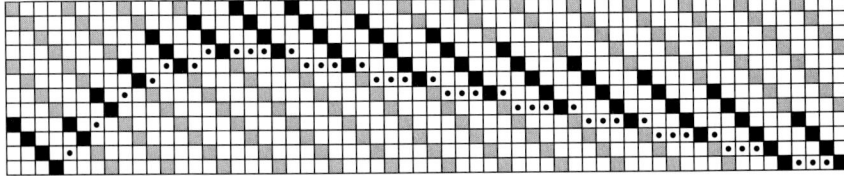

5c. Twill tie-up, 'flipped' treadling order

5d. Turned twill tie-up

Design a dobby peg plan.

Network drafting and computer-driven dobby looms are natural partners. Examine the dobby peg plan in *Figure 5e* Each horizontal row shows the shafts raised for the corresponding pick. For the first pick, for example, shafts 4, 8, and 12 are raised. There are 60 picks in *5e* that would require 28 treadles on a regular loom. With networked threadings, peg plans allow greater control over design detail. Computer-aided dobby looms, which do not require each row in the peg plan to be pegged by hand, allow quick design changes and encourage experimentation. Peg plans can be also used to indicate the sheds for table looms.

The pattern line used to generate the threading in *Figure 5b* is also used to derive the peg plan in *Figure 5e*. One side of the pattern line produces 1/3 twill and the other side of the pattern line produces 3/1 twill. Other interlacements can be included or substituted, such as plain weave, broken twill, etc.

5e. Dobby peg plan derived from the pattern line

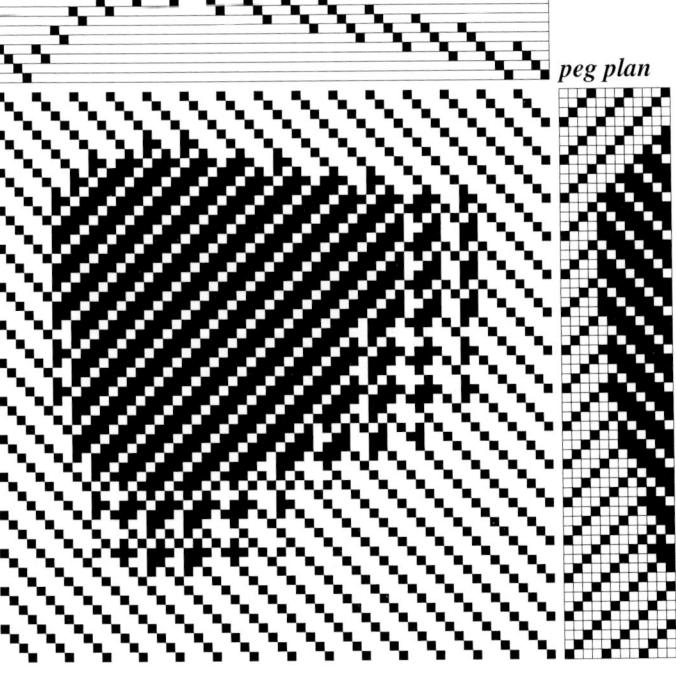

peg plan

Chapter 15
Understanding Fabric Analysis

Prepare the drawdown.

To analyze a fabric is to determine the threading, tie-up, and treadling order from the interlacement. This is relatively easy once the interlacement is graphed as a drawdown. What is not so easy is preparing the drawdown from a piece of fabric, since warp threads and weft threads bend out of their vertical and horizontal alignment when removed from the loom. Computer programs that advertise fabric analysis let you do the hard part.

Derive the threading.

Identify all warp threads that perform the same interlacement: they can be threaded on the same shaft. For example, with a ruler placed vertically on the drawdown in *Figure 1*, examine the behavior of the first warp thread. Notice that it is up for the first two picks and for the last two. Mark a *1* in the threading grid for this warp end. Why *1*? No reason except that it's the first thread we're examining and it would be odd to start with, say, 6. Look across the drawdown to find the other warp threads that do exactly the same job. The only other one like it is the last warp thread in the draft. Mark a *1* in the threading over it. Warp threads on shafts 1, 2, 3, and 4 are already marked in *Figure 1*. Look next for all of the threads that are exactly like the first thread marked *5* and write *5* in the threading draft above them. Continue until all of the threads in the draft are marked.

Derive the tie-up and treadling order.

To determine the shafts raised by each treadle, place a ruler horizontally to isolate the first pick. Looking across the row, find the shaft number for each warp thread that is shaded black in the drawdown (this is a warp drawdown). Write these numbers in the tie-up for the first treadle and put a mark in the treadling diagram to indicate that a weft is inserted

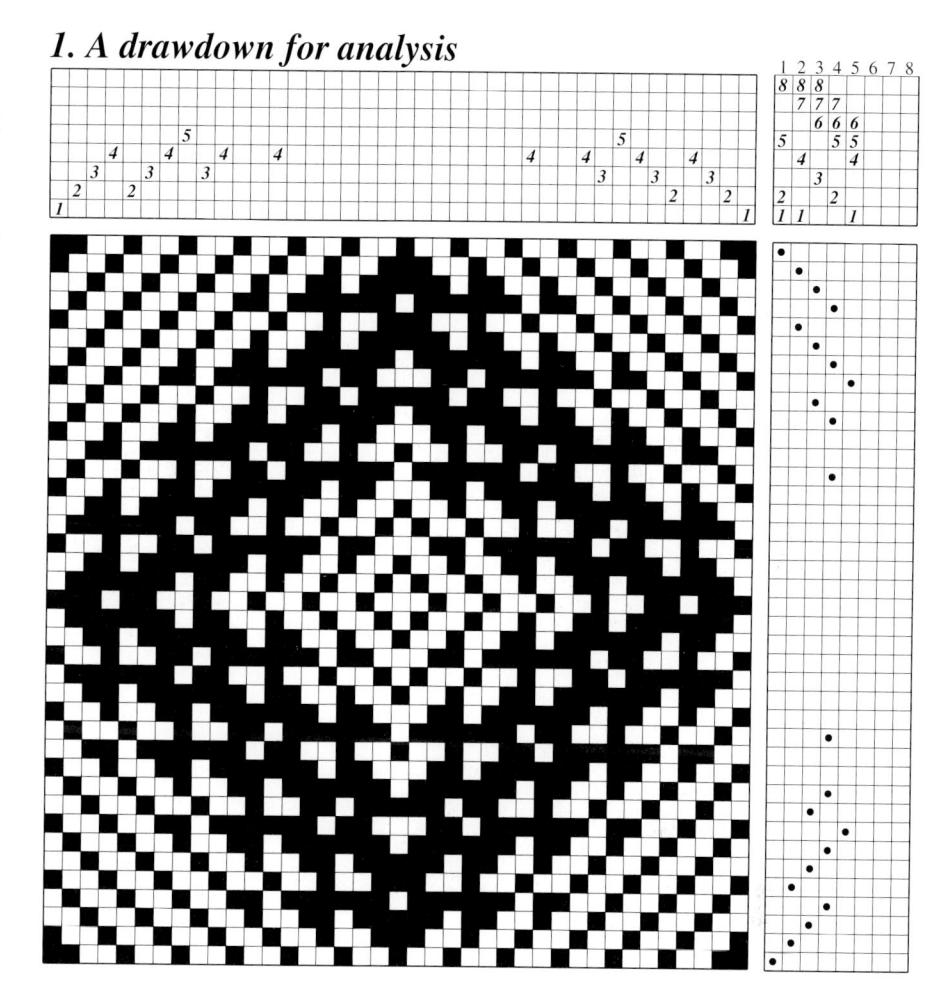

1. A drawdown for analysis

using this treadle. Then check to see if any other picks are exactly the same, since these picks can be inserted with the same treadle. The last pick is made in the same shed. Place a mark under the same treadle for the last row.

Next determine the shafts raised for the second pick. Write those numbers in the tie-up for treadle 2. Move the ruler down the drawdown grid to find any other picks that can be made with the same treadle. There are four picks inserted with treadle 2. The shaft numbers for treadles 1-5 are already written in the tie-up in *Figure 1*. Mark the rest of the picks inserted with treadle 5, then determine the shafts raised with treadles 6-8 to complete the treadling sequence. Check your analysis in the answer section, p. 125.

Note that although this 'skip' or 'progressive' twill draft looks a bit like a networked draft, the threading and treadling orders cannot be placed on a network made of any regularly repeating initial.

Answers

Writing Drafts

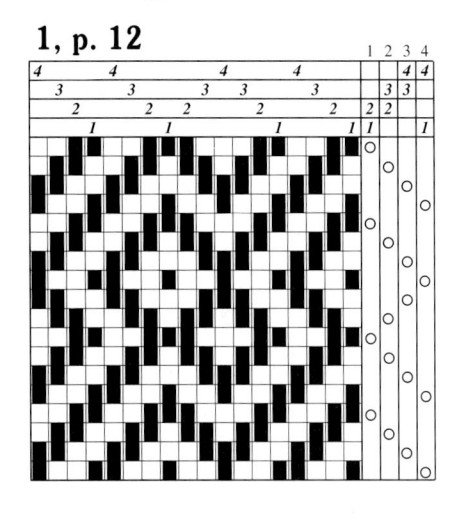

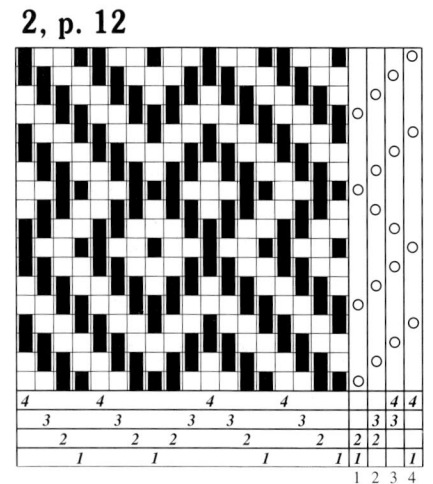

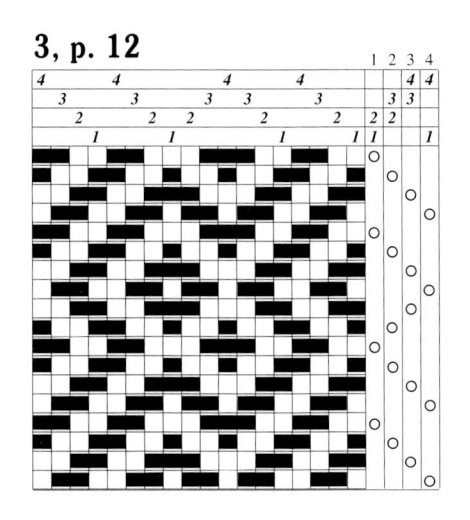

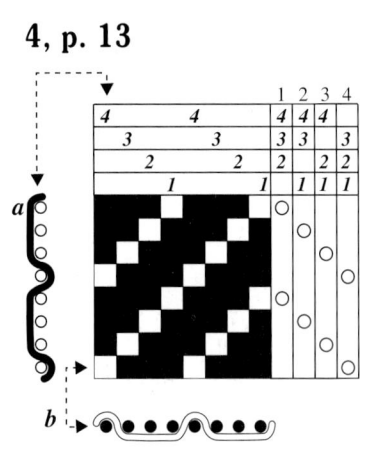

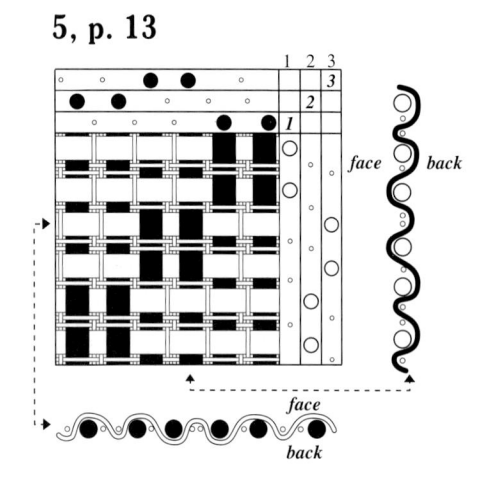

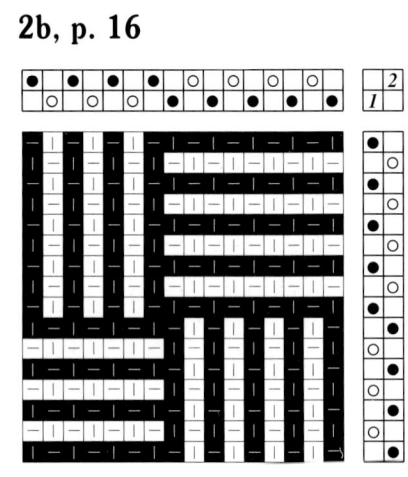

1, p. 12
2, p. 12
3, p. 12
4, p. 13
5, p. 13
2b, p. 16

Drafting Twills and Color-and-Weave

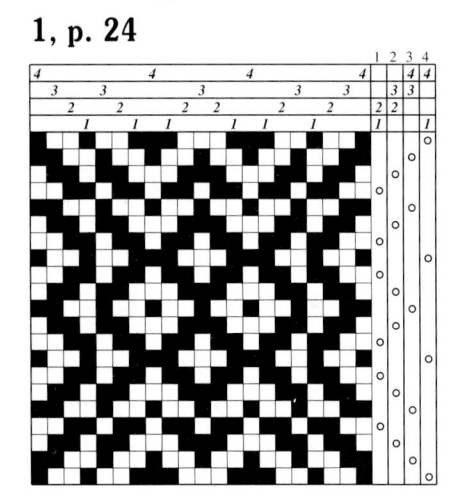

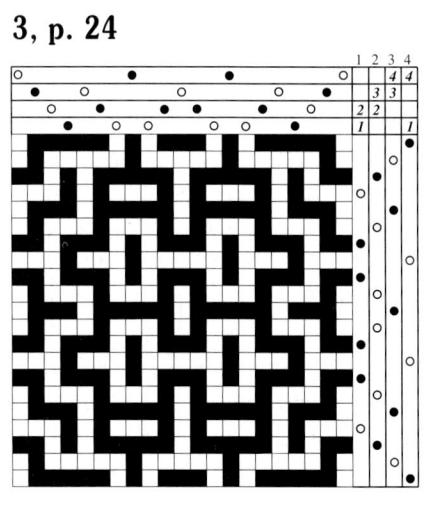

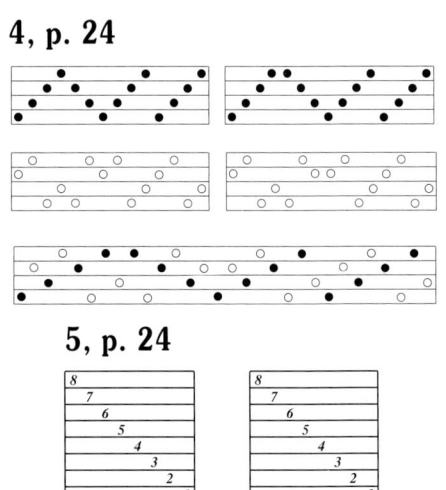

1, p. 24
3, p. 24
4, p. 24
5, p. 24

2, p. 24

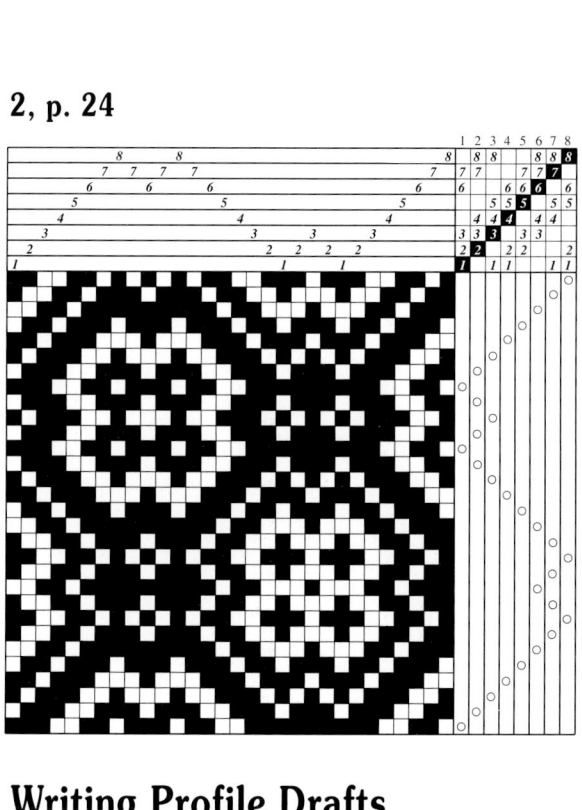

6d, p. 20

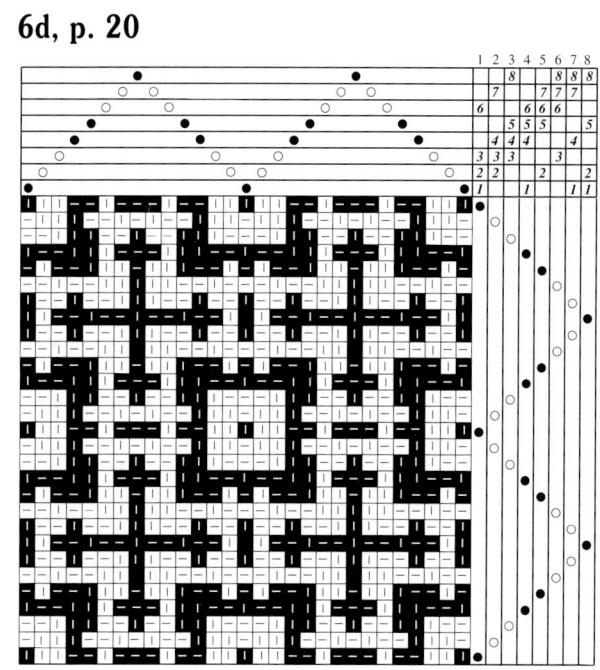

Writing Profile Drafts

1, p. 36

2, p. 36

3, p. 37

5, p. 37

4, p. 37

6, p. 37

Drafting Overshot

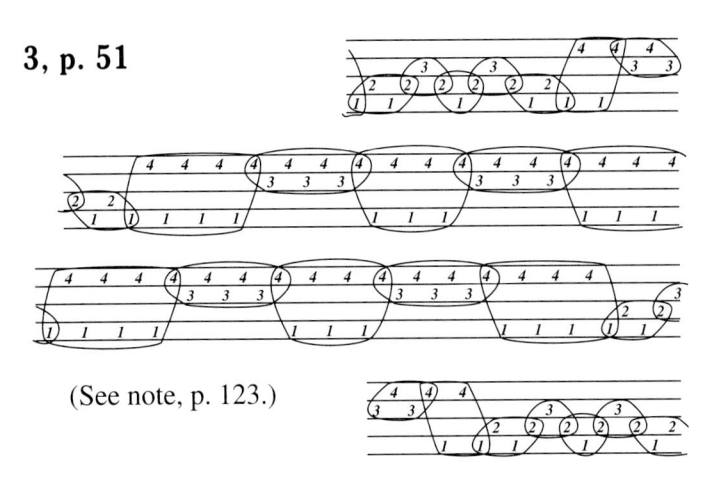

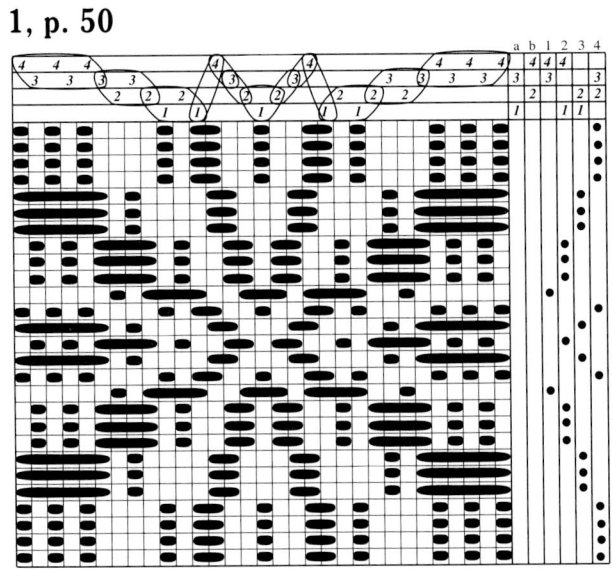

3, p. 51

(See note, p. 123.)

1, p. 50

2, p. 50

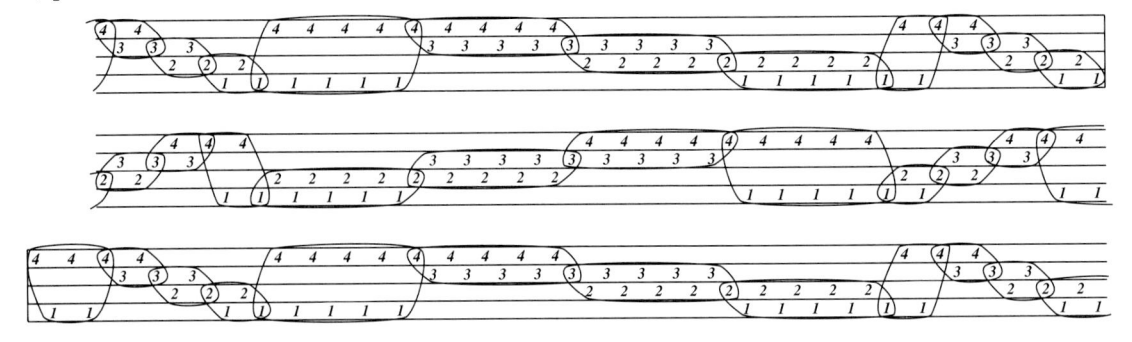

Drafting Lace

1b, p. 67

1c, p. 67

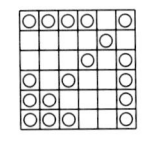

2b, p. 67

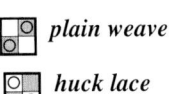

plain weave

huck lace

3, p. 67

design key

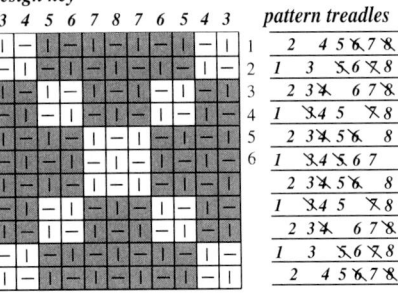

pattern treadles

tie-up

1a, p. 67

Bronson lace threading units:

1-8-1-8-1-2   1-8-1-8-1-2   1-7-1-7-1-2   1-8-1-8-1-2
1-7-1-7-1-2   1-8-1-8-1-2   1-8-1-8-1-2   1-8-1-8-1-2
1-3-1-3-1-2   1-4-1-4-1-2   1-4-1-4-1-2   1-4-1-4-1-2

1d, p. 67

Bronson lace treadling units:

1-8-1-8-1-2   1-8-1-8-1-2   1-7-1-7-1-2   1-8-1-8-1-2
1-7-1-7-1-2   1-8-1-8-1-2   1-8-1-8-1-2   1-8-1-8-1-2
1-3-1-3-1-2   1-4-1-4-1-2   1-4-1-4-1-2   1-4-1-4-1-2

2a, p. 67

Huck lace threading units:

2-7-2-7-2-1-8-1-8-1   2-7-2-7-2-1-8-1-8-1   2-7-2-7-2-1-8-1-8-1
2-7-2-7-2-1-8-1-8-1   2-3-2-3-2-1-4-1-4-1   2-5-2-5-2-1-6-1-6-1
2-7-2-7-2-1-8-1-8-1   2-5-2-5-2-1-6-1-6-1   2-3-2-3-2-1-4-1-4-1

122

Drafting Overshot

ANSWERS

4a, p. 51

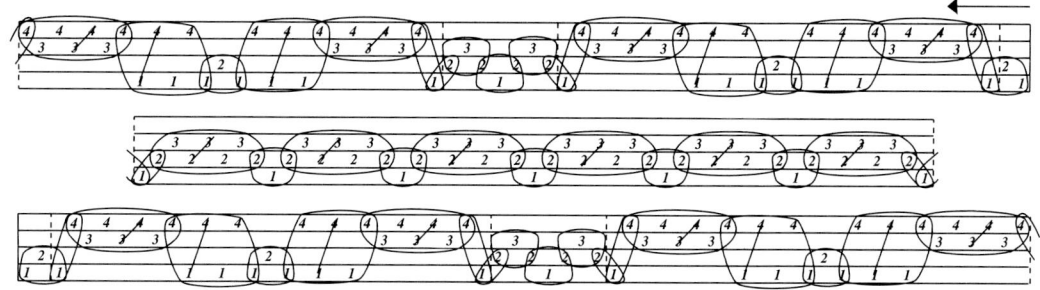

4b, p. 51

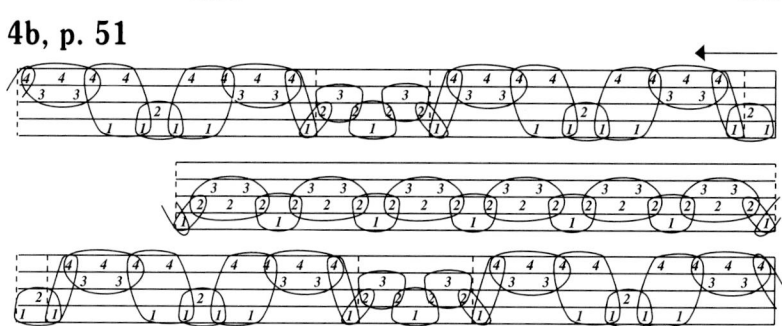

When deriving balanced thread-by-thread overshot drafts from profile drafts or shorthand drafts, add or subtract one warp thread from each turning block. When a thread is subtracted, the turning block has two fewer threads than when a thread is added. In the answer for *Exercise 3*, p. 51, a thread is subtracted from every turning block.

5, p. 51

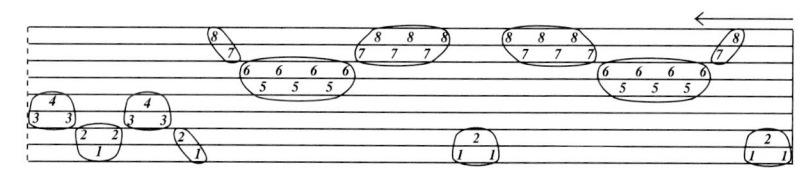

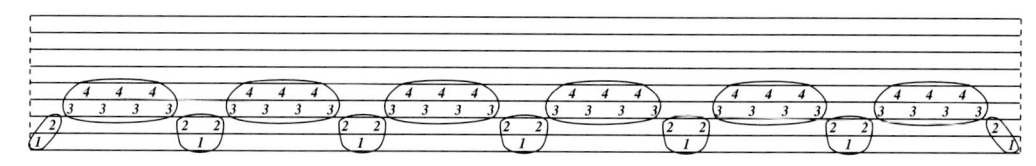

3b, p. 74

3a, p. 74

Drafting Damask

1, p. 74

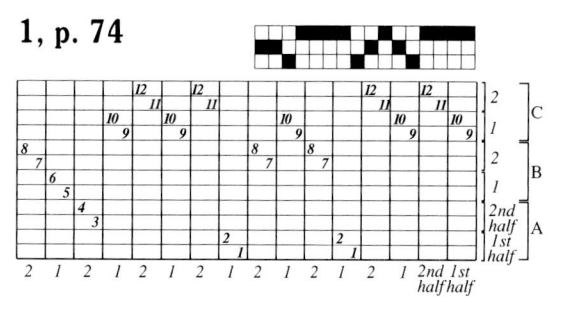

2, p. 74

Turned twill threading units:

9-10-11-12	9-10-11-12	9-10-11-12
9-10-11-12	1-2-3-4	5-6-7-8
9-10-11-12	5-6-7-8	1-2-3-4

3c, p. 74

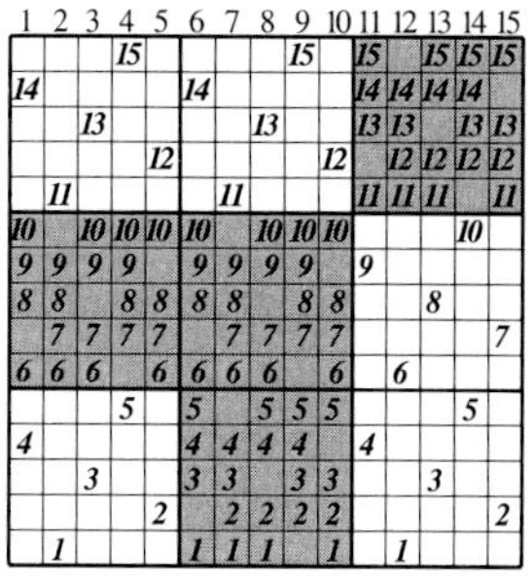

4, p. 74

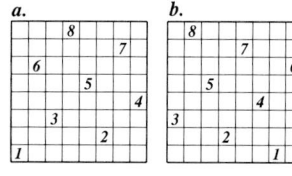

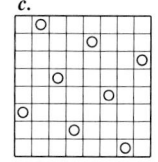

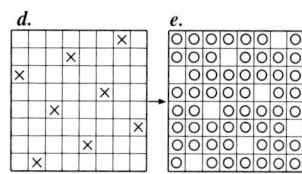

a. b. c. d. e.

123

Drafting Tied Unit Weaves

1, p. 93

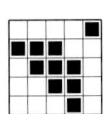

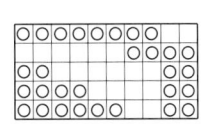

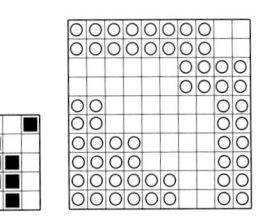

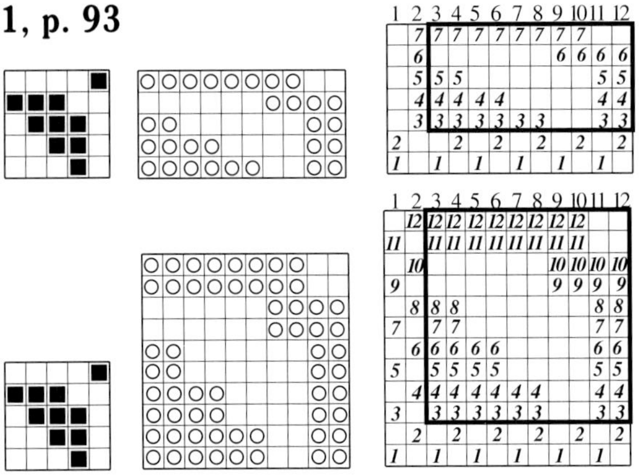

2, p. 93

1:2 extended summer and winter, full units:

1-8-7-2-7-8	1-12-11-2-11-12	1-12-11-2-11-12
1-12-11-2-11-12	1-12-11-2-11-12	1-12-11-2-11-12
1-12-11-2-11-12	1-12-11-2-11-12	1-4-3-2-3-4
1-4-3-2-3-4	1-6-5-2-5-6	1-6-5-2-5-6

3, p. 93

Bergman, quarter units:

1-6-3-6	2-8-1-8	3-8-1-8
2-8-3-8	1-8-3-8	2-8-1-8
3-8-1-8	2-8-3-8	1-4-3-4
2-4-1-4	3-5-1-5	2-5-3-5

4, p. 93

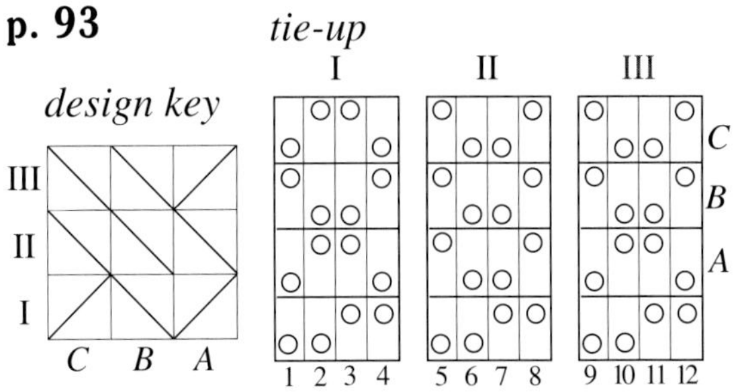

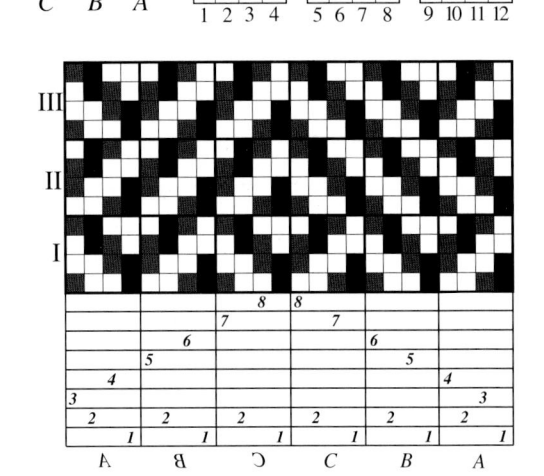

design key   *tie-up*

Drafting Double Weave

1d, p. 108

Double-weave threading units:

9(D)10(L)11(D)12(L)	9(D)10(L)11(D)12(L)	9(D)10(L)11(D)12(L)
9(D)10(L)11(D)12(L)	1(D)2(L)3(D)4(L)	5(D)6(L)7(D)8(L)
9(D)10(L)11(D)12(L)	5(D)6(L)7(D)8(L)	1(D)2(L)3(D)4(L)

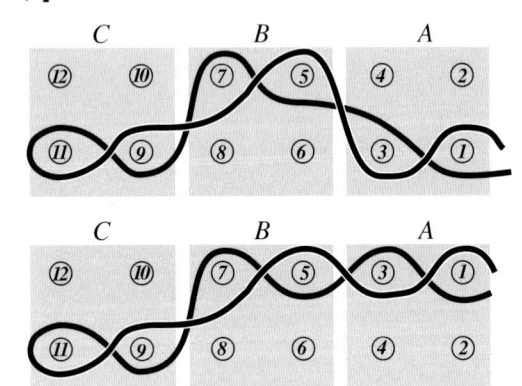

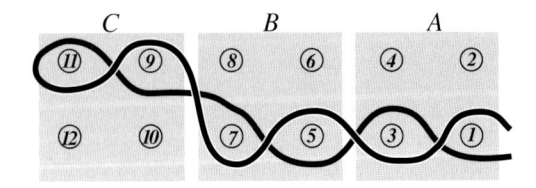

3, p. 108

4-block, 8-shaft double-weave threading units:

7-8-1-2	7-8-1-2	7-8
5-6-7-8	5-6-7-8	5-6
3-4-5-6	3-4-5-6	3-4
1-2-3-4	1-2-3-4	1-2

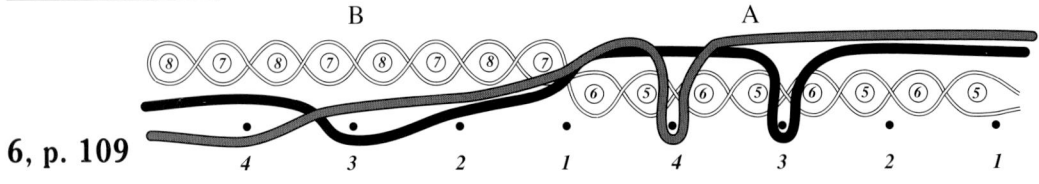

2, p. 108

6, p. 109

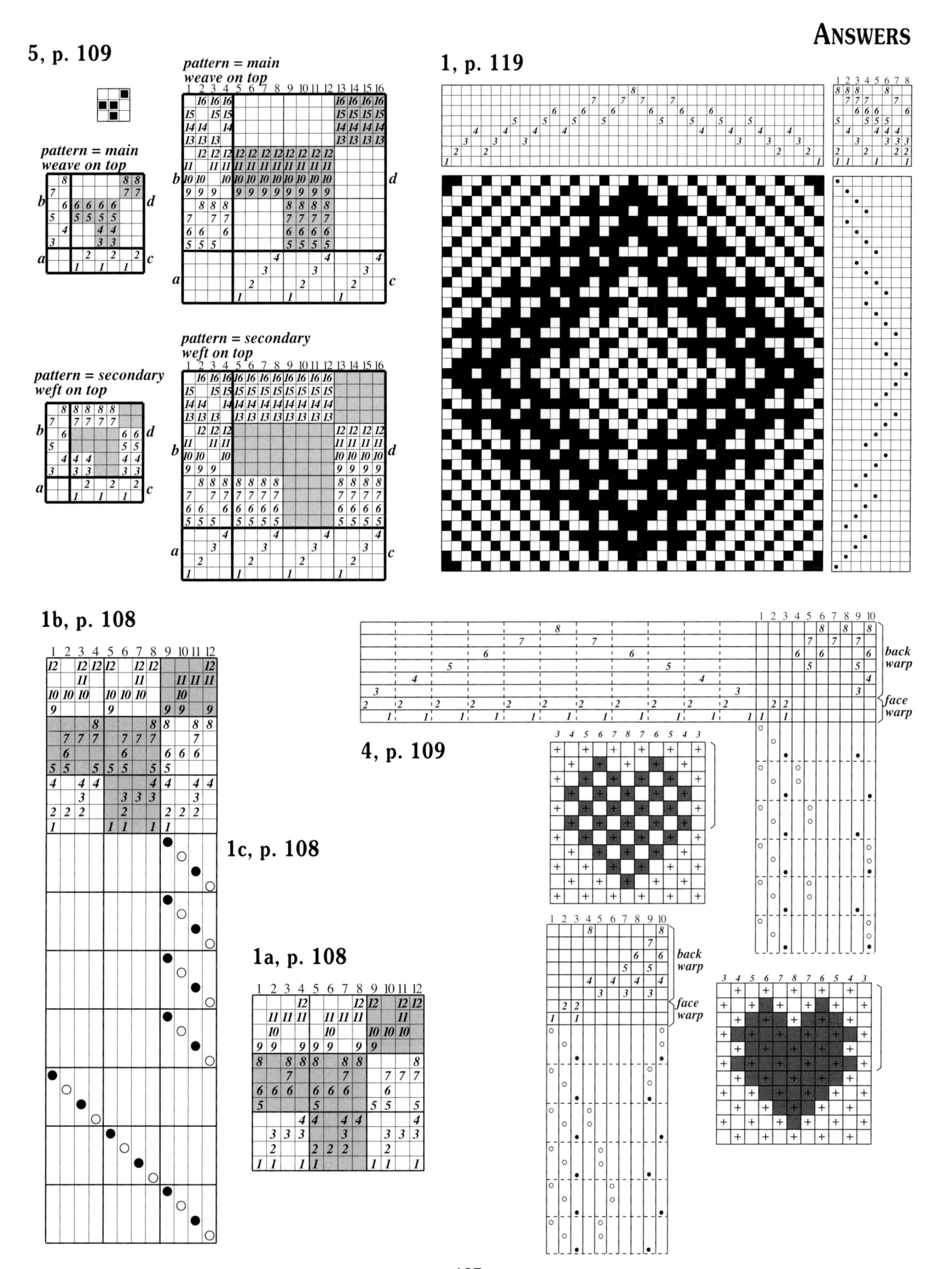

ANSWERS

5, p. 109

pattern = main weave on top

pattern = main weave on top

pattern = secondary weft on top

pattern = secondary weft on top

1, p. 119

1b, p. 108

1c, p. 108

1a, p. 108

4, p. 109

back warp / *face warp*

back warp / *face warp*

125

For Further Study

Parts III and IV will serve as a constant reference handbook of weaves, but you'll want to study a weave structure in greater depth to use it effectively. Included here are some imporant general texts and other reference materials. Under specific topics, find listed several special in-depth resources that can help direct your further study. Some of these books are no longer in print. Look for them in your guild or public library.

General

Atwater, Mary M. *The Shuttle-Craft Book of American Hand-Weaving*, Coupeville WA: Shuttle-Craft Books, 1986.

Black, Mary E. *The Key to Weaving: A Textbook of Handweaving for the Beginning Weaver*, New York: Macmillan, 1980.

Buschman, Isabel. *Handweaving: An Annotated Bibliography*, Metuchen NJ: The Scarecrow Press, Inc., 1991.

Cyrus-Zetterstrom, Ulla. *Manual of Swedish Handweaving*, Stockholm: LTs Forlag, 1984.

Davison, Marguerite Porter. *A Handweaver's Pattern Book*, Swarthmore PA, 1971.

Frey, Berta. *Designing and Drafting for Handweavers*, New York: Collier Books, 1958.

Redding, Debbie (Chandler). *Learning to Weave with Debbie Redding*, Loveland CO: Interweave Press, 1984.

Tidball, Harriet. *The Handloom Weaves*, Shuttle-Craft Monograph 33, Coupeville WA: Shuttle-Craft Books, 1984.

Wilson, Sadye Tune and Ruth Davidson Jackson. *Textile Arts Index, 1950-1987: Selected Weaving, Spinning, Dyeing, Knitting, Fiber Periodicals*, Nashville: Tunstede, 1988.

Textile history

Geijer, Agnes. *A History of Textile Art*, Stockholm: Sotheby Parke Bernet, 1979.

Wilson, Kax. *A History of Textiles*, Boulder CO: Westview Press, 1979.

Definitions and classification

Burnham, Dorothy K. *Warp and Weft: A Dictionary of Textile Terms*, New York: Scribner's, 1980.

Emery, Irene. *The Primary Structures of Fabrics*, Washington D.C.: The Textile Museum, 1980.

Zielinski, Stanislaw A. *Encyclopedia of Hand-Weaving*, New York: Funk and Wagnalls, 1959.

Industrial texts

Grosicki, ed. *Watson's Textile Design and Colour*, 7th ed., London: Newnes-Butterworths, 1975.

Grosicki, ed. *Watson's Advanced Textile Design*, 4th ed., London: Newnes-Butterworths, 1977.

Goerner, Doris. *Woven Structure and Design, Part 1: Single Cloth Construction*, 1986; *Part 2: Compound Structures*, 1989; Leeds, England.

Oelsner, G. H. *A Handbook of Weaves*, New York: Dover Publications, 1952.

Block designs

Atwater, Mary M. *A Book of Patterns for Handweaving by John Landes*, Hollywood: Southern California Handweavers' Guild, 1992.

Burnham, Harold B. and Dorothy K. *Keep Me Warm One Night: Early Handweaving in Eastern Canada*, Toronto: University of Toronto Press, 1972.

Holroyd, Ruth and Ulrike Beck. *Jacob Angstadt Designs Drawn From His Weavers Patron Book*, Pittsford NY, 1976.

Color-and-weave

Barrett, Clotilde. *Shadow Weave and Corkscrew Weave*, Boulder CO: Colorado Fiber Center, 1980.

Windeknecht, Margaret and Thomas Windeknecht. *Color-and-Weave*, New York: Van Nostrand Reinhold, 1981.

Twills

Voiers, Leslie. *Looking at Twills*, Harrisville NH: Harrisville Designs, 1983.

Landis, Lucille. *Twills and Twill Derivatives: Design Your Own, Four to Eight Harnesses*, Old Greenwich CT: 1977.

Overshot

Davison, Marguerite Porter. *A Handweaver's Source Book*, Swarthmore PA, l953.

Estes, Josephine E. *Original Miniature Patterns for Hand Weaving,* Boston; vol 1, 1956; vol II, 1958.

Wilson, Sadye Tune and Doris Finch Kennedy. *Of Coverlets: The Legacies, the Weavers*, Nashville: Tunstede, 1983.

Windeknecht, Margaret. *Creative Overshot*, Shuttle-Craft Monograph 31, Coupeville WA: Shuttle-Craft Books, 1978.

Weft-faced weaves

Barrett, Clotilde. *Boundweave*, Boulder CO: Colorado Fiber Center, 1982.

Collingwood, Peter. *The Techniques of Rug Weaving*, New York: Watson-Guptill, 1968.

Hoskins, Nancy. *Weft-faced Pattern Weaves: Tabby to Taqueté*, Seattle: The University of Washington Press and Skein Publications, 1992.

Lace weaves

Morrison, Ruth; Lynn Tedder; and Madelyn van der Hoogt. 'A Little Bit More Huck,' **Weaver's**, Issue 13, pp. 48-51.

Muller, Donna. *Handwoven Laces*, Loveland CO: Interweave Press, 1991.

Weaver's Magazine, Issues 10 and 21; Golden Fleece Publications, Sioux Falls SD.

Double weave

O'Connor, Paul R. *Loom-Controlled Double Weave: From the Notebook of a Double Weaver*, St. Paul: Dos Tejedoras, 1992.

Prairie Wool Companion, Issues 12 and 13; Golden Fleece Publications, Sioux Falls SD.

Sullivan, Donna. *Piqué Plain and Patterned*, Jacksonville FL: Sullivan Publications, 1988.

Tidball, Harriet. *The Double Weave, Plain and Patterned*. Shuttle-Craft Monograph 1, Coupeville WA, Shuttle-Craft Books, 1960.

Weaver's Magazine, Issues 1, 2, and 17, Golden Fleece Publications, Sioux Falls SD.

Weaves for eight or more shafts

Harvey, Virginia. *The Bateman Manuscripts*, Shuttle-Craft Guild Monographs 35-40, Coupeville WA: Shuttle-Craft Books, 1981-1989.

Strickler, Carol. *A Weaver's Book of 8-shaft Patterns*, Loveland CO: Interweave Press, 1991.

Shelp, Wanda Jean and Carolyn Wostenberg. *Eight Shafts: A Place to Begin*, Worland WY, 1991.

Keasbey, Doramay. *Pattern Devices for Handweavers*, Bethesda MD: 1981.

Tied unit weaves (inc. double two-tie)

Anderson, Clarita; Judith Gordon; and Naomi Towner. *Weave Structures Used in North American Coverlets*, Olney MD, 1979.

Barrett, Clotilde and Eunice Smith. *Double Two-tie Unit Weaves*, Boulder CO: Colorado Fiber Center, 1983.

Kelly, Jacquie. 'Designing Fancy Twills in Double Two-tie Unit Weave,' *Interweave*, VI:1, Winter 1980-1981.

Prairie Wool Companion, Issue 14; Golden Fleece Publications, Sioux Falls SD.

Sullivan, Donna. *Summer & Winter: A Weave for All Seasons*, Loveland CO: Interweave Press, 1991.

Tidball, Harriet. *Summer and Winter and Other Two-tie Unit Weaves*, Shuttle-Craft Guild Monograph 19, Coupeville WA: Shuttle-Craft Books, 1966.

van der Hoogt, Madelyn. 'Double Two-tie Unit Weave for Supplementary Warp,' **Weaver's**, Issue 8, pp. 32-37.

van der Hoogt, Madelyn. 'Twills in Double Two-tie Unit Weave,' *Handwoven*, VI:5, November/December 1985, pp. 64-68.

Xenakis, David. 'The Double Two-tie System Applied to Overshot,' *Prairie Wool Companion*, Issue 9, p. 7-11.

Xenakis, David. 'Figured Piqué Patterning with the Double Two-tie System,' *Prairie Wool Companion*, Issue 12, pp. 20-23.

Network drafting

Barrett, Clotilde. 'Introduction to Network Drafting,' **Weaver**'s, Issue 12, pp. 38-40.

Masson, Oliver and François Roussel. *Shaft Weaving and Graph Design*, Montreal, 1987.

Schlein, Alice. 'Network Drafting: More for Less,' **Weaver's**, Issue 6, pp. 28-32; 'Network Drafting: Part II,' Issue 7, pp. 23-29; 'Network Drafting: Part III: Double Weave,' Issue 8, pp. 50-56; 'Network Drafting with Lampas,' Issue 10, pp. 48-52.

Graph paper: 8 squares/inch

Graph paper: 10 squares/inch

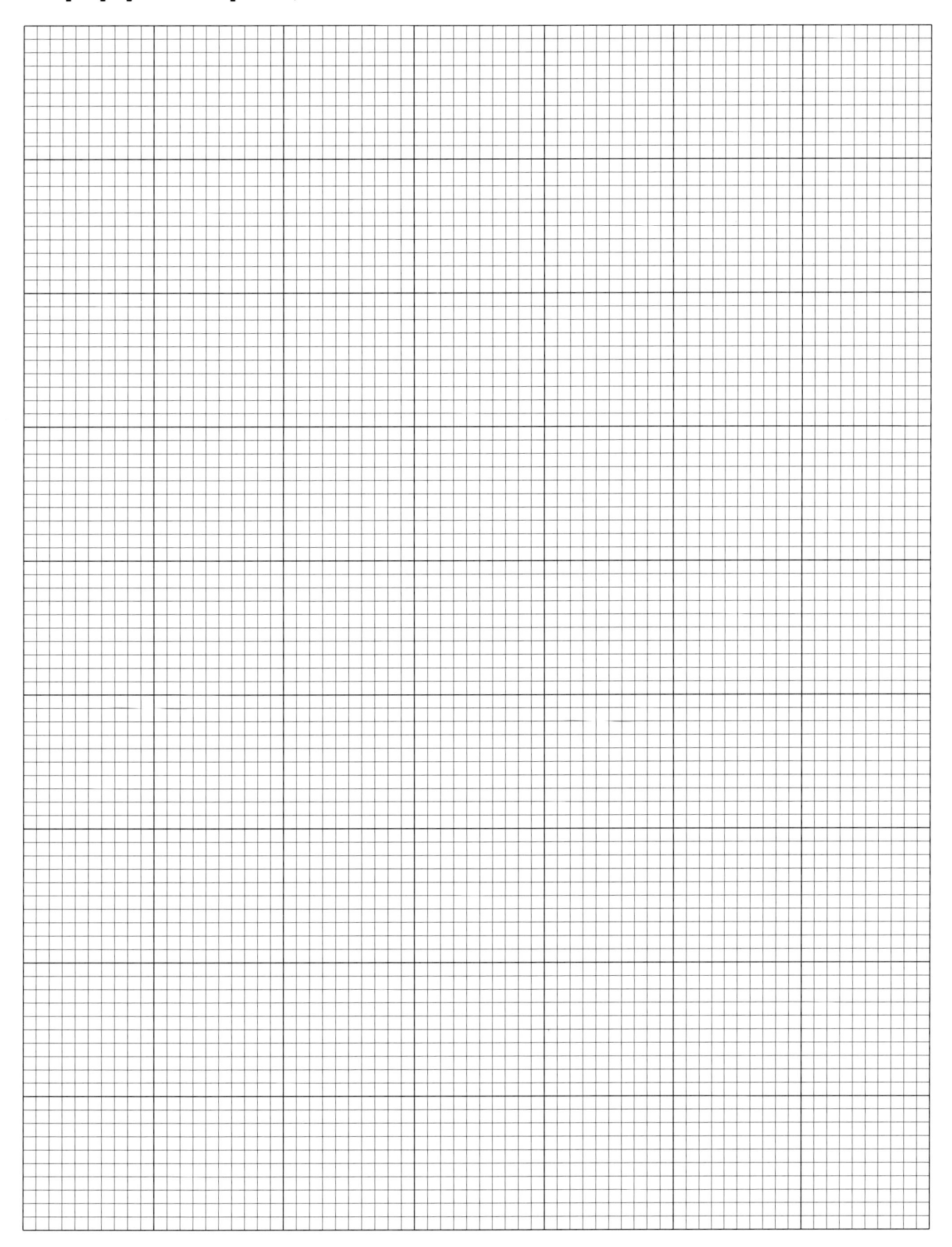

Piqué design paper

Huck design paper

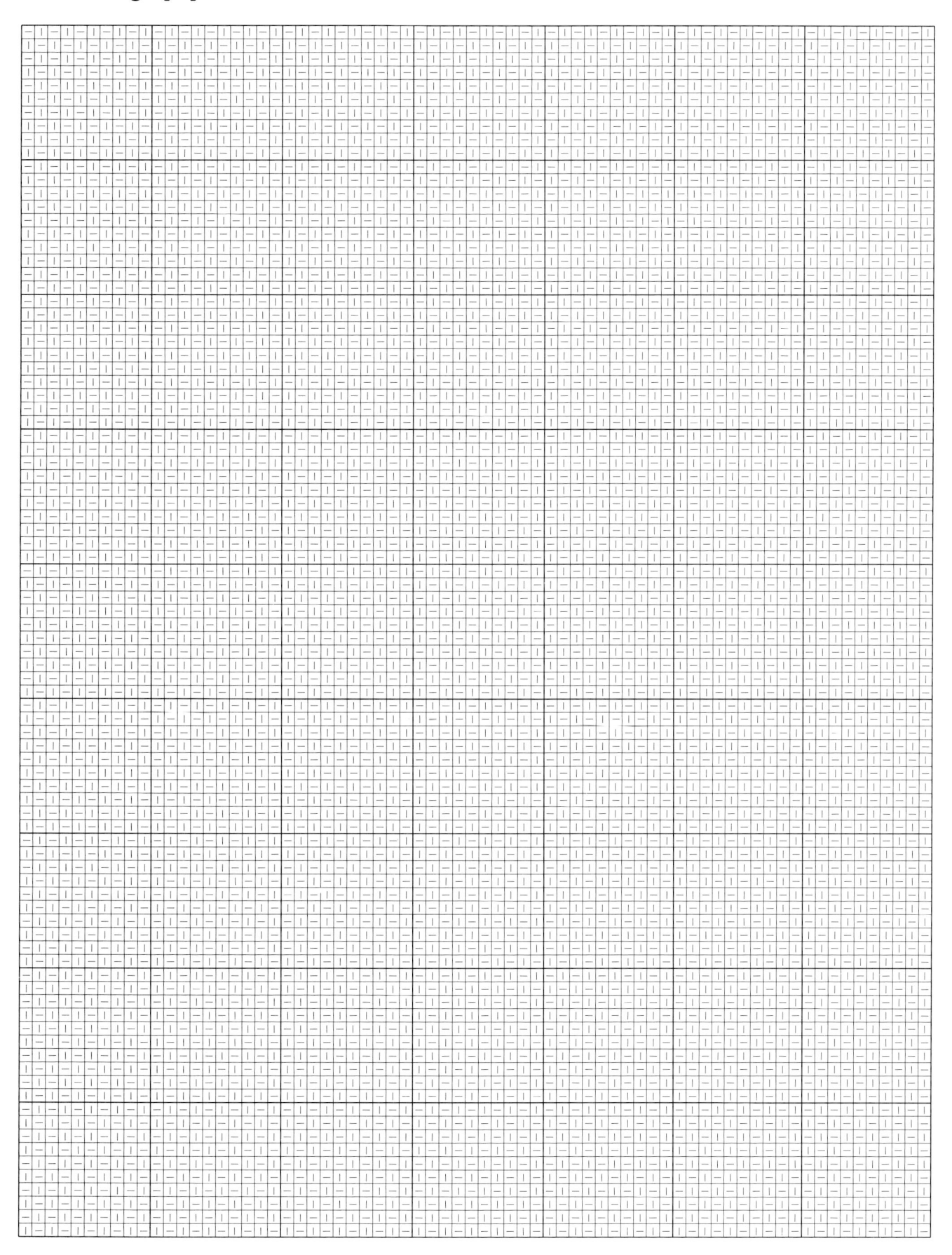

Double two-tie drawdown paper

Some networks for 8, 12, and 16 shafts

Index

As-drawn-in, *definition*, 25; blocks woven as-drawn-in, 33-34, *See* Star fashion

Asymmetrical threading and treadling, 35

Background, 28; *definition*, 25; in block weaves, *definition*, 52

Basket weave, 16; *definition*, 14

Bateman weaves, *definition*, 75

Beiderwand, *definition*, 94; *see* 'Keys,' 26-27

Bergman, 2, 87, 88; *definition*, 75; *see* 'Keys,' 26-27

Blended drafts, 114-115; *definition*, 110

Block weaves, 28-37; block, *definition*, 38; recognizing blocks, 53; block vs counterblock, *definition*, 52; combining blocks, 31; *definition*, 52; 'Keys to Block Weaves' chart, 26-27; recognizing combined blocks, 54; in overshot, 39-51; turning blocks, *definition*, 38; woven as-drawn-in, 33-34

Blooming leaf, *definition*, 38

Boundweaves, 2

Bronson lace, 29, 60-61; *definition*, 59; *see* 'Keys,' 26-27, 61

Clean cut, *definition*, 68

Color-and-weave, 16, 20-21; *definition*, 14; log cabin, 16, 20; shadow weave, 21

Color drawdown, 20, 21

Complementary warps or wefts, *definition*, 110

Compound elements, *definition*, 38

Compound sets of elements, *definition*, 94

Compound weaves, *definition*, 94

Counterbalance loom, 11

Counterchanged, *definition*, 68

Countermarch loom, 11

Crackle, 2; *definition*, 75; *see* 'Keys,' 26-27

Cross sections, 7

Damask, 2, 69-74; clean-cut damask, 70; *definition*, 68; designing damask, 71-73; damask diaper, *definition*, 68; double damask, *definition*, 68; dräll damask, *definition*, 68; half-units, 71; *see* 'Keys' 26-27, 72-73; twill damask, *definition*, 68

Definitions, *See* Words to Know

Design vs pattern, *definition*, 52

Digitizing, 116; *definition*, 110

Direct tie-up, 9

Double faced, *definition*, 110

Double two-tie unit weave, 90-92; *definition*, 75; drawdown paper, 132; for twill blocks, 90-92; *see* 'Keys,' 26-27, 90, 91

Double weave, 2, 95-109; *definition*, 94; figured double weave, *definition*, 94; patterned double weave, 97-99; translating overshot to double weave, 98-99

Drafts, 4-13; balanced draft, *definition*, 38; blended draft, 114-115; draft, *definition*, 3; direction of draft, 5; network drafting, 116-118; symbol variations, 8; turned drafts, 111-113

Dräll weaves, *definition*, 68

Drawdown, 4-10; color drawdown, 20; *definition*, 3; warp drawdown, 6; weft drawdown, 6; variations, 9

Drawloom, *definition*, 68

Drawups, 17

Even-tied overshot, *see* 'Keys,' 26-27

Extended point twill, 18, 19; *definition*, 14

Extended summer and winter, 80-81, 113; *definition*, 75; *see* 'Keys,' 81

Fabric analysis, 119; *definition*, 3, 110

'Family Tree of Weaves,' chart, 2

50/50 weaves, *definition*, 14

Four-tie unit weaves, 2, 89; *definition*, 75; *see* 'Keys,' 89

Gauze, *definition*, 59

Graph paper, 8" and 10", 128-129

Ground, *definition*, 75

Ground cloth, *definition*, 38

Halb-dräll weaves, *definition*, 68

Half dukagang, 82, 83; *definition*, 75

Half satin, *definition*, 75, 88; *see* 'Keys,' 26-27

Halftones, 46-48, 84, 85; *definition* 38

Harmonics, *definition*, 110

Harness, *definition*, 3

Huck, 62-66; *definition*, 59; design paper, 131; *see* 'Keys,' 66

Huck lace, 2, 65-66; *see* Huck *definition*, 59; *see* 'Keys,' 26-27, 66

Initial, 116; *definition*, 110

Interlacement, *definition*, 3

Jack loom, 10

'Keys to Block Weaves,' chart, 26-27

Lace weaves, 2, 59-68; *definition*, 59

Lampas, 2, 104-107; *definition*, 94; binder, *definition*, 94; *see* 'Keys,' 26-27, 107

Landes hybrid, 82, 113; *definition*, 75

Leno, *definition*, 59

Log cabin, 15-16; 20; *definition*, 14

Looms: counterbalance, 11; countermarch, 11; jack, 10

M's & O's, 2; *see* 'Keys,' 26-27

Matelassé, *definition*, 94

Monk's belt, 38, 45

Motif, 40, 41; *definition*, 38

Network, 116; *definition*, 110

Network drafting, 116-118; *definition*, 110; grids, 133

One-tie unit weave, *definition*, 75

Opphämta, *definition*, 110

Overshot, 2, 29, 39-51; balanced drafts, 42-43; characteristics of, 39; *definition*, 38; eight shaft overshot, 49; enlarge a draft, 43-44; halftones, 45, 46-48; *see* 'Keys,' 26-27; on opposites, 45; *definition*, 38; reduce a draft, 43-44; short draft, 41; thread-by-thread draft, 41-42; threading drafts, 40-41; threading from a profile draft, 43; treadling orders, 49; tied overshot, 84-87; *definition*, 76; turning blocks, 41; unbalanced draft, 41, 43; uneven-tied overshot, 113; *see* 'Keys,' 26-27

Paired-tie weaves, 82, 83; *definition*, 76

Pattern, 28; *definition*, 25; pattern (warp) ends, *definition*, 76; pattern weft, *definition*, 38, 76; pattern vs design, *definition*, 38

Pattern line, 116, 117, 118; *definition*, 110

Pattern shafts, *definition*, 59, 76

Patterned double weave, 95-99; *definition*, 94; *see* 'Keys,' 26-27, 97

Piqué, 2, 100, 102, 103; *definition*, 94; design paper, 130

Plain weave, 2, 15-16; *definition*, 2

Profile drafts, 28-37; *definition*, 25; profile drawdown, 28-31; profile threading, 29-31; profile tie-up, 29-31; profile treadling, 29-31; designing with, 33

Quigley weaves, 89; *see* Four-tie unit weaves, *definition*, 75

Rising shed, *definition*, 3

Rose, *definition*, 38; threading for, 41

Rose fashion, 34-35; *definition*, 25; in overshot, 49

Rosepath, 28; *definition*, 25

Samitum, 2; *definition*, 110

Satin, 2, 23, 69, 70; *definition*, 3, 68; half satin, *definition*, 75; warp-float satins, 69, 70; weft-float satins, 69, 70

Satin counter, 24, 69; *definition*, 14, 68

Shadow weave, 21-22; *definition*, 14

Shaft, *definition*, 3

Shed, *definition*, 3

Simple weaves, 2, 15-23; *definition*, 14; plain weave, 15-16; satin, 23; twill, 17-22

Sinking shed, *definition*, 3

Skeleton tie-up vs regular tie-up, 10

Spot Bronson, *see* 'Keys,' 26-27

Spot weaves, 2; *definition*, 59

Square the design, *definition*, 38

Star and diamond weaves, *see* tied overshot, *definition*, 76

Star, *definition*, 38; threading for, 41

Star fashion, 34-35; *definition*, 25; in overshot, 49

Stitched double cloth, 2, 100-103; *definition*, 94; *see* 'Keys,' 103

Straight draw, *definition*, 14

Structure, *definition*, 25

Summer and winter, 2, 29, 77-81, 113; *definition*, 76; double summer and winter, 90; extended summer and winter, 80-81; *definition*, 75; *see* 'Keys,' 26-27, 80, 90; summer and winter polychrome, *definition*, 76

Supplementary warp or weft, 112; *definition*, 110; *see* 'Keys,' 112

Supplementary weft, *definition*, 76

Symbols, threading, 7; treadling, 7; warp and weft, 7

Tabby, *definition*, 3

Tabby weft, *definition*, 38

Table, *definition*, 38

Taqueté, 2; *definition*, 110

Telescoping, 117; *definition*, 110

Thread-by-thread draft, 28; *definition*, 25; woven as drawn in, 33

Threading abbreviations, 7; symbols, 7

Threading draft, 4, 5, 8; *definition*, 3

Three-tie weaves, 2; *see* 'Keys,' 26-27, 88

Tie, to tie, *definition*, 76

Tie-down (warp) end, *definition*, 76

Tie-up, 4, 5, 9-11; *definition*, 3; direct tie-up, 9; skeleton tie-up, 10; standard formats, 10

Tied Latvian/Lithuanian, *see* paired-tie weaves, *definition*, 76

Tied overshot, *definition*, 76; *see* 'Keys,' 26-27, 86

Tied unit weaves, 77-92; *definition*, 76; drafting tied unit weaves, 78-79; *see* 'Keys,' 26-27, 80-83; 86, 88-90; single two-tie unit weave, *definition*, 76; translated to weave structure, 54; turned twill, 54; understanding the process, 55-57

Treadle as written, *see* tromp as writ

Treadling sequence/order, 4, 5, 6, 8; *definition*, 3

Tromp as writ, 33-34; *definition*, 25

Turned, *definition*, 68

Turned drafts, 111-113; *definition*, 110

Turned satin, *definition*, 68

Turning blocks, *definition* 38

Twills, 2, 17-22; balanced twills, 19; broken twill, 18, 19; *definition*, 14; cross twill, 68; *definition* of twill, 3; extended point twill, 18, 19; *definition*, 14; fancy twill, 18; *definition*, 14; point twill, 18; *definition*, 14; ratios, 17, 19; regular twills, 19; repeat twill, *definition*, 14; right twill vs left twill, 19; straight point twill, 18; turned twill, 55-57; *definition*, 52; *see* 'Keys,' 26-27; twill blocks, 90-92; twill circle, 17; in overshot, 40; twill diaper, *definition*, 68; variations, 19

Uneven tied overshot, *see* 'Keys,' 26-27; 113

Unit weaves, 53-57; *definition*, 52; unit, *definition*, 52

Velvet, 2; *definition*, 110

Warp, *definition*, 3; symbols, 7

Warp cross section, 7

Warp drawdown, 6; *definition*, 3

Warp end, *definition*, 3

Warp-faced, *definition*, 68

Warp-faced compound tabby, 110

Warp-faced vs warp-predominant, *definition*, 14

Warp-predominant satins or twills (warp-float satins or twills), *definition* 68

Weft, *definition*, 3; symbols, 7

Weft cross section, 7

Weft drawdown, 6; *definition*, 3

Weft-faced, *definition*, 68

Weft-faced compound tabby, *definition*, 110

Weft pick, *definition*, 3

Weft-predominant satins or twills (weft-float satins or twills), *definition*, 68

Whig rose, *definition*, 38

Words to Know Index

As-drawn-in, 25
Background, 25
Background in block weaves, 52
Balanced draft, 38
Basket weave, 14
Bateman weaves, 75
Beiderwand, 94
Bergman weaves, 75
Binder or binding warp, 94
Blended drafts, 110
Block, 25
Block vs counterblock, 52
Block weaves, 38
Blooming leaf, 38
Broken twill, 14
Bronson lace, 59
Clean cut, 68
Color-and-weave, 14
Combined blocks, 52
Complementary warps or wefts, 110
Compound elements, 38
Compound sets of elements, 94
Compound weaves, 94
Counterchanged, 68
Crackle, 75
Cross twill, 68
Damask, 68
Damask diaper, 68
Digitizing, 110
Distribution factor, 68
Double damask, 68
Double faced, 110
Double two-tie unit weave, 75
Double weave, 94
Draft, 3
Dräll damask, 68
Dräll weaves, 68
Drawdown, 3
Drawloom, 68
Extended point twill, 14
Extended summer and winter, 75
Fabric analysis, 3, 110
Fancy twill, 14
50/50 weave, 14
Four-tie unit weaves, 75
Gauze, 59
Ground, 75
Ground cloth, 38
Halb-dräll weaves, 68
Half dukagang, 75
Half satin, 75
Halftone, 38

Harmonics, 110
Harness, 3
Hopsack, *see* Basket weave
Huck, 59
Initial, 110
Interlacement, 3
Interruption factor, 68
Lace weaves, 59
Lampas, 94
Landes hybrid, 75
Leno, 59
Log cabin, 14
Matelassé, 94
Motif, 38
Network, 110
Network drafting, 110
One-tie unit weave, 75
Opphämta, 110
Overshot, 38
Overshot on opposites, 38
Paired-tie weaves, 76
Pattern, 25
Patterned (layer-exchanged) double weave, 94
Pattern line, 110
Pattern shafts, 59, 76
Pattern vs design, 52
Pattern (warp) ends, 76
Pattern weft, 38, 76
Pine, 38
Piqué, 94
Plain weave, 3
Point twill, 14
Profile draft, 25
Quigley weaves, *see* Four-tie unit weaves
Repeat twill, 14
Rising shed, 3
Rose, 38
Rose fashion, 25
Rosepath, 25
Samitum, 110
Satin, 3, 68
Satin counter, 14, 68
Shadow weave, 14
Shaft, 3
Shed, 3
Simple weave, 14
Single two-tie unit weave, 76
Sinking shed, 3
Spot weaves, 59
Square the design, 38

Star, 38
Star and diamond weaves, 76
Star fashion, 25
Stitched double cloth, 94
Straight draw, 14
Structure, 25
Summer and winter, 76
Summer and winter polychrome, 76
Supplementary warp or weft, 110
Supplementary weft, 76
Tabby, 3
Tabby weft, 38
Table, 38
Taqueté, 110
Telescoping, 110
Threading draft, 3
Tie, to tie, 76
Tie-down (warp) end, 76
Tie-up, 3
Tied Latvian, 76
Tied Lithuanian, 76
Tied overshot, 76
Tied unit weaves, 76
Thread-by-thread draft, 25
Treadling sequence, 3
Tromp as writ, 25
Turned, 68
Turned draft, 110
Turned satin, 68
Turned twill, 52
Turning blocks, 38
Twill, 3
Twill damask, 68
Twill diaper, 68
Unit, 52
Unit weaves, 52
Velvet, 110
Warp, 3
Warp drawdown, 3
Warp end, 3
Warp faced, 68
Warp-faced compound tabby, 110
Warp-faced vs warp-predominant, 14
Warp-predominant satins or twills, 68
Weft, 3
Weft drawdown, 3
Weft-faced, 68
Weft-faced compound tabby, 110
Weft pick, 3
Weft-predominant satins or twills, 68
Whig rose, 38